Arcus
Costātini

T.S.M.noua   Arcu Tin

orti hortessterism

Iouis Floton

L.S.Teodosii

T.S.Georgii

olinus

Piazzamontanara   S.Mariain Por

I.Marcelli

THE
ROMAN'S WORLD

AUGUSTUS AS PONTIFEX MAXIMUS
FROM THE VIA LABICANA, MUSEO DELLE TERME

THE
ROMAN'S WORLD

BY

FRANK GARDNER MOORE

BIBLO and TANNEN
NEW YORK
1965

The city which thou seest no other deem
Than great and glorious Rome, Queen of the Earth
So far renowned, and with the spoils enriched
Of nations. There the Capitol thou seest,
Above the rest lifting his stately head
On the Tarpeian rock, her citadel
Impregnable; and there Mount Palatine,
The imperial palace, compass huge, and high
The structure, skill of noblest architects.

Paradise Regained, 4, 44

PREFACE

Former generations studied "Roman antiquities," meaning everything connected with the ways and customs of the Romans, a field more recently restricted to "Private antiquities" and known for short as "Roman life." In the present work the aim has been to outline a larger picture of the world—social, cultural, and political—in which the typical Roman of one age after another lived. A vast fabric it was, still challenging modern interest and amazement, a tapestry of many colors and intricate pattern, interwoven with much that was borrowed in religion, in art, in letters, in every branch of knowledge. Yet for us of a later day it is still to be viewed as the Roman's world.

Columbia University
April, 1936

CONTENTS

ILLUSTRATIONS

MAPS AND PLANS

THE END PAPERS present a small section of a bird's-eye view of Rome in 1593, by the artist Antonio Tempesta. In the foreground, at the left, is the Capitoline, with the Church of the Aracoeli, on the site of the Arx. Behind the equestrian statue of Marcus Aurelius rises what in a former state was the ancient Tabularium. The center is occupied by the Campo Vaccino, not yet identified as the Forum. At the right are the Farnese Gardens on the Palatine. In the lower right corner the Theater of Marcellus appears as a medieval stronghold converted in the sixteenth century into a palace.

For the illustrations acknowledgment should here be paid to the photographers named on the plates; to the Metropolitan Museum of Art, New York; to Messrs. George C. Keiser and Thomas W. Price, of New York, and Mme. Tatiana Warscher, of Rome; also to the American Academy in Rome, the Touring Club Italiano, the Ministero Aeronautica, and Anton Schroll and Co., in Vienna. Special debts are due to the kind assistance of Mr. Thomas Wistar, Jr., of Philadelphia, while in Rome, and to the skill and experience of my daughter Janet Gaylord Moore, who has been my collaborator in drawing the maps and plans.

I
FROM VILLAGE TO CITY-STATE

HOC, QVODCVNQVE VIDES, HOSPES, QVA MAXIMA ROMA EST,
ANTE PHRYGEM AENEAN COLLIS ET HERBA FVIT.
                                    PROPERTIUS, 4, 1, 1

ROMVLVS AETERNAE NONDVM FORMAVERAT VRBIS
    MOENIA, CONSORTI NON HABITANDA REMO,
SED TVNC PASCEBANT HERBOSA PALATIA VACCAE
ET STABANT HVMILES IN IOVIS ARCE CASAE.
                                    TIBULLUS, 2, 5, 23

OUR most distant vista into the Roman past was opened little more than thirty years ago by the discovery of very ancient graves ten to fifteen feet and more below the level of the Forum valley as it was in the time of the Empire. This small section of a larger prehistoric cemetery had been covered up by successive strata of rubbish, dwellings, and paving, and long since forgotten when a dozen centuries later the lofty Temple of Antoninus and Faustina was erected, probably over the remains of many other primitive inhabitants laid away in the ground near the edge of the swampy valley which was to become the site of the Forum.

The location of this village of the dead near the Esquiline and opposite the Palatine suggests that here lay those who in that early Iron Age had lived in one of the villages established on those hills. Among some fifty graves a considerable fraction were round cavities to receive earthen urns containing ashes, while the rest were inhumation graves. Thus on the site of Rome, almost if not quite 1000 B.C., we find cremation and inhumation practised by the same small community, whereas in general every primitive tribe held consistently to its own custom, either that of burning bodies and burying the ashes or that of burying its dead intact. In this particular necropolis there appears to be no sufficient reason for supposing a lapse of time such as might account for a change of custom. More plausible is the inference that the villages contained at the same time two distinct races, each adhering to its own tradition.

This may be taken to mean that a part of the population, descended from tribes whose ancestors had been established along the Adriatic and over a good part of central Italy even before the Bronze Age, had inherited from them the

custom of burying their dead in the ground; that the rest of
the villagers, retaining their own habit of cremation, were
sprung from tribes which had migrated over the Alps, probably from the valley of the Danube and in successive waves,
until they had reached the Tuscan coast. Those who pushed
farthest south had even crossed the Tiber below Rome, to
settle on and near the Alban hills.

Thus we find in the earliest Rome two elements in the
population: the inhuming Sabine stock, of the same race
as the Picenes and Samnites, and established in much the
same region since the Stone Age; and the Latins, probably
more recent comers, practising cremation as their inherited
custom. The latter must be grouped with their kinsfolk farther north, the so-called Villanovans,[1] who by 1000 B.C. had
spread from the Alps across the Po and Arno, and then
over the Apennines to the sea and even as far south as Mt.
Alba—this before the coming either of Etruscan or of
Gallic invaders.

But as one turns away from this fragment of Rome's most
ancient cemetery, now filled in and covered by a pattern in
grass and concrete to show the plan of the Sepulcretum beneath, one is sure to be thinking less of conflicting opinions
of ethnologists and archaeologists as to the races in Italy
3,000 years ago than of the villages which we have to restore
in imagination on the neighboring hills, of the houses and
their occupants. Perfect models of the houses are furnished
us by those tombs which contained hut-urns of clay, each
the semblance of a real house (illus., p. 399). Such were
the round wattled houses daubed with clay and roofed with
thatch held down by timbers meeting at the rounded ridge

---

[1] This modern name, first applied to the prehistoric inhabitants of sites
near Bologna, has been extended to cover tribes, probably related, whose
tombs show the same customs and the same state of civilization, including
Umbrians and Latins; cp. p. 6.

and often adorned with fanciful horns. A wide door, sometimes flanked by posts to support a porch, made windows
needless, while vents in the roof, but not at the very top,
allowed smoke to escape. From such huts our villagers on
the Palatine and the other hills came out to tend their flocks,
to till the soil, or to fight off enemies. To them they returned
for the evening meal about a fire on the open hearth in the
center, and for sleep under rough-hewn beams, behind that
broad, closed door. If one wanders off the beaten track in
the Campagna today one may still see similar homes of
herdsmen.

Group such thatched huts in a hamlet, giving each household space for a yard and a fold, or for some simple out-
building, for which we have unfortunately no clay models;
surround such a village with an embankment, a stockade,
and a trench, and we have an image of any one of the units
which slowly combined, as is now supposed, to form the city
of Rome.

Villages of this type were nothing new in the Early Iron
Age, nor limited to this region. In such round or elliptical
huts men had lived in central and northern Italy and even
beyond the Alps, in the Bronze Age as well, and probably
still earlier in the Neolithic period, more than 2,000 years
B.C., when weapons and tools were still of stone and agriculture did not exist. That age, which after all was not
utterly barbarous, had yielded to the Bronze Age about the
time when the lake-dwellers were coming over the Alps and
establishing themselves around the shores of the Italian
Lakes, perhaps about 1700 B.C. This wave of immigration
was followed three or four centuries later by another and
a greater from the Danube country—these people also accustomed to burn their dead. But their villages, though not
set on piles over the water, were raised on posts over marshy
or even dry ground. Such dwellings on piles but not over

water are called *terremare.* Those who built them had brought down into Italy knowledge of agriculture and much skill in the working of copper and bronze. And they seem to have kept up communication with the land whence they came. This meant a very material advance and extensive trade not only in the Po Valley, where they had established themselves, displacing or absorbing the lake-dwellers, but also with regions farther south.

Another series of invasions from the Danube region appears to have taken place before 1000 B.C. These new invaders were probably akin to the men of the *terremare* and had the same custom of cremation. They are chiefly known from their settlements about Bologna, and are named from one such site, that of Villanova. But, as we have seen, they wandered southward and coastwise even beyond Rome. As they brought with them the use of iron it is with these immigrations that the Iron Age began for Italy, though bronze was still extensively used, except for weapons and tools.

As for Rome and its immediate vicinity, no evidence has yet been found for any settlements before the Iron Age, possibly because the volcanoes of the Alban region were not yet quite extinct. Our Proto-Romans of the hut-urns buried just outside of the future Forum were unmistakably of the Iron Age. The oldest of those remains may date from the eleventh century B.C., and are hardly less ancient than the similar cemeteries in the Alban hills. The latest graves of the Forum necropolis may be as recent as the sixth century B.C., shortly before the draining of the marsh and the laying out of the market place closed that chapter. Another less ancient necropolis on the Esquiline has yielded similar remains, chiefly of a time when the villages had combined to form a town, now defended by a wall that enclosed the different settlements.

Tradition gave priority among them to the Palatine, which certainly offered the best situation, combining nearness to the river with natural defenses which were supplemented by the marshes lying beneath two, and at times three, of its sides. But, the story of settlers brought from Alba to found a new city being discredited, probability favors the humblest and least romantic beginning in detached villages, at first quite independent of one another. Two of these were on the Palatine, for each of its two eminences, Cermalus and Palatium, was occupied by a primitive village of round thatched huts.

In one of these huts, or in the open when weather favored, we must imagine a few elders meeting to settle the affairs of their own village and differences between its families. Proximity made contacts with the other village and occasional conflict of interests inevitable, as when customary rights of pasture or other claims were disputed. An attack from without would demand united action in defending both positions and closing the slight depression which lay between them.

Other small settlements grew up on neighboring hills, perhaps first on the Esquiline, where many remains of its ancient cemetery have been found, near and beneath the line of the "Servian Wall." On the Quirinal was another village, inhabited apparently by Sabines, on the Capitoline another of the same origin, and still another, traditionally but uncertainly connected with Etruscan settlers, on the Caelian. Some primitive council of elders representing the several villages must be imagined as the earliest method of keeping the peace and maintaining order between the small communities. In the process of fusion the first step must have been the consolidation of the two Palatine villages into one, which would then be certain to take the lead, drawing the others gradually into some sort of federation, if that word may be used when the scale of everything was so minute.

Looking again at the separate villages we find them occupied in each case by a few clans (*gentes*). Each *gens* considered itself descended from a common ancestor, and in historical times this was supposed to be indicated by a man's *nomen,* the second of the three names usually borne by a Roman (p. 196). The *gentes* were thus made up of the older families, but such patricians had clients also and humble retainers, attached to the clan but not members of it. Each clan had its own religious cult or cults, and in many cases some custom or customs almost or quite peculiar to itself and maintained by long tradition. Thus the *gens Cornelia,* to which the Scipios and Sulla belonged, continued down to the time of the latter to bury its deceased members, following the more ancient practice of central Italy. Conservative as it was, with customs and practices of its own, the *gens* itself underwent changes, by degrees accepting as members some who could not claim the same ancestry.

The land, both arable tracts and pasture, was long held, it would seem, as common property of the *gens*. Assignments of extremely limited plots to individuals are mentioned very early, but so small was this *heredium* of two *iugera* (1¼ acres) that it was understood to have been merely a garden plot for a farmer who tilled a part also of the land held in common by all the members of his clan. Should he die without lawful claimants the *heredium* reverted to the possession of the clan. Later the individual lots were increased in size, and in the course of time collective ownership gave way to individual tenure.

In these rustic villages there were of course humble folk who were not attached even indirectly to any patrician clan. Obscure as is the origin of the plebeians, no suggestion that they may have been of a different race conquered and kept

in subjection by the patricians, as were the Umbrians by a
warlike Etruscan minority, comes to us from any ancient
authority.

The patrician *gens,* with all its heritage from a patriarchal system, did not have a patriarch at its head. The
elders carried on its traditions, and one of them may have
represented the clan in the senate—the king's counselors—
when that stage of development was reached. For times of
special danger brought the necessity of stronger rule.

At such critical moments the village elders, who were at
the same time spokesmen for their several clans, but often
beyond the age for active leadership, would select one or
two men capable of heading the forces hastily called out to
defend their homes from an enemy. Special fitness, signal
success, or a continued menace might result in a more permanent authority committed to a single chief. Such was
probably the origin of kingship at Rome.

The Romans themselves were unable to go back to the
sources of kingly power, which their historians supposed to
have lasted 245 years before the establishment of the Republic, at a date corresponding to our 509 B.C. Legends
had gathered about the founding of the city and the rule
of its kings, until it was impossible to sift out a few credible
facts from the accumulated mass of fiction. Especially was
this true of the founder, the most shadowy figure of them
all—the Romulus whose name is so obviously derived from
that of the city. Shadowy too was Titus Tatius, whom legend made a Sabine king, and then head of the Sabine element in the new city and a kingly colleague of Romulus.
Yet as a lesser figure he is usually omitted from the standard
list of seven kings. These seven reigns were said to have
covered nearly two centuries and a half, with no short
reigns (none less than twenty-four years) to lower the
incredibly high average of thirty-five years. A warlike

founder was followed in the legend by Numa, a Sabine and yet a man of peace, to whom could be ascribed the establishment of the national religion, its priestly colleges, and the calendar.

Tradition carried the institution of a senate, as advisers to the king, back to the foundation of the monarchy. Upon the death of a king it was to this council of elders that the supreme power (*imperium*) reverted. Not that the "fathers" (*patres*) were to exercise their authority except during a brief interregnum, pending their choice of a successor. And their choice required confirmation by an assembly of the people, voting by groups. Each of these groups was called a *curia,* probably taking its name from its place of meeting.[2] There were thirty *curiae,* each containing a number of clans, not to the exclusion of plebeians, however, since every free man seems to have been a member of a *curia,* sharing in its special religious rites at its particular shrine; and in time the right to vote in the assembly was won by the plebeians. It was this assembly of the *curiae* (*comitia curiata*) which confirmed the senate's choice of a new king. It was not yet a legislative body in a day when the king's authority was unquestioned in law-making as in everything else.

The thirty *curiae,* forming groups of *gentes,* were themselves accounted subdivisions of three ancient "tribes," Ramnes, Tities, and Luceres. These were thought to represent differences of stock, *i.e.,* respectively Latins, Sabines, and Etruscans. When an expression of popular approval was called for, action was taken by the assembly of the *curiae* voting as separate units.

Such differences of race as were obvious in the earliest period gradually disappeared in the process of fusion which went on while the slowly growing city maintained

[2] A hall for meetings, even the Senate House, was called a *curia.*

itself in the midst of enemies, making only a slight enlargement of its territory—down the left bank of the Tiber to the sea, but otherwise only five or six miles from the Palatine in several directions,[3] not toward the east, however, where Roman territory under the earlier kings extended only one or two miles from the city. Before the monarchy fell a diminutive domain of possibly fifty to sixty square miles had been increased by six or seven times.

This great expansion was due to the Etruscan supremacy in the last century of the kingdom. For this period the kings are less unreal, but the truth is still lost in the mazes of legend. The three traditional reigns of Tarquinius Priscus, Servius Tullius (his son-in-law), and Tarquinius Superbus (son or grandson of Priscus and son-in-law of Tullius) are embellished with picturesque tales, but through that purple haze one may discern the contour of Etruscan domination over a city-state which has prospered outwardly in spite of coercion. Legend, not altogether devoid of historical basis, represents this rule of enlightened kings as bringing both good and evil, until a day came when tyranny met its inevitable downfall.

After the revolution, and in immediate succession to the deposed monarch, tradition tells of the rule of magistrates, two in number, sharing equally that supreme power (*imperium*) which had formerly been lodged with the king. These colleagues for a single year at the head of the government were at first called praetors, as leaders of the army, and then consuls. They were elected by the people voting in groups, not in *curiae,* as in the older assembly of the *comitia curiata,* but by centuries, according to the elaborate classification attributed popularly to Servius Tullius, with its five classes graded by a property qualification and sub-

[3] As shown in part by certain religious rites still observed centuries later at the fifth or sixth milestone, *e.g.,* at the grove of the Arvals (p. 125).

divided into centuries [4] (pp. 449 f.). This assembly (*comitia centuriata*), meeting outside the city in the Campus Martius, continued through the whole history of the Republic to be the most important of the popular assemblies for the election of higher magistrates. Plebeians had the right of suffrage, but the group-vote system kept down their influence, except as more and more of their number by acquiring property gained registration in a higher class, thus adding weight to their votes.

If a dangerous emergency arose it became customary even in the early years of the Republic to create a single head of the state for a short term, during which the consuls laid down their authority. This single head was called a dictator and was regularly named by one of the consuls. That danger over, or in any case at the end of six months, the dictator and the master of the horse (*magister equitum*) whom he had himself appointed, resigned, and the consuls resumed their normal functions.

As for the city itself, it was generally believed that an ancient division into four wards called tribes (or regions),[5] dated from the time of Servius Tullius. Their names were local: Suburana (including the Caelian), Esquilina, Collina (including Viminal and Quirinal), and Palatina. These four, none of which embraced the Capitoline, were the city tribes or wards. More important politically were the rustic tribes, of which there may have been as many as seventeen in the early years of the fifth century B.C. Every citizen possessed of a piece of land belonged to one or the

[4] Including the knights (*equites*), there were 193 centuries. Those of the first class (80 in number) voted before those of the second class (20) and so on down. A majority was easily obtained if that very large class of the well-to-do agreed with the knights (18 centuries) in supporting the same man or the same measure.

[5] This division of the city remained until Augustus made his fourteen regions.

other of the tribes, the number of which was from time to time increased up to thirty-five. The older rustic tribes were named from well-known *gentes,* as Fabia, Aemilia, while those added later bore local names, such as Sabatina or Pomptina.

The first two centuries of the Republic were chiefly remembered for the heated struggles between patricians, who were at first in complete control, and plebeians, who though citizens and liable to be called out as soldiers were held down by the upper class, zealous to maintain its superiority by every possible means, including force. To gain one by one the rights refused them, to open the door to public office, to improve their economic situation, were the aims of the plebeian leaders in conflicts which tradition has painted in vivid colors and adorned with many picturesque details. It was a commonly accepted version of the tale that on three different occasions the plebs had organized what would now be called a general strike, except that it was political and not industrial. One of these so-called secessions was said to have occurred within fifteen years after the expulsion of the last king, that is, in 494 B.C. This was described as an armed withdrawal of all the plebeians to a hill outside the city, and a refusal to return until concessions were made. Though accounts differed, it was commonly supposed that the chief result was the establishment of special officials to safeguard the rights of the plebeians. These were the tribunes of the plebs, at first two or five in number, but presently ten, elected by the assembly of the *curiae.*[6] In 471 B.C. a law was adopted that the plebeian magistrates, that is, tribunes and the plebeian aediles (market officials primarily), should be elected by an assembly of the tribes. Thus a new assembly was created in which a citizen voted as member of a tribe, and the tribe itself voted as one unit

[6] As stated by Cicero with the evident approval of Asconius.

in the assembly. This *comitia tributa* was destined to play a
very important rôle in the history of the Republic, especially in legislation, in spite of the absence of any device by
which the citizen living at a distance could vote without
coming to Rome.

In the middle of the fifth century came a strong demand
of the people for a written code of laws, that legal knowledge might not be confined to patricians. A commission
was sent to Greece to prepare the way by a study of the
laws of Greek states. Upon the return of the three commissioners they were made members of a board of ten
(*decemviri*) empowered to draw up a code. Unlike commissions of the same type in modern times, this board was
not treated as a body of mere legal experts. They were to
be at the same time a "college" of chief magistrates, taking
the place of consuls and other magistrates for that year,
451 B.C. A similar board, containing some of the same men
and even plebeians, was set up for the following year. The
result was the so-called Laws of the Twelve Tables, the
tenth and eleventh tables being the work of the second
board of decemvirs, and in a different spirit, decidedly unfavorable to the populace. Thus there was to be no legal
marriage (*conubium*) between a patrician and a plebeian.

The new code—the only code Rome was ever to produce
—was not epoch-making in its content. In large part it consisted of old customary law merely reduced to writing and
for the first time made accessible to all on twelve bronze
tablets set up in the Comitium, at the speakers' platform
later known as the Rostra. Harshness of that customary
law was somewhat mitigated, though the debtor found his
unhappy plight much the same as before. The rate of interest was fixed, and the usurer treated as a worse criminal
than the thief. Some few improvements, such as the law
against extravagance at funerals and that which permitted

clubs and guilds, are said to have been copied from Greek laws, especially those of Solon. The great gain was in publicity, so that the way of the arbitrary magistrate, ready to oppress his inferiors, was made more difficult.

Nevertheless the temporary rule of the decemvirs, during which time there were neither consuls nor tribunes, nor any right of appeal from the sentence of a magistrate, produced much friction and ended in another revolt of the plebeians (449 B.C.). As a result the right of appeal was restored, as was also the tribuneship with added safeguards. Another provision of these Valerio-Horatian laws, passed by the assembly of the centuries, was that legislation by the plebeian assembly—the plebs assembled in their tribes—should be binding for the whole people. This seemed to give *plebiscita* the validity of *leges,* but the contest still continued. Even Publilius's law of 339 B.C., reaffirming the equal validity of plebiscites and laws (of the *comitia centuriata*), does not appear to have been effectual. It was not until 287 B.C., when the distress of debtors caused another secession of the plebs, that a law proposed by a plebeian dictator, Hortensius, at last effectually established the right of the assembly of the tribes to pass laws equally binding upon all citizens.

Long and bitter had been the struggles of the plebeians to secure their representation in the greater magistracies. A famous stage of advancement was reached in 367 B.C., when the tribunes Licinius and Sextius brought about the passage of a law that at least one of the two consuls must always be a plebeian, and that plebeians might be chosen members of one of the leading priestly colleges. A plebeian name had never before appeared in the list of consuls. The year 366 B.C. was accordingly a landmark in Roman history; but it was almost two hundred years before two plebeians were colleagues in that office (172 B.C.).

By slow degrees and through intense party strife the gulf between patrician and plebeian had been bridged. The clash which had been so largely political became henceforth economic—the poor against the rich, with crises intensified by the increasing number of slaves. It cannot be said, however, that the dominant element was in immediate danger of losing its control of the state.

A new class, for which there is no parallel in any modern state, was slowly taking shape as the disabilities of the plebeians were removed. This was a novel kind of nobility, to which a plebeian attained by holding public office of the higher grades. In strict usage *nobiles* were the sons or descendants of a former high official, but the term loosely applied covered also the "new man" (*novus homo*) who by political prominence first brought distinction to his family. Patricians also were of course included in the *nobilitas* as descendants of former magistrates. Thus the old aristocracy, enlarged and renewed by the new element which owed its rise to the success of individuals in elections and their consequent admission to the senate by the censors, became the dominant factor in the Roman government during the third and second centuries B.C.

From the beginning of the Republic two officials called quaestors had assisted the consuls in the administration of justice and of the public treasury. Shortly after the publication of the Twelve Tables their office became elective (447 B.C.), and to it candidates were chosen by the tribal assembly. The number was soon raised to four, then to eight, and much later to twenty by Sulla,[7] with the provision that a quaestor should become at once a member of the senate.

Higher in the scale were the aediles, that is, an older "college" of two plebeian aediles, originally assistants to the

---

[7] The number rose to forty under Julius Caesar, but was reduced to twenty by Augustus.

tribunes, and two curule aediles, at first patricians; but soon
the office was opened to plebeians. Both "colleges" were
elected by popular assemblies. They were street commissioners, having charge also of markets, temples, and baths,
as well as a share in responsibility for public works (p.
19). They had some police powers and later were charged
with the grain supply. A popular function of the aediles
was their management of certain greater festivals (*ludi*),
at which lavish expense on their part in providing entertainments was a highroad to success at the next election for
a higher office.

Frequent mention has been made of the tribunes of the
plebs as champions of the commoners. They were ten in
number and chosen by the popular assembly. By individual
action or jointly they could effectually block any action or
proposal of other officials, for their right to intervene as the
defenders of a plebeian in distress had developed into a veto
of almost unlimited range. The tribunes sat in the senate,
and while any one of them could punish a magistrate who
persisted in the face of his veto, his own personal safety
was assured. To attack his sacrosanct person was a capital
offense for which no trial was allowed.

Above tribunes and aediles and inferior only to the consuls were the praetors (at first a single praetor, from 366
B.C.). They were entitled to the official chair, the *sella
curulis,* resembling a camp stool, but with legs usually made
of tusks of ivory or adorned with ivory, and they wore a
toga bordered with purple, the *toga praetexta.* One of the
praetors, the *praetor urbanus,* might be called the chief
justice, sitting as such on a platform in the open Forum.
His colleague, the *praetor peregrinus,* heard cases in which
non-Romans were involved. The rest of the "college,"
which at different times under the later Republic numbered
eight, ten, and sixteen, were governors of provinces. After

the permanent courts were established, chiefly by Sulla, they were judges and then automatically in the following year provincial governors. As they stood next to the consuls, having some executive functions also, with at times the command of armies, they had the full authority (*imperium*) and were elected by the military assembly of the centuries. The *praetor urbanus* alone was attended by lictors, two in number.[8] Of the greatest importance in the development of Roman law was the edict reissued with changes by each new *praetor urbanus,* declaring in advance how he proposed to interpret the laws, with what tempering of the letter by his understanding of the spirit (p. 308).

At the top of the official ladder in normal times stood the consuls, holding office, like all the magistrates just named, for a single year. A consul had held in succession the previous offices (with an option as between tribuneship and aedileship), and must be at least forty-two years old. He was elected by the *comitia centuriata* and held the *imperium,* as was outwardly declared by twelve lictors always in attendance when he was on duty, to overawe the crowd by their bundle of rods, to which axes were added only when he left the city. Like the praetors the consuls had the *sella curulis* and wore the *toga praetexta.* They presided in the senate and in assemblies of the *populus,* as over some public festivals and other religious functions, offering sacrifices, taking auspices, and pronouncing vows. Financial matters and taxation added to their responsibilities. They raised and commanded armies, organized newly conquered territory, and might even govern a province. Later, under a rule established by Sulla, the government of a province followed the consulship. Between the two colleagues there was often occasion for friction, usually avoided by mutual agreement as to precedence for a month or other fixed term.

[8] In his province a praetor had six.

Their crowning distinction was to have their coupled names used to date events occurring in their year of office, in place of a date reckoned from the founding of the city.

In a great emergency it sometimes became the duty of a consul, as we have seen, to name a dictator (p. 12), and the temporary transfer of power to the hands of the latter was indicated by his escort of twenty-four lictors bearing axes even in the city. This extraordinary office with almost unrestricted powers was allowed to lapse after the Second Punic War. In a totally different form and without limit of time it was revived by Sulla and again by Julius Caesar.

Above the consulship in dignity but not in authority was the censorship. It was only once in five years that the state had censors, two in number (ex-consuls as a rule), for a term of a year and a half. They also were elected by the assembly of the centuries, and their duties included the census, the resultant classification of the citizens, assessment, the finances of the state, public works, such as aqueducts, bridges, roads, and buildings for public uses. In the interval between censorships the finances fell chiefly to consuls and quaestors, public works to aediles. Another function of the censors down to Sulla's day was the revision of the list of senators (*lectio senatus*), and of that of the knights, adding to both all names of the eligible and deleting those of the undesirable. In this way they were guardians of the public morals.

It was indeed a singular structure, that Roman state, with its annual officials grouped in boards or "colleges." The old and familiar in law or custom was always being bent and strained to meet new needs with the least overt departure from long-established practice, as summed up in time-honored phrase, such as *mos maiorum* or *mores antiqui,* impressive in their weight of feeling for the dignity of the past and for continuity as in itself a virtue.

The institutions which had sufficed for a small city and its very limited territory with a population largely rustic were being perpetually subjected to a process of distension and distortion, as frontiers kept advancing, at first very slowly, and then by leaps and bounds. A senate of 300 members, not enlarged until Sulla raised the number to 600,[9] remained the same in outward appearance, but by degrees came to be a body entirely made up of men who had served as magistrates, since the censors, who drew up the revised list of members, interpreted the law of Ovinius (before 312 B.C.), as making none but ex-magistrates eligible. From the dictatorship of Sulla the quaestor became immediately a member of the senate.

As a result of this method of making up the senate—a feature unique among parliamentary bodies—the direction of public affairs was in the hands of this large council of experienced men, able to give their whole time continuously to the task. Actual authority belonged rather to the short-term magistrates, but as senators they were sure to be influenced largely by their fellow members. Reënforced by the new "nobility," automatically raised above the plebeian plane by office-holding, the senate became the real government in the period of the great wars with Pyrrhus, with Carthage, with Macedonia and Syria. The apparent democracy finally achieved after the plebeians had captured every position defended against them by the patricians was in reality controlled by an aristocracy which combined high ability and extensive experience with social distinction, and only strengthened itself by admitting the exceptional man from the ranks.

The outward form of democracy was still to be seen in the popular assemblies. That of the centuries (*comitia cen-*

[9] This was the normal figure from Augustus's time, after a temporary increase to 900 by Julius Caesar.

turiata) had no organic connection with the tribes until about the end of the First Punic War, when a reform of this assembly diminished the preponderance which the "Servian" constitution had given to the well-to-do [10] (p. 12, n. 4). With the more democratic trend this assembly lost in importance, except for the election of the highest magistrates, and for a declaration of war, while the *comitia tributa* gained. Not that either assembly took a prominent part in the general conduct of affairs. Every increase of territory made it more manifestly impossible for the actual government to be taken away from the senate, since so small a part of the entire citizen body could express its will in assemblies that failed completely to be representative and on occasion so easily degenerated into mobs.

Legislation in such a body as the assembly of the tribes was feasible only in approving or rejecting a bill introduced by the presiding official. Such a bill was seldom presented if it was known not to meet the approval of leading senators conversant with the matters involved. Rare were the occasions when a leader was able to carry an important measure through a popular assembly in the face of disapproval by the senate. An example is the first agrarian law, that of Flaminius in 232 B.C., granting to citizens farms out of public lands along the Adriatic; and sane as this measure was, Flaminius was branded as a demagogue.

The reluctance of the dominant class, the optimates, as they styled themselves, to react to a changed situation, requiring some sacrifice of personal and class advantages to the real interests of the state as a whole, was largely responsible for the rise of later leaders of the people, such as the Gracchi, themselves members of the governing class, but unable to rouse it to share their vision of a better order,

---

[10] Each of the thirty-five tribes was now divided into ten centuries, two from each of the five property classes.

based upon a restoration of the middle class and a liberal extension of citizen rights. Their policies would have ended the rule of a selfish senate, with what result for the state, no one could venture to predict.

Corrupt and ignominious conduct by the aristocrats of a war in Africa against Jugurtha helped to make a popular hero of the plebeian victor, Marius, who presently saved the state from the great invasion of the Cimbri and the Teutons by his victories (102-101 B.C.), after previous generals had met with disastrous defeats. His unprecedented reëlection as consul for five successive years intensified the heated struggle of the day between the popular party and the *nobilitas*. Other leaders in the contest, such as Saturninus and Drusus, by further land laws and other measures in advance of their time aroused opposition and suffered violent deaths. The strange Social War, so called from the Italian allies (*socii*), who actually won Roman citizenship by the sword, was followed by civil wars between Marius and Sulla and by the dictatorship (82-79 B.C.) of the latter, attended by cruel proscriptions.

Reaction gave the popular party opportunity to curb the senate, which found important decisions wrested from it by demands for vigorous measures, as when the popular assembly (67-66 B.C.) gave almost unlimited powers to Pompey for the suppression of piracy, and again for the war with Mithridates. It was evident that the traditional form of government had completely broken down. Short-lived harmony fostered by Cicero between senators and knights could not really lessen the danger of further civil wars. Corruption in the government, especially evident in the provinces, had greatly diminished the prestige of the senate. No conservative was able to offer a solution. A radical could solve the problem only by force, and such a champion of popular rights was all but certain to turn tyrant as soon as he found himself in the saddle. Pompey or Caesar might at first be hailed as champion of the people, but this would be only a step toward supreme power, possibly in the form of a masked dictatorship, while traditional institutions were nominally preserved. With Caesar the design to rebuild the Roman state became increasingly apparent. It is idle, however, to speculate as to just how he would have ended the anomaly of a city-state attempting to control a world-empire with outworn machinery creaking at every joint.

With Octavian, Caesar's heir, came the policy of preserving with pious care what we should call an unwritten constitution in its time-honored forms, as a screen ingeniously pieced together. Behind this lurked an immense power, monarchical in all but the name. Nominally city-state and ancestral customs were still there, while senate and first citizen, the new *princeps,* appeared to divide amicably the burdens of responsibility for a world exhausted by civil strife and in need of nothing so much as recuperation. In reality empire has stolen upon the stage, and the old urban state has passed into history as truly as had the first thatched village on the Palatine, leaving underground its clay house-models for the twentieth century to recover.

II

MAKING AN EMPIRE

FECISTI PATRIAM DIVERSIS GENTIBVS VNAM:
  PROFVIT INVITIS, TE DOMINANTE, CAPI.
DVMQVE OFFERS VICTIS PROPRII CONSORTIA IVRIS,
  VRBEM FECISTI QVOD PRIVS ORBIS ERAT.

RUTILIUS NAMATIANUS, 1, 63

ARMORVM LEGVMQVE PARENS; QVAE FVNDIT IN OMNES
IMPERIVM PRIMIQVE DEDIT CVNABVLA IVRIS.
HAEC EST EXIGVIS QVAE FINIBVS ORTA TETENDIT
IN GEMINOS AXES PARVAQVE A SEDE PROFECTA
DISPERSIT CVM SOLE MANVS.

.   .   .

HAEC EST IN GREMIVM VICTOS QVAE SOLA RECEPIT
HVMANVMQVE GENVS COMMVNI NOMINE FOVIT
MATRIS NON DOMINAE RITV CIVESQVE VOCAVIT,
QVOS DOMVIT, NEXVQVE PIO LONGINQVA REVINXIT.

CLAUDIAN, DE CONSULATU
STILICHONIS, 3, 136

NAM PVLSIS, QVOD DI PROHIBEANT, ROMANIS QVID ALIVD QVAM BELLA
OMNIVM INTER SE GENTIVM EXISTENT? OCTINGENTORVM ANNORVM FORTVNA
DISCIPLINAQVE COMPAGES HAEC COALVIT, QVAE CONVELLI SINE EXITIO CON-
VELLENTIVM NON POTEST.

TACITUS, HISTORIES, 4, 74

THAT a village on a hill by the Tiber should have expanded into an empire encircling the Mediterranean and reaching far beyond its shores was even to the age of Augustus such a marvel as could be explained only by the divine will.

> His ego nec metas rerum nec tempora pono;
> imperium sine fine dedi

are the words in which Vergil's Jupiter promises that the future city shall have no limits to its power either in space or time. And the soberest of historians, Tacitus, the most willing to see the darker side of conquest, admits only a temporary *terminus* to Roman rule. Here however we may mark our field with just such provisional *metae rerum* as shall stake out for us the boundaries of Rome's advancing power at four significant dates.

The first line of such *termini* will include no more than Latium, with parts of Etruria on the north and of Campania on the south. The second will embrace Italy—the peninsula proper, but not the great plain overarched by the Alps. The third line, tracing vastly expanded frontiers, makes a complete circuit of the Mediterranean if we include the client states. Our fourth and final beating of the bounds must carry us around the outer borders of vast hinterlands, to Clyde and Forth, Crimea and Caspian, Euphrates and—for two short years—Tigris and Persian Gulf.

And marking as clearly the corresponding periods we shall have: (1) some four centuries, to 338 B.C.; (2) three-quarters of a century, to the beginning of the First Punic War, 264 B.C.; (3) two momentous centuries, to 63 B.C., thus including Pompey's conquests and reorganization of the East; (4) two more centuries from the decade which

saw Caesar at the Rhine and the Thames to the generation
which heard of Trajan at the mouth of the Tigris (115
A.D.) and, at the other extreme and a little later, of the
great defenses drawn across North Britain by Hadrian and
Antoninus Pius.

If we take our stand for the moment at the year 338 B.C.,
when the Latin League came to an end in the subjection of
all Latium to Rome, and look northward, we note that
already a good part of southern Etruria also was under
Roman rule. For the nearest of the Etruscan cities, Veii,
only twelve miles away, after a stubborn siege had been
destroyed in 396 B.C. and her territory parceled out to plebeians. Five years later Volsinii (Orvieto), the chief city
of the Twelve, had suffered a humiliating defeat, while
Ṣutrium (Sutri, north of the Lake of Bracciano) soon became a Roman frontier stronghold. A generation later the
important city of Caere (Cerveteri), a commercial center
within twenty-five miles of Rome, with two seaports, Pyrgi
and Alsium, was compelled to give up half of her territory
and accept an inferior grade of Roman citizenship.

Turning to the south at the same period we find the
Roman in possession of nearly half of Campania, with a
garrison established in 343 B.C. at Capua, which had been
wrested from the Etruscans by the Samnites perhaps a century before. Thus southward expansion beyond the limits
of Latium had begun, but far more progress had been made
toward the north.

Within Latium itself the old system of the League, confirmed as far back as 493 B.C. by a treaty engraved on a
bronze column, which Cicero could remember having seen
behind the Rostra, had given way to an undisguised Roman
supremacy based upon a notable victory over Latins and
Campanians at Trifanum in 340 B.C. There was an end of

incessant wars with neighbors such as Tibur (Tivoli), Tusculum (near Frascati), Praeneste (Palestrina) and the Vol-
scian Antium (Anzio), whose fleet, given to piracy, it was
said, surrendered to the Romans in 338 B.C. No more do we
read of perpetual wars with Aequi and Volsci, since these
tribes and their neighbors, the Hernici, now combine with
the Latins to form an enlarged Latium stretching from the
Tiber to the borders of Campania.

The final conquest of that larger Latium found Rome
firmly planted both in southern Etruria and the northern
half of Campania. It was a total range of about 150 miles
from northwest to southeast, while in breadth her territory,
narrow elsewhere, reached as far as fifty miles from the sea
only among the Aequi, eastward of Rome.

Of this stage of Roman expansion an ancient visitor to
the Forum and Comitium was reminded by the bronze
ships' beaks (*rostra*) from Antium, placed there as trophies
upon the front of the speakers' platform (p. 14) in that
very year (338 B.C.).

The long period here so summarily traversed included
chapters which must not be passed over without brief mention. For more than a century Rome was ruled by Etruscan
kings, the two Tarquins—so tradition said—separated by
the intervening reign of Servius Tullius (Mastarna). There
followed the age of the early Republic, with its two elected
magistrates, dividing the powers of the king. Again for a
time Rome was humbled by the Etruscans, though we may
never know the details of this second and briefer period of
foreign domination.

It was an age of struggles on the part of the patricians to
retain their privileges, on the side of the plebeians to gain
their rights, a share in the government, and better living
conditions. One of the most important concessions ever
made to the plebeians was the framing and publication, as

we have seen, of the Laws of the Twelve Tables (p. 14).

During the next century the menace of Etruria was much diminished. In fact the whole northern region was itself threatened by an invasion from beyond the Alps. Gallic tribes from the Danube country swarmed into the plains of the Po, seizing the Etruscan cities of the plain and by degrees advancing southward. In 390 B.C. (387 according to Polybius) they even descended upon Rome, defeated the army sent against them at the Allia, burned the city, and besieged the Capitol for months. But after accepting a ransom they returned to northern Italy, leaving a terrible memory and chronic dread of similar raids.

Our second line of *termini* we should establish only two generations later, shortly before the outbreak of the First Punic War in 264 B.C., and it would include nearly the whole of peninsular Italy. The northern frontier was an irregular line drawn across from the Adriatic at the little Rubicon, north of the new colony of Ariminum (p. 39) [1] to the Mediterranean twenty miles south of Pisae (Pisa) on the Arnus (Arno), the greater part of that valley lying outside of Roman territory. Within the preceding decade the last of the Greek cities of southern Italy had submitted to Rome, after the failure of Pyrrhus, King of Epirus, whom the citizens of Tarentum had invited to cross into Italy as a champion of the Greeks. Twice he had gained notable victories over the Romans with the help of his elephants (280 and 279 B.C.), but though he advanced within little more than twenty miles of Rome, he was unable to induce the senate to make peace. After losing two years in Sicily in an unsuccessful effort to unite the Greeks of Syracuse and other cities, he renewed the conflict with Rome, only to suffer a great defeat at Beneventum (275 B.C.). Fleeing to Tarentum he soon returned to his own kingdom,

---

[1] Previously the boundary was the river Aesis, northwest of Ancona.

leaving the Romans to settle scores with the Lucanians and other tribes, to capture Tarentum (272 B.C.) and complete the conquest of southern Italy, founding colonies and establishing themselves at the port of Brundisium (Brindisi).

Tangible evidence of this important stage of progress exists to this day in the oldest Roman silver coins, the *denarius* (ten asses), *quinarius,* and *sestertius,* first minted, if Livy and Pliny were correctly informed, just at this time. Of very nearly the same date was the Temple of Tellus on the Esquiline, containing a map of Italy (p. 287) and often used for meetings of the senate—a reminder to later ages of the city as it was before the First Punic War, but a mere name to us.

Before passing to the next period, however, we should cast one look backward into the last quarter of the fourth century B.C. and the first decade of the third. Thirty years of obstinate warfare with the warlike Samnites, interrupted by only six years of armistice, had ended in 290 B.C. with the submission of these dreaded mountaineers, who had inflicted one historic defeat upon the Romans at the Caudine pass (321 B.C.), not to mention less serious reverses. Several times in these years the Etruscans, Umbrians, and Gauls had increased the dangers of the struggle with the Samnites, while not a few cities subject to Rome rose in revolt. It was the end, however, of the Etruscan power, and before hostilities with Carthage began Roman rule in all its varied grades of subjection (including nominal allies and dependent states) had expanded with such amazing rapidity as completely to cover the peninsula proper, now united in a single federation.

The third period of expansion covers just two centuries and, if we include protectorates and client-states, the boundaries reached at the close of this age actually encircle the Mediterranean—a colossal addition to the territory which the Romans had possessed when they first ventured upon a war with Carthage two hundred years before. It was now *Mare nostrum* indeed, and on a voyage of circumnavigation a ship could have found no port of that sea not subject either directly to Rome or dependent in some degree upon her, as belonging, for example, to a client-state such as Egypt,[2] Mauretania, or Massilia. The year at which we pause for this amazing survey is 63 B.C., when Pompey with extraordinary powers conferred upon him for the purpose in 66 B.C. had driven Mithridates, King of Pontus, out of Asia Minor,[3] and was occupied in organizing new provinces and dependencies, and in permanently settling the affairs of the East, in preparation for a triumphant return to Rome in the next year. He was leaving behind a political geography extraordinarily complex, including besides actual provinces the territories of vassal princes and kings, of high priests who were at the same time princes, of city-states, some of them nominally free. It was the same kind of mosaic which was to remain characteristic of Roman rule in the East even under the Empire. The accession of so much new territory, embracing Syria, Palestine, and a considerable part of Asia Minor, enormously increased the revenues of the state, now acknowledged as the only world-power, with no possible rival except Parthia.[4]

This particular stage of conquest expressed itself visibly and tangibly at Rome in the great group of Pompey's mon-

[2] Left by will of Alexander II to the Romans in 81 B.C. There were Roman troops in Egypt from 55, though a provincial government was not set up until 30 B.C. Similar was the status of Cyprus (previously Egyptian) until it was formally taken over by Cato in 58 B.C. (cp. p. 46, for Cyrene also).

[3] Mithridates had been for many years the terror of the East and of Greece. Fleeing at last to the north shore of the Black Sea and still dreaming of an invasion of Italy by land, he was forced to suicide by his own son in this same year, 63 B.C., in the consulship of Cicero.

[4] For the new provinces of this period see pp. 46 ff.

rapidly was it occupied by new settlers from the eastern
shore of the Adriatic and from Asia Minor, after the native
Dacians had been driven out or exterminated. There had
been a rush to the gold mines and to the lands of a country
very recently opened to settlement after destructive wars.
Arrived at last at the Black Sea we should probably have
taken a coasting vessel for the Crimea, where the Bosporan
kingdom flourished under Roman protection, its Greek
cities having Roman garrisons and trading in wheat and
raw materials from what is now southern Russia. Continuing our coasting voyage, and touching at some of the Greek
towns similarly protected on the northeast shore of the
Black Sea, we should have landed at Phasis and journeyed
along the northern border of Armenia, at the foot of the
Caucasus, to the Caspian. Thence following the southeastern boundary of the same new province we should have
reached the Tigris and still another recently acquired province, Mesopotamia. By boat down the river we should come
at length to the Persian Gulf below Charax, where Trajan
was eager to take ship for India. Returning we should
travel by boat up the Euphrates, perhaps to Zeugma (p.
87) and then by caravan across the desert via Palmyra,
and then southward by a similar route to Petra in Arabia,
and so to the Red Sea. Crossing into Egypt at Berenice we
should again mount a camel for the journey across to the
Nile (p. 87). After a brief trip up the river to Syene
(Assuan) we should travel comfortably downstream all the
way to Alexandria. As for the provinces to the west of
Egypt, we should perhaps be satisfied with the knowledge
that they were all bounded on the south by the Sahara, and
taking ship at Alexandria we should coast along to the west,
stopping at the most important ports, such as Cyrene, Oea
(Tripoli), Carthage and Hippo Regius (Bône), long
enough to form some impressions of these cities and their

surroundings, and to make some short trips into the interior. Finally we should pause at Tingis (Tangier) in Mauretania, and thence across to our starting point beneath the rock of Gibraltar (Calpe).

Many months would have been spent in such travel, but we should have felt rewarded by the endlessly varied scenes in distant lands and peoples most diverse, yet strangely united, as never before. We should have realized too that there were other lands just beyond the pale and other peoples no less varied who were waiting without for an opportunity to force their way into Roman territory.

At one extreme were the savage Caledonians, at the other vast regions peopled by unconquered Parthians, proud heirs of the Persian traditions, and now eager to recover the ample territory recently torn from them by Trajan. With his annexation of western Parthia we have reached the culmination. Rome had found her farthest *termini,* only to have the new eastern boundaries given up by Hadrian upon his accession. Armenia was indeed restored to its former condition as a vassal-state.

For a tangible reminder of this fourth stage, in which Roman expansion reached its ultimate limit, we have only to study the impressive remains of Trajan's Forum (p. 387), his column, or the triumphs of peace on his arch at Beneventum (p. 341), on that highroad to the East, the Appian Way.

If in the long history of Roman expansion the later phases are the most amazing, the secret of success is rather to be sought in the methods of the forefathers, the causes of eventual failure in neglect of means formerly thought essential or in their inapplicability on so vast a scale. Naturally we ask ourselves "How was conquest so soon followed by assimilation that anything like unity could be achieved?" and "How under the Empire could assimilation prove possible at all?" These inquiries into the problem of absorption lead us back to the young Republic and a study of its methods of treating former enemies as allies united by treaty, of sending its own men out to form colonies, of drawing cities once hostile into organic relations with Rome as *municipia,* of organizing, governing, and defending conquered territories as provinces.

THE ALLIES

One method of stabilizing relations with defeated enemies was from earliest times that of alliance, as though between equals. A formal treaty (*foedus*) tactfully kept the fact of recent submission in the background. The new allies (*socii*) were guaranteed the possession of their lands, the use of their own laws, courts, and forms of government. They were exempt from tribute, but obliged to furnish a specified contingent of infantry or cavalry to the Roman army. Such an allied state (*civitas foederata*) was in theory outside of Roman territory and could shelter exiles from Rome. A very early example was Greek Neapolis (Naples), forced by siege to submit in 326 B.C. and required, as were other Greek cities later, to furnish ships for the navy in place of troops. With the end of that war in 290 B.C., the third against the Samnites, this entire people in its half-dozen subdivisions, Marsi, Picentes, etc., became *socii* of the Roman people as tribal units. Of allied city-states there were many, scattered from Etruria (Tarquinii, Perusia, Arretium, and others) to the far south (as Velia, Heraclea, Rhegium). Even in Latium there were such federated city-states as Tibur, Praeneste, Lavinium.

But these allies, though in name protected by a treaty, were at times obliged to accept a law or a decree imposed upon them by Rome. An outstanding instance is the famous

decree of the senate suppressing the Bacchic orgies in 186
B.C.—a police regulation which the allies were commanded
to enforce (p. 128). Similarly in 193 B.C. a law (*lex Sempronia*) prescribed the same treatment of debts for allies as
for citizens. And even a sumptuary law to restrain luxury
in feasting was made in 143 B.C. to apply to all the allies as
well. They were not safe from abuses at the hands of Roman
officials. Oppression and arbitrary treatment were not want-
ing, and violation of rights led to increasing ferment among
the allies. More strenuous were the demands for Roman
citizenship, as it became more evident that the nominal ally
was in reality a depressed subject. Gaius Gracchus proposed
to grant full citizen rights to all who then had the *Latin*
citizenship, and the rights of the latter grade to all *socii* in
Italy—this in the face of fierce opposition to any such increase in the number of citizens. No timely concession was
made, and the storm brewed until it burst in the Social War
(90-88 B.C.). This bitter and devastating conflict forced the
victorious Romans to grant the demands of the defeated
allies, first to those who had not rebelled and then to those
who had done so. From the year 88 B.C. there were no more
civitates foederatae or *Latin* colonies in Italy. It was now
an Italy of Roman citizens up to the Arno and the Rubicon.

COLONIES AND MUNICIPIA

In the gradual expansion of the Roman federation, as of
some modern empires, colonization played a very important part. It has even been said that the history of Roman
colonization is the history of the Roman state. But colony
as then understood has no counterpart in the modern world.
While it served incidentally the familiar purpose of more
recent colonies as an outlet for an overgrown population,
its real object was far less economic than military and political. Fresh territory gained by arms was thus to be

secured, held and cultivated. It was a town, usually a fortified town taken from an enemy, to become now not merely a
Roman stronghold, of military importance, but a center for
the whole region. Of the lands belonging to such a town
previous to the Roman occupation two-thirds were usually
left in the possession of the conquered, the remainder divided among the newcomers from Rome. The members of
the colony came out as a compact unit, their migration duly
authorized in every case by a decree of the senate and a law
passed by the people. This law determined the number of
the *coloni,* the position and amounts of the lands taken
from the enemy and now to be assigned by commissioners
named in the law. It was by a formal act of the state, not a
mere charter or patent, that these functionaries "led off"
(*deducere*) the veteran soldiers with their late centurions
and comrades, together with other citizens to form the new
colonia. They were to be exempt from further military
service except in defense, to repair the ravages of war, till
the soil, live among their former enemies and by degrees
Romanize them. They were not free to remove, and if they
were in an especially exposed situation residence restrictions were severe.

In a short time the outpost became a center of Roman influence, all the more effective in the slow process of unification because of its strategic position. Thus placed colonies
were, in Cicero's words, *propugnacula imperi,* "bulwarks
of empire," not mere towns. They took pride in every feature which increased their resemblance to the capital.

The earliest of these "little images" of Rome, as Gellius
calls them, were composed of full Roman citizens and
placed on the coast, to ward off an enemy's fleet or pirates
in case of attack. Ostia, at the mouth of the Tiber, was
ascribed by tradition to the time of the kings (Ancus Martius), but archaeology is unable to find traces of any settle-

ment more than a generation older than the establishment
of a colony there about the end of the fourth century B.C.
Antium received a colony in 338, Tarracina in 329 B.C.
Through the latter the Appian Way was presently carried
(p. 97), and strengthened by colonies at two points of danger, Minturnae and Sinuessa, in 296. And as early as 283
we find a colony sent to Sena Gallica on the Adriatic.

Many colonies possessing the inferior grade of citizenship (*Latinitas*), and made up of Latins and former Roman
citizens, were very old, as Signia, founded in 495 and Norba
in 492 B.C. Later came Ardea, 442; Sutrium and Setia, 383
and 382 respectively. In this class of *Latin* colonies special
interest attaches to Venusia, where an abnormally strong
colony (20,000 *coloni*) was placed in 291 B.C., to hold a
portion of the Samnite territory. Gradually the different
elements of the population, including Apulians, Lucanians,
and Romans, coalesced. Non-Latins were by degrees Romanized, and from such stock eventually sprang the poet
Horace, son of a former slave. Ariminum became a colony
of this class before the First Punic War, and Brundisium
during the war. There were thirty such *Latin* colonies in
Italy by the time of the Second Punic War, including Cremona and Placentia, just established as outposts on the Po,
in Cisalpine Gaul.

Roman colonies with full citizenship continued to increase in number, eight being sent out in the one year 194
B.C., among them that which went to Puteoli, destined to
become the leading seaport, and that to Salernum. In the
age of the Gracchi the *colonia* gained a new importance
from the increased stress upon its economic benefit in providing for the impoverished. Thus the Greek city of Tarentum was enlarged in 122 B.C. by a colony of Roman citizens.
In the same year it was proposed by Gaius Gracchus to send
another to the site of Carthage, strewn with ruins since the

year 146. But so radical a measure as colonization overseas, in part to encourage commerce, was violently opposed by the conservatives, who were able to force the abandonment of the plan. The very liberal land-assignments, however, were made to individuals, and 6,000 Romans actually settled about Carthage without the colony organization. The one Roman colony established as such outside of Italy down to the end of the second century B.C. was in southern Gaul, Narbo Martius (Narbonne), 118 B.C., a trade center and capital of the newly won province between the Alps and the Pyrenees. Sulla, following the example of Marius, was conspicuously active in founding on confiscated lands colonies for his 120,000 veterans at such places as Faesulae (Fiesole), Pompeii, Praeneste.

With Julius Caesar and the triumvirs begins a period of greater activity in sending out such colonies, for example, to Capua, Pisae, Pola, Tauromenium (Taormina) in Sicily, Corduba (Cordova) and Hispalis (Seville) in southern Spain. In Gaul should be named the Rhone cities, Arelate (Arles), Arausio (Orange), Lugdunum (Lyons), and others. In Macedonia, Philippi, and in Achaia, Corinth (rebuilt 44-43 B.C., after lying in ruins a hundred years), belong to the colonies of this period. Augustus, who also had hordes of veterans to reward, founded many, such as Augusta Praetoria (Aosta) in Italy, Valentia (Valence), Vienna (Vienne), and Nemausus (Nîmes) in Gaul, Augusta Emerita (Mérida) in Lusitania, Berytus (Beirut) in Syria. In Africa Carthage became formally a colony at the hands of Julius Caesar (45 B.C.) and was reënforced by Augustus, becoming in time one of the greatest cities of the empire. On the Rhine we find from 51 A.D. the colony which has left its name to Cologne (Köln), *i.e.,* Colonia Agrippinensis, the only real colony in the vast territory conquered by Caesar. Many chief towns of the Gallic tribes, however,

had the title *colonia* conferred upon them, *e.g.,* Augusta
Treverorum (Trier, Trèves). Even in Britain there were
four actual colonies: Camulodunum (Colchester), Glevum
(Gloucester), Eburacum (York), and Lindum (Lincoln).
Merely titular colonies in the East were such cities as Heli-
opolis (Baalbek), Caesarea, and Palmyra in Syria, Carrhae
in Mesopotamia. In Africa Leptis Magna (Lepcis), of special interest on account of recent excavations, was also a
colony only by courtesy.

Under the Republic and the early Empire the colony was
a very real thing and colonization the active and vigilant
handmaid of victory. "Wherever the Roman conquers he
dwells" (*Ubicunque vicit Romanus habitat*), said Seneca,
and the secret of Roman expansion could not be aptly expressed in fewer words, unless we may venture to apply to
the colonies the proverb *Romanus sedendo vincit.*

Hardly less important in their contribution to ultimate
unification was the third important class of cities and towns,
representing not the action of a centrifugal force, as did the
colonies, but a continuous centripetal attraction. These were
the *municipia,* city-states located on what had been foreign
soil, but now bound closely to Rome by the fact that they
had received as entire communities the rights of Roman
citizens. At the same time they retained to some extent their
own customs and in a limited measure their own laws, being
governed by magistrates elected by themselves. There was
no systematic attempt to reduce them to a uniform basis.
Their own language gave way but slowly to Latin and gradually the Roman law was substituted for the local. Though
lacking a nucleus of Roman population, such as the colonies had, the *municipia* too were slowly Romanized. Traces
of their independent origin, some cherished customs, and
local pride might remain. Aricia, Anagnia, Caere, and

Capua (later a colony of Caesar, 59 B.C.) may serve as examples of the *municipium* in Republican days. After the Social War all allied cities (p. 37) in Italy together with the *Latin* colonies were converted into *municipia* and enjoyed all the privileges of cities of that class, including the right to vote at Rome and, upon removal to the capital, to become candidates for public offices.

Taken together, *coloniae* and *municipia* made up the enlightened dual system by which the Roman city-state planted its essentially military colonies in strategic positions, and elsewhere drew cities and towns into close relations with itself by conferring upon them citizenship and other privileges as municipal towns, while leaving them a limited measure of independence. The system was adjustable, and in such flexibility lay its strength. Both of the methods could be applied and were applied to increasing distances, across all barriers of race and language.

Whenever mention is made of Roman conquest, legions and campaigns, permanent camps and frontiers instantly come to our minds. But under the Republic military operations were as a rule for the summer only, and professional soldiers did not exist until the time of Marius (p. 458). It was the all-the-year military colony, skillfully posted among the defeated, as a body of veterans peacefully tilling the soil while manning a front which slowly advanced beyond them, and it was the shrewdly favored town of their late enemies, now admitted to citizenship, that is, the newly acknowledged *municipium,* that with no seasonal interruptions carried on the process of Romanization for generations. Hence the so-called conquest of Italy was even more a continuous political undertaking than a series of intermittent military operations. Slowly to convert the several enemies by whom she was surrounded into federated neighbors—this was the policy upon which the development of a greater Roman state was consistently based. None of her outward and visible triumphs was so significant as her success in gradually awakening a consciousness of national unity. A much-divided Italy drew together in spite of bitterness and bloodshed and at length was one, not so much because of brilliant military successes achieved by celebrated commanders as because of the anonymous labors of those who by slow stages created the equally Roman art of political and social assimilation.

Beyond the limits of Italy, as the range of expansion steadily increased, the same system was to be applied with adjustment to new and more varied conditions. Federated cities and colonies and municipal towns were all to reappear in the new territory, but methods of organization and administration on a far larger scale had to be developed.

THE PROVINCES

With the acquisition of Sicily at the end of the First Punic War began the reaching out for lands separated by nature from the home country. And with such extension overseas or beyond mountain barriers came the need of a new type of officials, while the very word *provincia,* "sphere of duty," "assignment," took on a new meaning.

A province in the new geographical and administrative sense of the term was governed under the Republic as a rule by a proconsul or a propraetor,[7] commonly for the term of one year, and this governor was at the same time military commander and chief justice. The city-states existing in that country at the time of the conquest were preserved with little change and to them was conceded a limited amount of independence. Democracies were not viewed with favor. Aristocratic local control of these city-states was more to the taste of the senators at Rome. Among the

[7] At first the governors were praetors.

different communities there were several distinct grades, some more privileged, others more obviously in subjection to the conqueror, but all grouped under Roman control. None of them could make war, or even raise troops for local self-defense except with the approval of the government. From Italy came such troops as the province seemed to require, and the costs of administration and defense were met by different forms of taxes, among others *decumae,* tithes on crops, *scriptura,* a tax on cattle pastured on public lands, *portoria,* duties on imports and exports. Certain communities were favored by exemptions. Systematic reorganization and consolidation were not thought necessary or politic. Thus, as Italy was a mosaic of assorted colors, so it was with the provinces even under the Empire.

The first territory acquired outside of Italy was Sicily, exclusive for a time of the kingdom of Syracuse. The greater part of the island was won from Carthage by the peace of 241 B.C. A few years later the security of the Mare Tuscum, west of Italy, seemed to require the seizure of Sardinia from the defeated foe (238 B.C.) and that of Corsica, which had been claimed but not really occupied by the Carthaginians. These two mountainous islands, with no important towns, became a single province, the Roman settlements being virtually limited to the coast.

The Second Punic War added the remainder of Sicily, after the capture of Syracuse in 212 B.C., while the end of the war (201) brought the possession of a large part of Spain, where Hamilcar and Hasdrubal had reconquered an older Punic domain covering most of the south and east of the peninsula and had founded cities. Two Roman provinces were organized, of which Hispania Ulterior included the former Carthaginian territory and Hispania Citerior covered the whole region of the Hiberus (Ebro). The conquest of the rest of Spain, including the wild northwest, was slow and stubborn, being completed only in the time of Augustus, when a threefold division was made—Baetica in the south, Lusitania in the west, and Tarraconensis, more than half of the whole.

Already in the years preceding the Second Punic War the Romans had begun to gain a foothold in the plains of the Po, establishing military posts at Placentia and Cremona (p. 39). Within fifteen years after the war these colonies were reached by a military road, a northwestward continuation of the Via Flaminia (p. 98). A complete organization of that Celtic land between the Apennines and the Alps as the province of Cisalpine Gaul was not carried out until the time of Sulla. Somewhat similar was the history of the eastern shore of the Adriatic, for as early as 229 B.C. a part of the Illyrian coast was under a Roman protectorate, enlarged in 168 B.C.; and by 155 further operations in Dalmatia had brought that coast land under Roman domination. Illyricum, including Dalmatia, was governed not as a separate province but as an annex to Cisalpine Gaul down to the time of Julius Caesar. And not until Augustus's reign was Cisalpine Gaul reckoned Italian soil, so that the Alps henceforth marked the boundary of Italy, now divided into eleven regions.

The next eastward expansion came as a consequence of wars with Macedonia, which became a province, as did Achaia (Greece) in the year 146 B.C. The same year, branded by the destruction of Corinth and Carthage, saw a new province created directly across the Mediterranean, the former territory of Carthage becoming the new province of Africa. This first overstepping of the bounds of Europe and its islands was followed seventeen years later by the organization of the province of Asia (129 B.C.), embracing only the western part of Asia Minor. Attalus III, the last king of Pergamum, one of the most splendid of the

Hellenistic capitals, had bequeathed his kingdom to the Roman state.

This was directly followed by an important advance in the West. The immediate aim was to provide a land route from the Maritime Alps to the Pyrenees with the help of a faithful ally, the Greek city of Massilia (Marseilles). At the same time the safety of ships making the usual coasting voyage to Spain would be promoted by the occupation of that shore, its ports, and a sufficient hinterland. The Gallic territory from the Pyrenees and the upper Garonne about Toulouse to the Lake of Geneva was conquered in 125-121 B.C., and the new Transalpine province was called Gallia Narbonensis from its capital, the old Celtic city of Narbo (Narbonne). But Massilia still held a long stretch of the coast west of Nice (Nicaea, also a Greek city) and the lower Rhone Valley.

Slower progress through the medium of a protectorate is illustrated by the land of the warlike Thracians, north of the Aegean. Conquered by Marcus Lucullus in 72-71 B.C., they were ruled by their own kings as client-princes until Claudius organized the province of Thrace (46 A.D.). Thus, at first indirectly and then directly, Rome maintained a foothold on the west coast of the Black Sea.

In the East great accessions came a half-century and more after the occupation of "Asia." Cyrene, on the north African coast west of Egypt, was bequeathed to the Roman state by its king, Ptolemy Apion, in 96 B.C. And Bithynia became Roman by the will of King Nicomedes III in 74 B.C. Cyprus also came by bequest, under the will of the King of Egypt, but like Cyrene it was not immediately occupied (p. 32, n. 2). Crete was seized in the war with the pirates in 67 B.C. Far more important were the acquisitions made by Pompey in Syria (another of the great Hellenistic kingdoms), in Cilicia, and in Pontus. The last was now combined with Bithynia in a province organized by Pompey.

These impressive gains in the East were matched a few years later by Julius Caesar's conquest of northern and western Gaul. With the older Gallia Narbonensis as a base he conquered in nine years (58-50 B.C.) all the rest of Gaul, so that Roman rule now reached the Channel, the North Sea, and the Rhine. Even the Germans beyond that river and the Britons across the Channel had more than once fought the legions of Caesar on their own soil. As yet there was no real occupation either of any part of Britain or of territory east of the Rhine. Augustus endeavored to carry the frontier eastward to the Elbe (Albis), but abandoned the attempt after the loss of Varus and his three legions in 9 A.D. The recently conquered portions of Gaul were divided into three provinces: Aquitania, Gallia Lugdunensis, Gallia Belgica. The last reached the Rhine and required a large army to defend that frontier. Not until Domitian's time was the Rhine country on the left bank, with large tracts to the west and south of the river, set off from Gallia Belgica and divided into two strongly garrisoned provinces, Upper and Lower Germany.

In Spain the western coast (Lusitania) was subdued by Julius Caesar, the mountainous northwest by generals of Augustus, who carried on the same kind of warfare from one end to the other of the Alps, reducing a long line of small tribes and thus securing the roads over the passes. As a memorial of this last achievement he erected his *Tropaea Augusti,* a towering monument high above the Mediterranean near Monaco, inscribed with the names of forty-four conquered tribes (p. 356; illus., p. 429).

North of the Alps much new territory was gained by conquest during the same principate and governed as the two provinces of Raetia and Noricum, extending from the Alps to the Danube, and the much larger province of Pannonia, which was protected by the same river both on the north and on the east. Under Augustus also two more Danube provinces were added, Upper and Lower Moesia, so that the right bank was now Roman all the way down to the Black Sea.

Egypt had been a Roman protectorate, for twenty-five years garrisoned by Roman troops (p. 32, n. 2), when the death of Cleopatra in 30 B.C. brought to an end this last of the Hellenistic monarchies. Octavian converted it into a province, but devised for it a new type of provincial government. Impregnably fortified by nature and long accustomed to enlightened despotism, it presented a special problem. The Roman *princeps* was to step into the long line of ancient Pharaohs and recent Macedonian monarchs. But he must rule at a distance and by the hand of a deputy. No senator—a possible rival in a dangerously strong location— could be such a deputy, or even be permitted to enter the new province as a tourist without express permission. The government was therefore placed in the hands of a knight with the title of prefect, but unlike any other knight or prefect, he had two legions under his command.

The adjoining land of Arabia Petraea, reaching north as far as Damascus, and southeast along the shore of the Red Sea, became a protectorate shortly after Pompey's time and a province under Trajan in 106 A.D.

The most considerable increase of territory during the first century A.D. was due to the conquest of Britain, beginning in the time of Claudius. What Julius Caesar had contemplated and even prepared for by two expeditions in 55 and 54 B.C. (the second on a very large scale), but with no permanent results, was actually carried out in 43 A.D. by Aulus Plautius. Gradually the southern and western parts of the island were subjugated, not without serious resistance and one great rebellion, that of Boudicca (61 A.D.). By

Trajan's time England and Wales had been to a large extent Romanized, though a danger zone lay across the north. This had been pushed back by degrees, so that under Domitian a line of forts drawn across from the Forth to the Clyde by Agricola marked for a short time the northernmost bounds of Roman influence. Eburacum (York) was by that time the capital of the province—an imperial province of the first rank, garrisoned normally by three legions. Northern Gaul was thus more effectually secured by Roman control of the neighboring island. From a military standpoint the northern frontier of the empire may be said to have extended at the end of the first century A.D. across the north of England, with some lines of forts beyond,[8] and then on the Continent by way of the Ems,[9] the Rhine, and the Danube down to the Black Sea.

The first decade of the second century saw an important advance across the lower Danube, where the Dacians, a warlike nation, had inflicted serious losses on the armies of Domitian and constrained him to make a discreditable peace, involving annual payments to buy off the invader. This disgrace and the constant menace led Trajan to conquer Dacia in two wars (101-102 and 105-107 A.D.). A part only of the land thus acquired was organized as a province entirely beyond previous frontiers, unprotected by natural boundaries on three sides. For it does not seem to have reached either the Theiss on the west or the Black Sea on the east. This extramural province of Dacia was a marked departure, necessitating the removal of many of the inhabitants and extensive colonization (pp. 33 f.).[10]

[8] For the walls of Hadrian and Antoninus Pius cp. pp. 465 f.
[9] To include the Frisii.
[10] That Romanization followed is shown by the fact that Roumania still speaks a Romance language. The majority of the new settlers seem to have come from Dalmatia, Asia Minor, and Syria. For the story of the conquest as pictured on the Column of Trajan at Rome cp. p. 341.

In the East the rival empire of Parthia was a constant source of danger, with Armenia as a particular bone of contention. This kingdom was a Roman dependency and had some Roman troops, but the throne was regularly occupied by a Parthian prince. Friction led once more to war near the end of Trajan's reign (115 A.D.), and the Emperor in person led his army into Armenia, which promptly submitted and became a Roman province, while several tribes of the Caucasus were ruled by vassal princes. Advancing southward into Parthia Trajan soon possessed himself of Mesopotamia, which likewise became a province. In 116 A.D. the Emperor crossed the Tigris and annexed one more new province, Assyria, lying to the eastward of that river. Thence he led his army down the Euphrates into Babylonia, captured the Parthian capital, Ctesiphon, and other cities, and advanced to the mouth of the Tigris and its port of Charax. But while he tarried by the Persian Gulf several serious revolts occurred in the vast regions he had hastily subdued. These were quelled, however, and Parthia itself was boldly proclaimed a vassal of Rome, though much of its territory was untouched, stretching far away to the east and the borders of India. On his return journey to the west in the summer of 117 A.D. Trajan died at Selinus, a seaport of Cilicia.

Space has permitted the merest sketch of Roman expansion up to its maximum. From Hadrian's immediate abandonment of Trajan's new provinces of Mesopotamia and Assyria it did not follow that there would be no more attempts to extend the eastern frontier or to recover losses there or elsewhere. The northern part of Mesopotamia was in fact regained by the victories of Lucius Verus and Marcus Aurelius, to be again disputed in the third century between Rome and the new Persian empire, which had now succeeded the Parthian. There were struggles of course on the long Rhine-Danube frontier and in the north of Britain. Here, however, we may not follow the fortunes of the provinces through the age of decline and gradual loss, as the resources of the empire proved unequal to the task of defense against hordes of invaders.

PROVINCIAL ADMINISTRATION

We turn back to consider the general methods employed in governing the provinces, with special reference to the Empire, pausing first to note one feature of Roman rule in foreign parts which is strongly suggestive of India in recent times—the presence of protected princes whose territories fringed one or more of the provinces. Petty princes who had sided with the Romans in a war were often rewarded by an enlargement of territory, and such vassal states were especially desirable where an important frontier was to be guarded. An example is Deiotarus, a prince of Celtic Galatia, in central Asia Minor, who supported Lucullus and Pompey against Mithridates and later gave aid against the Parthians. With enlarged territory and now recognized as king of Lesser Armenia he fought for Pompey against Caesar, but after the latter's death he was to be found once more in possession of his kingdom. His successor aided Augustus in the pacification of Asia Minor, but upon his death (25 B.C.) this kingdom became the province of Galatia. This was the usual history of protected principalities. Mauretania is a typical instance in the West. In Augustus's time a protectorate under Juba II, whose son and successor Ptolemy was put to death by Caligula (40 A.D.), the country was then reorganized as two provinces, each governed by a procurator. Any vassal kingdom or principality tended to be converted sooner or later into a province. Thus Egypt (p. 48), Palestine, Cappadocia, and Thrace severally ceased to be protectorates and swelled the list of reg-

ular provinces. After Trajan's time the Greek Bosporan
kingdom, in and about the Crimea, remained almost the
only exception, and continued unchanged through the reign
of Constantine.

In the time of the Republic provinces were the special
charge of the senate, and actual service, first in the lower
grades (as quaestors) and then in the higher (as proprae-
tors and proconsuls), gave the senators opportunity to master all the details of provincial administration. And as the
civil career was not separated from the military, many of
the older and more influential senators brought to the discussion of any question connected with the defense or the
government of a province a range of practical experience
with different peoples such as could nowhere be paralleled
in any modern parliament or congress.

The senate was in effect a body of experts and in the face
of such competence the people, uninformed and inexperi-
enced, could have no effective voice in the management of
the provinces. A Gracchus might develop new policies to
make the provinces serve the needs of the masses under a
broader scheme of colonization (p. 39). But senatorial
opposition could usually be counted upon to defeat promising innovations. The exploiters of provinces, *i.e.,* the finan-
ciers and companies of *publicani* (tax-farmers), largely
knights and mainly interested in their foreign investments,
supported the senators in their far from disinterested policy
toward the provincials.

A governor normally remained in his province but a
single year, and served without salary.[11] He was accordingly
tempted to enlarge by every means the incidental profits of

[11] Longer terms sometimes resulted from a failure of the senate to send
a successor. For this reason Verres remained three years in Sicily, Quintus
Cicero three in Asia. On account of distance governors in Spain for a time
had a two-year term. Expenses of travel and outfit were provided by the
state.

his office, especially if he had previously contracted debts in securing election to office, looking forward to a provincial assignment as his opportunity to recoup himself. Lavish expense for public shows—plays, gladiators, and the rest—under a system which offered no regular compensation to magistrates and senators, left many a successful candidate in a position in which he was prone to accept whatever a province might be made to yield in his one short year. When more rigorous laws gave abused provincials the right to bring action against the late governor there was a temptation to escape condemnation by bribing the jury. For such reasons a corrupt governor, as Verres in Sicily, had a further motive for oppressing his province, that he might return with the necessary means to purchase a favorable verdict. That one famous case throws a flood of light on the helplessness of the Sicilians under the established senatorial practice—a mixture of corruption and connivance. Yet, thanks to the young Cicero, Verres was forced into exile to escape condemnation. We cannot safely infer that the average governor was equally corrupt. Honest and enlightened provincial governors were not unknown, but the system could not be thoroughly reformed until the Empire.

After the civil wars were over and their incalculable damage was to be repaired, not only in Italy but also in the provinces from Spain to Egypt, reconstruction of provincial government was a crying need. With great wisdom Augustus devised a new system which created a highly honorable career with a fixed salary and reasonably certain promotions and rewards. The peaceful provinces requiring no legions were left under the nominal control of the senate, from whose members the governors would be appointed. An ex-praetor would be named for one of the smaller provinces, an ex-consul for a more important governorship, and the term was one year. With each governor a treasury official

who as a rule retained competent executives in the same position for three to five years, often longer. The senatorial provinces were also effectively controlled, though less patently, by the same central authority. In other words they were senatorial in name rather than in fact. The *pax Romana,* at last achieved to the great relief of an exhausted world, and maintained successfully as times improved, depended very largely upon the workings of this new system, which provided a combined military and civil service as before, but vastly improved and beneficial both to the governors and to the governed. The former, if loyal and efficient, had every reason to expect due promotions and a gradual, but reasonably certain, mounting of the official ladder. If the governed sometimes found that the oppressor was not yet an extinct species, in the main their situation was immensely improved and their pride of membership in the Roman society of nations increased.

A special stimulus to this sense of unity was given under Augustus by the institution or reorganization of the provincial assembly, or *concilium,* meeting once a year and charged with the maintenance of the cult of the emperors (p. 129). It was a coveted distinction for a local magnate to be the high priest of a province, an honor not inexpensive to the incumbent. The assembly had other functions also and was to a limited extent a representative body. It could express its approval of a governor by a vote of thanks, or send in its complaints to the central government and cause him to be brought to trial upon his return to Rome. One of the best-known of these provincial assemblies is that which represented the Three Gauls (Lugdunensis, Belgica, and Aquitania) at Lugdunum (Lyons) and served to unite them in their gatherings about the Altar of Roma and Augustus. Council and cult of the goddess Rome and her "superhuman" ruler turned the thoughts of all in the direction of the capital. And yet they had frequent reason to know that the Emperor, even if occasionally human, kept in close touch with the interests and needs of his people in the provinces.

A new governor of a province brought out with him formal instructions for the conduct of his office. These *mandata* of the Emperor were at first no doubt issued to governors of imperial provinces only, but the custom must soon have been extended to the senatorial provinces, or wide divergences of practice would have been bound to occur. When in doubt as to the best means of executing these instructions, or uncertain in the face of unusual difficulties, a governor could write directly to the Emperor, setting forth his problem and requesting enlightenment, advice, or a formal decision. The Emperor's reply, called a rescript, had the full force of law and was preserved also in the archives of the province.

The fact of such correspondence, beginning with Augustus, suggests surprisingly direct relations between the man at the helm of the state and his scattered deputies. Of all this we have very interesting evidence in the letters which passed between the Younger Pliny, as governor of Bithynia and Pontus, and Trajan in ca. 111-113 A.D. This series of official letters deals with such questions as water supply and other public works, the suppression of guilds and clubs, the treatment of the now numerous Christians, and even the most routine matters. Their publication by permission of the Emperor, together with his rescripts, including also a few merely friendly notes, shows that they were useful for other officials and in form models for their imitation.

Such in outline was the system of government for the provinces of the Empire—an immense advance upon the methods developed under the Republic, when flagrant abuses were all too common and when provincials, however much they might owe to the stability of Roman rule, were daily made aware of their place in a world subject in every sense to the Roman. And they were sure to suffer from the rapid change of governors even when these were upright. The old evils of irresponsible control were largely eliminated when the first Emperor reformed the entire system. At the same time he gave young men both at Rome and in provincial cities incentive and opportunity to devote themselves to an official career divorced from politics.

Many descendants of Italian settlers in the western provinces rose to high positions in the state and founded senatorial families. A Trajan, coming from southern Spain, an Antoninus Pius from southern Gaul, could govern important provinces; and by an adoptive succession both reached the throne, to administer with great ability the vast system in which they had served their apprenticeship. Spanish in origin—in a similar sense—were Hadrian also and Theodosius.

That we cannot match these notable names by similar sons of the eastern provinces is only one among many striking proofs of the cleft between East and West—so deep and lasting that ultimate division was inevitable. To the eastern provinces many Roman merchants and capitalists had gone in Republican times, not to settle down in one place and Romanize their neighbors, but to make their fortunes in various ventures including the farming of the revenue. Scattered about and organized only for profit, they were themselves Hellenized and thus contributed to the forces which tended to make even the West less Roman in its mode of living and its whole view of life. The conqueror in the attractive cities of the conquered was himself captivated as Greek influences grew stronger. It was impossible for the East, enjoying a more advanced civilization, not yet enfeebled, to be Romanized, as was the West, where the whole trend was Romewards, so that enlightened provincials seconded the efforts of the government. A prominent Gaul could build at Glanum (Saint-Remy in Provence) a triumphal arch to commemorate Julius Caesar's recent conquest of the northern tribes, now added to the lands destined to prosper under Roman rule. Had we visited Britain in the time of Titus and Domitian we should have found a governor of the province, Agricola, encouraging the natives to erect public works in the Roman style—temples, market places, porticos, and baths. In southern and eastern Spain, as in southern Gaul, many cities were in outward appearance hardly distinguishable from those of Italy—this as early as the time of Tiberius. And North Africa is still visited for the impressive remains of its Roman towns of the second and third centuries, especially Timgad and Lambèse, and more recently Leptis Magna (Lepcis).

The empire, however, was not made up of cities possessed of stately public buildings and inhabited by a Latin-speaking or a Greek-speaking population, nor even of towns large or small. In marked contrast stood the countless villages where the native customs and language of the province still lingered on and it might prove that few could speak either of the languages of the cultivated.

In a large province it was possible that race feeling might tend toward independence, such as had its short-lived trial in connection with an uprising on the Rhine in 70 A.D. It was more to be apprehended that a well-garrisoned province might support the claims of a rival for the throne. Both of these dangers were met by the policy of subdivision—a policy revived by Diocletian and reduced to an elaborate system in which he raised the number of provinces from forty-seven to eighty-seven.[13] But the diminished provinces

[13] Fifteen provinces covered the map of Gaul and Roman Germany instead of six; and six replaced the three old provinces in Spain.

were now grouped in larger units called dioceses.[14] Complete separation of the civil from the military career was a cardinal point in Diocletian's system.

How this immense territory, the Roman *orbis terrarum,* could be won and then held for centuries by relatively small military forces, is a question which admits of no approach to an answer without a systematic study of the army, its organization and its resources. In our present chapter, however, space admits only the briefest outline.[15]

THE ARMY

From the early days of the Republic at least the Roman army was organized on the basis of a graded property qualification, so that the majority of the state's defenders consisted of those citizens who possessed a certain amount of land and were able to provide their own arms and equipment. Service in the cavalry was required of those best able to meet such expense. The infantry was composed at first of two legions, each having thirty maniples. Two centuries made a maniple, three maniples, the most important unit, made a cohort.

In battle the usual formation in that time was the Greek phalanx, with its many ranks and its immobility, the important weapon being a long lance (*hasta*). Out of this solid formation a more open order was slowly developed, allowing greater freedom of movement. A short javelin (*pilum*) took the place of the lance, and a short sword became the chief weapon, since the javelin was thrown in the first encounter.

[14] There were twelve of these, of which one was for Italy, organized in twelve districts, including its three large islands and Raetia. Gaul had two dioceses, Spain one, Britain one, while that of the Orient included sixteen provinces. Each diocese was governed by a *vicarius,* and between the *vicarii* and the Emperor stood the *praefecti praetorio.*

[15] Details concerning army and navy will be found in the Appendix.

The eventful conflict with Pyrrhus led to further improvements, in particular the three-rank maniple formation, in which the front rank of a legion was made up of ten maniples, with intervals behind each of which stood one of the ten maniples of the second rank, having similar intervals, each of them to be filled if necessary by the advance of one of the ten maniples of the third rank. With the addition of its light-armed troops a legion of that period normally had 4,200 men, and was commanded by six tribunes, taking turns in the actual command. The tactical unit was the maniple, under the orders of a centurion and having its own standard (*signum*) on a staff.

In regard to the arms and equipment of the soldier, discipline, the fortification of camps, the gradual changes in tactics, and many other matters we naturally have much more information during the first and second wars with Carthage, and again in the second century B.C., especially from the Greek historian and friend of Roman generals, Polybius.

Much attention was paid to the morale of the troops, encouraged to acts of bravery by a system of rewards, culminating in their participation in the general's triumph, should they win for him the highest of Roman distinctions (p. 454).

With the terror inspired by the German invasions and after the victories of Marius (102-101 B.C.) came a most important change by which the army ceased to be a body of citizens defending the state until, danger removed, they should return to their usual vocations. It was henceforth almost a professional army, reorganized and in every way better fitted for service. The significant unit was now the cohort, not the maniple, and the legion received for the first time a standard of its own—the eagle.

Under Julius Caesar the army reached a high standard of efficiency, notably in siege operations and other engineering works, such as bridging rivers, also in rapidity of movement. Legions now had names as well as numbers, and a single commander (*legatus*), the six tribunes serving as his staff.

The founding of the Empire brought the necessity of a permanent military establishment, providing a real standing army and a systematic defense of frontiers such as the Rhine or the Danube, together with proper reserve forces, and garrisons, where trouble was to be feared. This great task was committed to no more than twenty-five legions of about 5,000 men each, usually supported by about an equal number of auxiliaries. To all provinces thus garrisoned, with the single exception of Africa (p. 54), the Emperor sent out his *legati,* at once governors and generals in command.

Changes in the permanent stations of the legions were not infrequent under the successors of Augustus. New legions were raised from time to time to take the place of such as had met disaster or had been disbanded. But the number of legions, thirty in Galba's time, was no more than thirty-three in the critical reign of Marcus Aurelius. Frontier defenses alone made it possible to hold such extended fronts with an army of only 300,000. Earthworks, palisades, walls, forts and smaller posts and watchtowers combined to strengthen the frontiers particularly exposed to invasion.

None of these great works of defense is better known than the stone Wall of Hadrian from Newcastle to Carlisle (illus., p. 401). Less imposing but admirably placed was the earthwork of Antoninus Pius from Edinburgh to Glasgow. Magnificent in the distance covered (370 miles) was the series of fortifications connecting the Rhine with the Danube (pp. 465 f.).

At the beginning of the third century Septimius Severus manned frontiers in a different way, by settling soldiers, largely of German and Sarmatian blood, and their families on farms near the *limes,* in readiness to meet attack, they meantime raising a new generation of soldiers for the same service, now hereditary.

With Diocletian and Constantine came sweeping changes in the army, greatly enlarged and consisting almost wholly of men of warlike races, while few soldiers came from the thoroughly Romanized provinces. Nothing could have been more unlike the citizen army of the Republic.

Essential as was the army during the whole process of expansion, it was indispensable in the centuries in which the pressure from without was seldom long relaxed. But in the making of an empire, as we have seen, the characteristic Roman methods—accepting defeated foes as allies, sending out colonies of veterans for peaceful penetration and absorption, receiving to citizenship and municipal status towns lately acquired—had been factors more persistent and no less effective than armed advances, while the whole work of making and holding was crowned, after many failures and much oppression under the Republic, by an ably administered system of provincial government. That so few provinces ever of their own motion sought to break away proves that under the Empire Roman rule brought to the ruled advantages which as members, large or small, of a world-state they had no desire to exchange for the uncertain blessings of independence.

III

TILLING THE SOIL

SALVE, MAGNA PARENS FRVGVM, SATVRNIA TELLVS,
MAGNA VIRVM: TIBI RES ANTIQVAE LAVDIS ET ARTIS
INGREDIOR, SANCTOS AVSVS RECLVDERE FONTES,
ASCRAEVMQVE CANO ROMANA PER OPPIDA CARMEN.

VERGIL, GEORGICS, 2, 173

VOS, QVI MVLTAS PERAMBVLASTIS TERRAS, ECQVAM CVLTIOREM ITALIA VI-
DISTIS?

VARRO, DE RE RUSTICA, 1, 2, 3

VIVE BIDENTIS AMANS ET CVLTI VILICVS HORTI,
VNDE EPVLVM POSSIS CENTVM DARE PYTHAGOREIS.
EST ALIQVID, QVOCVMQVE LOCO, QVOCVMQVE RECESSV
VNIVS SESE DOMINVM FECISSE LACERTAE.

JUVENAL, 3, 228

ROME, at first a village of shepherds, was for several centuries a community of farmers, and to the very end the social structure showed no signs of shifting to an industrial or commercial basis. The free citizen, owner of the farm, was long unashamed to work with his slave or slaves. The latter carried on the labors of the farm, helped by members of the family, when the master was called away to serve in the army. Free laborers who could be hired at times were apparently scarce in the early period. As a rule it was the master and slave working together, aided by the older children. Later generations were edified by tales of senators of the early Republic digging and delving, of a Cincinnatus called from his plow—a literal plow—to be dictator, and returning after a brief campaign to his very small farm across the Tiber. A patrician at that time was not too proud to work with his hands and side by side with his slave. Free labor also was employed when available for the harvest and vintage.

Large farms begin to be mentioned before the First Punic War. In 291 B.C. Postumius, a consul and a very different type of patrician from Cincinnatus, aroused much indignation by ordering two thousand of his soldiers to cut down brushwood on his own estate, evidently a large tract to be brought under cultivation. At that time there seem to have been no examples of large-scale farming with a gang of slaves under a steward. Increase of population combined with patriotic duty led many farmers to join the colonies frequently sent out in this period. And these farmer soldiers continued to play their part in tilling and holding lands lately taken from the enemy (p. 38).

The end of the Second Punic War (201 B.C.) marks an

epoch in the history of Roman agriculture. Hannibal's army in fifteen years had devastated whole regions of Italy, and prolonged absence with the army had ruined many farmers. The end of the long conflict found deserted farms, many more neglected, a great number for sale at very low prices. The small-farmer class, hitherto the mainstay of the state, was now seriously threatened. Some, unable to restore their farms, joined new colonies. Others drifted to the city and being now landless were exempt from military service, but hard put to it to make a living. In Sicily Roman soldiers had first seen large farms worked by numerous slaves under the orders of a *vilicus*, himself a slave, while the Carthaginian owner seldom lived on the place and considered his lands in Sicily only an investment from which to gain the largest possible income. This was agriculture on an industrial basis, requiring considerable capital and experienced management. It had no place for the small farmer-owner, and its introduction into Italy boded ill for the tradition that had kept sword and spade in the same hands and had thus ensured an irresistible advance. Cato the Censor saw the change in its early stages, but was himself the practical, horny-handed farmer in the intervals of his public service. We look in vain in his book, *De Agricultura,* for descriptive touches from which to reconstruct a picture of his own farm with its olive-yard and vineyard, its sternly disciplined household, but we can be sure that thrift and strict utility reigned in every corner.

Large-scale cultivation was Hellenistic as well as Carthaginian, and was treated in accessible books on agriculture. Mago, the Carthaginian, was held to be so important an authority that after the destruction of Carthage the senate ordered the translation of his work into Latin.[1] And his

---

[1] Mago's date is unknown. His work in twenty-eight books was abridged and translated into Greek in 88 B.C. by Dionysius of Utica with additions

system was now to be imitated by wealthy Romans. Abandoned farms were bought up and combined in large holdings. Public lands also could be leased in large tracts. Wartime captives continued to be numerous, so that a gang of slaves could be purchased and placed under a *vilicus* who was himself a foreigner and a slave. The landlord regularly lived at Rome, but if wise frequently visited his estate, since a steward needed watching.

Great farms, known as *latifundia,* in time covered a large part of arable Italy and threatened the extinction of the small farm worked by its owner. On many such estates the olive and the vine were cultivated intensively where cereals had formerly been grown. Others were mainly in pasture; for grazing was found more profitable. There was little dairy farming in the modern sense, since butter was not used and refrigeration impracticable. For the production of wool and hides large flocks and herds were pastured on the slopes of the Apennines in summer, to be driven down to the lowlands, especially those of Apulia, for the winter. The numerous herdsmen and shepherds were slaves, and being armed against wolves and robbers were a menace to peaceable neighbors. The massing of slaves, many of them working in chains on the *latifundia,* was a potential danger to the state. Tiberius Gracchus on a journey to Spain found Etruria cultivated almost entirely by foreign slaves. Varro warned against having too many of the same race, for the fear of a slave uprising was seldom absent. A regular feature of any large estate was a prison, and escaped slaves often turned brigands. That slaves of mixed nationalities were gradually displacing the native farmers, who had at the same time been owners, voters, and soldiers, was ominous. No legislation of the Gracchi or other reformers was suc-

---

from Greek sources, and in this form became the standard work. It could be had also in a condensed form in Greek (six books) by Diophanes.

cessful in reviving the old type of small proprietor. Sulla rewarded his veterans with farms and all the leaders of armies in the successive civil wars followed his example. But years of soldiering had unfitted most of the men for farming. Cultivation was not improved by such influx, and it was useless to hope that the sturdy peasant class could be thus revived, even if small farms were now more numerous. Discontent and unrest were inevitable, even to the point of rebellion. Meantime the great estates seldom brought their proprietors profits comparable to other investments. The owner might be deeply in debt and yet would be unwilling to sell. For pride in landed property was an aristocratic tradition to which even the newly rich must bow. By the time of Cicero fashion demanded extensive villas and flower gardens, orchards and fishponds, thus throwing many *iugera* out of cultivation, to the distress of Horace.

Already in Cato's time the raising of wheat and other cereals in Latium had greatly declined, immense quantities of wheat being imported from Sardinia and Africa. More profitable were the olive and the vine, with a view to exportation as well. To forestall competition from a new province the senate later tried the policy of forbidding the raising of grapes and olives in Gallia Narbonensis. But on lands cultivated merely for profit and with little personal oversight nothing could make up for the loss of the old peasant devotion to the soil, a quality which still remained in distant or less accessible regions, as in the hill country or in the Po Valley, where olive-yards and vineyards continued profitable.

In Varro's work on agriculture (37 B.C., a century and a third after Cato) we see the efforts made by intelligent landlords chiefly near the city, to meet the demand for new fruits, such as the cherry, recently introduced from the East (p. 173), or new kinds of figs from Africa, to diversify their crops, to raise roses, violets, lilies, and other flowers, to breed fowls of all kinds, pigeons, thrushes and game birds, deer and other game, and fish for Roman tables. In general, however, farming conditions grew worse. The South still produced the best of wheat as well as the choicest wine and oil. Augustus, though he must have seen the need, did not venture upon agrarian measures beyond some relief to Egypt.

Vergil in his *Georgics* eloquently voices the call back to the land, the goodly land of Italy, which even during the ravages of the civil wars was to his mind a garden spot. Farming to him, true son of the soil, is a mission demanding a bit of land, a sturdy frame, and toil with one's own hands —unremitting toil, *labor improbus*—but is not without its sure reward, its peculiar satisfactions. Other poets reëcho the note of recall to the country and the simple life; Tibullus by his idyllic pictures of contentment and happiness on a greatly diminished estate, Horace by glowing descriptions of his farm in a Sabine valley.

For the century and more between the death of Julius Caesar and that of Nero we are well informed about the most approved methods of cultivation, thanks to the *Georgics* of Vergil and much more to the formal treatises on farming by Varro at the beginning and by Columella at the end of that period. Special stress was laid, as by Cato, on fertilizing, and upon rotation of crops (mentioned by Cato, as later by Pliny). Lupines, vetches, beans, or alfalfa (*medica,* an importation from the East) were planted after a crop of wheat to enrich the soil. The cereals also had their turns, or the field lay fallow. Grafting was extensively practised and there was evidently enlightened management of lands, especially where the olive and vine were cultivated. Excavations such as those of Boscoreale and a number of other sites near Pompeii, including the Villa dei Misteri, or of a large establishment in Istria, on the island of Brioni Grande, or even in Gaul and Britain, are continually shedding fresh light on the buildings and equipment of *villae rusticae* of various dates.

Varro's estate near Casinum in southern Latium, with its aviary and other features, must have been a model. Though he never seems to forget his urban market we are not informed as to returns from his investment. It was but one of several estates of a great landlord who was able to indulge in what we should call fancy farming. Gone was the simple life possible in Cato's time, but evidently slaves and beasts were now more humanely treated, and the plastering of a farmhouse did not spell degeneration, as Cato seems to have thought. In Varro's day only a small part of the wheat grown in Italy actually reached the Roman market, and still fields were being turned, he complains, into pastures. It was disquieting that Rome could be brought to the brink of starvation if the corn fleet of Puteoli or Ostia should be intercepted by an enemy or seriously delayed by storms. The decline of agriculture in Italy was obvious when the capital remained dependent upon African and other distant fields for its daily bread. Technical knowledge indeed was not lacking in spite of the absence of special schools or experiment stations. The causes of the decline are to be sought here and there, but not generally, in exhaustion of the soil or erosion, but much more in altered market conditions, overproduction, insufficient oversight by owners, and the slave-gang system. A large farm thus worked under a steward seldom proved very profitable, even where liberal use was made of capital in improvements and equipment. And free labor was not available with sufficient regularity.

A new system to displace slave labor was the inevitable result. As far back as 100 B.C. we begin to hear of tenants. At a much earlier date extant remains seem to show that the more powerful patricians had tenants from the humblest class in sufficient numbers to make drainage works possible together with irrigation and terracing on a large scale. In the first century B.C. some great proprietors, such as Pompey and Domitius Ahenobarbus, had large numbers of tenants. A tenant (*colonus*) was normally a free man of limited means, often a freedman, holding a small farm under a formal lease. The land might belong to the state, in fertile Campania, for example, or to a city or town. Horace's Sabine farm had five *coloni* with their families. But apart from the parcels worked by these tenants he held a portion (wheat fields, vineyard, garden, pasture) reserved for himself and placed in charge of a *vilicus* (a slave). In Horace too we have the delightful portrait of frugal Ofellus, a philosopher in homespun, formerly owner of the farm which he now works as tenant. As such he was protected by law and might have a few slaves of his own. Or slaves were provided by his landlord along with live stock and implements, according to the terms of his lease, which might stipulate *opus* also, meaning that in addition to rent the tenant should furnish a small amount of labor on that part of the estate retained by the owner. Sometimes tenants in arrears were given a new lease on the basis of shares in the crops in place of cash. Long tenancy was sure to convert a tenant, however humanely treated, into a humble dependent. Gradually gangs of slaves were replaced by the tenant system, while many impoverished owners sank into this humbler class. Under the Empire this was the prevailing system. An entire estate was often leased to one responsible tenant (*conductor*), who then would sublet to a large number of small tenants—a method more commonly used in the provinces than in Italy. A piece of land was sometimes assigned to a faithful slave as a virtual tenant (*quasi colonus*). Owners of course had at times troubles with their tenants, such as those of which we hear in the *Letters* of the Younger Pliny, who was an uncommonly considerate landlord and followed the wise practice of many large owners in having his estates scattered in different regions, thus diminishing losses from crop failures. More distant estates outside of Italy were common investments for capitalists such as Cicero's friend Atticus, who had large holdings in Epirus. Seneca had provincial estates, especially in Egypt. Sicily and the province of Africa were preëminently lands of absentee landlords, so much so that in Nero's time one-half of the latter province (that is, of its arable land) was held by six Roman owners, until their vast estates were confiscated by him and thus became part of the imperial domains. The latter were so widely scattered that hardly a province lacked estates of the Emperor administered by his procurators. Most such imperial possessions passed to his successor. Others belonged to his private fortune. Egypt, which was virtually the patrimony of the Emperor, contained many *latifundia* held by members of the imperial family and others, until the Flavian emperors adopted the policy of breaking up the large estates and leasing or selling to small farmers. In general, however, the emperors were continually enlarging their far-flung estates by inheritance, confiscation, and otherwise.

Yet the wiser heads were troubled by the gradual disappearance of the small farmer-owner, the progressive depopulation of Italy, and the unabated decline in agriculture. Most conspicuous were the efforts begun by Nerva and developed by Trajan and his successors to relieve orphans and poor parents and at the same time help hard-pressed landowners. An endowment was established from the interest received on money loaned by the state to owners of land. Among Trajan's various measures to improve agricultural conditions was the founding of colonies of veterans in Italy, and none were to be established elsewhere. Agricultural enterprise in the provinces was encouraged. Evidence abounds that on the left bank of the Rhine and in the valleys of the Moselle and the Meuse there were in the third and fourth centuries many estates systematically developed in the Roman manner.

Conditions naturally differed in the different provinces. In some much depended upon the proper maintenance of irrigation, especially in Egypt, for which we have abundant information from papyri, and in Africa. Prosperity in the provinces at times meant distress for Italy, which found her markets for oil and wine now well supplied by the provinces. Overproduction at home called for measures of correction, as in Domitian's proposal—this with a very modern ring—that half of the vineyards be destroyed and no new ones planted. Complaints, such as had been voiced by the poet Lucretius under the Republic, that the soil was becoming exhausted were repeated, with truth for some localities, but surely not as a sweeping generalization. Many writers on agriculture whose works have not come down to us reiterated the tale of impoverishment. It is explicitly denied by Tacitus, who has never been accounted an optimist. Others extended Mother Earth's senile sterility to the alleged failure of her quarries and mines!

Whatever were the conditions the lot of the tenant did not change for the better. Whether he sublet from the *conductor,* or head tenant, of one of the imperial estates, or leased a farm on similar terms from a private landlord, or from a city or town, he paid his rent in cash or in a share of the crops. That condition and general poverty made it more and more difficult for him to remove to another farm. By the third century the tenant-farmers, cut off from the advantages of the cities, though legally free were sinking by degrees into practical serfdom. Just as in industry the artisan was coming to find himself entrapped in a fixed hereditary occupation (p. 96), so it was with the *colonus*. Yet farms were sometimes abandoned and in Diocletian's time radical measures of reclamation were revived. His new system of government, with its great increase in the hierarchy of officials and its doubled army, required unbearable taxes. Pressure was needed to prevent wholesale migration on the part of tenants. Constantine in 332 A.D. put the fleeing *colonus* on a par with the runaway slave. This law had the effect of binding the nominally free tenant and his family to the soil he had been cultivating. Henceforth he was in fact a serf, thrown into chains if he tried to escape.

Near the frontiers much land about the military posts was tilled by the soldiers (p. 467), while barbarians were actually settled on the land, at times even in Italy, and that in large numbers. This was a policy of Marcus Aurelius at a critical moment, when war and pestilence threatened alarming depopulation.

So pressing had the labor problem become, and yet invention never came to the rescue. Farm implements remained what they had been for centuries. Plows were still too light to reduce seriously the labor of deep digging. Aside from olive presses and those for grapes we read of no machines in general use. If water had to be raised to higher levels for irrigation there were no new devices. A mechanical reaper was known to Pliny the Elder, but suited only to fairly level ground, being pushed by an ox trampling down the straw behind a machine which cut only the ears. It is described by Palladius in the fourth century, the last of our Roman writers on husbandry. For there were still readers of books on farming, and even in the second half of the fifth century, after the devastating waves of the Germanic migrations, we hear of bountiful tables and well-kept estates in Gaul, differing little if at all from those of Italy

in a happier age. Vineyards and olive-yards are mentioned
as a matter of course by Apollinaris Sidonius in his descriptions of well-stocked countryseats near Narbo and Nemausus
—these in a region already ruled by a Visigothic king at
Tolosa—while his own principal estate, Avitacum, in
Auvergne, tempts him to a detailed account of its charms
(p. 175).

IV
CRAFTS, TRADE, TRANSPORTATION

NON SINE CAVSA DII HOMINESQVE HVNC VRBI CONDENDAE LOCVM ELE-
GERVNT, SALVBERRIMOS COLLES, FLVMEN OPPORTVNVM, QVO EX MEDITERRANEIS
LOCIS FRVGES DEVEHANTVR, QVO MARITIMI COMMEATVS ACCIPIANTVR, MARE
VICINVM AD COMMODITATES NEC EXPOSITVM NIMIA PROPINQVITATE AD PERI-
CVLA CLASSIVM EXTERNARVM, REGIONEM ITALIAE MEDIAM, AD INCREMENTVM
VRBIS NATVM VNICE LOCVM.

LIVY, 5, 54, 4

PREMANT CALENA FALCE QVIBVS DEDIT
FORTVNA VITEM, DIVES ET AVREIS
MERCATOR EXSICCET CVLVLLIS
VINA SYRA REPARATA MERCE,

DIS CARVS IPSIS, QVIPPE TER ET QVATER
ANNO REVISENS AEQVOR ATLANTICVM
IMPVNE.

HORACE, CARMINA, 1, 31, 9

APPIA LONGARVM TERITVR REGINA VIARVM.

STATIUS, SILVAE, 2, 2, 12

DOWN to the era of the Etruscan occupation (p. 11) Rome· had the fewest possible industries and little trade with her neighbors. The Etruscans had developed arts, industries, and a commerce. Having occupied Praeneste (Palestrina), only twenty-three miles from Rome, and Campania as well, they left Latium almost an enclosed territory, exposed to gradual penetration or conquest. With the actual establishment of Etruscan rulers in Rome and other Latin cities a new period begins. Carthaginian ships brought their wares to the coast of Latium, as did Greek traders coming from Sicily and from their new colony of Massilia (Marseilles), which had opened an extensive trade with the tribes of Gaul and Spain. Massilian merchants were in this way enabled to offer tin from Britain (required for making bronze), iron, and from the shores of the Baltic, amber. Demand for these imports and other commodities, such as the earthenware of Corinth, from Greece and the ports of Ionia, was greatly increased as villages and towns grew into cities. Rome became a market also for the vases, bronze ware, and terracottas produced in Etruria, and later for the bronze mirrors and toilet boxes as well as jewelry made by Etruscan artisans at near-by Praeneste.

Already under the kings there were goldsmiths and coppersmiths, mainly Etruscan, at Rome. Tradition mentions guilds of these trades, as of the carpenters (builders), potters, tanners, shoemakers, and dyers. The building and adornment of temples and of the king's house had brought in Greek and Etruscan artists and skilled workmen.

Although a seaport was provided at Ostia there was the merest beginning of Roman commerce, since enterprising Carthaginian, Greek, and Etruscan merchants kept the control of trade in their own hands. And Latium with its rich farm lands, its complete lack of a seafaring population, its undeveloped native industry, was in no position to compete. In fact the removal of the stimulus given by Etruscan kings left Roman industry to languish for three centuries, except for the making of such simple implements as the farmer used, together with arms and armor for the soldier, domestic utensils, and the handicraft of some non-Latin artisans. On industries which had so declined no real commerce could be built up in the face of competition from the merchants of Carthage, as also of Syracuse, Massilia, and other Greek cities. Nevertheless there were Roman traders, since a treaty with Carthage in 348 B.C. excluded them from much of the Carthaginian territory.

Ostia, at the mouth of the Tiber, was a small town by the middle of that fourth century, but not yet a notable seaport. The Punic Wars, however, brought the necessity of transporting troops and supplies across the sea and thus aided in the development of a merchant marine. But at Ostia vessels of 100 tons (3,000 talents) could not enter the harbor. For all larger craft, from the second century B.C., the port of Rome was Puteoli (Pozzuoli), 150 miles away, on the Bay of Naples, much as Naples is today the real port of the capital, in spite of the nearer harbor at Civitavecchia. From Puteoli ships sailed for Sicily, Africa, and the East, but a large proportion of these were foreign vessels (p. 86). The wars with Syria and Macedonia led many merchants in the second century B.C. to venture into eastern waters, following in the wake of transports. Thus began a current of emigration toward Asia Minor.

INDUSTRY

For senators to engage in commerce seemed improper, especially to possible competitors, and by a law of 220 or

219 B.C. they were forbidden to own any ship that could carry more than about 225 bushels of grain (perhaps eight tons' burden).[1] At that time the principal exports from Italy were olive oil and wine, not the products of industry in the towns. The senators being chiefly interested in landed property and the produce of their estates, took no measures to promote commerce or to protect and encourage industry, though it was apparent that the free artisan suffered much from Etruscan and other competition and the extensive employment of slave labor.

There were trade guilds in increasing numbers, but they did not grasp at control of the trade nor secure more favorable terms for their members, nor even effectively voice their complaints, certainly not by refusing to work.[2] Even under the Empire the few actual strikes recorded were in Asia Minor.

As the strike—hopeless in view of the number of slaves—was conspicuously absent, so were measures designed to regulate and protect industry. At no time in Roman history was there anything like a patent or other stimulus to invention. Nor were there tariffs to meet ruinous competition from abroad.[3] The knights, who in time became capitalists with many investments, managed chiefly by freedmen and trusted slaves, seem never to have helped the cause of the free laborer or employee, or to have devised means of advancing the general interests of commerce. And the senators as great landlords looked down in scorn on trade in any form, on free labor as sordid and tainted by contact with slaves.

Industry was on a small scale. There were very few ma-

---

[1] This old law was revived by Julius Caesar.

[2] The only case of which we hear at Rome is that of the aggrieved flute-players, whose presence was required at religious ceremonies (312 B.C.). But we should not class them with artisans.

[3] For an exceptional prohibition cp. p. 68.

chines, and none more complicated than the loom. Typical of the system would be the shoemaker as he was among us two generations ago, making with his own hands, perhaps unassisted, the shoes which he himself sold to his customers. One stage further back was the tanner, who needed more space and more hands. There was no middleman to claim his profits from both. One shoemaker's pride in his craft has perpetuated itself upon his tombstone, now in a museum on the Capitol. Above his portrait in relief we see a sandal and a last, while the inscription takes care to name the location of his shop—at the Porta Fontinalis. And many such stones tell a similar story for various trades. Much selling was done in public places, especially on market days (*nundinae*, p. 114).

Almost every street in Pompeii has shops in which making and selling went on at the same time, and so it was in ancient cities from early times down through the later Empire. But there were larger establishments also, such as those of the fuller, the baker, or the tanner, as we may see at Ostia, Pompeii, and Herculaneum. The fuller finished and dyed cloth, cleaned soiled garments and whitened them with chalk or pipe clay. For these purposes he needed a plant with vats and tanks, space for drying, a screw-press, a number of slaves or free helpers. The baker too required space for his plant, for he was at the same time a miller. Yet the scale of all these industries was small. In fact though Pompeii had become in part an industrial town, no streets as yet excavated have revealed anything approaching a factory, nor was the place noted for products requiring much capital and a factory system.

Not far away was Capua, a real industrial center, but we are not informed as to the appearance and equipment of an ancient factory. Such establishments were to be found at Puteoli also (p. 39), an industrial city as well as a busy seaport. At Capua the Etruscans had developed a bronze industry, and its products, both the useful and the ornamental, were very widely distributed. The same city made elaborately wrought silverware, also pottery and furniture.

In the second century B.C. came important changes in commerce and industry when eastern territory was acquired with flourishing cities such as those of the province of Asia (p. 45), where the making of rugs and tapestries and parchment had led to the establishment of real factories. Contact with the East and its well-developed manufactures stimulated a taste for luxuries, including works of art, imported at high prices, and Tyrian purple. Importation of fine wares, furniture, and fabrics was soon followed by imitation. The influx of slaves from the East, many of them skilled artisans, made it possible to produce in Italy articles heretofore seldom if ever required for the Roman market. In spite of competing imports, often of superior excellence, production was encouraged by the general trend in the direction of greater comfort.

The trade guilds (*collegia opificum*) suffered a temporary eclipse owing to their part in political agitation and consequent legislation against them in 64 B.C. With few exceptions they were later suppressed by Julius Caesar, only to be revived by Augustus under fixed conditions (7 B.C.).[4]

Enterprising Italians with capital found new business opportunities in the first century B.C. in Africa, in southern Gaul, and in the mines of Spain. By that time there was a well-developed commerce between Italy and the provinces, and through the latter into countries beyond the frontiers. By far the larger part of it was the trade in necessaries of life, cereals, olive oil, fish, wine, wool and flax, or woolen goods and linen, metals, lumber, also manufactured articles in commonest use. Not that luxuries were neglected—the

[4] For their later history see pp. 93 ff.

finer fabrics, as silk and purple, other high-grade products, the choicer wines and best qualities of oil, perfumes, spices, precious stones and jewelry. For all of these and many others fashion steadily enlarged the market.

Industry still continued, as in China today, largely in the hands of the shopkeeper class with their small shops in which handicraft and selling were only different phases of the same trade. In some trades, however, requiring a number of workers in the same shop, division of labor had been introduced, so that we may speak of an incipient factory. Such developments were familiar to Roman travelers in the Hellenistic cities, and Italy was only adapting methods long in vogue in Greek lands.

Some towns were favorably situated for a particular industry and thus gained prosperity and a name. Yet raw materials were carried to a distance also. So the iron of the island of Elba, from which the Etruscan cities had long received their supply, was smelted at Populonia and shipped to Puteoli to be wrought into arms, cutlery, tools, etc. The clay of Arretium (Arezzo), one of the chief cities of Etruria, enabled it to develop an industry which from the time of Augustus to that of Vespasian sent its wares to every part of the empire. Imitating and reproducing the raised designs of silverware, as their predecessors of Samos had done before them, the potteries of Arretium produced an admirable red-glazed ware of attractive form and graceful ornament for everyday table use. Many of the moulds have been preserved, evidently made by skilled designers, usually freedmen of Greek origin. From such moulds the workmen then produced a large number of bowls, cups, and plates. Thus in this industry requiring much division of labor there was certainly a factory system.

The popular ware of Arretium was soon imitated in Gaul. A town on the western slopes of the Cevennes, Conda-

olive oil (both of these important exports from Greece also and from Asia Minor). In exchange she was receiving grain from Egypt, Africa, Sicily, and Sardinia, tin and lead from Spain and Britain, iron from Spain, Gaul, and the Danube provinces, woolen goods and pottery from Gaul, woolens from Asia Minor and Syria, linen, papyrus, and manufactures of every kind from Egypt, glass from Syria and Egypt, spices from Arabia, perfumes from Syria, sulphur from Sicily, lumber from the shores of the Black Sea, valuable woods and marbles from Africa, marbles from Greece and her islands, porphyry and granite from Egypt. The great seaports of Italy were Puteoli, Ostia with its new harbor, the work of Claudius, Aquileia at the head of the Adriatic. All of these and many other ports were full of ships, of which comparatively few were Roman. To complete the picture of Roman commerce and industry at their height, from Augustus to Hadrian, we must add the complicated network of trade carried on by the provinces with one another, and bear particularly in mind the prosperity of such centers of provincial industry as Alexandria and Antioch in the East, Lugdunum and Augusta Treverorum in the West. Nor should we neglect the foreign commerce not only with lands across the frontiers but also, through such intermediaries or else by sea, with lands still more remote, even the Far East. The interprovincial trade, as that of Italy with the provinces, was overwhelmingly a commerce of indispensable products. That with the most distant countries dealt prevailingly in luxuries for the sale of which the high cost of transportation with its risks was not prohibitive.

More important than any other long-distance commerce was the trade with India, from which were brought products of China also, as well as those of Ceylon, Burma, and the Malay Peninsula. With most of these Far-Eastern imports the Romans had had little or no acquaintance until their conquest of Syria. Pompey's successes in the East brought new contacts with oriental trade, and the spoils of his campaigns opened Roman eyes to undreamed-of luxuries. More epoch-making was the occupation of Egypt by Octavian, for Alexandria of the Ptolemies had been a great market for imports from the Far East. But even under the early Empire there was no direct trading with India. What the Greek merchants of Alexandria offered for sale as Indian wares had been brought as a rule by their ships from the southern end of the Red Sea only, and to ports in Upper Egypt (Berenice and Myos Hormos). Thence goods were carried by caravan across to the Nile at Koptos [6] and so down the river to Alexandria. They had purchased their cargoes in southern Arabia, especially at Arabia Eudaemon (now Aden), to which mart Indian ships had brought them by a long coasting voyage. The western trader thus met the eastern at the mouth of the Red Sea. And the "Roman" merchant, who very rarely went farther, was usually a Greek or a Greek-speaking Egyptian.

There were overland routes also from China and India, and other routes on which the coasting voyage from India to the Persian Gulf was succeeded either by a caravan trail across the desert to Petra and so to the Mediterranean in southern Palestine, or else by a river voyage up the Euphrates to Zeugma and then by caravan to Antioch in Syria, or continuing on across Asia Minor to the Aegean. One overland route left the upper valley of the Indus, crossed the mountains into what is now Afghanistan, then via modern Kabul over the Hindu Kush Mountains to ancient Bactra and modern Merv, thence south of the Caspian through Media to the Tigris at Ctesiphon, capital of Parthia, and by boat up the Euphrates. Chinese silks were often carried by this route. A more northerly route, espe-

[6] Over 250 miles from Berenice.

cially for silk, from western and northwestern China passed
north of Tibet, through eastern Turkestan to Maracanda
(Samarkand), then down the Oxus, and so to the Caspian,
where ship was taken for its western shore; thence by land
south of the Caucasus to the east end of the Black Sea.
These land routes, on which camels were the beasts of
burden, were in large part controlled by the Parthians and
subject to interruption. It was to their interest to prevent the
Chinese merchant from making direct contact with the
Roman.[7] The long sea voyage to the Red Sea, a course
known to Egyptian, Arabian, and Indian traders, had its
advantages, but direct contact was even less possible by that
route.

Commerce between Italy and India was greatly stimulated in the time of Claudius (41-54 A.D.), after a Greek
mariner, Hippalos, had rediscovered the secret of using the
monsoons for a direct voyage from the Red Sea to southern
India. This bold course kept a ship out of sight of land for
some forty days without the help of a compass. In all it
was seventy days from the Egyptian port of Berenice. The
steady southwest winds from May to September, and then
southeast from November to March, made a round trip
from Egypt to southern India possible—a trading voyage
requiring with all its delays less than a year. The result of
this improved open-sea navigation was a greatly enlarged
trade to meet the ever-increasing demands for oriental
luxuries.

While it was chiefly a commerce of high-priced articles
and still remained in the hands of Greek merchants, the
range of commodities is astonishing. It was by no means

[7] In the time of Nerva (97 A.D.) Kan Ying, a Chinese emissary of the
Han dynasty, did reach Syria, and it is interesting to imagine what might
have been the cultural results if the two empires had really come to know
each other.

limited to articles of dress and personal adornment, perfumes and condiments. Pearls had come to be in great demand, and for these India was the chief source. The general
use of seals required stones suitable for the engraver, and
India sent the best—sards and carnelians, also onyx and
sardonyx for cameos, often of great size. Beryls (aqua-
marines), sapphires, rubies from Burma, opals, amethysts,
and rock crystal, sometimes in large pieces for cups and
bowls, came from India, and rarely the diamond, except as
used for cutting other stones. Another mineral product was
asbestos, from which costly shrouds and garments and also
expensive lamp wicks were woven in Syria and elsewhere.
Chinese silks, silk yarn, and raw silk came by an overland
route, either directly from the land of the Seres,[8] *i.e.,* northwest China, across Parthia, or indirectly by way of the
marts of India, which had its own trade with China. The
extensive importation of this costly material, transported
over such vast distances, begins with Augustus. The weaving
was often done in Syria or Egypt, where silk yarn was also
interwoven with wool and linen. From China came furs and
skins, from India, cotton and the finest muslins. Roman
luxury in furnishings and decoration created a large market
for Indian ivory, competing with that from Africa, for
ebony (also from Africa), tortoise shell (the best from the
Malay Peninsula and Ceylon), and mother-of-pearl. For
the table the great luxury was pepper from southern India,
always costly, but one of the chief oriental imports. Ginger
came from Ceylon, while cinnamon in several forms was extensively imported from China and India, both for flavoring
and for incense. The leaf of the same tree was called *malo-
bathrum* and furnished a costly ingredient of perfumes and
ointments. Other perfumes on India's list were *amomum*
and spikenard (very expensive) and *costus.* Medicine made

[8] Hence silk is *Serica vestis* or *Serica,* whence comes our word.

much use of Indian plants and their products, even pepper, cane sugar (only in medicine), and indigo, chiefly used as a dye. Rice was imported from India and brought high prices.[9] Of the metals imported from the Far East the quantity must have been small, but the quality high. Especially was this true of the much-prized iron and steel of the Seres and of India.

Of all these varied imports and many others less noteworthy, as also of Roman exports, we have authentic lists in a trader's guidebook to the ports of the Red Sea and Indian Ocean, the so-called *Periplus Maris Erythraei,* written by a Greek merchant in Egypt nearly or quite contemporary with Pliny the Elder, whose *Natural History* gives much information about eastern commodities. An official list of imports for the guidance of merchants and customs officers in Egypt has been preserved in a rescript of Marcus Aurelius (ca. 180 A.D.), to be found in the *Digest* of Justinian. It includes costly articles imported from India, East Africa, Arabia, and also from China.

Turning now to the other side of the balance sheet, we are at once impressed not only by the limited number of exports from Roman territory, but also by their wide geographical range. For even Spain shipped lead to India, there to be alloyed with copper or tin for various uses, especially to be coined into money. Tin also was exported from Spain and Lusitania, and to a much smaller extent from Britain after 43 A.D., while lead bound for India was

[9] Wild animals were occasionally brought from the same country, tigers, leopards, panthers, lions, to be exhibited to the people or hunted down in the amphitheater. They seem to have been transported overland through Parthia. Elephants, which the Romans had first met in the army of Pyrrhus, came from Africa, but their drivers were mainly Indian. Among the marvels of India brought to the capital were snakes of great size, especially pythons. For pets parrots were brought in large numbers, and monkeys— these also by land.

shipped from Britain. Copper also was sent out from the western provinces, but mainly from Cyprus. Exports to the Far East were in part articles of luxury, including wines, especially the Italian and the Laodicean, red coral (to China as well), Tyrian purple, linen from Egypt, embroidered fabrics from Syria (especially to China), silverware, slaves trained as singers, slave girls for the harem. But in a much larger proportion the exports to India were glassware and crude glass (both of these to China also), clay vases and lamps, bronze vessels, cheap stuffs of various kinds. Transshipment at Alexandria was the rule.

So much more costly were the imports than the exports that the balance of trade was decidedly unfavorable to Rome. Ships returning to India must often have sailed in ballast. And the unfavorable trade balance had to be made up in gold and silver coin. Hence specie was listed among the exports. Loud were the complaints concerning this loss of currency that never returned, such as those of Tiberius in a letter to the senate, or of Pliny the Elder.[10] Hence it is not strange that thousands of Roman coins, especially of Augustus and Tiberius, have been found in India, particularly in the South.

With the Far North, or what was such to the Roman mind, that is, with the German tribes on the shores of the Baltic, there had been from prehistoric times a trade in amber passed along from tribe to tribe until it reached Mediterranean waters, mainly at the mouth of the Rhone or the head of the Adriatic. Under the Empire it was brought especially to Aquileia, the chief port of northeastern Italy, to be mounted or worked up into jewelry, toilet articles, etc. Roman merchants carried Italian wares

---

[10] Pliny deplores the fact that India drained away 55,000,000 sesterces every year, while the addition of what went to the Seres and the Arabians raised the annual loss of specie to 100,000,000.

into eastern Germany and even Scandinavia, either by sea
from Atlantic ports of Gaul or by land from Aquileia to
the Baltic. From unconquered Germany came hides and
slaves. From regions north of the Black Sea grain was
shipped to Greece, together with furs and hemp. All of the
northern imports were paid for in manufactured articles or
in wine and oil. As for Africa and its less accessible regions,
there was a trade in slaves, dates, and to some extent in
ivory, across the Sahara. But most of the products of Central
and East Africa came by way of the Nile or the Red Sea
to Alexandria—gold and ivory, spices, rare woods, wild
animals for the amphitheaters.

Of special interest to us is the traffic in marbles and other
valuable building materials, beginning in the last century
of the Republic and greatly extended under the Empire.
From the quarries of Greece and Greek islands came a rich
variety of colored marbles and the choicest of the white
(p. 348). Asia Minor furnished especially the Phrygian,
mottled with purple, Numidia the much-admired yellow
marble, Arabia, Syria, and Egypt their precious alabasters,
Egypt her green and her red porphyry, also granite. The
shaping into columns and other architectural members was
done in part at distant quarries by slaves or convicts, in part
at the ultimate destination. There were slabs for revetment
(p. 366) or pavements, blocks for the sculptor and the
carver of ornamental details, while the smallest fragments
found extensive use in mosaics. Many ships must have been
employed in this trade. Italy's own resources in marble were
never fully drawn upon, though the quarries of Luna (Carrara), located close to the sea, furnished much excellent
white marble, beginning with the time of Augustus.

Commerce and industry were not carried on by organized
capital in the form of companies. The independent manu-
facturer or merchant was the rule. There were small groups

forming a *societas* engaged in business, but these are hardly to be distinguished from firms. The nearest approach to a modern company is to be found in the operations of the *publicani* of Republican times, that is, the corporations of the knights to whom the censors let contracts for farming taxes and for public works, and who engaged in trade to some extent in the provinces. But the collecting of taxes by this method in the rich province of Asia was discontinued by Julius Caesar. The short-lived example of such companies seems not to have been imitated either in industry or commerce. Industry was only occasionally capitalized and conducted on a factory basis, either in a town or on some large estate where the raw materials were to be found or produced. Nevertheless business was far from simple, the papyri of Egypt showing a very modern complexity in contracts, business deals, and banking.

The banker (*argentarius*) at Rome was usually a freedman or a foreigner. He accepted without interest deposits from which payments could be made by a written order to transfer a specified sum to another's account—an approach to a checking system. Through his correspondents in distant cities he could arrange for payments in the provinces, though he did not issue a letter of credit. Often he was a money changer as well, and a lender and negotiator of loans at varying rates, six per cent being the normal, twelve per cent the legal maximum. In the eastern provinces the *publicani* made or arranged loans to princes, cities, and other creditors, often at high rates of interest.

TRADE GUILDS

The rôle of trade guilds in Roman commerce and industry has been touched upon above (p. 81), but their importance in the time of the Empire requires a fuller account of later developments under increasing government control. There were guilds (*collegia*) of shipowners (*navicularii*) and of merchants (*negotiatores*), with a wealthy membership. Most of the guilds, however, were recruited from the artisans. Actors and musicians, who frequently migrated, had guilds without local habitat. The vast majority of the *collegia,* however, were strictly local, with no organic connection with those of the same trade even in neighboring cities. Rich members were not excluded, nor were artists, nor freedmen, nor even slaves who joined with their masters' permission. In the Greek portion of the empire most of the trade guilds seem to have been first introduced by the Romans. Emperors such as Trajan were strongly opposed to them, as liable sooner or later to become centers of disaffection.

The internal workings of the guilds are amply illustrated for us by masses of inscriptions. Thus there was an initiation fee, a small monthly tax, and at times other burdens, with special contributions from officers or patrons. These last, along with other donors, often left endowments to keep their memory green by an anniversary feast, or they aided in the acquisition of property. Prosperous guilds had a hall (*schola*) adorned with statues and other special gifts. It was usually in the street or quarter of that trade or else in the market place. Each "college" had its patron divinity, linked by long association with the trade, and conducted its religious rites either at the *schola* or in a temple. Some had a temple of their own, most a common burial place, either a *columbarium* (p. 200) or a burial plot. Funeral expenses and a space in the common tomb were the limit of insurance offered by these guilds. Relief in illness or poverty, to widows and children of members, may have been practised to some extent, but evidence for any form of charity is lacking.

It was not the object of a guild to improve the trade by

encouraging invention or better methods. They did not combine to raise wages, reduce hours, regulate apprenticeship,
capitalize their industry, or secure a monopoly (p. 81).
There is small ground for comparing them either with the
medieval guilds or with modern unions.

However, these *collegia* filled a vacuum in the life of the
commercial and industrial classes, as is shown by the care
with which they framed their society on the lines of a state
or municipality.[11] The average membership may perhaps be
set at 100-300.[12] Pliny the Younger thought 150 a manage-
able number for a guild which he vainly hoped might meet
with Trajan's approval, to serve as a volunteer fire department for Nicomedia, in Bithynia. Women were not admitted until the fourth century, but had some guilds of their
own, *e.g.,* the *mimae.* The organization was democratic and
the greatest freedom of internal management was permitted by the state to licensed guilds until the third century,
when conscription altered the whole situation.

Some of the guilds had regularly performed a quasi-
public function, *e.g.,* those serving the state in the grain
supply (*annona*), or a municipality in lieu of a fire department. Three guilds found in almost every city in the western
provinces, as also in Africa, constituted the local fire bri-
gade. These were the *fabri tignarii* (carpenters or builders),
the *dendrophori* (dealers in firewood) and *centonarii,* who

[11] Their highest officials, *magistri* (one to twelve in number) were
elected for one year or for five, while the members grouped themselves in
"hundreds" under a *centurio* or in "tens" under a *decurio.* Next to the
magister stood a *curator* usually, then a quaestor, or treasurer, in charge
of the chest (*arca*). There was sometimes a praetor or an aedile, commonly also a *scriba* (clerk). There was also a color bearer (*vexillifer*),
since on gala occasions the guild paraded, and finally (from the time of
Alexander Severus) a *defensor* to represent the guild in court or before
the authorities.

[12] The largest known guild, that of the carpenters at Rome, seems to
have reached a membership of nearly 1,500. Another at Mediolanum
(Milan) had 1,200.

made coarse cloth out of secondhand materials. For as pumps were of limited capacity fire was fought also by smothering and by demolition. These were the principal guilds and in some towns combined in one. They had *praefecti* and a more military organization on account of their service at fires. Important in the service of the state were also the *navicularii,* including boatmen on rivers and lakes, and the *negotiatores* (merchants), and hence exempt from municipal burdens.

From the reign of Alexander Severus (222-235 A.D.) the trade guilds became state institutions and a trade no longer free employment but public service as truly as that of the soldier, and under increasingly burdensome exactions. It was a not unnatural outgrowth of the imperial system with its enormous number of functionaries. From furnishing the capital with grain at a low price or at times even free—a system requiring the organization of a great bureau, the *annona*—the government proceeded to other largesses, as wine and oil, and drifted further and further into the business of production, transportation, and distribution on an enormous scale, furnishing food for court, army, and civil service, besides manufacturing clothing for them. Guilds of cloth workers were established by authority and made hereditary. The same kind of control was extended to other industries, to mines, quarries, and many enterprises formerly conducted by private capital. Thus it may be said that in the third and fourth centuries the government commandeered the guilds in a rather general conscription of industry and commerce.

Membership in a guild was no longer a matter of choice, and once a member the novice found himself permanently attached to it with his family and his property. Escape was as impossible as for the soldier or the *colonus* (p. 467). And the son must follow the trade of the father, so that, except

in name, this hereditary servitude of the industrial and
commercial classes was almost worse than the ancient
slavery, which still existed unchanged. Political liberty was
as completely lacking as was economic freedom. By the time
of Diocletian (284-305 A.D.) the state bore a partial resemblance to a vast penitentiary, with only life sentences and
a hereditary feature unknown to prisons. Yet even after
there ceased to be emperors in the West something still remained of the guild system, to be revived for a short time
by Theodoric the Ostrogoth at Ravenna, and by other German rulers in their endeavors to retain Roman institutions.
In Constantinople the guilds, minutely and oppressively
regulated, survived until the fall of the Byzantine Empire.

THE ROAD SYSTEM

No contribution of Rome to the welfare of the Mediterranean world is more familiarly known than the remarkable
system of communications which linked the city with the
most distant provinces. If the proverb made all roads lead
to Rome, it was because road-building was inseparable from
Roman expansion. The first great highway—by no means
the first road—was a necessary sequel to the occupation of
northern Campania. Rather was it part and parcel of that
occupation. This was the Appian Way (Via Appia; illus.,
p. 405), bearing the name of its builder, the censor Appius
Claudius, who in 312 B.C. carried the "queen of roads" almost in a straight line southeastward through the Pontine
Marshes as far as the sea at Tarracina, and then, partly
along the coast, to Capua (132 miles), where there was a
Roman garrison. Later it was extended over the Apennines
by way of Beneventum and Venusia to the southern ports of
Tarentum and Brundisium (360 miles). In time the latter
developed into the port of departure for travelers bound for
Greece and the East, and thus the Appia became what we

should call the trunk line for eastern travel.[13] From Capua
lesser roads ran to Neapolis (Naples) and the much more
important seaport of Puteoli (Pozzuoli), also by way of
Salernum, Paestum, and Velia to the Straits of Sicily at
Rhegium (Reggio).

Toward the north there were three important routes made
necessary by campaigns and annexations in that direction.
Vying in celebrity with the Appia was the Via Flaminia,
built in 220 B.C. and named for another censor, Gaius Fla-
minius. It ran through the Campus Martius, crossed the
Tiber on the Pons Mulvius (p. 360) and again beyond
Mount Soracte, then on through Umbria and over the
Apennines to the Adriatic at Fanum Fortunae, ending at
Ariminum (Rimini) on the same coast and at that time still
a frontier town. In 187 B.C. it was continued as Via Aemilia
by Aemilius Lepidus in a northwesterly direction through
Bononia (Bologna), Mutina (Modena), Parma, and Placentia (Piacenza), and then, after crossing the Po, to
Mediolanum (Milan, 416 miles from Rome). Next in importance to the Flaminia-Aemilia route was the Via Aurelia, running down to the sea at Alsium and following the
coast of Etruria to Pisae (Pisa) and Luna (Carrara). Beyond that the extremely rugged nature of the coast made a
detour inland unavoidable, reaching a pass (2,000 feet)
north of modern Spezia, and so down to the coast again.
Following the Riviera the extended road passed Genua
(Genoa) and Nicaea (Nice), crossing the frontier of Gallia
Narbonensis at the river Var.[14]

[13] For after crossing to Dyrrhachium or Apollonia one took the Via
Egnatia, which led across the Balkan Peninsula to Thessalonica and Byzantium.

[14] Continuing as the Via Domitia the road ran on through Forum Iulii
(Fréjus), Aquae Sextiae (Aix), Arelate (Arles), and Narbo (Narbonne)
to the Pyrenees. Crossing these by a low pass near the coast it joined a

The third northern route was the Via Cassia, leading through the Etruscan cities of Clusium (Chiusi) and Faesulae (Fiesole near Florence) to Luca (Lucca) and the coast south of Luna.

For the regions east and northeast of Rome the chief roads were two: the Salaria, originally the road by which salt was carried into the interior, and the Valeria. The former traversed the land of the Sabines and Picenum to the Adriatic, following that coast to Ancona, while the latter led through Tibur (Tivoli) and Corfinium to the Adriatic at Aternum.

There were in course of time many other well-traveled roads in Italy, such as the Postumia, which ran from Placentia through Cremona and Mantua to Aquileia at the head of the Adriatic.[15] Of the Alpine routes the most used road to the west led from Mediolanum (Milan) via Augusta Taurinorum (Turin) over the pass of Alpis Cottia (Mont Genèvre) into the old province of Gaul, to Arelate (Arles) and the Rhone country or to Massilia. One could also journey by way of Augusta Praetoria (Aosta) to the higher pass of Alpis Graia (the Little Saint Bernard) and down the Isara (Isère) to Cularo (Grenoble),[16] and so to Vienna (Vienne) and Lugdunum (Lyons), then by way of the Arar and the Mosella (Saône and Moselle) to the Rhine. There was also the more difficult and still higher pass of Alpis Poenina (Great Saint Bernard), a route to

---

main road which led by the east and south coast of Spain via Tarraco (Tarragona) and New Carthage (Cartagena) to Gades (Cadiz, cp. p. 101).

[15] From the port of Aquileia roads diverged, one over the lowest of Alpine passes into Pannonia and so to the Danube, another eastward across the Balkan Peninsula toward Byzantium, a third down the east coast of the Adriatic.

[16] An alternative route diverged from the valley of the Isara above Cularo northward to Genava (Geneva).

the Rhineland,[17] but for the hardiest. Northbound travelers out of Italy could take the road from Verona to Tridentum (Trent) and over the Brenner pass into Raetia (Tyrol), and so to the Danube Valley.

These Alpine roads were very different from the modern highways in the same region. The Roman road in the Alps, designed chiefly for pack animals, was in places only five feet wide, seldom more than ten, and often very steep. In general Roman roads always seem to us very narrow. Specimens still exist in almost every corner of the empire, but are often concealed by the broader modern road laid down above the old, in which case the crossing of an ancient bridge may alone remind us of the Roman builders. The best-known examples still visible are near Rome, especially the Appia, Latina, Nomentana, and Ostiensis. The paving is of pentagonal blocks of basalt (*silex*) very neatly fitted and with a broad curb. The average width of the Appia in the excavated ten miles or more nearest the city is under fourteen feet, not including the curb. On a steep grade the main roads are wider—eighteen feet instead of fourteen or fifteen, and sometimes twenty-one feet or more on a bridge or high embankment. The paving naturally differed according to the stone available in the particular region, and not all roads were surfaced with stone blocks. Some had a surface of rammed gravel (*glarea*). Great pains were taken to secure drainage and a solid foundation, usually in several layers of broken stone of graduated sizes and often one or two layers of concrete, as prescribed by Vitruvius.

The straightness of Roman roads, mentioned by Plutarch, but only here and there very conspicuous, became a legend. In level country, as where the Appia makes its march to the sea (sixty miles), or in the plains of the Po, there were

[17] Via Viviscus (Vevey), near the upper end of the Lacus Lemanus, and through the land of the Helvetians.

long straight stretches. But curves were frequent in following the course of streams and in climbing, to avoid heavy grades. Bridges were generally arched in stone, and many such are still in use both in Italy and in distant countries, while others are impressive in their ruin. Some were adorned with a monumental arch spanning the roadway or with two such arches (p. 360). Rock cuttings, causeways and other engineering works were often necessary. Tunnels were driven through the rock, some of them of considerable length, as that at Pausilypon (Posillipo, near Naples), pierced by Agrippa.

In some regions, as Macedonia, Asia Minor, and Syria the Romans had only to improve and enlarge an already existing system of roads. Even Gaul before the coming of Caesar had not a few tolerable roads. By the time of Trajan the network covered every part of the empire and distances were marked by inscribed milestones, large numbers of which have been discovered, many of Republican date or of the early Empire. The focus of the entire system was the gilded pillar which Augustus had placed in the Roman Forum. A cursory study of the leading roads can be made in any good map of the empire. More impressive is an original document, a milestone from a distant country, or better still a contemporary itinerary engraved on a traveler's silver cup. Four such cups, probably of the time of Trajan, may be seen at Rome in the form of cylindrical milestones, with all the town names and distances from Gades (Cadiz), beyond Gibraltar, to Rome (p. 289).

Of great interest are the ancient guidebooks such as the *Antonine Itinerary* so-called, though it dates from the time of Diocletian and comes to us only in medieval copies. This lists all the main land routes throughout the empire (presumably from a map), giving distances from place to place, the *mutationes,* where horses were changed, and *mansiones,* where one could tarry overnight. No space is found for general information or useful hints. The *Jerusalem Itinerary* (333 A.D.), designed for Christian pilgrims to the Holy Land, covers the roads from Burdigala (Bordeaux) to Hierosolyma (Jerusalem) by way of Milan, Constantinople, and Antioch, adding some notes on places of interest, especially in Palestine. The distance amounts to 3,300 miles, and for the return another route is given by way of Macedonia and the whole length of Italy. The one extant example of a road diagram for the whole empire and beyond will be described in another ·context (p. 288). Even if we reduce our range and confine ourselves to the road system of a single province, such as Britain or Africa, or of a group of provinces, such as the four which made up Gaul or the three in Spain, the study is in every way rewarding. But space fails us to linger here over the vast net of roads which made a single central government possible and at the same time brought immense advantages to trade.·

TRAVEL

Travel was slow in comparison with modern times, but compared favorably with eighteenth-century conditions in England or France. Carriages were used especially for long journeys with frequent changes of horses. There were *redae* with four wheels and *cisiae* with two. Saddle horses and mules were at times preferred. Horace and a leisurely party of notables covered the distance from Rome to Brundisium in fifteen days at about twenty-five miles a day. Probably forty miles a day was the normal average for the ordinary civilian traveler on a long journey, as even officials traveling by post do not appear as a rule to have exceeded fifty miles a day except for short distances.

The post (*cursus publicus*) was first established by Augustus, following the example of the King of Persia, whose couriers are mentioned by Herodotus, and that of Egypt under the Ptolemies. It was no small burden to the towns through which it passed and to farmers along the road, frequently commandeered for repairs.[18] Its facilities were open only to officials, such as provincial governors and their attendants, a pass (*diploma*) entitling them to changes of horses at the *mutationes,* to food also and other accommodations at the *mansiones* (about twenty-five miles apart). Private persons by special favor of the Emperor or a governor sometimes received a pass. Couriers bearing official dispatches and reports used the resources of the post. But there was no post service for the public.

Of the speed of couriers, of private messengers, and individual travelers we have some notable examples, far beyond the average performance. Thus in January, 69 A.D., a message from Moguntiacum (Mainz) reached Rome in less than nine days.[19] A standard bearer rode from Moguntiacum a few days earlier to Colonia Agrippinensis (Cologne), 108 miles, in about twelve to fourteen hours. A letter to Cicero was brought by private messenger (*tabellarius*) from Brundisium to Rome (360 miles) in eight to nine days. Julius Caesar was particularly noted for his rapid journeys, as that from Rome to the Rhone in less than eight days at a rate of 100 miles a day. Another was from Rome to southern Spain in twenty-seven days (twenty-three according to Suetonius). Tiberius, summoned from Ticinum (Pavia) to the deathbed of his brother Drusus in Germany, is said to have covered the last stage of 200 miles in twenty-four hours.

Naturally a large part of the traveling in the ancient

[18] Towns in Italy were relieved of this burden by Nerva.

[19] By the most direct land route, via the Little St. Bernard and Milan, the distance was nearly 900 miles. But to avoid the Alpine passes in winter the messenger may have taken ship from Massilia.

world was done by sea or on rivers. Rome's lack of a permanent natural harbor for large vessels was met by the engineering works of Claudius and then of Trajan at Ostia. Trajan constructed a new harbor also at Centumcellae (Civitavecchia), reached by the Via Aurelia (fifty miles). But even in the second century B.C. the real port of Rome for vessels of size was Puteoli (Pozzuoli), in spite of its distance (p. 82). Reached by the Via Appia or the Latina, and then by a branch road, it prospered especially under the early Empire, when the annexation of Egypt had so greatly stimulated commerce with the East. The large grain ships came in great numbers from Alexandria to transship their cargoes at Puteoli to smaller vessels for the shorter voyage to Ostia. Lighter and more valuable freight could be carried to Rome by the Appia, with some use of the canal through the Pontine Marshes. Ships returning to Alexandria carried the products of Campanian industry, especially in iron, bronze, and pottery. The coming of the first grain fleet of the season from Egypt was eagerly anticipated. Seneca vividly describes the enthusiastic crowds on the docks when the approach of the ships was announced. To Puteoli came also many ships from Africa, bringing chiefly wheat, from Spain with cargoes of oil, wine, or metals, from Elba with iron. Near by at Misenum was the chief naval station under the Empire.

Before the middle of November navigation was usually closed and so remained until early in March. Not that ships never ventured to sea in the winter months. Down to 67 B.C. winter voyages were at times risked as less endangered by pirates. Necessity or the desire to make one more trip must often have prompted a voyage out of season. So also in the case of officials and of ships in the service of the post after its establishment. Yet the fact remains that ships were generally laid up, actually out of the water, for four months.

The graphic account of St. Paul's last voyage and shipwreck in the book of the Acts tells of a large ship of Alexandria with 276 persons on board attempting a westward
voyage in early winter, until driven on the coast of Melita
(Malta). After three months the voyage was resumed on
another ship from Alexandria which had wintered at the
island. The port finally reached was Puteoli, as usual in
that trade, the passengers journeying on to Rome by the
Via Appia.

Ships of such size, having but one mast with one very
large square sail, were able to tack only under the most
favorable circumstances, and excessive strain on the single
mast and its rigging in a storm was likely to open the seams.
The fore-and-aft rig, so much more serviceable in "beating," was limited, so far as our knowledge goes, to very
small boats, such as that pictured on a relief from Lamp-
sacus now at Constantinople. Ships with two masts are represented on Indian coins, probably depicting vessels in the
western trade, but we know nothing of them in the Mediterranean.

In good weather sailing was often done at night, guided
by the stars and lighthouses at many harbors. Most voyages
were coastwise and not long out of sight of land, except at
seasons of steady winds. The Etesian winds in the Mediterranean or the monsoons in the Indian Ocean (p. 88), blow-
ing for a season persistently from the same quarter, were a
partial compensation for the lack of a compass.

There were few comforts for passengers, who evidently
regarded roughing it as unavoidable at sea. Private yachts
were built and extravagantly adorned, but are seldom mentioned. No such luxuries were provided by any regular pas-
senger service. Transports after a long voyage delivered
their troops in poor condition for service.

For a passage from Puteoli to Alexandria at least eight

or nine days were required, and twice as many, or more, for the slow grain ships. A ship sailing from Ostia might reach Carthage in two to three days, Massilia in three to four, Tarraco in Spain in four to five, Gibraltar in seven to eight; but these are excellent passages, not averages. For Athens or Asia Minor one could sail from Ostia or Puteoli, but one normally made the long land journey by the Appia and sailed from Brundisium. At Corinth one crossed the Isthmus,[20] taking another ship from Cenchreae, and so to the Piraeus, and if bound for Asia, on across the Aegean. Twenty-one days was fast time for a messenger bearing a letter from Rome to Athens. Through ships for Asia or Syria sailed around the southeastern promontory of Greece, the Malea, noted for its dangers.

Long-distance travel usually combined land journeys with sea voyages or the use of boats on rivers or lakes. Gaul was particularly a land of river navigation, with much traffic across from the Mediterranean to the Atlantic and the Channel by the Rhone, Saône, Loire, and Seine; also by the Aude to the Garonne. In the same way the lower Rhineland was reached by the Saône and the Moselle. By the first-named routes lead, tin, etc., from Britain were transported across Gaul by water and by roads over the watersheds. Water carriage was highly developed on most of the great rivers, from the Tagus to the Euphrates. Boats were available on many lakes, such as Como, Garda, Constance, and Geneva.

As for canals, the best-known in Italy was that which ran parallel to the Appian Way through the Pontine Marshes. Passengers southbound, with better luck than fell to Horace, could sleep on the canal boat and breakfast at Tarracina. Far more important were the ancient predecessors of the Suez Canal—two canals across from the Nile to the

[20] The canal, begun by Nero, is modern.

Gulf of Suez, chiefly the work of Darius and Ptolemy Philadelphus, restored by Trajan. Yet most of the merchants in the India trade preferred the caravan route from Koptos, further up the Nile, to the Red Sea (p. 87).

Information in regard to travel by water was doubtless as accessible as that contained in the land itineraries. Some of these guides, if extant, would be of great interest. What we actually have are a maritime itinerary in Latin and brief books in Greek for merchants, naming the ports of the Black Sea or of the Indian Ocean, including East Africa, and listing the principal commodities to be sold or purchased at each. Such a trader's manual was called a *periplus*.

Convenience and comfort in travel increased otherwise, but had little effect in raising the low standard of the inns. The traveler might have a luxurious carriage and be attended by numerous slaves, mounted or in other carriages, not to mention much superfluous baggage, silverware and costly vessels, but where search for a *hôtel de luxe?* The inns (*deversoria, tabernae*) were usually very democratic, noisy, and of doubtful respectability, with little to choose between rival inns in the same town. As a result the rich, whose most frequent journeys were in making the round of their villas, often purchased halfway houses on or near the road, to escape the discomforts of the public taverns. Cicero owned several of these. Inns had signs—elephant, camel, eagle, cock, and the like—while some showed inscriptions inviting the wayfarer to tarry. Those of a somewhat better grade were found in places especially frequented by merchants, or at the many mineral springs—the numerous *Aquae,* carefully set down in the itineraries or on maps, *e.g.,* Aquae Sextiae (Aix-en-Provence), Aquae Sulis (Bath). Such resorts were visited by the well-to-do in quest of health, but no one thought of residing even at the best inn.

Among the inconveniences of travel should be mentioned

the danger of being robbed. Brigands (*latrones*) were dealt with very summarily by the law, which gave the authorities power to hunt them down without waiting for an accuser. Yet they were never altogether suppressed, particularly in certain regions, such as the Pontine Marshes, or lonely districts in the mountains or near the frontiers. Corsica and Sardinia, parts of Greece and Asia Minor, and the province of Africa were especially infested with bandits and kidnapers (*plagiarii*). In general, however, the average traveler met with no such adventures. Those constantly on the road, as St. Paul, might recall the encounters of the highway.

The total volume of traffic by road and by water was very large, since movements of troops were not infrequent, while army officers, governors, procurators, and other officials were liable to transfer involving travel over great distances. And the merchant of ancient times found long journeys indispensable. To Horace the *mercator* is a restless wanderer, boldly racing over every sea, undeterred by shipwrecks. But the proportion of Romans among the merchants steadily declined. In general they were Greeks from Asia Minor or Egypt, and Syrians—not Jews, who were chiefly to be found in industry and small trade.

Another class of travelers was made up of tourists, largely young men who were finishing their studies and seeing the world. Some of them had been serving on the staff of a provincial governor and were now returning at a leisurely pace by a circuitous route to visit famous cities. The best example of this enthusiastic touring on release from official duty is that of the poet Catullus, cruising homeward from the Black Sea on his small yacht and furnishing a motto for all of his class—

ad claras Asiae volemus urbes.

Poets traveled also to recite their verses, witness Archias, the Greek poet. Other persons took long journeys to see and hear literary celebrities, as the man who came from Gades to see Livy and, that done, at once returned satisfied. Much more frequently seen on the roads were actors, musicians, athletes, entertainers of every description, artists on their way to execute commissions or in search of such. Philosophers and rhetoricians traveled extensively. Journeys for scientific purposes or to gather materials for a history were less common than among the Greeks. Roman historians felt no urge to visit battlefields and other noted scenes. Polybius, a Greek, acquainted himself with the Alpine passes before writing of Hannibal's crossing into Italy. Not so Livy, though born within sight of the Alps. Many visited Egypt [21] to see the pyramids and ancient temples or toured through Greece and parts of Asia Minor; but the explorer was the rarest of birds.

Journeys for health, especially to noted resorts, such as Baiae, were common, including seasonal migrations. And as their patients went to take the cure at this or that medicinal spring, physicians also were addicted to travel. Religion itself was responsible for much traveling *en masse,* to festivals at Rome, Olympia, Eleusis, and for the Jews, to Jerusalem. Less conspicuous were the repeated journeys of missionaries of several oriental religions rapidly spreading in the West (pp. 114, 130 ff.), but few of these bringers of new faiths can have rivaled the travel-range of the apostle from Tarsus.

[21] For a senator this required the Emperor's permission.

V

GODS AND MEN

EXAVDI, REGINA TVI PVLCHERRIMA MVNDI,
INTER SIDEREOS ROMA RECEPTA POLOS;
EXAVDI, GENETRIX HOMINVM, GENETRIXQVE DEORVM,
NON PROCVL A CAELO PER TVA TEMPLA SVMVS.
RUTILIUS NAMATIANUS, 1, 4

ET PEREGRINOS DEOS TRANSTVLIMVS ROMAM ET INSTITVIMVS NOVOS.
LIVY, 5, 52, 10

NEC ME EX EA OPINIONE, QVAM A MAIORIBVS ACCEPI DE CVLTV DEORVM
IMMORTALIVM, VLLIVS VMQVAM ORATIO AVT DOCTI AVT INDOCTI MOVEBIT.
CICERO, DE NATURA DEORUM, 3, 5

THE religion of the Romans was at first that of a primitive community of shepherds and rustics, with neither sacred books nor religious teachers. Immemorial rites observed with the utmost care in every detail were for centuries the sum and substance of religion. A multitude of vaguely conceived spirits—to be placated lest something untoward happen—could hardly be called gods. Certainly prayer and worship in such a religion were possible only in a sense all but unintelligible to us. As the city-state grew by conquest new divinities more human, rites more appealing, and religious ideas less primitive were imported. Meanwhile the older religion, a feeble light, was further dimmed by the luster of Greek divinities, either accepted as the virtual counterparts of old Italic deities or quite displacing them. This new and composite religion, more Greek than Roman in its outward manifestations, helped to bring Rome within the pale of the civilized nations, and in time proved capable of stimulating national consciousness and patriotism. It is with this phase of Roman religion that the classical literature acquaints us, rather than with the ideas and practices of the earliest period.

But with changing times a religion which combined elements so diverse had little real meaning for the masses, while the cultivated turned rather to philosophy, outwardly accepting the state religion as a useful institution commended by the forefathers. It was indeed an imposing mechanism controlled by the government, and ingeniously enlarged or readjusted to new conditions from time to time by the senate and later by the emperors, Augustus being the most active of all in his efforts to revive time-honored observances. The failing motive power, however, could not

be permanently replenished. Foreign cults, first Italic, then
Greek, and in one case Phrygian, had been accepted and
domesticated. Then came the Hellenistic worship of the
ruler and finally the widespread propaganda of oriental
religions, offering a consolation in sorrow and distress, a
hope of salvation for the individual, not to be found in the
Roman religion, to which positive beliefs and definite doctrines had always been uncongenial. At last in the fourth
century the strange conglomerate gave way to Christianity.

Corresponding somewhat to the Christian year, with its
calendar of feasts and saints' days, the Romans had their
Fasti, or calendar of festivals, preserved for us by inscriptions of the early Empire, and indicating for each month
the Kalends [1] (sacred to Juno), Nones and Ides (the latter
sacred to Jupiter); also the market days, that is, every
eighth day (*nundinae*). By initials, F or C or N, they
showed respectively whether the day in question was a day
for business, judicial or otherwise, or one when the *comitia*
(pp. 20 f.) might be held, or a day of ill omen, on which
worldly affairs were forbidden. Further the calendar included the festivals for each month (p. 137). The divinities
named in the Fasti are often those which had become little
more than names by the end of the Republic, such as An-
gerona, Carmenta, Furrina, Portunus, Volturnus. Thus
were preserved the memories of an early time before the
importation of Greek divinities, Apollo and the rest.

Besides Jupiter and Juno the chief gods of that period
were Mars, at first not so much a war god as a spirit of
springtime, Quirinus, a war god (or another form of
Mars), Vesta, the goddess of the hearth, and Janus, god of
the door, with prayer to whom every sacrifice began, and

---

[1] *I.e.,* the first day of the month. The Nones and Ides fell on the fifth
and thirteenth respectively, except in March, May, July, October, when
they fell respectively on the seventh and fifteenth.

whose priest, ranking above all the others, was called Rex sacrorum, as successor to the king in his religious duties. Other gods were believed to concern themselves with agriculture: Saturn at seedtime, Ceres while the crops were growing, Consus and Ops at harvest time. Fruit trees and their fruits were the province of Flora, and later in the season of Pomona. These clearly show the Roman idea of divinities as having each a definite action at a definite time, before and after which they are no concern of men. They were not imagined in any form, human or other, being simply vague impersonal spirits, with nothing defined about them except the narrow limits of their activity. And so specialized were their functions that it was of great importance for one to know which divinity he must address at the particular moment, and where, with what offerings, and in what set form of words. Such stereotyped prayers and proper instructions were to be had from the pontifices, who themselves officiated on important occasions. These priests did not instruct the people on the nature of the gods, and as state officials they were not connected with a particular temple or cult.

Among the most ancient divinities was Pales, a deity of shepherds, but so far from being conceived as personal that whether a god or a goddess was debated. In fact in the oldest phase of the Roman religion the spirits had no form or attributes, and hence no sex. Later, when human features and qualities were gradually assigned to them, uncertainty as to sex sometimes remained. And as an error of any kind in a prayer was thought to nullify the entire ceremony certain evasive formulas for addressing such ambiguous gods were invented by the priests, such as *sive mas, sive femina* or *sive deus, sive dea*. Nothing could show more clearly how slow the Romans were in coming to imagine their deities, as the Greeks and others did, in human form. Imag-

ination had had no place in the earliest animistic religion,
except in peopling the world with invisible spirits or forces
without shape and void of all but the special activity which
tradition had ascribed to each. A minute subdivision of
labor, which we think of as marking a very advanced stage
of human civilization, characterized the earliest-known
Roman conception of divinity, as handed down from remote ancestors, probably of the Stone Age.

As these spirits needed no dwelling places there were
for centuries no temples. Sacred places there were, as groves
and caves, sacred trees and altars; but the first temple at
Rome, that of Jupiter on the Capitoline, was not built until
the last years of the monarchy and was due to Etruscan
influence (p. 373). Not until then were images of gods to
be seen there, though familiar to those who had visited
Etruria or the Greek cities of the South. Jupiter had been
honored in stones, trees and bushes, but not in an image.

The early Romans had felt little need of supplying their
gods with legends or a genealogy or myths in any form,
such as were indispensable to the Greeks and in a later age
to the Romans. No venerable tales are known which had
helped to bring their gods nearer to man. Abstract forces
lacking personality in the nature of things could inspire no
myths. Even Juno was an impersonal force similar and
parallel to another called Jupiter. Only in a later stage
were they thought of as husband and wife, in imitation of
Greek Zeus and Hera. In the primitive religion prayer to
an impersonal something could be only a matter of form—
a strictly regulated form, as an essential part of ceremonies
which were virtually the whole of religion. More spiritual
elements than such dry bones of ritual can hardly have
existed in that early period. And yet even where the old
rites had ceased to be understood and some of the gods had
become empty names fidelity, however blind, to the tradi-

tions of the fathers was a moral force which had a leading part in the development of Roman character.

It was difficult for them to imagine a god of general powers when the whole tendency was to link a particular activity with some mysterious power supposed to preside over that activity and that alone, hence to be supplicated or placated at that particular time and not again until the circumstances repeated themselves. Thus almost every significant moment in human life from birth, and even before birth, to death was conceived of as under the influence of a special spirit whose activity was confined to that moment. The names of these momentary divinities, if we may so call them, were either nouns of agency or otherwise of obvious derivation from common words—practical labels that could not be misunderstood. The fact that they were so many and their specialization so minute suggests that the lists which have come down to us, the so-called *indigitamenta*,[2] while correctly representing the older religion in general—that religion of Numa, as it has been called—have been systematized and edited by the pontiffs. As examples we may take a few of those supposed to control particular moments of infancy, as Rumina presiding over the baby's nursing, Edusa and Potina over his eating and drinking respectively. His first efforts to speak were aided by Fabulinus and Farinus. Statulinus helped him to stand, Abeona and Adeona respectively when he first stepped forth from the house and when he returned, while the older child was similarly guided by Iterduca and on the way home by Domiduca. When he has grown up and is taking a wife the latter spirit will escort the bride to his house. A whole group of these specialist spirits was assigned to the marriage day, others to ensure fidelity and harmony of the wedded. At the end comes another group concerned with death and the

[2] From a verb of the same meaning as *invocare*, "invoke."

funeral, including Morta, and last of all Nenia while the dirge is chanted. Not only is the whole of life thus parceled out among these spirits, but places and things are similarly protected, the threshold by Limentinus, the hinges by Cardea, mountains by Montinus, hills by Collatinus, valleys by Vallonia, the Aventine by Aventinus. And the farmer must reckon with a long series of such hazy divinities, each representing some particular action—one for the first plowing, Vervactor, one for the second, Redarator, one for the sowing, Insitor, one for harrowing, Occator, and so on until harvest time brings Messor, followed by others for carting and storing; Promitor when the grain is taken out of the granary, and Mola when it is ground at the mill. All of these and many more of their kind were thought of as present in some very impersonal fashion in the particular activity which concerned them. What mattered was the exact performance of the specified rite for that occasion with the most meticulous care to avoid a possible mistake.

To monotheists of a later age, especially to the Church Fathers, such as St. Augustine, this extreme specialization seemed the height of absurdity. To pour contempt on Roman religion they had only to conjure up a small army of these one-track spirits from the pages of Varro or some other antiquary who wrote on the primitive religion of the Romans. But the same tendency to specialize showed itself even in the case of the greater gods when the second stage was reached. There were different Jupiters of special habitat or particular function. As tutelary divinity of the Viminal Hill there was a Jupiter Viminus; a Jupiter Feretrius to whom were dedicated the *spolia opima* [3] in a very small temple on the Capitol; a Jupiter Lapis, from the flint kept in that temple; a Jupiter Fulgur, from his thunderbolt; a Jupiter Stator, who was said to have stayed the flight of

[3] Spoils taken by a Roman general after slaying the general of the enemy.

the Romans under Romulus in battle with the Sabines. And the number of such general divinities with a particular application kept on increasing. Probably the average Roman seldom troubled himself to inquire whether these were separate divinities from Jupiter Optimus Maximus of the Capitol.

Another class of deities are those which have sometimes been interpreted as personifications of abstract ideas: Honos, Fides, Spes, Pietas, Concordia (Honor, Loyalty, Hope, Devotion, Harmony) and others—in reality impersonal spirits which produce these desirable qualities in men. These too in time received their temples.

A different group of divinities comprises those borrowed by the Romans from their neighbors or acquired by conquest. Before the end of the monarchy one Italian goddess, Minerva, had been honored with a shrine—a separate cella —in the first of Roman temples, that of the new trinity, Jupiter, Juno, and Minerva, displacing an older trinity of Jupiter, Mars, and Quirinus. Another newcomer, probably later, was Diana from Aricia, whose temple on the Aventine was to be a central fane for all Latins. In this way the numerous ranks of native gods, the *di indigetes,* were from time to time increased by new divinities, the *di novensides.* Conquest brought in other deities, since the gods of a beleaguered city were solemnly invited to desert the enemy, with promise of equal or greater honor at Rome. Juno Regina of Etruscan Veii was thus "evoked," to use the technical term, and transported to the Aventine in 396 B.C., and Vortumnus from Volsinii (Orvieto) in 264. The capture of Tibur (Tivoli) in 338 B.C. brought Hercules to Rome. The prescribed ritual for "calling out" the god or gods of an enemy was used by Scipio the Younger before Carthage, to win over another Juno. In such ways conquest involved a hospitable reception for foreign deities.

For the real roots of Roman religion we turn to the rites practised in every household. The head of the house was priest for his own family and responsible for keeping up the traditional ceremonies. In the same way the clan had to keep up its traditional cult, its ritual customs, of which our knowledge is very limited. And that enlarged household, the city-state, had its officially recognized gods, whose cult must be maintained according to the customs of the fathers, except for such changes as were duly authorized by the priestly colleges or the senate.

Each household had its domestic divinities, a Lar, the Penates, and its Genius. The Lar, or *lar familiaris,* was a protecting spirit, thought by some scholars to have been an ancestor spirit, though this view cannot be proved. It would naturally give us a plurality, whereas until the first century B.C. we hear only of a singular Lar. More probably he was originally a protector of the fields. In the household offerings were made to him, as later to the Lares, three times each month, besides those on the days of family festivals, and lesser offerings every day. The Penates were in early times guardians of the larder (*penus*). Later the little images of the Penates, kept with those of the Lares in a small shrine called the *lararium* (p. 162), represented no longer the old-fashioned impersonal spirits, but such divinities as Jupiter, Minerva, Mercury, according as the head of the house might have chosen to name them. Another figure in this house chapel, often no more than a niche, was the Genius, the guardian spirit of the *paterfamilias,* linked with the head of the house and attending him through life. Each member of the family had such a spirit, a Genius or a Juno according to the sex of the person,[4] but that of the

---

[4] Earlier this personal deity, or patron saint, had no sex, that is, a woman's also was called Genius. A thing too might have its Genius, a place its *genius loci.*

pater received the offerings of the household. Vesta was
reckoned among the household gods, and originally the
most important of them, since the keeping of the fire on
the hearth was essential, and her function included not this
only, but also the grinding of cereals and preparation of
meals. Hence the domestic worship of Vesta was in the care
of the matron.

There was a cult of the ancestors as spirits, called *di
parentum* or *divi parentes*. It was for them to punish un-
filial conduct or other violations of the unwritten law of the
family, as well as to watch over the household. The closing
month of the year, February, had its Parentalia (13th to
21st), a public festival in honor of deceased members of
the family. There were other seasons when very ancient
rites were practised in connection with ghosts of the dead,
especially on the three days of the Lemuria in May (9th,
11th, 13th). The head of the house was supposed to "lay"
the ghosts by quaint ceremonies at midnight, including the
spitting out of nine black beans one after another on his
way through the house, which was thus supposed to be in-
sured against spectral visitors for another year. That the
shades had any abiding-place beneath the ground was not
an idea that originated at Rome.

Offerings to the household gods were simple, reflecting
the ways of the forefathers and their meager resources,
namely, spelt (a variety of wheat) pounded and salted, or
a porridge of the same cereal, beans, cakes of special kinds
or bread, cheese and milk, fruit, honey, or a dish sent from
the table, that the gods might not be forgotten by the family
at its meals; for special occasions a kid or a sheep, a pig,
an ox. Such victims were slain at an altar on which portions were burned, while the greater part was eaten. Often
a certain victim had been promised in a vow which was now
to be fulfilled.

For public sacrifices the offerings were of the same kinds but more lavish. There might be three victims, a pig, a sheep, and an ox (the *suovetaurilia*), or the number might be increased. White cattle were preferred, except for gods of the lower world, whose victims must be black. But the ritual cakes, humble as they were, were not scorned even on the most solemn occasions. At all formal religious ceremonies a flute-player was present, not that his music might stimulate devotion, but to drown unlucky words or sounds which, if heard, might nullify the ceremony. Such was the care that nothing should mar the rite. Silence was commanded in the words *favete linguis*,[5] in itself a euphemism. The least variation from prescribed rule, a slip in pronouncing the words of a prayer, rendered the whole ceremony void.

In some sacrifices strange customs from a primitive age lingered on, often survivals of magical practices. On the 15th of April at the Fordicidia thirty-one pregnant cows were sacrificed to Tellus (Earth), one for the state on the Capitol and one for each of the thirty *curiae* (p. 10). The unborn calf was torn from its mother's womb and burned. The sacrifice was supposed to increase the fertility of crops and cattle. Six days later the sacrificial ashes were distributed by the Vestals to be used as a means of purifying the flocks and shepherds at the Parilia (p. 137). With the ashes was mingled the blood of the so-called October horse, carefully preserved from the sacrifice of a winning horse in a chariot race in honor of Mars in the Campus Martius on the Ides of October. Dogs were the victims in some special rites, as the Lupercalia, February 15, and the Robigalia, April 25, when Robigus, the spirit causing rust in grain, was placated by the offering of a dog and a sheep. Human sacrifice was practised when expressly ordered by the Sibyl-

[5] "Favor with tongues!" "No unlucky words!" virtually "Be silent!"

line books, and cannot be proved to have been Roman in its
origin.

Underlying most offerings, as also prayers and vows, was
the idea that the strict conscientious performance on the
worshiper's part laid the particular god addressed under
obligation to grant the petition. The relation was felt to be
almost that of a legal contract. In making a vow one solemnly promised that if the god heard and answered the
prayer the petitioner would at a specified time make the
gift just promised; and legal precision was applied to the
exact definition both of the thing promised and of the ante-
cedent condition. The solemn vows of magistrates or priests,
praying for the safety of the state or its head are conspicuous examples, but in private life as well the vow played
no insignificant rôle. Prayers for health, recovery from illness or injury, success, a prosperous journey, a safe voyage,
rescue from shipwreck, or for any blessing craved, very
often took the form of vows. As a token that the prayer had
been duly granted the grateful petitioner at least placed an
ex-voto in the temple of the god. This might be a small
terra-cotta arm or leg or other part of the body, an ox or a
cow, etc. Thousands of these have been preserved. Or it
might be a small picture painted to order or even ready-
made—a wreck at sea, a recovery from illness, an accident
escaped, and the like.

For the general conduct of religion there was nothing
comparable to a clerical order, no numerous centralized
profession. In place of the king, originally head of the state
religion, was the Rex sacrorum, the priest of Janus. Of
more real power was the Pontifex maximus, who with two
other pontiffs formed the first college of priests. Their number grew to nine in 300 B.C. and to fifteen by 81 B.C. To them
were entrusted the regulation of the calendar and the general conduct of the national religion. The Pontifex maxi-

mus was legally a father to the six Vestal virgins and lived
near their residence, eastward of the Forum. These nuns,
as we may call them, tended the sacred fire in the Temple
of Vesta, the hearthstone of the state, and were present at
most of the important religious ceremonies. Under a vow
of chastity enforced by a death penalty in case it was not
kept for the thirty years of their term of service,[6] these
daughters of prominent families lived under the immediate
direction of the Vestalis maxima in the Atrium Vestae,
which in time became a palace (p. 375). At the end of
their long term they returned to their families, free to marry
if they wished. They wore a distinctive dress, including the
toga and woolen bands about the head, which was partly
covered by white drapery purple-bordered (the *suffi-
bulum*). On the street the Vestals were escorted by a lictor.

While Vesta had her six priestesses Jupiter contented
himself with one priest, the Flamen Dialis, for whom life
was made a burden by the number of things he might not
do. He must be married, and that by the old patrician ceremony (p. 198), and was forbidden to divorce his wife, the
Flaminica, whose life was also hampered by ancient restrictions, while in case of her death he must lay down his
office. There were flamens of Mars also, of Quirinus, and of
twelve more divinities, among them some of the dimmest
luminaries, such as Carmenta and Furrina, and two that
were so obscure that their names have not been handed
down to us.

Unlike the flamens, who stood alone in the conduct of
their several cults, the other priests formed groups called
colleges, such as that of the very ancient priesthood of the
Salii, the dancing votaries of Mars who carried in procession the twelve sacred shields (*ancilia*), one of which—
never to be identified—was said to have fallen from heaven.

[6] The unfaithful virgin was buried alive.

This procession might be seen several times in March and once in October. Another ancient college of priests was that of the Arval Brothers (Fratres arvales), revived by Augustus (p. 129) and devoted to the worship of a nameless goddess akin to Tellus or Ceres, but merely called Dea Dia. The archives of this brotherhood have been partly preserved, including an unintelligible hymn, to be compared with the obscure fragments of the chant of the Salii. The augurs formed another college, concerned with predicting the future. Though taking their name from that form of divination which pretended to obtain omens by observing the flight of birds in a designated part of the sky (the so-called *templum*), they were the official interpreters of signs from thunder and lightning, as also from the way the sacred fowls ate their food—in fact of all the forms of divination except that from the entrails of victims. This last method was the art of the *haruspices,* who came originally from Etruria. By observing minutely the form and condition of certain internal organs, especially the liver, and comparing diagrams of their own invention, suggestive of the phrenologist's charts of today, they professed to reveal the future and the will of the gods.

Another college of priests had much to do with the gradual Hellenization of the national religion. These were charged with the oversight of sacrifices and hence called *duoviri sacris faciundis.* But from a membership of two their number was increased to ten in 367 B.C. and three centuries later to fifteen (*quindecimviri,* even when there were more). It was to this priestly college that the mysterious Sibylline books were entrusted, not to be consulted by them, however, without the express command of the senate. Legend had it that the Sibyl of Cumae had herself brought these books and constrained Tarquinius Priscus (others said the Younger Tarquin) to buy them. They seem to have come

from Cumae with the worship of Apollo, but not before the
fifth century B.C. They were kept at first in the Capitoline
temple of Jupiter, but from the time of Augustus, in his
new temple to Apollo on the Palatine. The contents were
Greek verses, in small part oracular, giving obscure predic-
tions, while the great majority had to do with rites and
ceremonies, expiations, and other means of appeasing the
anger of the gods. When the senate in time of famine, pestilence, or defeat ordered these custodians to consult the books
of the Sibyl it was not to inquire into the future, but because ominous occurrences, such as a shower of stones, the
sweating of a statue of a god, a monstrous birth, and the
like had been reported. Such portents and prodigies were
believed to indicate that some divinity had been offended.
How that deity was to be placated, was to be discovered
from the secret books, literally or freely interpreted by this
priestly college. At times after solemn deliberation they
went beyond their ordinary prescription of specified sacrifices and temple gifts to the old national divinities, and
ordained the introduction of a new cult. Foreign deities
thus officially accepted and domesticated brought with them
their own rites and priests, who were attached to the new
temple.

Apollo, transported from Cumae, was given an altar or
grove, or both, in the Campus Martius; and on that site at
a later date (431 B.C.) his first temple was dedicated in fulfillment of a vow made in time of plague. The older religion had lacked a god of healing, as it also lacked a god
of trade. Hence the adoption of the Greek god of merchants, Hermes, under the Latin name Mercurius (from
merx, "ware," "merchandise"). His temple on the Aventine was dedicated in 495 B.C., to be the seat of worship of
the guild of merchants. The chief trade at that time was
probably the importation of grain, as we may infer from

the building of the Temple of Ceres at the foot of the same hill, near the northwest end of the Circus Maximus. This too was an adoption of a Greek cult, that of Demeter, Dionysus, and Persephone, under the names of Italic divinities supposed to correspond to them, namely, Ceres, Liber (Bacchus), and Libera. The new cult was ordered by the Sibylline books, as the priests construed them, in time of famine, and the temple with its Etruscan and Greek decorations was dedicated in 493 B.C. (p. 320). Other Greek deities were similarly invited to Rome, among them Aesculapius, the physician of the gods, in 292 B.C. This was in consequence of an epidemic, and near his new temple on the island in the Tiber something like a primitive hospital was erected.

Under such Greek influence it was felt that the older national gods also needed temples. They were indeed beginning to be imagined in human form, and a temple must have its statue of Etruscan or Greek workmanship. And if they required dwelling places they might be honored by the semblance of a human feast. Their images were made to recline upon couches (*lecti*), while food was placed before them. This new ceremony of the *lectisternium* for a group of gods was another Greek importation, ordered as far back as 399 B.C. by the Sibylline books.

As Greek rites with more appeal both to the eye and the imagination exerted their influence on the Romans, many of the impersonal spirits were slowly relegated to a dim background and then forgotten. Others were saved from extinction by identification with a Greek divinity, as Semo Sancus and Dius Fidius with Hercules. The process of identifying Italian gods with those of Greece having somewhat similar functions went on until the fusion was complete.

The failure of the state religion to meet the needs of the people became evident in the grave crises of the Second

Punic War, when disaster after disaster led to extraordinary efforts to sustain the morale of the people and the
army. Most significant was the appeal, as of last resort, to
a divinity scarcely heard of before, whose outlandish rites
could not otherwise have been accepted. This time it was
an Asiatic goddess, the Great Mother of the Gods (Cybele),
that was solemnly brought from Phrygia to Rome, in 204
B.C.—not a statue but a black stone, evidently a meteorite.
This foreign and in every way strange saviour of the state
was brought in by order of the mystic books. A temple for
her was built, not outside the city but on the Palatine (p.
373), and before it could be dedicated a great festival, soon
famous in the annals of the Roman stage, was established in
her honor (p. 137). With the Phrygian goddess came her
emasculated priests to conduct the wild orgies none had witnessed before. Naturally no Roman was permitted to enter
that priesthood (but cp. p. 131).

No less exotic were the mysteries of Dionysus, when from
Campania and Etruria in 186 B.C. there rolled a wave of
uncontrolled enthusiasm for this cult of Bacchus—a wave
that quickly broke in gross crimes and immoralities, re-
pressed by the senate with great severity. The stern decree
which resulted in thousands of executions is still preserved
on a bronze tablet, while the beautiful frescoes of a room
in the Villa of the Mysteries near Pompeii (p. 329), painted
more than a century later, revived the memories of a religious movement which in its inception was viewed with
great alarm.

All through the second and first centuries B.C. Greek
philosophy was doing its part in weakening the hold which
even the greatly modified and Hellenized religion, now enriched by many spiritual and aesthetic elements, had on the
minds of the educated, who came to see in the religion of
the state little more than an elaborate system designed to

impress the masses. Scipio the Younger could still meditate and commune alone in Jupiter's temple, but for most men of his kind nothing was left but stately forms, impressive but unconvincing.

In the last century of the Republic the so-called religion of Numa—the pale gods of the *Indigitamenta*—hardly concerned any but antiquaries such as Varro. As for Spes and Pietas, Concordia and Honos, what sincere devotees were they to find for their decaying temples in an age of civil wars? Yet religion itself was far from dead. There were conservatives who sought to maintain the ancient customs. Such was Julius Caesar as Pontifex maximus, and such in a higher degree Augustus, holding the same office (from 12 B.C.). In Augustus's policy of regeneration of the state a revival of the religion of the fathers was a cardinal feature. To Apollo and Mars he showed special veneration, the former as having aided him to victory at Actium, the latter as helping him to avenge the death of Julius. Apollo, placed virtually on a par with Jupiter of the Capitol, was honored by the erection of a splendid temple on the Palatine, Mars the Avenger by another in Augustus's new Forum (p. 381). Vesta too received a new temple near his house on the Palatine. Eighty-two temples in the city were restored by his orders in one year (28 B.C.). Institutions such as the lapsed priesthood of the Arval Brothers were revived and long vacant offices, such as that of the Flamen Dialis, filled after a lapse of seventy-six years.

With this reëstablishment of religion and its utmost state and ceremony went the beginnings of the worship of the emperors living and dead. In the city Augustus refused to have such divine honors paid him as were familiar to all who in Egypt or the East had lived under a Hellenistic monarchy. In the provinces and in some towns in Italy he was worshiped as a god even in his lifetime, usually in connection with the new goddess Roma. In the city he ordered that his Genius (p. 120) as that of the *pater patriae* should be placed between the two Lares in the shrines at the street corners. Thus his Genius was venerated rather than the *princeps* himself. Julius Caesar had been officially deified in 42 B.C. and had his temple in the Forum (p. 380). Augustus was similarly honored after his death in 14 A.D. as were most of the good emperors among his successors. Not a few members of the imperial family were also deified. Emperors thus consecrated after death received the title *Divus* and had their temples. Livia, mother of Tiberius, was deified by Claudius. Faustina, wife of Antoninus Pius, was the first empress to have a temple of her own, shared with her husband after his death (p. 390).

Among the many different nationalities and as many diverse religions, the worship of the emperors everywhere was a conspicuous force making for unity, in each separate province a pledge of its loyalty. Meantime the old state religion was in theory local, and the ancient religious law, *ius sacrum,* did not apply to the provinces. Outwardly and legally speaking, the official religion was not affected by the advent of various unrecognized oriental cults, until the Edict of Caracalla, in 212 A.D., in extending Roman citizenship to all free-born *peregrini,* effaced the lines of legal distinction between the national and the foreign religions.

Lack of space forbids more than the briefest mention of the chief oriental religions—*externae superstitiones* they were, to conservative Romans. These followed the way of traders to Rome or were carried by soldiers from eastern provinces to distant frontiers. The Egyptian goddess Isis, duly Hellenized at Alexandria, had her votaries in Rome in the first century B.C., but the authorities more than once pulled down her shrines and altars. Augustus forbade their erection in the city and Tiberius destroyed her temple.

Caligula, however, appears to have built her a temple, rebuilt by Domitian, in the Campus Martius. This religion was especially popular with women. But that even the official attitude toward eastern cults was changing, is shown by the fact that on the eve of their triumph over the Jews Vespasian and Titus spent a night of vigils in the Temple of Isis. Her worship consisted chiefly of daily morning and evening prayers and offerings, with venerable hymns and litanies intoned by white-robed priests with shaven heads. A further attraction was the hope of immortality promised in her mysteries, into which initiates were admitted by successive stages. Penance for sins, unknown to the state religion, was practised. In the closing days of October a passion play was acted commemorating the death of her husband Osiris and his resurrection, followed by wild rejoicing—a triumph over death.

The worship of Cybele, introduced officially in 204 B.C., began after two centuries and a half to become popular. By that time the priests and priestesses of the Great Mother were citizens, and the central feature of the cult from the time of Claudius on was based upon the myth of Attis, a beautiful youth who was said to have unmanned himself and to have died of his wounds. Elaborate ceremonies centering at her temple on the Palatine (p. 377) for several days in March, with wild grief and then unbridled rejoicing, recalled the life, death, and resurrection of Attis, and seemed to the votaries to prove that the goddess could raise them also from the dead. This then was another cult having mysteries and giving assurance of a life beyond. It had likewise a baptism, but of blood, the so-called *taurobolium*.

Much more widespread, in fact in every part of the empire except in Greek lands, was the worship of Mithras. This too was a religion of mystery, originating in Pontus, the land of Mithridates, and in Cappadocia, likewise offering salvation in some form. It reached Rome and the West before the end of the first century A.D. A masculine religion, it was popular with soldiers, whose movements carried the cult to distant regions, and also with slaves from Asia sold or removed to the West. It was like early Christianity in gaining its first converts among the lowest classes and in the small size of its places of worship, called grottoes (*spelaea*), that is, underground halls, with an apse or niche at the farther end, providing space for the conventional relief of the god Mithras in Phrygian dress slaying a bull. A convert was initiated into one degree after another—three preliminary stages and four advances—each initiation involving a test of the candidate's courage. Not unlike Christian rites were some practices, such as baptism and a form of sacrament with wine and loaves of bread marked with a cross. But women were not admitted to the mysteries. In origin this religion was Persian. In Asia Minor and Armenia, however, it had acquired some barbaric and some astrological elements; and as a god of light Mithras was later identified with the sun.

Sun gods were in the ascendant in the third century, especially the chief divinities of Palmyra and Emesa in Syria. The worship of the sun was fanatically and fantastically promoted by the Emperor Elagabalus, himself a Syrian and priest of the Emisene god whose name he bore. And Aurelian after conquering Palmyra (273 A.D.) sought to make its sun god the supreme deity for the whole empire, building for him as Sol Invictus a splendid temple in the Campus of Agrippa (p. 382). Its festival fell on the 25th of December.

The future, however, belonged to another oriental religion, with somewhat similar promises of regeneration and salvation—the religion of Christ, which was officially recognized by the edict of toleration in 311 A.D. But the old fabric of Roman religion as renewed by Augustus lasted on as before, and primitive ideas of manifold minor divinities of very special functions had not disappeared. Even under several of the Christian emperors the old gods still had their temples and their priests, supported by the state until 382 A.D., when Gratian, who had been Pontifex maximus, disestablished the ancient religion, leaving its support to private generosity. For a time there were loyal defenders of the traditions of the fathers; but ultimately, within another century, even these were absorbed by the Church, while some ancient pagan ideas and rites and certain popular festivals tended to survive.

VI

FESTIVALS AND DIVERSIONS

O COLENDI
SEMPER ET CVLTI, DATE QVAE PRECAMVR
TEMPORE SACRO,

QVO SIBYLLINI MONVERE VERSVS
VIRGINES LECTAS PVEROSQVE CASTOS
DIS QVIBVS SEPTEM PLACVERE COLLES
DICERE CARMEN.
                    HORACE, CARMEN SAECULARE, 2

NAM QVI DABAT OLIM
IMPERIVM FASCES LEGIONES OMNIA, NVNC SE
CONTINET ATQVE DVAS TANTVM RES ANXIVS OPTAT,
PANEM ET CIRCENSES.
                    JUVENAL, 10, 78

QVID NERONE PEIVS?
QVID THERMIS MELIVS NERONIANIS?
                    MARTIAL, 7, 34, 4

THE most conspicuous feature of the state religion for the mass of the people was the series of recurring festivals. Four of the annual festivals were observed with particularly elaborate entertainments of various kinds: the Megalesia in April, in honor of Cybele, after the introduction of this foreign cult (p. 128); the *ludi Apollinares* in July, the feast of Apollo; the *ludi Romani* in September, in honor of Jupiter; the *ludi plebeii* in November. These festivals were presided over by magistrates, who as a rule contributed generously or even lavishly of their private means, that their year of office might be memorable for the splendor of gladiatorial shows, races, plays, and other entertainments provided for the populace.

Other popular festivals were: in February, the Lupercalia, for what divinity is not clear; in April, the Cerealia, for Ceres, Liber, and Libera (Demeter, Dionysus, Persephone); also the Parilia, for Pales; in December, the Saturnalia, a reminder nominally of primitive simplicity when Saturn ruled gods and men, but really a season of general festivity.

In all of these the religious element was present, but overlaid with stately ceremonial on the one side and holiday-making on the other. The number of holidays grew both by the lengthening of festivals and by the insertion in some years of protracted thanksgivings (*supplicationes*) for notable victories or conquests. In the fourth century the normal holidays in the year had reached a total of 175.

Introducing Greek customs, some of the emperors established *ludi* with athletic and other contests recurring every four years, in one case every five years (p. 154). On a different cycle, and one of impressive length, was the secular festival, recurring after the lapse of a *saeculum*, a century or, as the Etruscan reckoning made it, 110 years. In actual fact the period was somewhat erratic, subject to the caprice of politicians who happened to be priests, and later of the emperors. The most memorable occurrence of this jubilee was that under Augustus in 17 B.C., the tenth anniversary of his principate, celebrated with great splendor and the most imposing religious ceremonies.[1] Under Claudius these *ludi saeculares* were observed with similar rites and entertainments; again by Domitian and once more by Septimius Severus; finally for the thousandth anniversary of the city by Philip the Arabian (248 A.D.).

THE CIRCUS

Races formed a part, and easily the most popular part, of the varied entertainments provided by the magistrates at some of the religious festivals. No form of sport or recreation gained a hold upon the popular mind at Rome to compare with horse-racing. At first the narrow, level valley between the Palatine and the Aventine, in early times still divided by a small stream, furnished a natural race course. Turning posts were placed at each end, and the race was largely a matter of skill in making these very sharp turns successfully. Breeding and training proved of such consequence that professionalism soon ousted the venturesome citizen who drove his own horses. The necessity of providing races, together with plays and other shows, at seasons of festivity led the authorities to make contracts with those who could furnish drivers, horses and chariots. The demand was for a very short season—a day at the end of a festival, or at most a few days; but soon came another festival and then another. Hence a steady supply was provided by com-

---

[1] Details are preserved for us in a famous inscription in which Horace's ode is mentioned.

panies or syndicates of knights and other capitalists who owned and maintained racing stables, manned by slaves of the company and freedmen attached to it. Among the latter were the successful jockeys (*aurigae, agitatores*), who often had earned their freedom by winning races. Such a company was called a *factio* and was distinguished by its color. In the first century B.C., if not earlier, there were the "reds," the *factio russea* (or *russata*) and unquestionably others. In the first century A.D. we begin to hear of the "greens," "whites," and "blues," *i.e.,* the *factio prasina, albata* (or *alba*) and *veneta* respectively.[2] These were named from the colors of the tunics and caps worn by the jockeys, probably the colors of the chariots also and of some part of the harness (illus., p. 407). And in a loose sense the faction included the multitude of its partisans.

The Circus Maximus (p. 388) grew with the population and its increasing taste for the excitements of a sport far more dangerous than our races. Successive enlargements and improvements replaced cheap and temporary structure with stone and marble; but many of the upper tiers of seats were always of wood. The arena was divided for about two-thirds of its length by a low wall, the "backbone," and just beyond each end of this *spina,* on a semicircular base, stood three conical *metae,* the turning posts, of wood until Claudius replaced them in gilt bronze. Owing to the divergence of the *spina* from the axis of the arena the *metae* nearest the starting point were closer to the seats on the left (northeast), thus allowing more room on the right for the chariots crowded together in the first few seconds of the race. The spectators were reminded of the fact that even the circus had to do with religion by the presence on the *spina* of a number of small shrines, some of them to almost forgotten

[2] Domitian added a golden and a purple faction, but these were short-lived.

divinities of the farmer.[8] There were statues also similarly placed, and from the time of Augustus an Egyptian obelisk, to which was added another in 357 A.D.

A striking feature was the suspense of the great crowd up to the moment when the presiding magistrate from his box over the western entrance dropped a white cloth as a signal. Instantly the grilled double doors of the *carceres* (stalls) were thrown open and the chariots, usually four, one for each color, but often more, dashed out all at once. These marble archways (*carceres*), as rebuilt by Claudius, were just large enough to hold one chariot and its horses (commonly four) entering from outside and concealed from sight until the signal was given by the magistrate in charge. As a rule a race (*missus*) required seven laps (*spatia, curricula*) around the *spina,* ending at a white line (*calx, creta*) drawn across the sand, probably at or near the western *metae,* so that the finish was straightaway. How many laps had been run, was indicated by the removal each time of one white egg (*ovum*) from a row of seven supported by two columns on the *spina.* A similar device at the other end of the *spina* had seven metal dolphins, one of which was probably swung around like a weather vane at the end of each lap.

The wild enthusiasm of the shouting crowd—possibly 150,000 in the second century A.D. and later—was not that of disinterested sportsmen favoring only the swiftest and best, but the frenzy of violent partisans, madly devoted in advance to one particular color and ready to mob the victor of a rival faction. There was much betting, also bribing of jockeys to ensure the defeat of rivals, since an *auriga* was allowed to head off a competitor, any foul being accounted fair. For these reasons and owing to the skill required to

---

[8] Sessia, Messia, and Tutulina (spirits of seedtime, harvest, and garner respectively).

make sharp turns in a very light chariot without losing too much speed, accidents were very frequent, applauded or mourned according to the faction favored by the spectator. For protection the driver had thongs wound many times around his body and wore leggings (illus., p. 407). Among the thongs he carried a curved knife ready to cut the reins around his waist or the traces of his horses in case of an upset. Successful charioteers were idolized and enriched, as is shown by their proud epitaphs, often recording great profits and victories in the thousands.

The horses were largely bred and trained in the provinces, Sicily, Africa, Spain, Cappadocia, and brought at great cost and no small risk to the stables of the factions in the Campus Martius, near the Flaminian Circus (p. 374).

So popular a sport was of course not limited to the capital. Besides the three circuses in Rome there were in the suburbs two on the Appian Way (that of Maxentius, and a second at Bovillae) and one five miles down the Tiber at the grove of the Arval Brothers (p. 125). Other cities in Italy had at least one, Mediolanum (Milan), for example, and Asisium (Assisi). In Gaul we may name Massilia (Marseilles), Arelate (Arles), Arausio (Orange), Lugdunum (Lyons), Augusta Treverorum (Trier); in Spain, Corduba (Cordova), Emerita (Mérida); in Africa and Numidia, Carthage, Hadrumetum (Susa), Thugga (Dougga). And there were many more.

The factions continued their wild rivalry of the colors. By the end of the third century the red had become subsidiary to the blue, the white to the green. Transplanted to the hippodrome of Constantinople they became more dangerous politically and caused even greater excesses in riot and bloodshed, culminating in 532 A.D. under Justinian in an outbreak which cost 30,000 lives. In the same reign the last races were run in the old Circus Maximus at Rome

(549 A.D.)—a concession to the populace of a half-ruined
city by its captor, Totila the Goth.

Especially in the time of the Republic entertainments in
the circus (*ludi circenses*) had included various other shows
besides races. Gladiators often fought in the circus in that
period. There were exhibitions of daring riding, perform-
ing horses, cavalry evolutions, and on special occasions the
Game of Troy (*ludus* or *lusus Troiae*). In the last boys of
prominent families took part on horseback in a sham battle,
preserving, it was imagined, a custom brought from Troy
by Aeneas. More frequent and more exciting were the hunting scenes (*venationes*), realistically enacted by trained men
(*bestiarii*) in the long arena of the circus. These hunters
were often condemned criminals, sometimes unarmed.
There were not only bullfights, but also fights with lions,
tigers, bears, panthers, leopards, elephants, and other wild
beasts, often in large numbers. At the dedication of his
theater (p. 378) Pompey is said to have provided 600 lions
and nearly a score of elephants, only to find that the populace, for once moved to pity, cursed him for his inhumanity.
Caesar's games were not less prodigal of wild life procured
at vast expense, and the emperors followed his example.
But the *venationes* of the emperors were generally held in
an amphitheater.

Entertainments in the circus were preceded by a procession (*pompa*) which wound its way from the Capitol
through the Forum and the Velabrum and entered the Circus Maximus at its west end, to march around the arena,
pausing for a sacrifice. The magistrate who gave the games
headed the procession in the costume of a triumphing general. Besides his civil and military escort there was a long
column of charioteers, wrestlers, dancers, and all the other
performers; then the ceremonial contingent—censer bearers
and bearers of sacred objects, priests and religious corpora-

tions, images of the gods, borne aloft or on the sacred vehicles (*tensae*) driven by boys; also under the Empire images of the dead emperors.

THE THEATER

At the major festivals of the year in the classical period plays were regularly performed. The theater had been developed very gradually out of oddly assorted materials both native and foreign. To the former belonged the primitive banter at harvest and vintage festivals; and its successors, crude verses alternately recited, were called *versus Fescennini* from a Faliscan town in southern Etruria. Later they were restricted to weddings.

Etruscan performers were first imported, we are told, in 364 B.C., when a plague was to be stayed by unusual rites and ceremonies. The traditional horse races, the only spectacle down to that time, were to be supplemented by a novel performance, probably staged likewise in the circus. It was not a play, however, but an interpretative dance without words to the accompaniment of a flute. In imitation of these pantomimes the young men at Rome were led to combine with mimetic dancing crude Saturnian verses of the Fescennine stamp, largely improvised and lacking a definite plot. Whether this infancy of the drama really produced a definite form deserving its own name as *satura* ("potpourri"), is still matter of controversy.

Beyond dispute is the type of play known as the *Atellana,* taking its name from Atella, an Oscan town near Neapolis (Naples). This had a plot, restricted by the use of stereotyped traditional characters, very suggestive of Punch and Judy or the popular *commedia dell' arte* in Italy today. There was Pappus, the old man to be fooled, Dossennus, the sly hunchback (a caricature of a schoolmaster or philosopher), Maccus, the stupid, and Bucco, a puffy-cheeked blockhead. Rustics, small-townsfolk, and certain trades were ridiculed in these plays, in which the actors were Roman. citizens wearing masks, while the professional performers (*histriones* or *ludiones*) were social outcasts, freedmen or slaves. This Oscan *Atellana* reached Rome from Campania, as reoccupied during the Second Punic War (211 B.C.). It attained to a literary form by the time of Sulla, when the poets Pomponius and Novius wrote plays of this character. Many titles of Atellan plays have been preserved, but few fragments. They were farces of the broadest kind in rustic and vulgar Latin, coarse enough to retain their popularity under the Empire, especially as interludes or as after-pieces (*exodia*) at the close of regular plays.

Even more popular were the mimes, which were also farces similar to the Atellan in length and in use, as also in their loose construction. In these women's parts were taken by women (*mimae*). By the time of Julius Caesar the mime had come to have a text written by a competent poet, such as Laberius, a knight, and Publilius Syrus, a freedman. But their best efforts failed to elevate a performance which catered to the lowest tastes of the populace, for whom no language was too gross. Great freedom of speech was permitted, as in the *Atellanae,* even when aimed at the emperors.

The legitimate drama, as we should call it, had its beginning in 240 B.C., when the first tragedy and the first comedy were brought out by Livius Andronicus (p. 224). He had translated and adapted these plays with much freedom from the Greek and, so far as rather primitive conditions permitted, they were performed after the manner familiar to the many Romans who had visited Greek cities in the South or in Sicily. Such were the tragedies and comedies [4]

---

[4] The borrowed Greek names, *tragoediae* and *comoediae,* stamped these as importations, while the latter were also called *palliatae* on account of the use of Greek costumes.

as developed by the dramatic poets, especially Ennius, Naevius, Pacuvius, and Accius for tragedy, and Plautus, Caecilius, and Terence for comedy. Less frequent were serious national Roman dramas, called *praetextae* from the *toga praetexta* worn (p. 186) by the actors. For these the scene was laid in Italy and they were based upon Roman history or legend. Parallel to this national tragedy (for it was such, though not called by that name) was the comedy of local color, the *togata,* dealing with everyday life in Rome or some Italian town. This was a later development than the borrowed *palliata* and was chiefly cultivated in the second half of the first century B.C. by Afranius, an imitator of Menander. Yet the real stock in trade consisted almost entirely of plays based on Greek originals.

Though classic tragedy was never popular, such a drama contributed to the stateliness of the festivals, especially when unlimited display converted it into a spectacle. If the return of Agamemnon from Troy was accompanied by an interminable procession bearing the richest spoils of a recent campaign in the East, including perhaps a white elephant or a giraffe, all eyes at least would be concentrated upon a pageant that could be seen nowhere else in the world. After this order were the amazing displays with which Pompey dedicated his theater. What if Tragedy herself was strangled in all her pomp?

The plays staged were largely the oft-repeated works of the early masters mentioned above, though tragic dramas of merit continued to be written, as by Varius, Ovid, and the Younger Seneca, but commonly that they might be read to appreciative critics and admiring friends rather than for performance on the stage. The interest of the great public was elsewhere, and probably even the cultivated were more concerned with the acting and the lavish production.

Actors had begun at last to win social recognition by the

time of Sulla. Roscius in comedy and Aesopus in tragedy were citizens and friends of prominent men such as Cicero. Yet the status of an actor was usually little above that of a gladiator, though he was often rewarded richly. Not until the fourth century were the female parts in tragedies and comedies taken by women, as they had been regularly in the mimes. Since actors competed for the favor of the audience and at times for prizes, rivalry among their supporters occasionally led to riots.

There was no daily performance of plays even for a short season and of course no commercialized theaters with incessant repetition of the same play. As a rule dramas were brought out at the stated festivals. Each time there would be a series of plays for a few days only, and then no performances until the next festival or some extraordinary occasion, such as a state funeral, a dedication, a triumph, or the fulfillment of a vow. And yet under the Republic dramatic entertainments were more frequent than gladiatorial shows or races, which were more to the taste of the masses.

In early times dramatic performances were staged in the circus or on an improvised platform in front of the temple of the divinity to be honored at the particular feast, as that of Cybele on the Palatine (p. 373). At first it was customary for the spectators to stand. In the second and first centuries B.C. temporary wooden theaters were erected only to be removed at the close of the festival. Opposition to Greek customs delayed the building of anything more permanent until, in 55 B.C., Pompey gave the city a theater in stone and marble. In many cities of Italy and the provinces notable remains of Roman theaters still exist: that of Marcellus at Rome (illus., p. 408), those of Ostia, Pompeii, Fiesole (Faesulae), Orange (Arausio), Arles (Arelate), Mérida (Emerita), Aspendus (in Asia Minor), Timgad (Thamugadi in Numidia), and others. The level orchestra was

occupied by the seats of senators and dignitaries. Over its
entrances to right and left were two boxes (*tribunalia*) to
be occupied by the presiding magistrate (later shared with
the Emperor) and the Vestal virgins. The first fourteen
rows of the semicircular seats (*gradus*) were reserved for
knights, above whom sat the people, women and the lower
classes in the uppermost rows. Similar distinctions were
observed in the provincial theaters. Partial protection from
sun and rain was furnished by awnings (*vela*), sometimes
blue and spangled with stars.

As tragedy declined its place was gradually taken by the
revived pantomime, beginning early in the reign of Augustus. In this a single versatile performer (*pantomimus,
histrio, saltator*) impersonated with dance and gesticulation
the various characters in the plot, the female as well as the
male rôles, to the accompaniment of a chorus singing words
suited to the action of the moment, or, during a pause for a
change of costume and mask, supplying narrative in the
manner of a recitative. For instrumental music, the pantomime added lyres, Pan's pipes, cymbals, and other instruments to the traditional flutes. Female performers (*panto-
mimae*) were rare until the later Empire. The text was
usually excerpted and adapted from some tragedy, for the
comic pantomime rapidly declined and disappeared. New
texts also were written for the purpose, as by Lucan and
Statius. Mythology, not excluding Roman legend, furnished
most of the themes. Specially favored were such romantic
subjects as Venus and Mars, Venus and Adonis, Dido,
Pasiphaë. Such pantomimes, now favored, now frowned
upon as a cause of disorder by the emperors, were artistic
performances appealing chiefly to the upper classes, while
the mimes charmed the lower.[5]

[5] A more elaborate production was the *pyrrhica,* a lavishly costumed bal-
let, representing bacchanalian scenes, adventures of Bacchus in India, sham

GLADIATORS

More popular than any theatrical performances were the combats of gladiators, often held in the Forum or in the circus, but under the Empire regularly in an amphitheater. The custom was borrowed from Etruria and was long associated only with funeral honors, this strange link with mourning being explained as derived from the primitive custom of sacrificing slaves and captives at the tomb. The first known performance in Rome was at the funeral of Brutus Pera, 264 B.C., and given by his two sons in the Cattle Market (Forum Boarium). By the time of the Second Punic War a more elaborate funeral—that of Aemilius Lepidus—was marked by gladiatorial combats in which forty-four gladiators took part in the Forum (216 B.C.). Scipio the Elder gave such a show at New Carthage (206 B.C.) in honor of his father and uncle, who had fallen in Spain, the combatants in this exceptional case being volunteers. Exhibitions of this kind (*munera*), with increasing numbers of contestants, were not limited to notable funerals, such as the historians thought worthy of record, but might be provided for in the will of the deceased.

Official exhibitions of gladiators began in 105 B.C., when after immense losses in battle with the Cimbri and Teutons the consuls Rutilius and Manlius gave a gladiatorial show, a tribute to the fallen and an object lesson in the use of arms. The possession of such dangerous slaves in droves by Julius Caesar led to restrictive legislation, thus curtailing the display intended by him as aedile in 65 B.C. and reducing the number he could produce to 640. Augustus, who thought further restrictions necessary, gives the total number of

battles with wooden weapons, or the Judgment of Paris. Of the last, as it was given in Corinth, we have a full account from the pen of Apuleius (p. 265).

gladiators exhibited by himself at eight such shows during his long reign as about 10,000.[6] This high figure was reached by Trajan in a single festival lasting four months, after his second triumph over Dacia (107 A.D.).

It was primarily for the combats of gladiators, and following the example of towns in Campania, that amphitheaters began to be built, at first in wood. Such structures were erected by Curio in 52 B.C. and Julius Caesar. Pompeii, in Campania, had its permanent amphitheater forty years before the first stone structure of the kind was built at Rome in the Campus Martius by Statilius Taurus (30 B.C.). This last was replaced in wood by Nero after the great fire. The Flavian emperors erected the huge stone amphitheater which bears their name, but is more familiarly known as the Colosseum (p. 384). A much smaller Amphitheatrum Castrense was added on the eastern edge of the city in the second or third century A.D. As provision had to be made for the hunting scenes (venationes, p. 142) in the same buildings, there were dens for wild beasts under the arena of the Flavian and other amphitheaters.

Of these great buildings scattered over Italy and the provinces only a few examples may be mentioned in a list containing merely such as still show imposing remains: Verona, Capua, Pompeii, Puteoli, Casinum, Syracuse, Pola, Arelate (Arles), Nemausus (Nîmes), Thysdrus (El Djem in Africa), Corinth. Smaller and less permanent were the amphitheaters in most of the eastern provinces, where the sport, although introduced into Syria by Antiochus Epiphanes (175 B.C.), was never so popular. In the West few cities of any size lacked their gladiators and the proper

---

[6] Gladiatorial combats were occasional, rather than regular, being provided at a triumph, at the dedication of a public building, on a birthday, for a state funeral, or other special occasion. After previous attempts to give them a permanent place in the calendar had failed, Domitian established them on ten dates in December, including the Saturnalia.

arena, though the remains of their amphitheaters (Paris, Trier, Mérida, Fréjus, Nice (Cimiez) and many others) may now be scanty or hardly to be mentioned with those named above.

The gladiators were slaves, often owned by their manager (*lanista*), or captives or condemned criminals. In a small minority were such freemen as hired themselves out in spite of the stigma attached to such a calling. Under the Empire there were some senators and knights and rarely even women of rank who on occasion displayed their swordsmanship in the arena. Emperors were known to pride themselves on such skill, so that Commodus even appeared as a gladiator in public contests. Some criminals were condemned by the courts to fight with gladiators or with wild beasts, with the requirement that they must be slain within a year. Others were sentenced to gladiatorial schools (*ludi*), from which they might emerge so skilled as to earn their freedom in the course of time. These training schools were at the same time barracks, with training tables and brutally rigorous discipline. An establishment of this kind may be seen at Pompeii. Rome had such *ludi* under government control—four of them (from Domitian's time), including one for the hunters (*venatores*).[7]

Among the different types of gladiators were the so-called Samnites, armed after the manner of that people, but from Tiberius's time known as *hoplomachi*. They carried a large oblong convex shield, a helmet with visor, crest, and feathers. The right arm was protected by a padded sleeve (*manica*) with thongs and perhaps some metal, and the left leg by a greave (*ocrea*). A belt (*balteus*) held the very scant garment (*subligaculum*) worn in place of the tunic. Their weapon was the short sword. The Thracians owed

[7] A procurator was in charge, and officials of the same grade superintended similar schools elsewhere in Italy and the provinces.

the name to their type of shield, a small *parma* (round, square, or triangular) and a curved sword (*sica*), also Thracian, having sometimes an obtuse angle instead of a curve in the blade. Both legs were protected by greaves, the right arm by a "sleeve." In combats they were paired against the Samnites (*hoplomachi*), sometimes against other Thracians or lighter armed *Galli*.

Retiarii carried a net (*rete*) to be thrown over the head of the antagonist, who was fully armed while the net-thrower wore no helmet and carried no sword. His legs were partly protected by thongs, his left arm by a *manica* and the left shoulder by a piece of armor or stout leather (*galerus*) rising high enough to guard the neck. If successful in entangling the adversary in the net the *retiarius* attacked him with his trident or at close quarters with a dagger. Gladiators paired against the net-throwers often had a crest in the shape of a fish and from its Greek name they were known as *murmillones*. Another type in this contest were the *secutores*, apparently more lightly armed than the rest.

At times mounted gladiators were to be seen, and there were also charioteers (*essedarii*), fighting after the manner of the Britons and matched against each other with spectacular effect. As a combat of gladiators was a spectacle lavishly staged, the helmets, greaves, and other pieces of armor were show pieces, elaborately ornamented, as is proved by specimens recovered from the school at Pompeii. A striking difference from the armor of the soldier was the absence of anything like a breastplate, so that the upper part of the body was quite exposed.

Contests were announced in advance by notices painted on house walls, as we see them at Pompeii, and manuscript copies were sold on the streets.

Fighting in pairs was the rule, but group combats were occasionally to be seen—real battles on a small scale. More commonly a sham battle or a series of sham duels with wooden or blunted weapons was the prelude to real fighting. When a gladiator was seriously wounded he put down his shield and raised one finger of the left hand to beg the presiding magistrate or the crowd for his life. A plucky fight or conspicuous bravery would often win the spectators over to mercy, indicated by waving napkins (*mappae*). But if they thought him a coward, or were otherwise displeased, their gesture, probably with thumbs turned down, was a command to the victor to despatch his fallen antagonist. Attendants garbed as Mercury or Charon were at hand to remove the body. As for the victors, they might become notable champions and popular favorites. Partisanship or local rivalry led at times to riots, as at Pompeii in Nero's time. Yet no regular factions were developed as in the circus (p. 139).

It may be said that a gladiatorial show presented examples of remarkable skill, enviable pluck, endurance and real fortitude worthy of a better field. Cruel it was and inhuman, as Cicero admits. And yet others as well as he could praise the trained courage of gladiators, their steadfastness to the bitter end, thugs or barbarians though they might be. The inhumanity impressed the spectators the less in proportion as wholesale slavery and frontier wars had cheapened human life. To them it was *vilis sanguis,* largely barbarian captives, slaves, and criminals. Soldiers had of course a professional interest, and legions of the Empire often owned bands of gladiators, to be exhibited at more or less permanent amphitheaters at their winter quarters.

The only vigorous protest against the barbarity of the gladiatorial combats in any extant Roman writer is to be found in the Younger Seneca, especially in one of his *Letters,* written after he had witnessed the noonday interlude, when in the absence of most of the multitude, who had gone

Rome in 186 B.C. by Fulvius Nobilior with Greek athletes. Later on Sulla, Pompey, and Julius Caesar gave others with athletes imported from the Greek cities. Augustus followed their example by establishing at Nicopolis, near Actium, a series of athletic and musical contests, to be repeated every four years in commemoration of his naval victory and to rival the old Olympian Games. At Rome also there was during his reign a quadrennial festival including athletic with other contests. Caligula and Claudius gave *ludi* at which athletes competed. Nero's short-lived five-year cycle of contests, his Neronia, after the Greek manner included music, poetry and oratory with athletic competitions and chariot races. These gave encouragement to athletes, amateurs as well as professionals. Domitian's four-year cycle brought a recurring festival, the Capitoline Agon, which lasted for centuries. For this purpose he provided in the Campus Martius both a stadium (p. 386) and a music hall, his Odeum. The athletes continued to come from Greek lands. Boxing, wrestling, and running were indeed popular even before the introduction of Greek training; but Romans of the upper classes long looked with disfavor on sports so directly associated with the idleness and dubious morals of the Greek gymnasium. The great public baths, however, offered opportunities for physical exercise, notably ball-playing in several different games, also for bowling, running, jumping, etc. Amateur interest in athletics thus slowly increased as prejudice was breaking down, while the professionals who won victories were still almost exclusively from the Greek cities. Such Italians as did compete were not subject to the stigma which had long attached to actors (pp. 145 f.), but they provoked the sarcasms of Seneca, Tacitus, Pliny, and Juvenal. Galen, the famous physician of the second century, repeatedly shows this attitude (p. 294). He admits, to be sure, that Marcus Aurelius regularly made enlightened use of the exercises of the *palaestra* at the close of his overburdened day.

THE BATHS

More than athletics in any form the bath with its attendant diversions came to fill a definite place in the well-ordered day of the city-dweller (p. 193). Whence the custom came, is made clear by the names borrowed from their Greek neighbors to the south. By the time of the Second Punic War baths were open to the public. We are not informed how far they were municipal, how far privately owned. They were duly inspected by the aediles, such as Cato and Fabius Maximus, who were none too well pleased that foreign customs were making headway. At first few in number, these *balneae* were far from luxurious—how simple, we can best judge from Seneca's detailed description of a private bath of the Elder Africanus. It was at his seaside villa near Liternum, where the victor over Hannibal lived in voluntary exile. This bath was cramped and dark, with slits rather than windows in the thick walls, a plain ceiling, a cheap floor. Heating was by charcoal braziers, for there were as yet no furnaces. Equally primitive at first were the baths open to the public at Rome and in other cities, very bare, only moderately warmed, and with a limited supply of hot water. About 80 B.C. a great improvement, the hypocaust (*suspensura*),[9] was introduced by a well-known epicure, Sergius Orata. This innovation consisted in supporting a concrete floor on many short pillars set on the sloping pavement of a very shallow cellar (two to three feet), so that hot air from a wood furnace adjoining could be forced to circulate under the floor. By placing tubular tiles or flat tiles with rounded projections near their

---

[9] Vitruvius gives full directions for constructing this system, and there are many extant remains.

corners against the walls, hot air was also circulated all around the walls of the room. The baths at Pompeii, largely rebuilt just at that period, show this method of heating, while some rooms were still warmed by charcoal braziers. Two of the Pompeian baths made provision for women by duplication of their facilities, placing the furnace and boilers for hot water between the hot bath for men and that for women.[10] In some places a different time-table made it possible for a single establishment to serve both sexes. There were also baths for women exclusively, some of them frequented by ladies of the highest class.

Balneae were usually managed by a *conductor,* who received a small admission fee, a *quadrans* for men, probably more for women, as fewer in number. Some such baths and all of the large public establishments called *thermae* had space for athletic exercise, a *palaestra* which had room for various games, including bowling with stone balls, and often for a swimming pool in the open. The essential features of any bath used by the public were an *apodyterium,* or room for undressing and dressing, a *frigidarium,* or cold bath with its tank (*piscina*), a *tepidarium,* moderately heated and sometimes containing a tub or tank, finally a *caldarium,* the hot bath with its basin of warm water at one end and at the other a small basin for tepid or cold water.

The number of *balneae* in the capital kept on increasing until in 33 B.C. Agrippa as aedile, wishing to please the public by his munificence, found 170 such baths which he could maintain free of cost to the public, probably for that year only. But Agrippa later built in the Campus Martius the first of the great Thermae, opened in 19 B.C., and conducted to it a new aqueduct (p. 382). Yet the number of smaller baths increased as exercise and bath became a daily

[10] A complete plumbing equipment for a small bath may be seen in the museum at Pompeii.

ritual. In provincial towns public baths were often built and endowed by some rich citizen. Their conveniences and their decorations are known from many widely scattered remains and from detailed descriptions such as we have from Lucian in the second century. Houses of the wealthy and their villas of course had well-appointed baths. Of these also many interesting remains exist in different countries, not to mention extant descriptions, such as those of Pliny the Younger.

Fads and fashions, or it might be the advice of a noted physician, ruled the customs of the bath—a changing sequence of hot and cold, rubbings, anointings, etc. Lounging, games, conversation, and other diversions of a modern club were enjoyed in the baths. Wine and refreshments were to be had, and quiet was at a discount. Neighbors and those who lodged in the upper stories of *balneae,* as Seneca at one time, naturally complained of the noise. The great Thermae provided halls for reading and lectures, libraries, and every facility for athletic contests as well as for exercise.

Agrippa's example was imitated by Nero in the same region of the city, and by Titus, who built his Thermae on the Esquiline over a part of the Golden House of Nero. Adjoining these Trajan erected his Thermae on a far larger scale, providing for the first time wide, open spaces on three sides (illus., p. 409). Thus a Greek gymnasium was reproduced, but with Roman elaboration of the baths proper. Another novelty was the projecting *caldarium,* to catch every ray of sunshine. The invention of window glass in the first century A.D. had made it possible to flood baths with sunlight. Caracalla's immense Baths, lavishly adorned (illus., p. 410), and the still larger Baths of Diocletian provided greater luxuries at nominal cost to vast numbers (pp. 391 ff.). Last in the series were those of Constantine on the Quirinal (p. 394). In his time, in spite of the huge Thermae of the emperors, the smaller *balneae* reached the number of 856. Many of these must have been frequented by women, since for them the huge Thermae made no separate provision so far as is known. An allusion in Martial shows that some women wearing a minimum of bathing suit went to the men's baths. There were those still more emancipated who made no concessions to modesty, in spite of imperial orders against promiscuous bathing.

In the provinces, as everywhere in Italy, there were public baths and the smaller private baths as well. Many such establishments still speak for themselves in extensive ruins, as at Paris, Trier, Nîmes, Aachen, Bath, Leptis Magna, Ephesus, at Saalburg and other frontier posts, even along the Walls of Hadrian and Antoninus Pius in Britain.

VII
THE PATERNAL ROOF

EN TIBI DOMVS VT POTENS
ET BEATA VIRI TVI:
QVAE TIBI SINE SERVIAT
(O HYMEN HYMENAEE IO,
    O HYMEN HYMENAEE)

VSQVE DVM TREMVLVM MOVENS
CANA TEMPVS ANILITAS
OMNIA OMNIBVS ADNVIT.

CATULLUS, 61, 156

PVRIS LENITER ADMOVENTVR ASTRIS
CELSAE CVLMINA DELICATA VILLAE.
HINC SEPTEM DOMINOS VIDERE MONTES
ET TOTAM LICET AESTIMARE ROMAM
ALBANOS QVOQVE TVSCVLOSQVE COLLES
ET QVODCVNQVE IACET SVB VRBE FRIGVS.

MARTIAL, 4, 64

AT MIHI CONTINGAT PATRIOS CELEBRARE PENATES
REDDEREQVE ANTIQVO MENSTRVA TVRA LARI.

TIBULLUS, 1, 3, 33

THE Roman house had a long and varied history, beginning with the circular or oval hut with thatched roof and walls of interlaced branches or reeds daubed with clay. One example of such a *casa* was piously renewed from time to time on the Palatine (p. 378), another on the Capitol. For us the model is preserved in hundreds of primitive round or elliptical hut-urns (p. 4), once receptacles for the ashes of the dead, and closely resembling habitations of the living in the early Iron Age.[1] A rare form, probably Umbrian in origin, is rectangular, with wide eaves and an oblong opening in the highest part of the roof through which smoke escaped and a modicum of light might enter. Etruscan tombs hollowed out in the rock show the form of their dwellings, not essentially different from their temples. It was thus from the north that a new type of house reached Latium, to displace the thatched huts with dwellings which combined Umbrian with Etruscan elements.

This plan was essentially that of a farmhouse—a small court through which one reached the rooms, usually three in number, at the farther end. As other rooms were added around the court the latter became smaller and was roofed over except in the center, thus becoming a hall, called *atrium,* lighted from above, since windows, if any, were very small. Rain dripped from the inward-sloping roofs and their eaves all around the oblong opening, called *compluvium,*[2] into a shallow tank in the pavement, *impluvium,* and thence into a cistern. This type of house was adapted to

---

[1] The *urna capanna* has been found everywhere in Central Italy and even beyond the Alps. Herdsmen in the Campagna still build themselves huts of thatch.

[2] This term was sometimes applied to the whole space under the opening, and *impluvium* is not always clearly distinguished from *compluvium.*

use in cities and towns, with gradual encroachment upon intervening yards and even upon the narrow strips prescribed by the Laws of the Twelve Tables, until the houses were directly adjoining.

The atrium was really a large living room, for there stood the hearth and altar, there were the household gods, there meals were eaten, there spinning and weaving went on, there opposite the door was the marriage couch. A narrow hall (*fauces*) led from the door directly into the atrium. At the opposite end of the latter, toward the garden, the atrium claimed the full width of the house, having on either side an *ala* ("wing"), about the size of one of the smaller rooms. Beyond the *alae* the central room, the *tablinum,* retained its importance with all subsequent enlargements. It was flanked by a room on each side and usually there was also a narrow passage (*andron*) leading to the garden. The tablinum was separated from the atrium only by a curtain, or later sometimes by low folding doors resembling a screen (illus., p. 411). And toward the garden it usually had a wide door, or at least a broad window. Any one of the three rooms just mentioned could serve as a dining room after the family ceased to gather in the atrium for their meals, while another of the same group became the principal bedroom.

Near the tablinum stood the strong box (*arca*), and in the alae, if the family was distinguished, were cases (*armaria*) containing wax masks of the ancestors, and later busts or statues. In the tablinum were usually kept whatever there might be of family archives. Conspicuously placed, commonly in the atrium, was a household shrine (*lararium*), for the very small images of the Lares and Penates (p. 120). This often had two diminutive columns and a pediment—a modest suggestion of a temple.

The kitchen was a very small room, with a raised cube of masonry on which charcoal fires were lighted under the

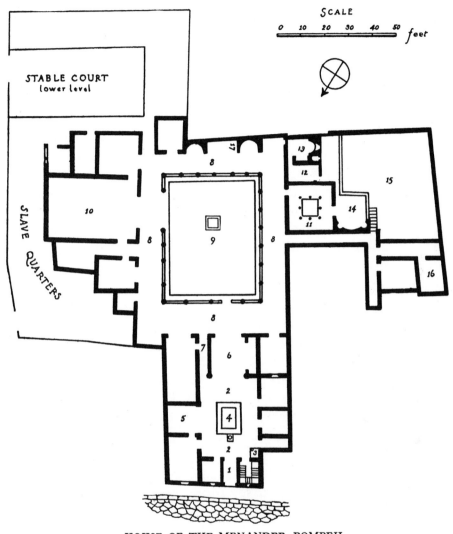

HOUSE OF THE MENANDER, POMPEII

The front part of this house, about the Tuscan atrium, dates from not later than 200 B.C. Enlarged in the time of Sulla by the addition of a peristyle, it was further extended in the time of Augustus (especially the bath, 11-14), and again about 50-65 A.D. Quarters for the slaves and procurator, also the stables, are on a lower level. See p. 411.

1 FAUCES	9 GARDEN (WITH FOUNTAIN)
2 ATRIUM	10 TRICLINIUM
3 LARARIUM	11 ATRIOLUM
4 IMPLUVIUM	12 APODYTERIUM
5 ALA	13 CALDARIUM
6 TABLINUM (WITH ARMARIUM)	14 HELIOCAMINUS (SUN TERRACE)
7 ANDRON	15 GARDEN (LOWER LEVEL)
8 PERISTYLE	16 KITCHEN

17 PORTRAIT OF THE POET MENANDER

pots, supported either by low brick uprights or by iron trivets. Directly adjoining, for the sake of a water supply and drainage, was the *latrina*.

As for its construction, the house was usually built of sun-dried brick, with much use of wooden framing, down to the time of Augustus. Shingle roofs early replaced thatch and had in turn given way to tiles before the First Punic War. Floors were in early days of rammed earth, then of concrete, later of marble mosaic, composed of small cubes (*tesserae*), or pavements of marble slabs, often showing an elaborate design.

Increasing population, not only in Rome, but in other walled towns, led inevitably to taller houses and cramped quarters for the poorer classes, and in time for the whole middle class as well. Already in the third century B.C. there were tenement houses of three or more stories at Rome, with staircases leading up from the street. A limit of three stories, in the second century B.C., was not regularly enforced. For the inhabitants of these houses there were few increases in comforts, while the dwellings of the prosperous grew more and more luxurious during the second and first centuries B.C., and such houses in the latter century were of stuccoed concrete.

Luxury in novel features, as in decoration, including marble columns, paintings, sculpture, furniture, was encouraged by the examples of Catulus, Lucullus, Scaurus, and others, and had come to be quite general with the upper classes in the age of Cicero and the early Empire.

The simple Tuscan atrium had become more stately, often imposing in its height. Or four columns, commonly of imported marble, one at each angle of the impluvium, supported the roof timbers.[3] Another kind of atrium, the

---

[3] A small atrium often had its compluvium close to one wall, and four or five columns around three sides of the impluvium.

so-called *displuviatum,* was high in the center around the
compluvium, but had its roof sloping outward. A rarer type
(*testudinatum*) had the same hip roof, but no opening in
the center,[4] and must have received its light from the sides.
Near the impluvium stood a stone or marble table—a reminder of the family meals formerly eaten in the atrium,
also a marble wellhead out of which water could be drawn
from the cistern.

Former garden space was now converted into a Greek
peristyle, usually with rooms all around it, and here was
lived the more intimate life of the family. The Tuscan-
Roman house—an atrium surrounded by smaller rooms,
and everywhere rather dark—was thus enlarged by the addition of an open, colonnaded court, enclosing a small garden with sculpture, fountains, and a pool, and giving access
to the rooms which encircled it. The tablinum now opened
on the peristyle as well as on the atrium; and opposite, at
the farther end of the peristyle, was in many cases a corresponding room, but more stately, called the *oecus.* This
served for festive occasions, being sometimes adorned with
columns which might support a vaulted ceiling or a clerestory, with an upper row also of columns or pilasters.

Greek fashion brought in Greek terms for these newer
features of the Roman house. Beyond the oecus there might
still be left a small garden, at least enough for a summer
triclinium for dining under a vine-covered pergola, while
the blank wall would be frescoed with trees and flowers.
Even before the days of such expansion the house had received a second story, partial or complete, with some of its
rooms looking out on the street or projecting over it in half-
timbered construction—a *maenianum.*[5] Dining rooms were

[4] Rooms over the atrium were thus made possible.

[5] Herculaneum had some houses with projecting second stories, supported
by columns or piers on the edge of the sidewalk.

so frequently upstairs that second-story rooms came to be known in general as *cenacula*. Above the columns of the peristyle there was often an upper tier of columns making an open gallery part way or entirely around the court. A similar colonnade was sometimes to be found on the street front at the level of the upper story, as seen in recent excavations at Pompeii (illus., p. 403).

At the entrance there was usually no porch—nothing more than a shallow recess (*vestibulum,* in early times an open space). A double door opening in gave access, if the porter (*ostiarius*) saw fit to admit you, to the narrow hall leading into the atrium. Near the door the mosaic floor might offer a friendly greeting in the word SALVE or a less hospitable CAVE CANEM, reënforced by a mosaic picture of a savage dog.

Private houses often had baths of their own near the kitchen (from about 95 B.C.), also a library, a picture gallery, etc. But even an imposing house frequently had shops on the street, while the dwelling occupied the center of the block. And parts of the second story, reached by stairs from the street, might be let to tenants. At Pompeii many houses have one or more shops opening into the dwelling, showing that here the owner disposed of the produce of his lands or of wares made by his slaves, while the other shops were rented, with lodgings for shopkeepers in the second story or a mezzanine (*pergula*). In less aristocratic quarters there were also whole rows of shops and poorer lodgings over them.

In Rome spacious houses with peristyles were chiefly to be found on such favored heights as the Palatine, Esquiline, and Quirinal. Only the very wealthy, a Sallust or a Maecenas, could have gardens of any size. The middle and lower classes even before the end of the Republic were forced to content themselves with apartments, often in lofty, crowded, and unsubstantial buildings, in constant danger from fire. Four stories were common, six perhaps not unheard of. For Augustus limited the height of houses to seventy feet, a

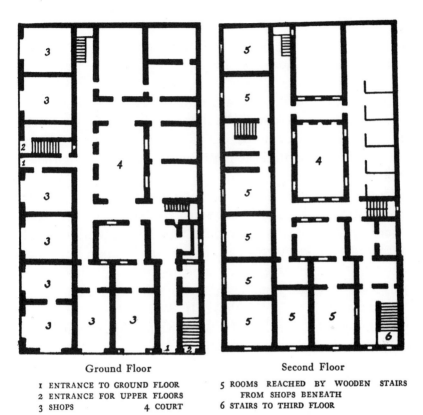

Ground Floor   Second Floor

1 ENTRANCE TO GROUND FLOOR
2 ENTRANCE FOR UPPER FLOORS
3 SHOPS   4 COURT

5 ROOMS REACHED BY WOODEN STAIRS
    FROM SHOPS BENEATH
6 STAIRS TO THIRD FLOOR

AN APARTMENT HOUSE AT OSTIA
Casa di Diana (see p. 404)

figure somewhat reduced by Nero after the fire; and Trajan established sixty feet as the limit.

Of these apartment houses or tenements we get our best idea from excavations of recent years at Ostia. There we see well-built houses of standard types, dating from 100 A.D. and later, closely resembling modern street fronts, with shops on the ground floor, balconies and loggias on upper stories (illus., p. 404). Only a few have a central court of any size.

At Rome recent excavations with the demolition of modern structures have revealed buildings of the same type, in fact a short street of such architecture.[6] It is now clear enough that the Rome of the Empire, with an overwhelming proportion of such beehives, was very different in appearance from such towns as Pompeii, and that many streets must have closely resembled those of modern Italy. Hence we know that, except for the wealthy, apartment life was the rule at the capital, as it probably had been for the last two centuries B.C.

In the provinces there was much greater variety in house architecture, as local traditions still influenced private dwellings long after public buildings had taken on the official Roman style. Africa can show many Roman houses differing little from those excavated in Italy. In the northern provinces necessary concessions to climate made heating arrangements similar to those of Roman baths very common in houses and villas. In Britain and Gaul houses often had their rooms ranged in a row along a corridor like a veranda. Others had a court with a colonnade along one of its sides. In northern regions the peristyle was uncommon. The eastern provinces as a rule followed the Greek house plan. But the court might have columns on one side only, as in Syria, where everything was of stone.

Returning to Rome and the palaces of the emperors on the Palatine, we may study many impressive remains showing the ultimate limit in the development of the Roman one-family house. The best preserved example of a great palace, however, is that of Diocletian at Spalato (Split),

---

[6] The ancient Via Biberatica. Other shops are shown in the illustration on p. 439.

on the Dalmatian coast. Rising directly out of the harbor
on one side in a lofty substruction surmounted by a long
arcaded gallery terminated by towers at each end, it
strongly suggested on the other three sides a fortified city.
But within these frowning walls and their monumental
gates were arcaded courts, many sumptuous apartments, a
temple and a mausoleum, now the cathedral (illus., p. 433).

THE VILLA

Country life played an increasingly important part for
the upper classes in the last century of the Republic and
the early Empire. Even the Elder Scipio had retired in 187
B.C. to a seashore villa at Liternum, north of Cumae. This
is the earliest villa described for us, and was suggestive of
a stronghold, as it seemed to Seneca, who found it and its
dark baths incredibly primitive (p. 155).

The old families had long been large landholders, and
economic management of these important investments required at least frequent visits. Pride in well-tilled fields,
well-kept gardens, and an economic return was very general. Many owners took great pains to have the best breeds
of cattle, the best varieties of fruit trees, often recently imported from the East. For most of the owners it was no
mere fancy farming.

Older farm buildings, the *villa rustica,* became more
habitable with successive enlargements and the gradual introduction of city comforts. Or a new residence, *villa
urbana,* was erected, but separated from the farm by gardens and vineyards. Such a country home might be suburban, easily reached when the business day in the city was
over. But, unlike the commuter's home of today, it usually
had a farm, or at least a vineyard and orchards. There are
remains of many such in the Campagna, among them the
villa of the Empress Livia, on the Via Flaminia above the

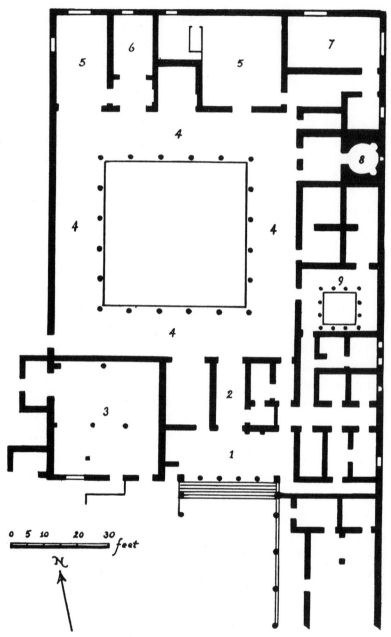

VILLA AT BOSCOREALE

1 VESTIBULUM   6 CUBICULUM
2 FAUCES   (METROPOLITAN MUSEUM)
3 VILLA RUSTICA   7 SUMMER TRICLINIUM
4 PERISTYLE   8 CALDARIUM
5 TRICLINIUM   9 ATRIOLUM

Tiber meadows, still retaining a vaulted room with remarkable garden frescos (p. 332).

Favorite locations at a distance of fifteen to twenty miles
were on the Alban Hills, near Tusculum (Frascati), or on
the edge of the Sabine Mountains, near Praeneste (Palestrina) or Tibur (Tivoli). Others preferred the seaside,
where many villas lined the same shore. Such were the
villas of Pliny the Younger near Ostia, of Cicero at Antium, of Pollius at Surrentum (Sorrento), described by the
poet Statius, of Trajan at Centumcellae.

The Bay of Naples attracted many of the leisure class,
especially in winter or spring. Baiae, on its northern shore,
was the most notable of Roman watering places, but there
were many villas all around the Bay—on the Capo Miseno
(the villa owned in turn by Marius, Lucullus, and Tiberius,
and that of Julius Caesar) ; also at Cumae (Cicero's), Herculaneum (Piso's), Pompeii (Cicero's), Capri (several
villas of Tiberius), to mention but one owner in each local-
ity. Even in the far South there were villas at Tarentum.
At the head of the Adriatic, around Pola, seaside villas are
known, especially on the island of Brioni Grande, where a
very interesting combination of a palatial villa with a large
agricultural establishment devoted mainly to the production of olive oil has been excavated.

In the provinces, even in Germany and Britain, many
examples are known, showing adaptation to climate and to
available building materials. Special interest attaches to a
suburban villa at Uthina (Oudna), near Carthage, with
elaborate mosaic floors, common in Africa. A villa often
had towers and in its defenses sometimes resembled a castle,
as pictured for us in African mosaics. In the south of
France, on the Garonne, at the foot of the Pyrenees, near
Martres-Tolosanes, we may visit an immense establishment,
notable for its sculptures.

Around Pompeii several villas deserve special mention, including that at Boscoreale, represented by a series of frescos and one entire room in the Metropolitan Museum of Art, New York City (p. 324). Most remarkable of all is the Villa dei Misteri, an old suburban villa (200 B.C.), both *rustica* and *urbana,* much enlarged and decorated with frescos, a single series of which is of the first order of importance (pp. 329 f.). In the Sabine Mountains one may study the foundations of the comparatively simple villa generally identified with the famous Sabinum of Horace (illus., p. 413). Under the later Empire a villa often had to serve as a place of refuge.

The emperors of course had their villas, relatively unpretending in the case of Augustus or of Antoninus Pius (the latter at Lorium, on the Via Aurelia), or lavish, as was that of Domitian near Albano. Caligula had not only his villas but also his extravagant houseboats, recently recovered from the bottom of the Lake of Nemi. Eclipsing all others was the villa of Hadrian below Tibur, where he incorporated some earlier countryseats in a vast complex of buildings very irregularly grouped in the midst of extensive gardens, and adorned with much sculpture and mosaic pavements of rare excellence. But here, as in the case of many smaller villas, formal gardening was one of the outstanding features—the type of landscaping revived during the Renaissance and still known as the Italian garden. Terraces, long *allées* and bordered walks, hedges, rows of statues or herms, pools and fountains, canals and other water works, aviaries, game preserves, fish ponds, were among the conventional features. Trimming of trees, often into fantastic shapes, was much in vogue—that art of the *topiarius.* Ilex and plane (the oriental plane) were favorite ornamental trees. The perfume of flowers was much sought after, as also scented shrubs such as laurel, myrtles (with white, sweet-scented flowers), box, and rosemary. Ivy often covered foundations, retaining walls, and other masonry.

New fruit trees and plant and flower species had been brought in, first from the Greek cities of the South, from Sicily and Africa, and later, beginning with Lucullus, from Asia Minor. Such were the cherry, quince, pomegranate, plum, peach, mulberry, almond, and walnut; also such purely ornamental trees as the cypress and the "unwedded plane" of Horace, not serving to support grapevines, as did the much-trimmed elm. So also among flowers, the lily, rose, and violet. In fact this extensive domestication actually changed the face of the Italian landscape in the more habitable regions, while Horace and others shook their heads over the many acres no longer plowed for useful crops. Such products of the Far East as oranges and lemons were still lacking.

Building, enlarging, improving became in the first century B.C. a polite mania, with marked symptoms of individual caprice. A part of the villa might achieve formal symmetry, especially in a colonnaded front, approached through a garden. But the remainder and subsequent additions might be placed with sole regard either to exposure to sun and wind, or to capturing a charming view from a higher level or a different site. Thus a villa as pictured for us in Campanian frescos was often an irregular group on several different levels. "Cottage" or "casino" is hardly the word for the detached habitations (*diaetae*) [7] irregularly placed, and yet may suggest their separation from the main building and from one another. The family could occupy, as comfort or fancy prompted, those quarters which were especially inviting at the particular season. The scant furni-

[7] Also used for a single room (*diaeta*), or several rooms forming an apartment.

ture of the inhabited rooms made it easy for the owner to turn nomad within the limits of his villa.

In many cases some of the outlying portions were reached by an open portico, or by a vaulted corridor (*cryptoporticus*) partly underground and hence cool, with windows on at least one side. Such a corridor often buttressed a terrace, and its vaulting might be decorated in stucco or with mosaic.

Where ample ground permitted, an elongated garden took the form of a circus, its arena chiefly occupied by plantations of trees and shrubs. Such a nominal hippodrome Pliny describes at his Tuscan villa, and a familiar example is that of an imperial garden on the Palatine, the so-called Hippodrome (p. 384). A palaestra often invited guests at the villa to exercise, as did garden seats or semicircular sheltered benches to conversation or readings. Lesser features much in vogue were small pavilions, diminutive temples, fountains, especially in the form of a *nymphaeum,* or hall, with fountains amid statues of nymphs and river gods, flowers and plants. A simple villa lacking such fashionable accessories seems to Cicero to preach against the follies of other villas, meaning the very novelties which Marcus and his brother were making all haste to imitate.

From such letters of Cicero and the more detailed descriptions of Varro and the Younger Pliny a large part of our information on this subject was formerly derived. Pliny alone offers himself as a real guide, first to his Laurentinum, below Ostia, on a site now covered with oaks in a royal game preserve, and then to his Tusci, in the upper valley of the Tiber. But these letters fail to give a single dimension, so that the many published plans of the two villas are only ingenious attempts to solve a problem obviously insoluble except by the spade. Side lights we have from other writers, such as Ausonius, and glowing pictures in descrip-

movable belongings was much smaller relatively to the floor
space. Rearrangement of rooms was simple and moving
must have had few terrors. Heavy pieces were practically
confined to the couches in the dining room, a massive table-
top, wardrobes (*armaria,* used for books also), a strong box,
and a few tables of marble. With us a dining room is always
just that, while for a Roman meals were more migratory,
and the triclinium for summer use might serve another purpose in winter. With us library, drawing room, and bed-
rooms are permanent, while the lightness of most Roman
furniture and the very few pieces required to furnish a
room made frequent changes easy. A study needed only a
couch or sofa (*lectus*) and an armarium for books and writing materials, with the option of an easy chair (*cathedra*)
or two. It became at any moment a bedroom by the addition
of a chest or another armarium for clothes. The ubiquitous
couch or sofa made the term *cubiculum* serve for any room
which offered privacy. Individuality was given to the different rooms by their fresco decorations, mosaic floors, the
artistic quality of chairs, couches, and other pieces, often
by small works of art, especially in bronze. Movable pictures (wooden panels, *tabulae*) were uncommon in private
houses, except in the most luxurious. Miscellaneous bric-a-
brac was not in favor. A rich house possessed many real
treasures: sculpture, paintings, silver, rare Corinthian
bronzes, crystal and glass, costly tables, other pieces inlaid
with tortoise shell or mother-of-pearl, and sumptuous tex-
tiles. Rugs, rarely used on floors, and tapestries were frequently hung on the walls, especially in the triclinium. But
the domestic note was spaciousness and freedom from in-
cumbrance, as in our most modern interiors, which, with
all their novelty of forms, have much about their simple
and flexible arrangement to recall the ancient house. Fashion was not without its part in dictating changes of detail,

as when the conquest of Egypt produced an influx of Egyptian decorative motives, just as Napoleon's campaign in the same land gave the sphinx a new lease of life in the West. But in general changes of mode were slow.

The wooden furniture of antiquity, that of Egypt excepted, has been known to us chiefly from paintings, sculpture, and books; and for ornamental features we have had many small bronze details similar to the applied metal ornament of our so-called Empire style. But now Herculaneum is yielding excellent specimens in wood, to be carefully protected by glass from further carbonization.

Beds were usually of wood and often had legs made of narrow boards edged with concave curves sawed and carved. Elaborately turned legs, rather heavy as compared with Greek designs, were common, and in this case the legs rested upon two narrow, flat and moulded crosspieces on the floor. A wooden bed might have bronze legs. Another graceful type was entirely of bronze, except for the long wooden rails encased in the same metal, often inlaid with silver and copper. Even silver beds are mentioned. The mattress was supported by straps, sometimes of thin metal. To support the pillows there was a headboard. If this was carried around the back and across the foot the bed was said to have "walls" (*parietes,* the back alone being called *pluteus*). A bronze bed had headboard and footboard faced with bronze and gracefully curved. The upper part of this curved *fulcrum* usually took the form of a mule's head, while a medallion adorned the lower part, the intervening panel showing silver inlay. Many examples of such details have been preserved. Another type of couch, with comfortably curved ends and a back of the same height against the wall, closely resembled our sofa and may even have been at times upholstered, though evidence for any kind of upholstery is not clear. On such a sofa one reclined on the left side while writing or reading. The waxed tablets on which one wrote were held in or rested against the left hand. A sheet of papyrus was doubtless supported in the same position by a thin board. No mention is made of anything like a writing desk. A reader thus reclining used both hands to hold his book in the roll form. No one sat at a table or desk to write or read. Thus sedentary occupations did not exist except for certain trades, and we have repeatedly to remind ourselves that a very active people made a limited use of chairs and none of desks, reclining to read, study, write, or do any kind of paper work, as well as to dine. Thus Suetonius pictures Augustus rising from his dining couch to lie down on his study lounge for a very long evening of what we should call office work, and finally to bed.

Dining couches had banished the earlier custom in which the family sat at meals. First the father reclined, while the others sat, but in time the later Greek fashion was domesticated. Each of the three broad couches regularly furnished places for three reclining diagonally, the left elbow resting on a pillow slightly above the level of the low table (square, later round) about which the couches were placed, leaving one side open for the service. Following the fashion for round tables came (in the first century A.D.) a new semicircular couch (*sigma, stibadium*), with space for from five to eight, the other semicircle being left open. In both cases the couches were approached from the outside, which was lower. Expensive coverings and draperies, often of purple, were in vogue, as in general couches of all kinds were considered incomplete unless handsomely covered with fabrics of silk or other costly materials.

For chairs much use was made of the same sawed and turned leg forms as for couches, especially for high-backed chairs with or without arms. These were the *solia,* the "thrones" of the Greeks. Cushions were loose or held in place by straps. Other chairs had curved solid sides and back, resembling the modern armchair, except in the absence of upholstery and of feet. Wicker chairs of this form were not unknown. A more ornate type of *solium* had claw feet or made use of other animal forms in its heavy carving. Light and graceful bronze chairs ending in hoofs or paws are known to us from paintings.

A chair the name of which has lived on in history, surviving the particular form to which it applied, was the *cathedra,* notable for the comfortably rounded and sloping back, also for the graceful concave curve of its legs and the absence of arms. It was at first the fàvorite chair of women, but soon found a more general use. It was the chair of teachers as well as of authors when they gave readings (p. 241), also of some of their auditors. Seated statues preserve this form for us. Much more frequent was the *sella,* with its four turned legs and no back, pictured in Pompeian frescos (*e.g.,* at the Villa dei Misteri), as are also light bronze forms with tasteful details. The folding chair with crossed legs (and rarely a low back), often made of bronze or iron, was much used. This was the form of the official curule chair, with no back, but made of ivory or adorned with ivory. There were short benches for two persons (*bisellia*), and others for more than two (*subsellia*); also low stools, much used on account of the height of beds and chairs.

Tables (*mensae*) were of various forms. An oblong top was often supported by two legs at one end and one leg at the other. A table top of the same shape rested upon two vertical slabs, heavy and richly carved. Extant specimens are of marble and are usually found in the atrium near the impluvium, but lighter wooden tables of this pattern no doubt existed. Small round tables with three legs were much used and as tripods bore the name of *delphicae.* Wooden examples with carved legs are being found at Herculaneum, and many in bronze are in the museums. The metal tripod was at times collapsible, so that the height of the table could be easily regulated.

The equivalent of the modern sideboard or console was the *abacus*—a rectangular top of richly grained wood or veined marble supported in various ways, for example by two carved sphinxes or other figures. A favorite type had a single support in the shape of a herm or a statuette. This type was the *monopodium* (or *trapezophorum*), admirably illustrated by a recent discovery at Herculaneum. Here the figure of Attis in his Phrygian cap supports the marble slab. On such a console were displayed drinking cups, mixing bowls, and other silverware. A lower shelf was sometimes provided.

The round dining table, which gradually displaced the large square form, was also supported by a single leg in the center. In luxurious houses this support was often of ivory. But the chief evidence of fastidiousness in a triclinium was the table top (*orbis*) of thuja wood, a cypress, usually from the Atlas Mountains in Mauretania. Being a cross section of a trunk near the ground, rarely as much as four feet in diameter and up to six inches in thickness, it was very costly. Such an orbis with rich grain brought out by a high polish might cost from 500,000 to 1,400,000 sesterces. The former sum had been paid by Cicero for a table still to be seen in Pliny's time.[8] To reduce the cost, or to make a larger table, smaller pieces were joined together, and veneered tables were much less expensive, but were used even by Tiberius. Other woods also were employed, especially curly maple.

[8] For a comparison we may note that Atticus, who lived well in his old-fashioned house on the Quirinal, managed to limit his current housekeeping expenses to 36,000 sesterces a year, in other words could pay such domestic bills (not including service) for fourteen years out of a sum which his friend Cicero spent for a single table top.

The glistening surface was not concealed by a cloth until fashion began to change in Domitian's time. It was covered, however, by a large tray (*repositorium*) brought in at the beginning and removed at the end of each course.

In strange contrast with such luxury was the lack of any efficient lighting system. A palatial home had no lack of candelabra of artistic design and costly material, but the many small lamps they supported produced what would seem to us a feeble light and an inordinate amount of smoke, so that ceiling beams, gilded or of noble woods, and their panels veneered with ivory, were soon blackened.

The candelabrum, which at first supported only candles, became in time a stand for lamps burning olive oil. In form and height it showed great variety, sometimes being made of wood, but preferably of bronze. A slender shaft rose from a tripod base to a top suggestive of the capital of a column, the upper part of the shaft sometimes sliding up and down to adjust the height of the lamp. The modern counterpart is the bridge lamp, but in place of an arm carrying a shaded light of forty or more candle power there was only a single smoky flame of two or three candle power precariously perched on the top. A more elaborate kind had two or more branches, to increase the number of lamps. Monumental marble candelabra with reliefs and much acanthus ornament adorned palaces and villas, such as that of Hadrian, as also temples, without furnishing what we should call adequate illumination. This stately type has been frequently copied in modern times. Other lamps hung from the ceiling by chains and resembled our chandeliers, especially where a large ring-shaped lamp had many wicks.

For use on tables there were low stands on which to place single lamps. Or a statuette served as a lamp-bearer; or a small column or tree trunk in bronze provided support for several lamps. Though more ingeniously varied in form and quaint charm, these table lamps differed little in their practical service from the so-called "Roman lamps" of modern Italy down to the present century.

A very large proportion of the lamps themselves were of moulded clay with designs in low relief, such as scenes from the circus or the amphitheater or out of mythology. Most of them had but one hole for a wick and one for the frequent replenishing of the oil. Others had two or three or even more wicks. In richer homes many of them were of bronze or silver.

Heating had advanced much further than lighting, but even after central heating had .been introduced into the baths (p. 155) and had come to be employed in private houses for a few rooms only, the charcoal brazier (*foculus*) was still indispensable, in spite of its deadly monoxide. In form it was simply a bronze bowl or other receptacle for coals, often rectangular, and raised on feet. Actual fireplaces (*camini*) with flues were not common in private houses, except in cold regions.

To the furnishing of a Roman house or apartment, though space is lacking for details, we must add all the cooking utensils in earthenware, bronze, and silver, including forks, which were not used at table; also the tableware in tasteful Arretine pottery (p. 84), glass, and silver both chased and plain. Gold services were forbidden in the reign of Tiberius. Many specimens of silverware have been found, notably at Boscoreale, on the slopes of Vesuvius, and recently in the House of the Menander at Pompeii, including many cups, porringers, pitchers, and other such pieces, also spoons—examples both of the pointed *ligula* and of the small, round-bowled, straight-handled spoon called *cochlear,* used both for eggs and snails—but no forks (illus., p. 414). Some Roman generals carried entire silver services with them on campaigns against the barbarians of the North, to which fact we owe the well-known Hildesheim treasure now at Berlin and others in Paris. Times had changed since old Fabricius in the first half of the third century B.C. had allowed a general in command no silver except a *salinum* (saltcellar, counterpart of our Victorian castor) and one plate (*patella*) used in offering salted meal to the gods.

In short Roman houses and apartments were furnished with a more than Spartan simplicity until the second century B.C., when eastern expeditions brought new contacts with the Hellenistic world. The advent of fine furniture and costly fittings was dated by the Roman historians from the return of an army from Asia and a particular triumph, that of Manlius in 187 B.C. Then began fashion's demand for bronze couches with costly coverings, for monopodia and abaci, chased silverware, and cloth of gold. Lucullus too, in his time, and Pompey brought home the best. In this respect as in others conquered Hellenism proceeded to capture Latium.

FAMILY AND DRESS

In the midst of such surroundings lived the Roman household (*familia*). Its head might be a *pater familias,* with married sons and their children living under the paternal roof, and all subject to his authority—that *patria potestas* of which the Roman law made so much. Or he might himself be under the *potestas* of his father, though not living in the latter's house. Thus *familia,* regardless of residence, suggested something quite different from what we mean by family. It included the large circle of all those related through males, that is, the so-called *agnati.* But as a daughter on her marriage passed into the family of her husband, blood relations (*cognati*) who were not at the same time *agnati* were not reckoned members of the *familia.* The son under paternal authority became his own master (*sui iuris*) on the death of his father or by emancipation, and was thereafter a *pater familias* himself, though he might have no children or were himself a child requiring a guardian. An adopted son or daughter (until her marriage) belonged to the family as truly as did own children. With the growth of the city and the increase of apartment living patriarchal establishments became rare and most homes must have sheltered only a narrow circle.

The *patria potestas* still nominally gave the *pater* power of life and death over his children regardless of age, with the right to sell them into slavery. But public opinion and gentler manners had softened the rigors of ancient customary law, so that would-be domestic tyrants found sentiment arrayed against that old unlimited authority as exercised even over adults.

A different name was given to the always more limited authority exercised by a husband over a wife. This was known as *manus,* "hand," a form of authority to which the bride submitted at the time of her marriage, either voluntarily or at the behest of her father, since marriages were usually arranged by parents. Her dowry passed into her husband's control. In case he was not yet independent (*sui iuris*) she too with dowry or other property came under the *potestas* of his father. Literally interpreted the law placed a wife in what forefathers had thought a becoming subordination, but as customs grew more humane her actual status improved. Even Cato the Censor sagely observed, "We rule all men, but our wives rule us." Yet many a wife avoided that legal, if nominal, subjection. It was a quaint provision of the Laws of the Twelve Tables that if a wife who was married by the simplest form, called *usus,* absented herself for three successive nights each year she should not come under her husband's *manus.* By this evasion she could hold property and retain her connection with her own family, instead of passing into that of her husband. By the time of Marcus Aurelius that particular form of marriage (*usus*) was obsolete, and fewer and fewer were the wives under authority.

There had been in fact three forms of marriage. That by the old patrician ceremonial of *confarreatio* [9]—a very formal occasion requiring the presence of the two highest priests and ten witnesses—was falling gradually into disuse, except as maintained by ancient rules that certain priesthoods could be filled only by men who were the children of such marriages and had been themselves wedded by the same ceremony. The second form was that called *coemptio,* "purchase," from the primitive ceremony of a pretended purchase of the bride from her father or guardian in the presence of five witnesses and a man to hold the scales with which money had formerly been weighed. In this mock sale the symbolic price was a copper coin. This rite also, like *confarreatio,* gave a husband the power called *manus.* The third form, the latest and most plebeian, was that called *usus,* already mentioned. By this the bond was legally complete only after the couple had lived together for a year. At the end of that time the husband acquired *manus* provided the wife had not been absent three nights in succession.

Whether the wife was legally under the full authority of her husband or not, she held a very important place as mistress of the Roman household and in the early education of the children. Her home had no secluded women's quarters, as had the Greek house, nor did customs seriously hamper the freedom of the matron or limit her influence.

On the street and in public places she had much more liberty than was allowed to wives in a Greek city, while it was customary for men to make way for her—a gallantry

[9] Named from the offering of a cake of spelt (*far*) to Jupiter.

much older at Rome than that of addressing her as *domina*.
Her dress at once indicated that she was a matron, the distinctive garment being a *stola,* a long woolen tunic reaching to the feet. It was worn over a shorter tunic, was kept
from trailing on the ground by a girdle, and had short
sleeves and a particular kind of hem (*instita*). Under the
Empire the *stola* was less fashionable, gradually giving way
by the third century to a long-sleeved *dalmatica* of linen,
wool, or silk, worn by men also at that period in place of a
tunic. Over her *stola* a matron wore on the street a wrap,
usually the *palla,* corresponding to the Greek *himation*. It
was a large rectangular piece of cloth draped about the
figure with much attention to the arrangement of the folds.
As it was not seemly for a matron to appear in public with
head uncovered, and hats or hoods were not commonly
worn, she would draw the *palla* over the top of her head.
On going forth she changed her sandals (*soleae*) for shoes
(*calcei*).

Not less meticulously draped than a matron's palla was
the toga of her husband, the cumbrous, formal outer garment of the Roman male citizen. In shape as in the method
of draping it differed in different periods with the changes
prescribed by fashion. In general it approached the form
of an ellipse, the corners of a large, rectangular piece of material having been cut off, at different angles or in curves
according to the style of the time. In length it was twice the
height of the wearer and might be worn doubled. It was of
wool and white, requiring much attention from the fuller,
who whitened it with pipe clay. Boys and girls also wore
the toga with a broad purple hem (*toga praetexta*), which
in the case of men indicated a magistrate of the higher
grades or a priest.

Beneath the toga was worn a belted woolen tunic reaching just below the knees, and this was the preferred gar-

ment at home, in the country, or in any kind of work, while beneath it a *tunica interior* was often worn. Senators and knights wore two vertical stripes on the front of the tunic and two more on the back—broad stripes (*lati clavi*) for a senator, narrow (*angusti clavi*) for a knight. For cold or stormy weather there were outer garments of various shapes. The *lacerna* was a mantle fastened at the shoulder or over the breast with a brooch. It was much worn by soldiers, but also by dandies, who preferred gay colors and fine materials. There was likewise a cape, the *paenula*, of heavy stuff, felt, or even leather, and with a hood; the *laena*, circular, often brightly colored; and the *cucullus*, a heavy cloak with a pointed hood, worn mostly by slaves, workers, and for travel.

Hats were not usually worn on the streets of the city. The broad-brimmed *petasus* (sometimes tied under the chin) and the similar *causia*, both introduced from the Balkan Peninsula, were in use chiefly among travelers, messengers, and country people. The felt cap (*pilleus*) had been the usual headgear in early times, as in Etruria, but except at the Saturnalia it was worn only by the lower classes, especially freedmen, since the gift of such a cap was part of the ceremony of emancipation. There were other caps, some of which formed part of the costume of priests.

At home sandals (*soleae*) were worn, or when one went out to dine; but in general they were not thought proper for the street. With the toga one must wear the equally Roman *calceus*, a close-fitting shoe with thongs wound around the leg and tied in front. Patricians and senators could be distinguished by their shoes, those of the former having an ivory crescent.

SLAVES

Much of the clothing worn by members of the household was made at home. Spinning and weaving went on under the direction of the matron, though home industry tended to decline as increasing luxury brought a demand for finer fabrics. But whether slaves were thus employed or busied only in housekeeping duties or in attendance upon the master and his family we must not fail to reckon slaves—a large number of them in many houses—as members of the *familia* in the Roman sense of the word. Faithful slaves who had been manumitted and were now freedmen (*liberti*) must also be included, though not always housed under the same roof. Less closely linked with the home were the clients, not sharing its shelter, but protected by the head of the house as their patron.

Among the slaves those who had been born in the house (*vernae*) were specially favored and often pampered as having grown up with the children. Especially in earlier times, down to the days of Cato the Censor, the relations of master and slave were friendly. Eating with the family and admitted to the fireside the slaves were included in the *familiares,* "members of the household." In the country, as in smaller towns, these customs no doubt lasted much longer than in the city, where they were still revived annually in the festal days of the Saturnalia (p. 137), when master waited on slaves at table, as the *domina* served her maids on the first of March, the Matronalia.

The number of slaves to a household had kept on increasing, at first on the farm and then in the city housekeeping, where formerly one or two slaves had sufficed. By the end of the second century B.C. it was accounted poverty to have no more than six slaves. Increasing refinements in domestic service made it a note of extreme simplicity when Horace prides himself on having a frugal, solitary dinner served by only three slaves. A prefect of the city in Nero's time had four hundred slaves living in his house. But in general owners of slaves by the hundreds and even thousands kept the great majority of them employed either on their scattered estates or in industry and commerce at home and abroad.

A *familia urbana,* the domestic slaves of a *domus,* or town house, were under the orders of an *atriensis,* later on of a procurator, who was often a freedman. In the same way in the management of country estates a procurator was higher in the scale than a *vilicus* (pp. 67 f.). Where the number of domestic slaves was large their labors were minutely specialized, as many tombstones show. Some had charge of furniture, others of tableware, of storerooms, of wine room, of sculpture or paintings, wardrobe, jewelry, the toilet; others were personal attendants, litter bearers, letter carriers, not to mention the staff required for the kitchen and service in the triclinium, or the daily maintenance of the house. A memory specialist was the *nomenclator,* who accompanied his master on the street and in public places, enabling him to greet by name any citizen whose salutation it was tactful for the man in public life to return. More highly trained were the house physician, keepers of accounts, secretaries, copyists, librarians, readers, entertainers. Needless to say, the average middle-class homes and many of the upper class contented themselves with a much smaller number of slaves, of the less expensive sort at that.

Legally speaking, slaves were chattels, absolutely subject to the authority of the master (his *dominica potestas*), so that if he should kill one it would be no murder; and to sell an old or incapacitated slave was not thought inhumane. Kindlier feeling toward slaves, as commended by the philosophers, did increase under the Empire, as we see from the *Letters* of Pliny. Claudius, Hadrian, and Antoninus Pius curtailed the rights of a master over the lives of his slaves, but Constantine was the first to treat the willful killing of a slave by his master as murder. The marriage of slaves was not formally protected by law and was merely called *contubernium,* but it came to be treated by the jurists as an institution to be safeguarded. Similarly in theory a slave could hold no property, but in practice was allowed to save where he could and accumulate a *peculium* with which he might ultimately purchase his freedom. He might also use his savings to buy a slave of his own (*vicarius*). As for the slaves' food, they commonly had their rations (*demensum*), chiefly of wheat, weighed out to them by the month or by the day (*diaria*). The master furnished each slave with at least tunic, cloak, and wooden shoes—this in the country, as prescribed by Cato. Town slaves were likely to be better dressed and shod with more regard to the ears of the family.

DAILY LIFE

In our effort to visualize the Roman home life, as lived by these members of the household, thus garbed and in the midst of the setting already described, it remains for us to follow in brief the daily routine, and then to describe the most important incidents which sooner or later were to be recorded in the annals of a normal family.

In nothing did habits differ more than in the daily timetable. Most Romans were early risers—a habit established before the introduction of sundials and water clocks, when everything was regulated by the sun. In winter schools began before sunrise, by which time slaves, artisans, and other workers had begun their daily tasks, as had officials, while clients gathered thus early for the morning call upon their patron. Before they were admitted he had made an offering to the household gods at the domestic shrine and attended to matters about the house, giving orders and planning his day.

Sunrise, noon, and sunset were the cardinal points of a day before timepieces of any kind were devised, noon being announced by an attendant of the consuls when from the door of the Senate House he could see the sun just to the left of the Rostra. First came the sundial (*solarium, horologium*), brought with other spoils of war from Catina in Sicily in 263 B.C., and used for a century before it was displaced as far from correct, having been made for a very different latitude. But the corrected sundial of 164 B.C. was extensively imitated and many examples have been found. Instead of a vertical gnomon casting its shadow on a flat surface, as in the modern instrument, the common form had a horizontal pointed bar at the top of a block of marble and projecting over a bowl-like excavation in its surface approaching a quarter-sphere, tilted at a proper angle for the given latitude, and scored with eleven lines like meridians, one for each hour. There were also two arcs of small circles (tropics) to indicate the solstices and an equator for the equinoxes.[10]

Five years after the first correct sundial came the first water clock, showing the hour by the height of the water in a vessel from which it slowly escaped, to be refilled after twenty-four hours. But since in the latitude of Rome the longest day is more than six hours longer than the shortest a correction had to be applied except at or near the equinoxes; and this seems to have been made possible by adding a graduated scale engraved on the outside of the glass vessel.

[10] This sundial indicated the season and the hours, as they varied in length with the changing seasons. Another type, more like ours, with straight lines, could indicate only equinoctial hours—was accurate, in other words, only at the equinoxes. A third type was the portable sundial for travelers' use.

While there was a civil day from midnight to midnight, the natural day began at sunrise and ended at sunset. This day was then divided into twelve hours longer or shorter according to the season. The one fixed point, noon, was marked as the sixth hour, meaning the close of the sixth hour. Daylight saving needed no legislation. It was already there, being automatically produced and again insensibly discontinued by the mere increase and decrease in the length of the hour, from forty-five minutes at the winter solstice to an hour and a quarter six months later. Thus the third hour, in the middle of the morning, was our 9:46 at the winter solstice, but 8:13 at the summer solstice.

By the end of the second hour the patron would usually have finished the morning reception of his clients. Then came, when not served earlier, a light breakfast (*ienta-culum*), consisting commonly of dry bread with honey or salt, or bread dipped in wine, with olives or raisins and sometimes cheese. With the third hour many public duties began in the Forum and elsewhere. Elections might begin as early as the second hour; and in general a notable feature of Roman life was the transaction of so much business, public and private, in the senate, the courts, and everywhere else in the early hours of the day.

Hence during the greater part of the Republican period the principal meal of the day (*cena*) was at noon, the sixth hour, to be followed by a supper (*vesperna*) at the end of the day. With the increasing demands of city life, prolonging business past midday, a luncheon (*prandium*) took the place of the *cena,* and the latter as a major event in the day's program was postponed until the leisure hours.

A *prandium* consisted of meat, warm or cold, or fish, vegetables, bread, fruit, and wine, but might be more frugal. Especially in summer luncheon was followed if possible by a siesta (*meridiatio*). From the eighth hour, if duties permitted, exercise was taken in the Campus Martius, including running, jumping, and different games with a ball. As the Baths grew more luxurious this part of the afternoon often found the Roman of the Empire a regular habitué, enjoying the facilities for physical exercise before bathing, also the social advantages, comparable except in the absence of exclusiveness to those of a modern club.

After recreation came dinner (*cena*), around the ninth hour or even the tenth. From the simplicity of early times, when meat was only for holidays and everyday fare consisted of the most ordinary vegetables and *puls,* a mush of spelt (a kind of wheat), with bread and wine, dining at Rome came to be a well-appointed function long before the end of the Republic, and an agreeable recreation even for those who led a comparatively simple life. Most entertaining took the form of a dinner—the normal way of meeting one's friends, to linger with them at table for several hours, since the comfortable couches of the triclinium made it unnecessary to migrate to another room. A special garment, the *synthesis,* light, gay in color, and often changed between courses, added to the air of festivity.

The old-fashioned dinner had had but two courses: *cena* proper and *secunda mensa,* "dessert." It is safe to assume that even under the Empire simple meals were not rare in many homes even among the well-to-do. Of these we are seldom informed. But the familiar accounts of lavish entertaining and sumptuous repasts, especially of the parvenus, do not prove that simpler living and refined taste had been banished altogether. It is worth while, however, to picture to ourselves a formal dinner in upper-class society as it was in the latter part of the Republican period and for a century or two of the Empire.

When the guests had reached the table there was in some houses at least a prayer to the gods. After washing of hands in basins brought in by slaves—a process frequently repeated on account of the absence of forks—came the *gustatio*,[11] an ample array of *hors d'œuvres*, including every variety of salad, especially lettuce,[12] artichokes, olives, leeks, mallows, asparagus, cucumbers; and with these came mushrooms, snails, oysters fresh or cooked, sardines and other fish salted or in oil. Soft-boiled eggs had once been so conspicuous a feature of the *gustus* that the most elaborate dinner menu could be covered by the proverb *ab ovo usque ad mala*. Wine sweetened with honey was served with this course, hence the name *promulsis*.

Next followed the *cena* in its narrower sense, itself often subdivided into several *fercula*, virtually separate courses. Here the details would be endless, since the Roman market in that period offered an unlimited variety, including game and fish of every sort and ranging from peacocks to sea urchins. Cooking had become a fine art commanding the most varied resources in spices, such as pepper from India, in sauces to every taste, in condiments without end. The highest commendation which a cook book could append to one of its notable recipes was "No one will recognize what he is eating."

In the interval following this *cena* proper there was a call for silence while salted meal and bits of food from the table were solemnly sent to the hearth to be thrown into the fire as an offering to the Lares, and a flute-player blew at least a few notes, the necessary accompaniment of any religious act.

Then came the *secunda mensa*, the *bellaria* ("sweets"), consisting of fruits both fresh and preserved, and cakes, brought in, sometimes at least, on small, round, three-legged tables. Wine was served both with the dinner proper and

[11] Also called *gustus* or *promulsis*.
[12] Down to Augustus's day lettuce was served with dessert.

with dessert, warm water or cold water or even snow being mixed in the cups. After a general hand-washing guests called for their sandals and departed.

If the occasion was a more formal one the prolonged dinner might be continued without appreciable interval by a supper party (*comissatio*) to which additional guests had been invited. This was often a separate function and might be at a different place. For such a supper the hair was perfumed and a garland worn on the head. An *arbiter* (or *magister*) *bibendi,* chosen by a throw of dice, prescribed both the proportion of water to be mixed with the wine in a large mixing bowl and the quantity to be drunk. Healths were prefaced by such words as *bene tibi,* or *bene te,* or *vivas.* Musicians were there to play or sing; other performers were dancing girls or acrobats; there might be an actor or a reader; or the host might read a production of his own.

At a dinner with guests the host's wife and one or more of the children were regularly present, which was not the custom in Greece. Under the Empire they might even witness or take part in the convivial supper party, for which no one could claim that it was a school of manners or morals.

DOMESTIC EVENTS

From the daily life of the household we turn to the rare events which loom large in family history—birth, the assumption of the *toga virilis,* marriage, and death.

A birth in the family was made known to passers-by by a wreath hanging at the street door. The baby was first brought to the father and laid on the floor at his feet. If he lifted it up (*suscipere, tollere*) that act was an acknowledgment of parentage and a promise that the child should be reared and cared for. If he refused because of some physical defect or other reason the infant was exposed. This was his legal right by virtue of the *patria potestas,* but the inhumanity of the practice which exposed innocence to the risk of death, misery, slavery, and shame, gradually led to its abolition, not, however, until the third century A.D., when exposure was first treated as murder.

In the happier normal case, congratulations and gifts to the mother were immediately in order, even from the slaves. For seven or eight days there were offerings to Juno Lucina, as goddess of childbirth, and to primitive patronesses of infancy. The name was not given until the *dies lustricus,* the eighth for a girl, the ninth for a boy. It was the occasion of a family gathering and included religious ceremonies and a sacrifice. The name given at this time to a boy was simply a *praenomen,* Gaius, Lucius, Publius, etc., for under the Republic he would of course add the *nomen* (gentile name [13]) and *cognomen* (family name) of his father. Among the lower classes there was great diversity of names, while the list of first names in use among well-known families was a surprisingly short one. Under the Empire the older system of three names gave way to the widest range of freedom. A girl in Republican times might be given her father's *praenomen* in feminine form, Gaia, Lucia, Publia, or a more individual one, such as Rutila, from the color of her hair, Maxima or Prima as being the eldest daughter, Tertia as a third daughter. And these might be followed by the gentile name of her father, as Pompeia, Cornelia. Usage in the time of Cicero and Caesar inclined to the gentile name alone, as Pomponia, Tullia, Iulia. Under the Empire, as with names of men, there was the greatest freedom in combining names from both sides of the family.

To guard against malign influences and the evil eye amulets were tied about the neck of the newborn; or in the case of a senator's child or a knight's the amulets were enclosed

[13] *I.e.,* common to the whole *gens,* or clan.

in a gold *bulla* ("locket"), to be worn until the boy put on the *toga virilis* or the girl was married.

The end of boyhood and entrance upon the duties of a citizen were marked by the assumption of the white toga with ceremony and rejoicing. No fixed time was assigned for this function. When it was directly followed by military service for the Republic the seventeenth or eighteenth year was preferred. This was reduced to the fifteenth and sixteenth under the Empire, when the whole ceremony had lost much of its meaning in relation to a citizen's duty. Year and precise date were determined by the father or guardian. On the appointed day, often the 17th of March, as the feast of Liber and Libera (p. 127), the boy discarded before the household shrine (*lararium*) his *toga praetexta,* with its purple border, and his *bulla,* hanging up the locket as a gift to the Lares. He then put on for the first time the toga of manhood over a tunic. If his father was a senator or knight the tunic of the boy also showed the broad or narrow stripes already mentioned (p. 187). And now as a man and to be registered as a citizen the youth was escorted by family and friends to the Forum, to have his name entered on the official list of the tribes. An offering on the Capitol and feasting followed.

For a wedding it was necessary to choose a date with great care to avoid all unlucky days, such as the Kalends, Nones, and Ides, and the day next following each of these, or an anniversary of unhappy memory, as that of the battle at the Allia; also the festivals, many and prolonged. May was an unlucky month, while the second half of June was thought the most favorable season. Betrothal (*sponsalia*) with more or less formality, as evidence of parental consent, had preceded, sometimes in childhood, for the age of marriage was normally only thirteen to fifteen for a bride, while the groom was usually some five years older.

On the eve of the wedding the bride laid aside the purple-bordered toga she had been wearing in girlhood and dedicated it and her dolls to the Lares or other divinities, putting on a white tunic (*tunica recta* or *regilla*) and a flame-colored veil (*flammeum*), both of which she was to wear at the wedding. This tunic was long, like the *stola* of a matron, and held in place by a girdle (*cingulum*) tied in a particular knot which took its name from Hercules. Her costume also included a mantle (*palla*) of the same yellow-red as the veil and shoes of that color as well. Her hair was parted with a spear point and arranged in six locks with fillets (*vittae*). For the groom there seems to have been nothing more festive than the inevitable toga and a garland.

Preliminary to the ceremony, if a formal one, came the taking of auspices; or other methods were employed to find that the gods approved, though this became the merest form in many cases. The family and guests are assembled in the house of the bride's father, and the garlanded bride is escorted into the company by a matron, her *pronuba*. If there is a marriage contract it is certified by having witnesses affix their seals. Some formula was no doubt used by both groom and bride. One such for a bride has been preserved for us in the Greek of Plutarch—the quaint assurance, "Where you are Gaius, there I am Gaia." The *pronuba* then joined their right hands.

If the rite was the old patrician *confarreatio* there were more ceremonies. A spelt cake and salted meal were offered in the presence of the Pontifex maximus and the Flamen of Jupiter; and the couple then marched around the altar while prayers were said. In that ritual a sacrifice also was required, possibly at a temple. In any case, regardless of the precise form, there was usually a feast (*cena nuptialis*) at the house of the bride, and cakes of a special kind (*mustacea*) flavored with must and bay were served.

At nightfall, after the bridegroom's pretense of tearing
the bride from the arms of her mother, the whole company,
by torchlight even if it were not yet dark, escorted the pair
to the house of the groom to the accompaniment of flutes.
The bride was led, however, by two boys, each holding a
hand while a third held a torch before her. The groom also
carried a torch and scattered nuts to the crowd. Songs were
sung—the libelous and often indecent Fescennine verses—
while the crowd shouted *talasse,* a joyous cry of uncertain
meaning. Our most familiar picture of all this is in the
charming lyric of Catullus, in which Greek customs are
freely interwoven with Roman, and which closes with the
beautiful epithalamium, not a normal feature of a Roman
wedding.

On reaching her future home the bride hung woolen
fillets at the door, anointed the doorposts, and was carefully
lifted over the sill to avoid a possible omen if she should
stumble. Within she received fire and water from her husband, symbolic of her entrance into a new family, and was
sprinkled with the water. In the atrium opposite the door
stood the marriage couch (*lectus genialis*), and thither after
her prayers to gods and goddesses of marriage she was conducted by the *pronuba.*

Needless to say, many weddings were less elaborate, not
to mention local differences of custom for which we have
almost no sources. It is impossible here to give more than
a typical example, with a warning against too broad generalization. And the same must be said of funeral ceremonies, where our detailed information is virtually limited
to the upper classes.

During the classical period cremation prevailed except
for the poorest, very young children, and some conservative families (p. 8). By the second century A.D. burial was
coming to be preferred by many, as shown by the increased

number of sarcophagi, and with the fourth century under Christian influences cremation ceased altogether.

In the interval between death and cremation or burial the body was anointed, and, besides aromatics, various kinds of preservative were used, even embalming, but with no Egyptian mummy wrappings. All this was in charge of the undertakers (*libitinarii*), whose place of business was at the Temple of Venus Libitina (probably on the Esquiline), where deaths were recorded. They contracted in fact for the whole funeral including cremation or burial.

The corpse was laid on a lofty couch (*lectus funebris*) in the atrium, placed with its foot toward the door, and decked with rich coverlets and pillows. A former magistrate would be clad in his *toga praetexta* with other insignia, a citizen of less importance in a white toga, a woman in her best, often with gold embroidery and purple, and wearing her jewelry. Garlands of gold, if the deceased had won such as honors or prizes, or of flowers, were placed on the head, and a copper coin in the mouth to pay Charon's fare. Flowers and wreaths were scattered over the couch; candles and lamps were kept burning. Outside the door were branches of cypress or fir, while from within could be heard wailing and lamentation and music, especially of flutes; and this continued around the corpse lying in state for several days.

Provision for the costs of a funeral was often made by the lower classes through the medium of a burial society (*collegium funeraticium*), which in consideration of monthly dues paid in advance undertook to defray part of the expense or even to arrange for everything, including the assignment of space for the urn in a common tomb belonging to the society, that is, a *columbarium* ("dovecote"), named from its many small niches. For such funerals, as in general for persons of moderate means, there would be an interval of only one or two days before the final interment.

If a funeral was to be marked by unusual ceremony, as that of a prominent man, a herald went about announcing the fact, especially if it was to be followed by combats of gladiators or the performance of plays. A procession (*pompa*) formed before the house. There were musicians with their flutes, trumpets, and horns, attended by torch-bearers, even in broad daylight. Mourning women (*praeficae*) followed, singing their dirges (*naeniae*) in praise of the departed, and sometimes there were dancers and actors, one of whom might even impersonate the departed with travesty and jests.

Most characteristic of a Roman funeral in high life was the procession of the forefathers. The masks (*imagines*) religiously preserved in the atrium were brought out from their cases, or copies of them were made for the occasion. These were worn by men garbed in the robes of office, triumphal attire, and other distinctions formerly belonging to the ancestors represented, and attended by lictors. In a distinguished family this meant a long array of notables in chronological order, vividly recalling many pages of Roman history as these solemn figures were borne along, reclining, apparently, on couches carried by bearers.[14] Deeds of the deceased himself, if he had been an eminent commander, were called to mind, as in a triumphal procession—spoils of war, models of captured cities, figures representing conquered peoples, inscribed tablets, etc., all borne in procession. Then the lictors in black with lowered fasces, and freedmen emancipated by the will, if there were such, each wearing his new *pilleus* (p. 187).

Next followed the corpse with face uncovered, lying on a costly couch carried on a bier (*feretrum*). Near relatives were the bearers in early times, later friends or freedmen. Following the bier came the relatives and friends in dark

[14] In early times wagons seem to have been used.

or even black clothing. From the first century A.D., white came to be the mourning color for women. Insignia of rank or office and all ornaments were omitted. Men of the family covered their heads; women had their hair loose, beating their breasts, tearing their faces and their hair, rending their garments, wailing and calling the name of the departed.

For a man of special distinction, rarely for a woman, the procession would wend its way to the Forum, halting there before the Rostra for a eulogy (*laudatio funebris*) delivered by a son or other near relative. It was addressed like any other *contio* to the citizens in general, with that interspersed vocative *Quirites* ("fellow citizens"). Praises of the ancestors, solemnly represented by those *imagines,* were combined with eulogy, often extravagant, of their descendant. For a state funeral ordered by the senate the *laudatio* was pronounced by a magistrate. *Naeniae* were heard again after the oration, perhaps before it as well. And the mimes and dancers performed.

The procession then made its slow way to a spot (*ustrina* or *ustrinum*) outside of the city, where the pyre had been set up, usually near the tomb. The pyre itself might be large and elaborately adorned with rugs, paintings, and cypress boughs. Gifts of all kinds, embracing food, vessels, clothing and favorite articles, such as a hunting outfit, were placed upon the pile, together with incense and perfumes. Lighting the fire was commonly the duty of a relative, who turned his face away as he applied the torch. Dirges were sung once more while the fire burned down. Water or wine was poured over the coals, the bones and ashes were gathered, sprinkled with wine and milk, dried on linen, and laid with perfumes and a coin for Charon in an urn. The deposition of the urn in the tomb might take place on another day.

Regarding an elaborate funeral ceremony where the body

was to be buried or placed in a sarcophagus we have no adequate information, but in view of the increasing prevalence of that custom under the Empire we can only conjecture, knowing the general tastes of the time, that the laying away of a body in one of those sculptured marble sarcophagi did not lack state and ceremony, including the triple farewell, the sacrifice to dedicate the tomb and that to purify the family, defiled by contact with death, the meal at the tomb, and other customs known to us in connection with cremation funerals.

Tombs were for the most part located along the roads, with a marked preference for those with the greatest traffic, where many more would pass and perhaps note at least the new or the striking monument. Republican inscriptions sometimes bade the passer-by pause and read the epitaph. Many monuments displayed portraits in relief to the passing throng. Some were stately mausolea of impressive size, bearing beautifully lettered inscriptions, as that of Caecilia Metella on the Appian Way, or that of the Plautian family on the road which led to Tibur (Tivoli). Many were of more modest size, but bore no less noted names and memorable epitaphs. Today the names have in most cases disappeared; marble blocks, delicate mouldings, and sculpture, if they remain at all, are broken or in fragments, leaving a naked core of concrete.

The road by which a Roman traveled from his city house to his villa was often one that passed the family tomb which he perhaps erected in his lifetime, one of those now shapeless masses, it may have been, which still line the Queen of Roads mile after mile in the silence of the Campagna. Ancient travelers along the road were invited by him to remember: the modern visitor cannot forget.

VIII
SCHOOLS AND MASTERS

MARCVS PORCIVS CATO DIXIT LITTERARVM RADICES AMARAS ESSE, FRVCTVS IOCVNDIORES.

DIOMEDES, 1, 310 K (A PROVERB)

TAMDIV DISCENDVM EST, QVAMDIV NESCIAS; SI PROVERBIO CREDIMVS, "QVAMDIV VIVIS."

SENECA, EPISTLE 76, 3

INTEREA MVSIS, ANIMVS DVM MOLLIOR, INSTES
ET QVAE MOX IMITERE LEGAS, NEC DESINAT VNQVAM
TECVM GRAIA LOQVI, TECVM ROMANA VETVSTAS.

CLAUDIAN, DE IV CONSULATU HONORII, 396

ROMAN education was directly based upon the *patria potestas,* so that responsibility for a child's training always rested upon the father or guardian. The state never interfered either for the general good or in the interest of the individual. As in most of the Greek states, except Sparta and in a measure Athens, lawmakers did not consider education, aside from physical training, one of their problems. Any proposed system of required public education would have been rejected as opposed to the national customs. A statement of this incompatibility is put by Cicero in his *Republic* into the mouth of the Younger Scipio. And Scipio's friend Polybius, the Greek historian, thought this indifference to public schools the only matter in which one could charge negligence against Roman institutions. But through the whole classical period Roman education was something apart from the state. Single edicts might hamper teachers for a time; generous emperors and enterprising communities or private benefactors might provide salaries for eminent masters, but government regulation and central control were unthinkable. If parents were ignorant or poor or both the possibilities of training for their children were meager indeed. Against such inequality of opportunity, such neglect to provide at least rudimentary education for the masses, the Greek critic's protest stands alone.[1]

Of an enlightened father's personal interest in the training of his child we have a vivid picture from the household of old Cato the Censor.

As soon as the boy showed signs of understanding [says Plutarch], his father took him under his own charge and taught

---

[1] Plutarch indeed thought Numa less wise than Lycurgus in this matter of public education.

him to read, although he had an accomplished slave, Chilo by name, who was a school-teacher, and taught many boys. Still, Cato thought it not right, as he tells us himself, that his son should be scolded by a slave, or have his ears tweaked when he was slow to learn, still less that he should be indebted to his slave for such a priceless thing as education. He was therefore himself not only the boy's reading-teacher, but his tutor in law, and his athletic trainer, and he taught his son not merely to hurl a javelin and fight in armour and ride the horse, but also to box, to endure heat and cold, and to swim lustily through the eddies and billows of the Tiber. His History of Rome, as he tells us himself, he wrote out with his own hand and in large characters, that his son might have in his own home an aid to acquaintance with his country's ancient traditions. [Perrin.]

The intelligent mother also bore an important part, especially in the first years, as we know from Tacitus's picture in the *Dialogus*. After speaking of the old-time matron as nursing and bringing up her children, and of her pride in the care of the household and her maternal devotion, he adds:

Or an elderly female relative was chosen, and to her proved and well-known character all the children of the same household were entrusted. In her presence it was not permissible to say an indecent word or do an improper act. And by the respect and awe which she inspired she controlled not only the children's lessons and duties, but also their recreations and games. In this way, we are told, Cornelia presided over the bringing up of the Gracchi, Aurelia of Caesar, and Atia of Augustus, and they reared their sons to be leaders.

From the mother or aunt the boy then passed to the care of the father. While few fathers continued Cato's practice of taking complete charge, it remained the custom in most of the leading families for the father to accept the direction of his son's education and to give up much time to these cares. It is safe to infer that in the Younger Scipio's time a large part of the instruction was given in the home by a slave or freedman, often a person of excellent education from some Greek city in the South. Scipio's own training, as described by Cicero, was the usual combination of home instruction with a smaller proportion of book learning. Under the personal care of a distinguished father, Aemilius Paulus, he had profited by an upbuilding and informing home life reënforced by family traditions. This was the real meaning of *educatio* at its best, and quite distinct from formal schooling. But Paulus had brought home from Macedonia a Greek library and had a Greek philosopher, Metrodorus, in his house. No wonder that the son exerted a marked influence in that age of transition.

Elementary schools of some sort must have existed from early times. Fresh impulse in the direction of school training had come with the close of the First Punic War and the beginnings of Roman literature (p. 224). Hence the first period in the history of Roman education, a period of training largely parental and strictly Roman, may be said to have closed about 240 B.C., when increasing contacts with the Greeks and the necessity of learning their language had brought in new ideas of education for the upper class.

With the second period we begin to have definite information about regular schools (*ludi*) : that a master was called *litterator* or *ludi magister;* that, like the private tutor, he was as a rule a slave or freedman, receiving his meager fees monthly (for his owner if he was a slave) ; that presents at certain festivals were customary; that holidays were numerous in a school year which began in March. As to a summer vacation, we have no positive information.

The subjects taught were reading, writing, and elementary arithmetic. Before actual reading came memorizing of the most used syllables. In connection with the reading lessons it was customary down to Cicero's time to memorize

and recite the venerable Laws of the Twelve Tables (p.
14), also maxims, famous sayings, and whole passages
from the poets dictated by the master. As the children read
and recited at the top of their voices the noise of a school
could be heard far and wide. For the writing lesson words
of wisdom and brief passages were set as models. Among
the first aids to penmanship a board with the letters incised
was recommended.

Arithmetic with Roman numerals was simple enough
until one advanced beyond addition and subtraction, the
latter largely a process of cancellation. Multiplication and
division offered serious difficulties, enhanced by the absence
of a zero and the habit of using complicated fractions on
the duodecimal system. The larger part of arithmetic was
accordingly reserved for the older pupils under a special
and more highly paid teacher outside of the school. This
calculator taught both the use of the *abacus,* a calculating
board indispensable in trade (still in use in many countries), and a method of reckoning by signs made with hands
and fingers—a system used by lawyers in court.

The discipline was strict, enforced by a *ferula* to strike
the hands and a *scutica* for whipping. One martinet of a
schoolmaster has been immortalized by a pupil in Horace's
oft-cited phrase, *plagosum Orbilium.* Later there were
those who condemned corporal punishment, as Quintilian
and Plutarch. On the way to and from school each pupil
was accompanied by a slave, the *paedagogus,* not a teacher,
but commonly a Greek, able to help in the mastering of his
language, which many children of the upper class learned
to speak in infancy, often before Latin. In early times they
had been taught Etruscan.

Next above the elementary school of the *litterator* was
that of the *grammaticus.* An innovation dating from the
time of the Second Punic War, this school represented the

new desire to supplement old Roman traditional training by as much as possible of Greek culture. At first the *grammaticus* taught only in private families, as Livius Andronicus (p. 224) had taught in the house of his former owner. Ennius was another poet who taught in the same way. But the coming of Crates the philosopher as an ambassador from Pergamum (probably 168 B.C.) and his lectures on Greek literature gave a marked stimulus to Greek studies. And so by the year 150 B.C. regular schools of the *grammatici* had been opened. The central feature in their course of instruction was the reading and interpretation of Homer, as in the schools of Greece. Soon there were Latin schools of the same type in which the place of Greek poets was taken by Livius Andronicus's translation of the *Odyssey* into rough Saturnians, by Ennius, Terence, and other poets, as later on by Vergil and Horace.

The *grammaticus* must not be confused with a grammarian, since the teaching of grammar was only a part of his task. Rather should we call his subject literature, as in fact Quintilian does, and his range was very wide. He taught his pupils to read with expression, correcting their errors of pronunciation. He discussed with them matters of grammar and style, the poet's art, including meter. He must explain allusions and enlarge upon the subject matter wherever knowledge of geography or astronomy, philosophy, music, mythology or history was involved. Thus all these subjects were cursorily handled as they happened to come up in the particular text then being read, but with no systematic instruction in these several branches, much as the teacher might stimulate inquiry and private reading.

The detailed comment upon the author being finished, the teacher would require his class to memorize the passage, or to make it the basis for an exercise in composition. Some essentials of rhetoric were thus introduced at this stage, although the *grammaticus* gave less instruction in that subject after the rhetorical schools had been established.

There were no attractive school buildings, no adjoining playgrounds, and certainly the equipment afforded little more than one chair and plain benches. Though the *grammaticus* was somewhat better paid than the elementary teacher, he too had to hold his school wherever he could find a place, sometimes not entirely enclosed. Girls might receive the same instruction, and even in the same classes with the boys, though this was not generally approved, as contrary to old customs. As a stimulus much was made of rivalry for the first place in the class. Discipline was strict, as in the elementary school, and the hours were long, beginning very early and resuming after the midday meal. A *paedagogus* still accompanied these older children, while another slave (*capsarius*) sometimes carried the books and a portfolio containing tablets and other writing material. Horace, though himself the son of a freedman, was thus attended, and his father went along.

For some studies, notably advanced arithmetic, geometry, and music, the pupil had to depend upon instruction outside of the school. With the addition of these studies he was understood, on completing the course under his *grammaticus,* to have finished the studies commonly known as the *artes liberales,* namely, those which befitted the freeborn man not of the humbler classes.

On the physical side Roman schools made no provision. It was for parents to provide in their own way for proper supervision of the traditional exercises in the Campus Martius or elsewhere. These were running, jumping, boxing, wrestling, riding, throwing the javelin, and swimming. To these was added the discus borrowed from the Greeks. Physical exercise thus remained under the father's direction. And on leaving school a boy became his father's companion, daily learning from him something of his future duties to the family and the state. At this age or later he might be entrusted to the guidance of some prominent man noted for his gifts in the conduct of public affairs or in law or as a speaker.

For a young Roman of good family the one conceivable profession was public life, law and the official career being almost inseparable. It was inevitable that natural ability schooled by long practical experience in public speaking should some day be thought insufficient. The increasing demand for special training was met by new schools opened by teachers of rhetoric, the *rhetores,* at first Greeks teaching only in their own language. Cato the Censor, who possessed great natural gifts as a forceful speaker, had mocked at formal training and summed up his convictions in two famous maxims. He defined the orator as "a good man skilled in speaking" (*vir bonus dicendi peritus*) ; and in his "Grasp the subject, and the words will follow" (*Rem tene, verba sequentur*) he gave a comforting assurance not invariably sustained by the results. Character, practice, and mastery of the subject in hand could not always ensure the most effective expression in words.

Two generations after the death of Cato, in the boyhood of Cicero, that is, there were Latin teachers of oratory, *rhetores Latini,* as well as Greek. And with this new emphasis upon rhetorical training we have reached a third period in the history of Roman education, beginning 100-90 B.C. The school of the *rhetor* became the third stage of advancement for the pupil. The rhetorical schools were frequented by youths who had finished their course under the *grammaticus* and, having as a rule donned the *toga virilis* (p. 197), were now treated as young men preparing for

public life and destined to speak before the senate, the law
courts, and the people gathered before the Rostra.

The innovation was met by strong conservative opposition, resulting in 92 B.C. in the suppression of the schools
kept by Latin *rhetores,* and this by order of the censors,
though one of the latter, Crassus, was himself a celebrated
orator. Cicero at fourteen wished to hear Photius, the first
rhetor Latinus, but was dissuaded by his father's friends,
who thought the Greek training better. The prohibition of
such schools was of short duration. Declamation, as practised in them, had its vogue, so that eminent visitors often
attended the master's exhibition of his skill in oratory, not
in mere elocution. As an exercise it was designed to prepare
the student for public speaking. The imaginary speech
tended to artificiality, courting applause rather than aiming
at honest persuasion. At its best it helped even the seasoned
orator to keep in practice. Cicero often declaimed (in this
sense) before his friends, and that both in Greek and Latin.
Augustus visited rhetorical schools when there was to be a
public declamation, as did his distinguished friends.

The teachers of oratory (*magistri dicendi, rhetores*) were
at first freedmen, but by the time of Augustus we hear of a
knight, Blandus, in this profession. The chief forms of
rhetorical exercise were two: the *suasoria* and the *controversia* (p. 247). The former, usually assigned to the
younger students, purported to urge some historical character to action, or to dissuade him from an intended action.
The *controversia* was for the more mature, simulating as it
did an actual case before a court, the pupil pleading for
his client. But the supposed situations were often highly
romantic and improbable, far removed from drab reality.
Logic was apt to be subordinated to immediate effect. It
was a poor preparation for actual practice at the bar according to Tacitus and other critics. If everyday realities

were ignored in such exercises history also suffered many a distortion, being accounted chiefly a mine for illustrations and anecdotes, carefully collected for use in the schools and later—*e.g.,* by Valerius Maximus (p. 247).

From the early Empire on, much emphasis was laid upon the art of pointed, epigrammatic utterances, such as could not fail to attract attention and win applause, especially if tactfully placed at the end of sentence or paragraph. These so-called *sententiae* became a veritable mania in the rhetorical schools, in which Cicero was by that time quite out of date, partly because he used the now fashionable device so seldom. Point more than any other quality in speaking earned admiration for the budding orator, and from the schools it made its devastating way into the literary style of the Silver Age (p. 252).

Cicero's ideal for the perfect orator, that all-inclusive *humanitas* which presupposed a universal interest in everything that concerns mankind, and hence the study of all branches of knowledge, had been narrowed within two generations to a routine course, ending in most cases with the rhetorical school. And yet among the teachers of oratory were able and broad-minded men, chief among them Quintilian (p. 255), the Spanish master who labored and wrote on behalf of greater breadth of interest, wider range of reading, and sound taste based upon the best models. And his own age paid him high honor, as in general the teachers of the liberal arts were duly respected under the Empire.

On leaving the rhetorical school a young man of the upper class often traveled, hearing the philosophers and rhetoricians at Athens, Rhodes, Smyrna, and other centers. Under the Republic such opportunities added finish to the public speaking of not a few young men whose rise to high position in the state was largely due to their oratory. Under the Empire cultivation of the same gift was no less ardent, since few positions of high rank in the vast administration, which was less open to political aspirants but far better managed, failed to demand some gift of public speech. The emperors, not a few of whom spoke well, appreciated the luster shed upon their reigns by such orators as Messalla and Pollio in the time of Augustus, or Tacitus in that of Trajan.

In general Roman education did not lack its critics, especially after the home life had undergone gradual changes, and parents had come to be less constantly aware of their responsibility, while the school remained incapable of filling the place vacated by the father. Thus we hear under the Flavian emperors that many homes of the socially prominent were no longer nurseries of virtue for their children; that the nurse and *paedagogus* were often corrupting influences; that the slaves with whom the children came in contact were frequently vicious; that children were pampered and spoiled. For this decline our chief witness is Tacitus, among whose friends, however, the highest type of family life could still be found.

With the death of the historian or that of Trajan (the latter in 117 A.D.) a fourth period in Roman education may be said to begin. Corrupting influences continued, but were much less felt in the smaller cities of Italy. Many eminent men had their early schooling in such towns, *e.g.,* Vergil in Cremona and Mediolanum (Milan), Livy in Patavium (Padua), Horace in Venusia. Local schools were sometimes partly supported by an endowment such as that which the Younger Pliny gave to Comum (Como). In the provinces, especially in southern Spain and southern Gaul, there were excellent schools from which came conspicuous names in Roman literature and oratory. Particularly one recalls Corduba (Cordova) and its rhetorical schools (p. 247),

Nemausus (Nîmes), and Massilia (Marseilles). For the later period the schools of Carthage were famous, while in Gaul in the fourth century Burdigala (Bordeaux) and Augustodunum (Autun) were much resorted to by students from a distance. With every advance in Romanization, in Britain, for example, went the establishment of the *grammaticus* and the *rhetor,* still without institutional backing.

In the eastern provinces the schools of course remained Greek, though some provision had to be made for the teaching of Latin as the official language. So in Egypt fragments of Latin textbooks tell their story, even for village schools. And besides Alexandria, other important eastern centers for studies were Smyrna, Tarsus, and above all Athens. In the range of study there was no enlargement, no tendency to try new methods.

Higher education under the Empire was largely dependent upon municipal liberality, encouraged by the example of individual emperors, rather than sustained by systematic government support. Vespasian first established chairs of Greek and Latin rhetoric at Rome, with generous salaries paid out of the imperial treasury. Under Trajan and Hadrian the privileges of rhetoricians and philosophers were increased, the latter emperor erecting an Athenaeum, that is, an amphitheater in our academic sense of the word, for their lectures and readings, and also providing pensions for the retired. At Athens Marcus Aurelius founded a chair of oratory and four chairs of philosophy, one for each of the four schools, Stoic, Epicurean, Academic, and Peripatetic. New chairs established by Severus Alexander in Rome included even astrology. Yet there were no faculties in the modern sense, nor anything quite resembling a college or university. The words existed, but in the sense of "guild," "company," and at Arelate (Arles) at least there was a guild of teachers of rhetoric and philosophy. There was no

ordered grouping of subjects directly leading to a professional training to be pursued in a school for that specialty.
There were no organized schools of medicine or architecture, professions commonly practised by Greeks and freedmen. No instruction in agriculture was to be had, and even
schools of the law came only with the later Empire—
chiefly at Rome, Constantinople, and Beirut (Berytus) in
Syria. We are prone to speak of Athens, Rhodes, Marseilles,
and some other Greek centers as virtually university towns,
much resorted to by young men able to travel and prolong
their years of study (p. 108). But all this was without the
institution which it remained for the Middle Ages to devise.

In the fourth century, when the schools of Gaul were
especially flourishing, if any still thought of Cicero's cath-
olic and unlimited *humanitas,* it was as an unattainable
ideal. Education ended for most students in a rhetoric more
artificial than ever, and from its traditional routine there
seemed to be no escape. Yet very able men continued to
teach oratory even in the fourth and fifth centuries. And
with the fresh impulse of the new religion some of them—
such men as Lactantius and Augustine—gave up their
schools, entered the service of the Church and made Christian history.

Looking back over the four periods of Roman education
one is impressed chiefly by three facts: the scope of the instruction, narrowly restricted in some directions and yet
broad enough to be thoroughly bilingual; the absence of
anything like centralization or even provincial standard-
ization; the fact that elementary schools were of so little
concern to the government, with the result that systematic
education was only for the middle and upper classes.

As we have seen, a number of important subjects always
remained outside of the regular school course and required

private instruction or special classes out of hours, or for maturer pupils attendance upon lectures for which the school could make no provision. Yet what was for them the most important foreign modern language occupied a central position around which the rest of the course may be said to have revolved. From such emphasis upon Greek came that bilingual habit which remained for several centuries a notable feature in the life of the cultivated classes.

There were no ministers or commissioners of education, no superintendents; nor did the state otherwise exert itself to secure inspection, whether pedagogical or sanitary; to regulate the course of study or organize an orderly preparation for the several professions; to furnish funds, with the exception of the salaries granted by Vespasian, Antoninus Pius and other emperors to distinguished professors, following an earlier tradition of municipal enterprise, especially in the eastern provinces. The emperors, beginning with Hadrian, granted important immunities to a limited number of *rhetores* and *grammatici* in the cities, as they did to physicians. Inevitably those who received salary and immunities became subject to approval, and if unsuccessful could be removed by the municipal authorities. On the other hand when salaries were in arrears all grades of teachers could carry their complaints up to the governor of the province. Diocletian in his short-lived scheme of price regulation issued a scale of fees which might be charged by teachers, but this does not prove that education was really centralized.

Finally there was no system of elementary education under state control and reaching the humblest class. Lower schools were a concern of the municipality or the village, and not until the second century A.D. was the necessity of encouraging them impressed upon cities and provinces by the central government. Instead of receiving immunities

IX
IN A ROMAN LIBRARY

RVRIS BIBLIOTHECA DELICATI
VICINAM VIDET VNDE LECTOR VRBEM.

MARTIAL, 7, 17, 1

EDICTA VETERVM PRAETORVM SEDENTIBVS FORTE NOBIS IN BIBLIOTHECA
TEMPLI TRAIANI ET ALIVD QVID QVAERENTIBVS CVM IN MANVS INCIDISSENT,
LEGERE ATQVE COGNOSCERE LIBITVM EST.

GELLIUS, 11, 17, 1

QVAM BREVIS IMMENSVM CEPIT MEMBRANA MARONEM!
IPSIVS ET VOLTVS PRIMA TABELLA GERIT.

MARTIAL, 14, 186

COULD we have entered the library of Sallustius Crispus, grand-nephew and adopted son of the distinguished historian whom we know as Sallust, we should certainly have found a spacious room luxuriously appointed, in keeping with the splendid villa and extensive gardens inherited from that great-uncle and in the possession of this heir for more than fifty years, until his death in 20 A.D.[1] The collection of books would have done no discredit either to the literary repute of the family or the luxurious tastes of the owner, a very influential figure at the court and confidential adviser to Augustus and Tiberius.

Around the walls of the library, but raised two or three steps above the floor, we should see bookcases about six feet high, closed by solid doors, each case filling its own niche in the wall. Above these were busts of eminent authors in bronze or marble, where simpler libraries had medallions in stucco on the walls. Space may have remained for a few statues, a Minerva, a muse, a famous writer or two, in this case probably the historian himself. The cases (*armaria*, p. 176) were no doubt of valuable woods, possibly adorned with ivory, and numbered. On opening the doors of a case we should see each shelf supporting its own pile of *libri*, papyrus rolls, stacked like firewood, one end of the roll facing outward, displaying its attached tag (*titulus*). This was a parchment label bearing the name of the author and his work; also, if the work was of any length, the number of that particular *liber* ("book" in the sense in which we

[1] The villa lay outside of the Servian Wall near its northern gate, Porta Collina, the gardens extending westward and northward to the Pincian. The ruins there are those of later structures built by the emperors, who had acquired the property.

speak of a book of Vergil). We should note the absence of anything like a desk for writing and the presence of couches for reading in comfort, also a few easy chairs (*cathedrae,* p. 179). Adjoining this large and lofty room there would be one or more smaller rooms almost filled with cases, in the center as well as around the walls, for storing a large number of rolls. From the library proper we might also stroll out into a secluded court with columns all around, a normal feature of public libraries.[2]

As an admirer of earlier writers, especially Cato, the historian Sallust had undoubtedly gathered copies of the most important writers of Latin prose and verse down to his own time. Such a series began with Livius Andronicus, a Greek captive from Tarentum, slave and then freedman of a Roman Livius. He translated Homer's *Odyssey* into the native Italian meter, the quaint Saturnian. On some shelf among books seldom disturbed we should find a part at least of that version remembered with pain by those who, as Horace and probably Sallust also, had had to memorize it at school. Some of Livius's plays also—mostly tragedies with titles that recall Homer and the Greek tragedians— would be found on these shelves as incunabula of the Roman stage. When peace came at last at the close of the First Punic War and there was a demand for plays, Livius Andronicus produced the first adaptation of a Greek tragedy and a Greek comedy in 240 B.C., with which year Roman literature is commonly said to begin. Other translations of this type he produced and the playwright served also as actor. In old age (207 B.C.) he wrote a processional hymn for a chorus of maidens—one of the earliest of Latin

---

[2] On the arrangements of the library in a palatial villa light is thrown by the remains of two at the villa of Hadrian, near Tivoli—one of them apparently his private library. An example of the "stack" room is that in the villa of the Pisos at Herculaneum.

lyrics. And with this Livius began the guild of poets which met in a temple on the Aventine.

In that same *armarium,* but showing more evidence of use, we should quickly note that many tags bore the name of Naevius and with it the title of a play; that seven rolls made up an epic poem, his *Bellum Punicum,* or poetical narrative of the first war with Carthage, in which the poet had himself served. A Latin by race, he was possibly born in southern Latium, and gave most of his life to the writing of comedies (thirty and more) and seven tragedies, all of them freely adapted from Greek originals, the first being produced in 235 B.C. But venturing to introduce free-spoken criticism of the magnates he suffered imprisonment and exile. His strong national feeling showed itself in a new type of play, the *praetexta* (p. 145), a national drama drawn from Roman history. Two such plays are mentioned as his work, and it is likely that Sallust possessed at least the *Clastidium,* celebrating Marcellus's victory over the Gauls in 222 B.C. While all these plays were written in Greek meters, the epic composed in his old age returned to the native Saturnian and was thus national in form as well as in spirit. At the beginning of the poem the coming of Aeneas from Troy was recounted and other legends helped the writer on his way to the conflict with Carthage. For us there remain only meager fragments of this vigorous and independent poet, who died in exile in Africa, perhaps in 199 B.C.

Near that first of Roman epics, the *Bellum Punicum,* of Naevius, we should doubtless find the eighteen rolls of a poem called *Annales,* each book bearing the name of Quintus Ennius, commonly called the father of Roman poetry. Born in 239 B.C. in the extreme South, at Rudiae, a small town beyond Brundisium (Brindisi) in Calabria, he was half Greek, half Oscan, speaking three languages. Not until he was thirty-five did he come to Rome, being brought from military service in Sardinia by Cato. In his epic of Roman history Ennius introduced for the first time the Greek heroic measure, dactylic hexameter. It was a formidable task for an innovator, who could not avoid many prosaic lines, many unsuccessful experiments in rhythm. Yet the poem as a whole, with its intensely Roman spirit and some true poetry, exercised a great influence on later masters, such as Lucretius and Vergil, who were under constant obligations to him. In place of the eighteen books, quite complete, one must assume, in the Sallustian library, we possess only fragments, in quantity less than any one of them. More than twenty tragedies also, largely imitations of Euripides in his *Medea, Iphigenia,* and other dramas, were the work of Ennius. He may have written two *praetextae,* following in the footsteps of Naevius. His comedies, few in number, were evidently inferior to his tragedies. The latter continued to be performed long after his time. He had also written miscellanies in various meters, and these were called *Saturae* in the sense of a medley, not of satires. None of the other early writers was so incessantly quoted as Ennius, but it was chiefly as an epic poet that he handed down a highly honored name to posterity.

Probably Sallust had an entire armarium filled by the works of the comic poets of the early period. Plautus would require at least twenty-one rolls, allowing none for the many plays uncertainly attributed to him. Of these canonical plays, according to the verdict of Varro, we have all but one. Plautus, who was perhaps fifteen years older than Ennius, came from an entirely different region, being born in the Umbrian town of Sarsina, near the Gallic frontier and only lately conquered. After a long struggle with poverty he became in middle life the leading comic poet of his day, that is, of the period following the close of the Second

Punic War, down to his death in 184 B.C. Imitating Greek poets of the New Comedy, but with a very free hand, he made the plays of Menander, Diphilus, and the rest live again in another idiom, and live a more rollicking life at that. Greek are the scenes, the characters, the life depicted, but local allusions, not less amusing because entirely illogical, are frequently made, and the Roman, particularly in his uniquely vigorous speech, is everywhere coming to the surface. It is the racy popular speech of a stirring age and is almost phonographically preserved by the greatest of Roman playwrights.

A few of the numerous comedies of Caecilius Statius would surely be shelf-neighbors to the Plautus rolls, since some critics considered him the foremost writer of Latin comedy, though by birth an Insubrian Gaul from the upper Po country. Younger than Plautus by upwards of thirty years, he imitated Menander more closely, but is lost to us except for fragments.

Near Caecilius and Plautus we should find the six comedies of Terence, whom Caecilius encouraged in his early efforts. Publius Terentius Afer, was, as his cognomen announced, from Africa. Born at or near Carthage, he came to Rome as a slave, there to be educated by a Roman master, a senator whose name he bore as his freedman. Scipio the Younger and his intimates befriended and encouraged him to bring out plays in the years following the conquest of Macedonia (*i.e.,* 166-160 B.C.). These comedies also were adaptations of familiar plays of the Attic New Comedy, with an almost complete exclusion of anything which could be called a Roman allusion. Less of a genius than Plautus, he was a more finished artist, a perfect master of refined colloquial speech. His plays were always less popular, their delicate humor and restrained action not for the masses. Six comedies—all that he produced—have been preserved.

He had projected additional comedies when death overtook him on a trip to Greece in 159 B.C.

Other *palliatae,* or Greek comedies in Latin versions (p. 144, n. 4) after the pattern of Plautus and Terence, were probably to be found in Sallust's library in considerable numbers, but their authors are mere names to us. More reason have we to regret the complete loss of another type of play in which everything was Roman or Italian and native dress was indicated by the term *togata.* In this field Afranius, who flourished ca. 120-90 B.C., influenced by Terence and borrowing from Menander, was preëminent. We have the titles of forty or more of these comedies that wore the toga, and some fragments. Sallust probably possessed many of them, as valuable for their portrayal of low life in the second century B.C.

Among the dramatists in this section of the library we should doubtless find an honored place assigned to Pacuvius, then reckoned the greatest tragedian of Rome. Like his uncle Ennius, he too was a Calabrian (from Brundisium). He grew up during the troubled years of the Second Punic War, and at Rome he practised two arts, as painter (p. 321) and playwright. At eighty he was still producing. Fifty years younger, and highly honored as author of tragic dramas (two *praetextae*), was Accius, whom Cicero knew as an old man. Of both these poets mere fragments remain.

Closely related to comedy was satire in the new form given it in the second century by Lucilius (180 to about 102 B.C.), from Suessa Aurunca, in Latium but on the borders of Campania. For years he lived on terms of intimacy with the Younger Scipio and his famous group of friends. He retained the older idea of *satura* as a medley both in form and content (p. 226), but after earlier experiments in other meters finally chose the dactylic hexameter. His *Satires* (really *Miscellanies*) were published from time to time till they reached a total of thirty books, from which we have many fragments, often very brief. Sallust the historian must have been familiar with these vivid pictures of social and political life in the half century which included the last war with Carthage and the age of the Gracchi. There was much unsparing criticism of notables, much pointed comment, not always caustic, upon the follies of the day. For us the fragments are mainly of interest in our study of his imitator and critic Horace, a more genial and far more finished satirist, who found in the lines of Lucilius all that was necessary for an engaging portrait of the man.

In the library of a historian of unlimited means we should naturally expect to find ample space assigned to history. Thucydides was surely there, much read and often imitated by Sallust. The series of Roman historians of course began with the narrative of Fabius Pictor, written in Greek, since Latin prose in that period of the Second Punic War, in which Fabius served, was still in its infancy. Covering the whole story from Aeneas down to the end of that war, it was the earliest attempt of the kind at Rome. A Latin version existed, and this too Sallust may have had, though both are lost to us, as is also the work of the Roman historian in Greek, Cincius Alimentus.

The real father of Roman history—we may say the father of Roman prose also—was Cato the Censor. Born at Tusculum in 234 B.C., Marcus Porcius Cato saw active service in the war with Hannibal. A confirmed opponent of all who by introducing Greek ideas were breaking down the customs of the fathers, he was extreme in his narrowness. And yet, while outwardly contemptuous of culture and literature, he himself produced a large amount of prose at a time when there were hardly any books in Latin except in verse. The range of subjects treated was also astonishing. Most important of all was the unique historical work in seven books, his *Origines,* owing its name to the fact that the first three books gave the story of the founding and early fortunes not only of Rome but also of the other city-states of Italy. Such extraordinary breadth of scope was not matched by any of his successors. The fourth and fifth books were devoted mainly to the First and Second Punic Wars, while the last two covered another half century, to the year of his death (149 B.C.). In these he included some of his own speeches, and many others had been separately published by him, so that Cicero knew of 150. Of all these, as of the priceless *Origines,* we possess mere fragments, some of them, however, of great interest. Sallust, with his deep respect for Cato, surely prided himself on owning all the best-known works of the old censor, including the one which has reached us, his work *On Agriculture,* written with the most practical aim and in a quaint style. Though this book shows no sense of form, fragments of the orations prove that Cato was a master of direct and forceful speaking, a terror to his opponents.

In history Cato was followed in the same century by a series of annalists, Cassius Hemina, Calpurnius Piso, Coelius Antipater, who wrote with more finish and on a larger scale. Sempronius Asellio eschewed dry annalistic detail in his quest of underlying causes. In the period of Marius and Sulla came Claudius Quadrigarius, who set legend aside and began with Rome rising from her ashes after the Gallic invader had been expelled; also Valerius of Antium, who went back again to Troy for his starting point and wrote at least seventy-five books, marked by much exaggeration. To a younger generation belonged two more historians, Cornelius Sisenna and Licinius Macer. Known to us only from fragments and allusions, these men were the predecessors of Sallust in history, and we may well assume that they were sufficiently represented on his shelves. A whole case may have been filled with materials he had used in his own historical writing, especially the memoirs of public men such as Aemilius Scaurus, Rutilius Rufus, Lutatius Catulus, and Sulla—all of these long since lost.

The most memorable example of a work of this type which claimed a place rather as material for future historians than as finished autobiography was the famous *Commentaries* [3] of Julius Caesar, covering his campaigns in Gaul and in the civil wars against Pompey and his generals. These were supplemented by some of Caesar's officers who with far less skill completed the narrative of the campaigns in Gaul and those of the civil wars through the final battles in Spain. Best-known to us from centuries of schoolroom use is the *Gallic War,* restrained and sober in its direct style, aiming to let unvarnished facts leave their own impression. While making no claim to be writing formal history, avoiding the methods by which historians charmed their readers, for example, by inserted speeches cast in the best rhetorical moulds, or by descriptive passages or entertaining digressions, Caesar went his own way in tracing from one stage to another the conquest of a people ripe for Romanization and soon proud to call themselves Romans. Speeches become as a rule mere outlines in indirect discourse, as if noted down in brief by a faithful secretary at the moment. Descriptions, digressions, and other concessions to a reader's weakness are all but eliminated. But this clear, unadorned tale, never designed for youthful readers, will continue to hold its place, both as our prime source for a momentous chapter in human history and as a document for Latin speech at its peak. These works and many others on the history of the period were certain to be found in Sallust's collection, along with published orations and monographs of which we have no knowledge.

[3] Not meaning "comments" or "observations," but "materials."

The orations, perhaps filling another bookcase, would doubtless include most of the important names in Roman oratory from Cato's time down. Prominent among them would be the Younger Africanus, his friend Laelius, and Gaius Gracchus, all of whom attained a higher degree of finish in their vigorous speeches than was possible for Cato. Then came Antonius and Crassus, the leading orators of Cicero's boyhood; and then Hortensius, his somewhat older rival, followed by Julius Caesar, Calvus, Brutus. All of these and many others could be read no doubt in Sallust's house, at least in selected speeches, while for us there are scanty fragments. Cicero's orations would be found in such a library, if not the whole collection (the fifty-seven that we have and about as many more), at least the most celebrated, such as the Verrine series, representing his first success in prosecuting Verres, a notoriously corrupt governor of Sicily; the oration for the Manilian Law, recommending Pompey as generalissimo against Mithridates, King of Pontus; the four against Catiline, dealing with the suppression of a conspiracy in the orator's consulship (63 B.C.); those in defense of Murena, of Archias, a Greek poet, and of Milo; finally the fourteen *Philippics* against Antonius in the last two years of Cicero's life.

The other works of Cicero would claim considerable space on the shelves, even if in a generous selection rather than entire. The *Letters,* always valued as historical sources and prized as models for letter writers, may well have been more fully represented than in our eight hundred in the four extant collections. The philosophical works probably included some that have not survived, especially the *Hortensius,* a popular introduction to philosophy. The *Republic,* six books on the theory of the state, would have been there entire—not, as it is for us, a broken and in part fragmentary text. In this dialogue Cicero while imitating Plato constructs no imaginary ideal commonwealth, but prefers to let the Younger Scipio and his friends demonstrate that the Roman state practically combined the best elements of monarchy, aristocracy, and democracy. He closes with the fictitious *Dream of Scipio,* in which is set forth in prose on its highest plane the certainty of an immortal life to reward the statesman's services. To complete his political philosophy Cicero then added another dialogue, his unfinished *De Legibus,* in imitation of Plato's *Laws.* These works were written in his prime, before retiring from public life, to seek consolation in feverish literary activity.

To that last period belong nearly all of the philosophical works, likewise in dialogue form with a few exceptions, and aiming to popularize the subject. Yet he included so difficult a theme as the theory of knowledge, devoting to it his *Academica.* Less abstruse and carefully finished is the work *De Finibus,* on the ideal of conduct, the *summum bonum.* Much more popular are the very readable *Tusculan Disputations,* reporting imaginary discussions at his favorite villa on the heights of Tusculum, beginning with the thesis that death is not an evil and ending with the self-sufficiency of virtue for the happy life. The views of the different schools on the nature of the gods are set forth in the dialogue *De Natura Deorum,* supplemented by a lesser work, *De Divinatione,* on the various forms of divination, including augury. In *De Officiis* we have a popular work on ethics addressed to his son, and not in dialogue form. This treats of duties and their apparent conflicts, of what is honorable, and what expedient—a book which exerted much influence for centuries and was highly rated by Voltaire. The brief dialogues *On Old Age* and *On Friendship* are more widely known as essays of great and permanent charm.

As a student of style with a marked gift for oratory in his own historical works the elder Sallust would have had most of the rhetorical works of Cicero, if not perhaps his youthful *De Inventione,* or the other lesser writings, such as his translation of Demosthenes *On the Crown* with its preface (preserved for us while the translation is lost). Most admired was the *De Oratore,* a clever dialogue in which the leading parts are taken by Crassus and Antonius, the foremost orators of Cicero's youth. All the most important secrets of success in oratory are treated and the need of the soundest and broadest education is stressed, that one may prepare oneself for a most exacting art. This masterpiece, perhaps the greatest of Cicero's works, was followed a decade later by the *Brutus,* in which he traced the history of eloquence, briefly for Greece, more fully for Rome, with estimates of the abilities of a large number of orators, including Julius Caesar and himself, his training, his competition with Hortensius. In the *Orator* he treated of the ideal orator, who by the most thorough training and closest attention to every detail should reach the summit.

A carping critic, Sallust the uncle would surely have bought Cicero's poems, if only to rail at certain oft-quoted lines. In other verses he would perhaps have admitted reluctantly that a master of form had been at work. In his youth Cicero translated astronomical poems of Aratus and wrote a poem in honor of Marius. After his consulship, and with the same lack of inspiration, he versified contemporary history.

Poetry in the age of Cicero and Caesar was most effectively cultivated by Lucretius and Catullus. Lucretius was slightly younger than the masters of prose, and though probably born at or near Rome took no part in public life, devoting most of his years to the study of philosophy, especially the teachings of Epicurus, and to the writing of a hexameter poem *On the Nature of Things,* setting forth the Epicurean system. With all the fervor of an apostle he seeks to convert his countrymen, promising them escape from their blind fear of the gods and of death, and explaining in vigorous language how all nature (the human soul and the gods included) is produced by combinations of invisible atoms. A purely scientific theme is handled with every effort to be severely logical; but relief comes in many interludes of truest poetry, particularly in apt and vivid illustrations proving the close observer. This unfinished didactic poem *De Rerum Natura,* in six books, strongly influenced later masters, as Vergil and Horace. It outranks any other single work of Republican poetry and deeply moves his modern readers. The poet complains indeed of the poverty of the mother tongue, yet no one but Cicero handles it with equal persuasiveness or did more to make it the eventual language of philosophy and science.

Catullus, whose place among the immortals is permanently assured, was of Verona by birth, but wrote at Rome. There in the whirl of gay society he lost his heart to his Lesbia, who in real life was Clodia, sister of Cicero's enemy Clodius. Widely read in the artificial poets of Alexandria, especially Callimachus, he produced highly wrought poems in imitation of their learned and labored works. The reader, however, is all the while conscious that the young Roman is no copyist, that under all the Hellenistic polish there is native force unspoiled. Two lovely epithalamia, the unique Attis—its frenzied rhythm perpetual motion, the impassioned episode of Laodamia and that of Ariadne, the touching laments for his brother—all these leave an impression which nothing can efface. It is in the short poems on the other hand that his own passion carries him to the cloudless peaks of lyric and elegy. The language of this heart aflame could not be simpler nor more direct. Nor could his epigrams be more biting. A short life—thirty-three years at most—accounts for the limited output of the Shelley of

Roman literature, who died in 54 B.C., a year later than Lucretius.

Few collectors of poems as they first appeared in that day of versatile writers, when public men, Julius Caesar among them, could unbend and try their hand at epigram and other forms, would fail to put a copy of Calvus on the same shelf with Catullus. Though an eminent orator and busy lawyer Licinius Calvus wrote poems of such excellence that his name was constantly coupled with that of Catullus. One poet of the same generation lost to us was of unusual interest as the first bard from beyond the Alps. This was Varro Atacinus, born in Gallia Narbonensis, near the river Atax (Aude, the river of Carcassonne). Hence it was not strange that he should write an epic on Caesar's campaign against Ariovistus and his Germans. Satires also and elegies were written by him, but he was better known for his adaptations from Apollonius of Rhodes and other Alexandrians.

A much more celebrated Varro, whose prose writings were almost incredibly voluminous, wrote poetry also in quantity. His *Menippean Satires* reached the number of 150 books, a mixture of various kinds of verse with prose, treating of almost every theme connected with life in Rome. It was a medley, only in part satire in the sense in which we apply the term to Horace and Juvenal. As an antiquarian, rather than as a real historian, he accumulated a vast amount of information in regard to the Roman state, national customs of every kind, the state religion and its many cults—all this in a work in forty-one books, *On Antiquities,* of which only brief fragments remain. For these we are indebted mainly to the Church Fathers, who found the work an arsenal full of weapons to be turned against the old religion (p. 118).

One of his most important works dealt with the Latin

language, its syntax as well as etymology and inflection. Sallust's library probably had the twenty-five books of this *De Lingua Latina,* of which only six have been preserved. More widely read was the extant work of his old age, *On Agriculture* in three books, each in dialogue form, revealing practical experience, a high regard for those who serve their country by tilling the soil, and a deep love of Italy. He had himself been born in the Sabine country, at Reate. A long life (eighty-nine years, to 27 B.C.) and tireless industry enabled him in spite of activity in military and public service to produce many other works, historical, antiquarian, legal, geographic, critical, philosophical, mathematical, educational—a veritable library in themselves.[4] Among them was the earliest known example of an illustrated work in Latin [5]—his *Imagines,* or *Portraits,* in fifteen books, containing likenesses (at least alleged) of 700 eminent Greeks and Romans, with brief notices in prose and inscriptions in verse. Among the few private libraries of the Augustan Age that could own this costly work was surely that in the Gardens of Sallust.

Younger, but in the same generation, was the biographer and historian Cornelius Nepos, from Cisalpine Gaul, and a friend of Catullus and Cicero, also of Atticus, whose life he wrote. The last is much the best, as it is the most detailed, of Nepos's surviving biographies. These are sketches of famous Greek generals, the Carthaginians Hamilcar and Hannibal, and one Persian. There is a life of the Elder Cato, though the larger biography of the censor has perished, along with a life of Cicero. The whole series in some sixteen books may have been on Sallust's shelves. A rarity in Roman literature was Nepos's brief outline of universal history, his *Chronica* in three books, lost to us, as are the

---

[4] In all about 74 distinct works in some 620 books.
[5] Illustrated books had been known in the Alexandrian period.

Exempla, five books of inspiring or impressive incidents from Roman history, and likewise a work on geography. The Sallusts could have had no high opinion of the unfinished style in which Nepos wrote—a striking contrast to that of the historian uncle.

The complete works of the latter were unquestionably displayed with pardonable pride, probably in *éditions de luxe*—rolls of the best papyrus made of larger sheets, thus yielding broad margins. The *Histories* of Sallustius Crispus surely held the place of honor—a brief work covering in its five books only a dozen years, from the death of Sulla in 78 to 67 B.C. Extant are mere excerpts, that is, four speeches and two letters, besides lesser fragments. In addition to this his masterpiece there were his earlier works, two monographs, *On the Conspiracy of Catiline* and *On the War with Jugurtha.* These are of great historical and literary interest, examples of narrative prose of a very high order, with occasional speeches inserted. In both the author was greatly influenced by study of Thucydides and of Cato's *Origines.* Thus we find in these and in what little remains of the *Histories* Greek finish combined with something of Latin homespun at its best. And vividness is linked with an almost inimitable rapidity—his "immortal velocity," as Quintilian phrased it. Sallust, like Varro, had come from the Sabine uplands, his birthplace, Amiternum, lying near the highest of the Apennines. After a stormy career he spent his last years in this sumptuous villa among his books and in his gardens.

In our imaginary hour in the celebrated historian's library, as enriched by an enlightened and long-lived heir, we have surveyed the authors of the Republican period, and pass now to those of the Augustan Age.

Among all the writers of that Golden Age of Roman letters the first place belongs beyond question to Vergil, prophet of a new paradise in the *Fourth Eclogue,* an early poem, devoted son of the soil, calling his countrymen to labor that Italy might be still more productive, and finally singer of the lay of Aeneas, interweaving the Troy of legend with Augustan Rome and her unbounded future. He was born in a peasant family near Mantua, 70 B.C., when that whole northern region, Cisalpine Gaul, still lay outside the boundary of Italy and, during the poet's youth, was ruled by Julius Caesar as provincial governor. Educated at Milan and Rome, he suffered by the confiscation of lands about Cremona to reward Antony's veterans, and preferred to live mostly at Naples while slowly writing his *Georgics,* a didactic poem in four books on agriculture, glorifying labor and Italy. His remaining years (29-19 B.C.) were given to the *Aeneid,* the epic in twelve books left unfinished at his death. Few were the private libraries which did not contain this Roman iliad (in reality an odyssey followed by an iliad) and the more highly finished *Georgics,* together with the pastorals (*Bucolics* or *Eclogues*) and some other short early poems.

Younger by five years than Vergil was Horace, and like him of humble origin, but born in the South, at Venusia, on the Appian Way. He too came to Rome for his education, and that under the devoted guidance of a father who had been born in slavery. Later he went to Athens to continue the study of philosophy and rhetoric with young men of the best families. When Brutus came to Athens after the death of Caesar, Horace with many of his fellow students joined the army of the "Liberators" and became a military tribune (p. 459), sharing the final defeat of Brutus and Cassius at Philippi, 42 B.C. Pardoned by Octavian he supported himself at first by a clerkship in the office of the quaestors at Rome. His early works, the *Satires,* in two books of hexameters, and the *Epodes* (mainly iambics) won him an assured position and the patronage of Maecenas, who was virtually a prime minister. The *Satires* (*Talks* he preferred to call them) were only in part imitations of Lucilius, for Horace worked also a vein of his own and made much use of animated dialogue. The *Epodes*, coarse at times or bitter, were suited to the tastes of the day; but real poetry is not lacking. Then came the *Odes*, finally the *Epistles*. For the lyrics he chose as his models the best of the Greek lyric poets, Sappho, Alcaeus, Anacreon, and employed a wide variety of meters. Many of these poems show strong national feeling and an aim to uphold Augustus in his restoration of the state. Some were written at the behest of the *princeps*—six at the beginning of the third book, and the *Secular Hymn* for the jubilee festival of 17 B.C. (p. 138). In all they made four books and one unattached ode—the *Carmen Saeculare*. The *Epistles* in two books (hexameters) are only in a few cases real letters and tend to become essays in epistolary form—longer essays in the three which make up the second book. These are on literature, the third being best known under a later title, *Ars Poetica*. The others reveal in a delightful way the critical but genial observer of life, the mature and kindly man of the world—deservedly the pocket companion of many modern readers. His meticulous care for every detail of form and finish, his unerring taste in the choice of models marked Horace as a consummate artist rather than an inspired poet.

One department of poetry which has vanished for us, but was represented on the bookshelves of Augustan readers, was that of contemporary tragedy. This field was cultivated by a few men, such as Varius, the friend of Vergil and Horace, and one of the editors of the *Aeneid*. His *Thyestes* was highly praised, but the author turned rather to epics on the deeds of Augustus or Agrippa or to elegies, and only a few verses have survived to our time.

A great name among the versatile celebrities of the reign of Augustus was that of Asinius Pollio, a man of extraordinary independence who refused to bow the knee; but as writer and critic and patron he promoted Augustus's policy of encouraging letters. A triumph over Dalmatia, not long after Vergil had written the famous *Fourth Eclogue* in his honor, gave him the means of founding the first public library in Rome (p. 246, n. 6). He introduced the Greek custom of giving public readings of his works. These were tragedies from the Greek, an important history of the civil wars, probably down to 42 B.C., and published orations; for he was accounted one of the foremost orators of his day, along with Messalla Corvinus, the patron and friend of Tibullus and other poets. Both orators would surely be represented among the books of the younger Sallust, though meager fragments alone are extant.

Undisputed primacy among the prose writers of this period belongs to Livy—Titus Livius of Padua, one more son of Cisalpine Gaul. He was born at Patavium, lived apparently at Rome, but, unlike the men just named, took no part in public life. He wrote on philosophy after the manner of Cicero, also on rhetoric, works that were totally eclipsed by his great history of Rome from its founding. This immense undertaking saw the light in groups of five or ten or fifteen books covering particular periods, for orderly arrangement was a conspicuous feature. The total was 142 books, bringing the narrative down to the year 9 B.C. It was a prose epic of Rome, with marked poetic coloring, and we may feel sure that Sallust the nephew possessed at least large portions. Remaining to us are forty-five books— the first ten, and then the period from the beginning of the Second Punic War through the conquest of Macedonia, books 21-45. He admired the old Republic too fervently to be a eulogist of Caesar and Augustus. Yet the moral effect of his vast canvas, glowing with color, must have been hardly less than that of the *Aeneid* in its stimulus to revived patriotism. His style, less severe and more genial than that of Sallust, more distinguished than that of any other predecessor in Roman history writing, marks an epoch in Roman prose, the full development of the ample, periodic manner in narration. As for the age of this master of style, he was a decade younger than Vergil, whom he outlived by thirty-five years, surviving all the great Augustans, except Ovid, and dying under Tiberius in 17 A.D.

A very important department of poetry in this best period was the elegy. Cultivated under the Republic by Catullus and Calvus, it reached its culmination under Augustus in the poems of Cornelius Gallus, Tibullus, Propertius, and Ovid. All of these were much under the influence of Alexandrian poetry, especially that of Callimachus; but amatory elegy had its own course to run at Rome. The poems of Gallus, born in southern Gaul and the first prefect of Egypt, were admired by his friend Vergil, but have perished. Those of the gentle Tibullus remain, showing a deep love of the country and of rustic simplicity in the company of the beloved. Yet the form and finish reveal the master craftsman. In one memorable poem he rises to strike the national note, venturing to call Rome the Eternal City (the first known occurrence of the phrase), in a passage which recalls in a few vivid verses the tale of Aeneas, of Romulus, and the founding of the city that was to be a greater Troy with an imperial destiny, and this before the publication of the *Aeneid*.

Propertius was not a greater artist than Tibullus, but a more original genius. From Umbria and probably Assisi (Asisium) he came to Rome and found there his inspiration in a poet's granddaughter, Hostia, the Cynthia of his poems, whom he honors with all the Alexandrian artifices, not with the pure fire of a Catullus. And yet the learning and artificiality are redeemed by deep feeling and the mastery with which he finds new resources in the mother tongue, new possibilities in the music of the traditional couplet. If with the passing of his love for Cynthia his powers seemed to decline, still there are few greater poems than his last, the elegy on the death of Cornelia, a matron of the noblest type and stepdaughter of Augustus. For a time he gave up erotic elegy to serve the cause dear to the heart of Maecenas, his patron, by writing in a patriotic vein a series of poems dealing with venerated shrines, quaint cults, and their legends—idylls of early Rome and a romantic past, as a foil for the new grandeur of the Augustan city. But these are not his best. Short-lived, as were most of the elegists, he died but a few years after Vergil and Tibullus, hardly later than 16 B.C. when we lose all trace of him.

The last master of elegy was Ovid, the unrivaled story-teller and facile versifier who broadened the field while bringing the couplet to a too mechanical perfection from which it never again contrived to escape. Born in 43 B.C. at Sulmo, in the Abruzzi, he studied at Rome and Athens, traveled, and became the favorite poet of gay society until, for reasons never quite cleared up, he was suddenly exiled at the age of fifty to Tomis, in a wild country on the west coast of the Black Sea. From this dismal lot death alone released him ten years later. His love poems were endlessly varied; the *Amores,* and love letters of ancient heroines (the *Heroides*), the *Art of Love* and his *Remedies* for that malady—all in elegiac couplets showing the same facile wit and lightness of touch. For his most ambitious work he turned to epic and produced fifteen books of *Metamorphoses.* These *Changes* are legends of transformations,

properly tales of maidens or nymphs turned into birds or
trees, and similar legends. So freely, however, does he interpret his title that he begins with the creation—chaos
metamorphosed into matter and the visible world—and
ends with the deification of Caesar. Here and there he includes famous stories vaguely linked, if at all, with the idea
of a changeling. All are ingeniously interwoven, and digressions lightly inserted, so that the whole is one vast tapestry
of brilliantly colored scenes in endless succession, an inspiration to story-tellers and artists in every age. ·

A work which might have found favor with the Emperor
was the *Fasti* (*The Calendar*), designed to contain a book
for each month. Only six, however, were published, since
exile cut short Ovid's labors in this field. For the form he
reverted to the elegiac couplet, and in the treatment of his
material he imitated Callimachus, whose work on venerable
cults and sacred spots had been the model for Propertius
in some of his elegies. The feasts of the month he set down
in order, with explanation of the rites and customs, rehears-
ing their respective legends in his inimitable manner. Light-
heartedness becomes at times gross irreverence; but after all
we have here the religion of his people, quaint and incon-
sistent, yet real to the humbler classes.

Exile in a cold and distant country did not altogether
chill his fertile gift. From the Black Sea he sent back for
publication *Tristia* and *Epistolae ex Ponto,* together making
nine books of letters in elegiac form, bewailing the miseries
of exile and urging every argument for pardon, still with
the old fluency but with diminished charm. The attempt of
some false friend to injure him called forth the *Ibis,* a bitter
attack in elegiac measure. All of these extant works were
no doubt to be read in the Sallustian library, almost certainly his lost tragedy also, a *Medea,* highly rated by the
Roman critics.

No library of today lacks an encyclopedia, a want felt as early as the time of Augustus. We may fairly assume that the younger Sallust possessed the encyclopedic dictionary produced by Verrius Flaccus, a freedman, who as tutor to the young princes lived on the Palatine. This ample work was alphabetical in its arrangement and entitled *On the Meaning of Words*. It was a mine of information on words and customs, antiquities, religion, and what not. For us it is reduced to an epitome of the second half in twenty books made by Festus, probably in the second century, while for the first half we have only an abridgment of an abridgment, from the hand of Paulus Diaconus in the eighth century.

To the literature of information belongs also the extant work of Vitruvius *On Architecture,* written in an age of incessant building and rebuilding, but before some of Augustus's greatest public works, such as the Theater of Marcellus (p. 382). This is the only extant ancient treatise on the subject, and in its ten books it includes even aqueducts, sundials, and machines of different kinds. We read of a basilica at Fanum (Fano) which he had himself erected. Though the style of the book is that of a practical man of limited training and borders upon the popular speech, it exercised a great influence on Italian architects of the sixteenth century in their study and imitation of Roman structures.

A PUBLIC LIBRARY UNDER HADRIAN

From a large private library of the Augustan Age we pass to a public library in the time of Hadrian (117-138 A.D.). This creation of Trajan, like some others, was divided into two parts, one building for Greek and one for Latin books. Both of these halls were built directly against the northwest wall of the Basilica Ulpia (pp. 387 f.). The two faced each other across a small court in the center of which rose the huge Column of Trajan (*ibid.*) with its spiral band of colored reliefs, strongly suggesting an unrolled book of pictures. Just beyond lay the Temple of Trajan in its colonnaded court, so that the library was named from this temple, and also, perhaps unofficially, Bibliotheca Ulpia. Public libraries often sought the protection and seclusion of a temple court, as later that of a church. One of these halls has very recently been excavated and shows the typical disposition of an ancient library—the podium, or narrow platform, three steps above the floor, to support the bookcases in their niches, while a row of columns divided these wall spaces into alcoves. Busts of famous authors must be presumed, and other decorations in keeping with the stateliness of Trajan's Forum.[6]

We must confine our attention to the Latin library, and passing over its valuable archives and its law books, its collection of the edicts of the praetors, we may simply glance at the works of the principal writers whom we should expect to find in these bookcases and not in those of Sallust the Younger. These would be the authors belonging to the Silver Age, covering the period from Tiberius's reign (14-37 A.D.) to that of Hadrian. Needless to say, many writers of the earlier periods were also to be found in this imperial library.

One poet, Manilius, and a writer on rhetoric, Seneca the Elder, serve best to connect the Golden Age with the Silver. Manilius's astronomical, or rather astrological, poem was

[6] Other public libraries were those of Asinius Pollio, the oldest, not far from the Curia; of Augustus on the Palatine (Temple of Apollo); of Augustus in the Porticus Octaviae; of Tiberius near the Temple of Augustus (possibly identical with that called Bibliotheca Domus Tiberianae); of the Temple of Peace in the Forum of Vespasian; of the Capitol (the Capitolina); in several of the Thermae. Evidently conversation was not forbidden, as we read of a learned discussion in that of the Domus Tiberiana. Books could be drawn, as is proved by a letter of Marcus Aurelius to Fronto.

probably published very early in the reign of Tiberius. It is a didactic poem of six books in hexameters, carrying on the tradition of Lucretius and the *Georgics* of Vergil, but lacking their inspiration. Interest in astronomy was further shown by Germanicus Caesar's verse translation of an astronomical poem from the Greek of Aratus (p. 281). This version and Manilius's poem have come down to us.

As for Seneca the Elder, with him begins what one might call the Spanish chapter in Roman literature. Spain, as the oldest over-seas possession, and in its southern province the most completely Latinized, now produced a whole group of brilliant writers, three of whom belonged to one knightly family from Corduba (Cordova)—Seneca and his son, the philosopher, and a grandson, the poet Lucan. The Elder Seneca wrote a history (now lost), and out of his extensive knowledge of the rhetoricians and their schools, aided by a phenomenal memory, he wrote for his sons two rhetorical works, the *Suasoriae* and the *Controversiae,* recalling verbatim the arguments which had been used years before by many noted speakers on the traditional themes of the rhetorical schools (p. 214), with judicious prefaces and interesting comments in his own sane and sober language. That he himself taught rhetoric is possible, but not proved. He died under Caligula (37-41 A.D.), over ninety years old.

In an age more and more susceptible to pointed expression and terse aphorism proverbial wisdom was in demand. Such maxims were collected from the mimes of Publilius Syrus, written in the time of Julius Caesar, but perhaps never published. The maxims (*sententiae*) were in single iambic lines, useful as quotations or as models for the orator and the student of oratory.

Under Tiberius a collection of anecdotes in nine books was made by Valerius Maximus, drawing his material from Roman and foreign history. Students of rhetoric and other speakers were thus to have their illustrations ready to hand (p. 215). These are frequently marred by extravagances of expression and other signs of a decline from Augustan standards.

That prose was changing, and not for the better, is evident in the historical compend of Velleius Paterculus, a high officer of Tiberius in his northern campaigns. Hence there are unrestrained flatteries and excessive praise of his former chief. Much of the first book has been lost, while the second, beginning with the influx of luxury after the fall of Carthage, continues the story down into the Empire, including some fifteen years of the reign of Tiberius. The style is labored and entangles itself in overambitious periods.

To the same age, probably, though the writer is a mere name to us, belongs Quintus Curtius's *History of Alexander*. Originally in ten books, of which two at the beginning and some lesser portions are lost, it is romance, rather than history, but contains vivid descriptions, well-told stories, dramatic situations, sententious speeches—all these after the manner of Livy.

A writer less frequently read for entertainment, but doubtless often consulted by readers in Trajan's library, was the encyclopedist Celsus, who followed Varro's method rather than that of Verrius Flaccus (pp. 237, 245) in writing separate treatises on several different fields of knowledge. Of these only the extensive work *On Medicine* is left to us (p. 293).

Among the books on geography and travel we should have found Pomponius Mela, who was born near Gibraltar and thus represents the Spanish school. In three books he produced a handbook which makes the circuit of the Mediterranean and then takes up the remaining lands. His information is largely drawn from Greek books, with few traces of fresh knowledge, as reported by Roman officials from distant provinces. Venerable errors, such as that the Danube empties into the Adriatic, are left uncorrected. The necessary mass of names crowded into this outline is now and then relieved by a rhetorical description or a brief digression into myth or marvel. The brilliant style of the Spanish writers is almost wholly lacking.

In an age barren of poetry after the death of Ovid comes the Greek Phaedrus, a slave from Thrace, who used the free iambics, familiar in comedy, for fables. Many of these were borrowed from Greek prose current under the name of Aesop, some are drawn from Roman life. A considerable number have been lost. While speech on the lips of beasts and birds follows the convention of the fable, the follies and foibles of men and women, genially satirized under thin disguise, are true to nature. A moral is carefully attached at the beginning or end, but the reader's interest is focused on the story told in simple, direct style, free from most of the fashionable faults of the day. This was not a new field in Roman literature, since one of the best fables we have is due to Ennius, and in Horace we have several admirable examples. Phaedrus, however, was the first to publish a whole series (five books) and nothing else.

Minor poets of the time of Claudius and Nero could have been found in such a library. For us they may be represented by the *Laus Pisonis,* in which an unknown youth eulogizes the Calpurnius Piso who later, in 65 A.D., headed a conspiracy against Nero. Its smoothly flowing hexameters are probably typical of much verse-writing at that period. A more notable example is found in the seven *Eclogues* of Calpurnius Siculus, imitations of Vergil, but not without some charms of their own, and claiming a modest place in the long history of the pastoral. In these poems we have again the prophecy of a Golden Age now beginning under a youthful ruler, Nero. Here should be mentioned also the extant poem *Aetna,* uncertainly attributed to a friend of Seneca residing in Sicily. This is a didactic poem about as long as a book of Vergil, written while Vesuvius was still thought to be an extinct volcano and Roman knowledge of eruptions was less intimate.

Whoever came to Trajan's library to read up on agriculture or gardening would find there the Spanish authority, Columella, born at Gades (Cadiz), but a resident of Italy, in which he had estates. His *De Re Rustica,* written under Nero, contains twelve books, of which the tenth, on gardens, is in hexameters, as a supplement to the *Georgics* of Vergil. He names many authorities on farming, Greek and Roman, and the Carthaginian Mago (p. 66); and most of these, we may assume, could be consulted at the public libraries of Rome. Columella, though Spanish, avoids much of the rhetoric of his fellow provincials, writing usually in a clear and direct style.

Fiction would be represented by the *Satyricon* of Petronius, a court favorite of Nero. This ample work, of which we possess only a small part in excerpts, and that in a mangled condition, is the oldest extant example in Latin of a romance. It is a series of adventures and incidents, the dramatic, the highly colored, the sensual, including the famous dinner party of a boastful parvenu, Trimalchio, with much delightful satire of the newly rich and their extravagances. Poems, largely parodies and some of them of considerable length, inserted at intervals, show in this medley of prose and verse the influence of Varro's *Menippean Satires* (p. 236). The language is unique in its range from cultivated conversation to the popular speech of the streets. One may well believe that library copies of Petronius were well-thumbed. For us he is a mine, as we gather material to show how Latin became Romance, or to picture the manners of the time, or to trace the history of the novel.

The foremost place among the authors of the reign of Nero belongs beyond question to Seneca the philosopher, who, like his father (p. 247), was born at Corduba in Spain. His life of some seventy years began a few years before the Christian era and extended to the year 65 A.D. It included five years on the loftiest eminence to which a private citizen could rise, and before that eight years of exile in the wilds of Corsica. On his recall from banishment (49 A.D.) he became tutor to the young Nero, and when the latter came to the throne Seneca, with the help of Burrus, prefect of the praetorians, was virtually regent for five years. Then came waning influence, attempts to give up his immense wealth, retirement, followed by charges of complicity in the conspiracy of Piso, finally enforced suicide.

Seneca's prose works exercised a very wide and lasting influence, both in their sane philosophy—a humanized Stoicism—and in their brilliant epigrammatic style. The most readable are the 124 *Letters,* in reality essays in that form. Addressed to his friend Lucilius in Sicily, they often touch upon some current event, to draw from it sage counsel. The larger works are *On Benefits* (seven books) ; *On Clemency* (two books) ; the *Natural Questions* (seven books), dealing with earthquakes, winds, lightning, meteors, comets, etc., with ethical digressions; *On Anger* (three books). Briefer works treat of *Providence,* the *Steadfastness of the Sage, Peace of Mind,* the *Happy Life,* the *Shortness of Life, Leisure;* and there are three essays consolatory, one of them to his mother Helvia. In a totally different vein is a satirical medley in prose and verse under the title *Apocolocyntosis (Pumpkinification)*, a burlesque of the official apotheosis of the deceased Claudius.

In addition to these still extant writings of Seneca,

Trajan's library must have had some of his lost works, such as the biography of his father, a work on Egypt and its religion, published orations, and more letters. Seneca had achieved a style of his own, marked by staccato sentences, striking antitheses, words from the language of the street, and a wealth of quotable utterances (*sententiae*). It is in fact the acme of the sententious style, extensively imitated in later times.

An even greater influence on European literature was exerted by Seneca as a tragedian. Nine of his dramas remain, all based upon Greek themes but not mere versions of plays by the Attic masters, of whom Euripides was most frequently his inspiration. They are obviously academic pieces, suited rather to public readings than to the theater, and they fall far below the standard of Sophocles and the rest. And yet with all their faults of excessive realism and uncurbed rhetoric, especially in declamatory speeches, they long represented the classic tradition for generations ignorant of Greek, and so were undisputed models for more talented dramatists such as Corneille and Racine.

Trajan's great collection must have contained other book-tragedies, *Medeas* and *Phaedras* that never saw a stage and no longer exist. With these have perished also some national dramas (*praetextae*, p. 225), valuable as poetic interpretations of historic events and famous personalities. Thus we know that a tragic poet, Maternus, wrote a *Domitius* and a *Cato,* the former a historical play of the civil war between Pompey and Caesar, the latter ending presumably with the suicide at Utica. A single example of this type of play remains—the *Octavia,* dealing with the tragic story of Nero's young wife, and preserved with the tragedies of Seneca. That the prime minister is assigned a rôle in this play seems sufficient proof that he was not its author.

More Roman than tragedy was satire, and in this field

the age of Nero produced one promising but short-lived satirist, Persius, a son of Etruria, who died at twenty-eight in 62 A.D. Being an ardent Stoic he based his six satires upon the teachings of that school and was a zealous champion of goodness. In manner he imitated Lucilius and Horace, but the latter would have been incensed at his willful obscurity. In spite of that grave defect and a rare austerity he won a deserved place among the Roman satirists. His work was admired by Lucan, whose epic, the *Pharsalia,* must have been far more frequently called for by visitors to the library. Lucan, the precocious nephew of Seneca the Younger, was born at Corduba, but brought as an infant to Rome. As a young man he was favored by Nero, who made him quaestor and thus a senator. Their rivalry as poets, however, developed into bitterness, ending in Lucan's impetuous participation in the conspiracy of Piso; and thus he was forced to take his own life. Certain minor works, including *Laudes Neronis,* also a narrative of the great fire in Rome, and letters, were perhaps treasured by the libraries as rarities, but have not been preserved. His *Pharsalia* in ten books (the last incomplete) on the civil war of Caesar and Pompey with subsequent events in Egypt, is an epic on a new plan, in which the gods no longer intervene. The poet's sympathies are with Pompey and the Republic, his opposition to Caesarism evident. In style the poem shows the results of overtraining in the rhetorical schools, poetry being often lost in the elaboration of devices whose sole aim was display. The exaggerated, the ghastly, the harrowing are overdone, as also the flash of the glittering *sententia.* Quotability was a prime consideration, as with Seneca, and as a result many familiar quotations and oft-repeated phrases are from Lucan, among the latter his *furor Teutonicus.*

Readers of Cicero's orations who sought a clearer understanding of a particular case or of the political situation must often have come to the library to look into the voluminous commentary of Asconius, a fellow townsman perhaps of Livy. His historical notes were based on careful research, but only a small part of this learned and judicious work of Nero's time has escaped destruction. Lost also is his brief book defending Vergil against carping critics.

A friend in need to the man who came to a library for information was Pliny the Elder, filling a whole shelf with his *Natural History,* an encyclopedia in its range, but not planned for ease of consultation nor helped by alphabetical order. This northerner from Lake Como, born in the middle of Tiberius's reign, was no mere editor. He led a very busy life in military service, in provincial posts suited to his knightly rank, as counselor to Vespasian, finally as admiral of the fleet at Misenum (p. 469). In this last capacity he risked and lost his life in the eruption of Vesuvius (79 A.D.). His studious habits, tireless industry, and appalling economy of time are known to us from a letter of his nephew, who gives a careful catalogue of his works. None remains except the *Natural History,* complete in thirty-seven books, dedicated to the crown prince Titus. This treats successively of astronomy, geography and ethnology, anthropology, physiology, zoölogy, botany, agriculture, materia medica, and lastly mineralogy and metallurgy, including their relation to medicine. Through this same door enters a whole history of art, since the arts use materials provided by nature. By incessant application, though not a master of any of the sciences, he had collected information to a vast amount, mostly by excerpting from previous writers, almost five hundred in number. It was to later ages a vast storehouse of facts, real or alleged, and even now remains of great value to students of the ancient world. As a writer Pliny suffered from the failure to digest and assimilate his endlessly varied materials. His is a curiously unequal style, often smacking of the unrevised notebook, sometimes indulging in a pointed observation or in a rhetorical flight out of keeping with the context or the main purpose of informing rather than impressing the reader. As for his numerous earlier works (no longer extant), the same library would have contained the most important of them; a history of all the wars with the Germans (twenty books); a history of Rome in thirty-one books, beginning where a lost historian, Aufidius Bassus, had dropped his pen; an unusually ample biography of a tragic poet, Pomponius Secundus, his friend and at one time commander of an army on the Rhine; a manual for the student of oratory; a work on doubtful or incorrect word forms and other questions of grammar.

These last works were cast completely into the shade by the *Institutio Oratoria* of Quintilian, a complete treatise on the education of the orator in twelve books. This eminent Spanish master of Roman speech was born at Calagurris on the Ebro about 35 A.D., but educated at Rome, where his father was a teacher of rhetoric. Returning to Spain and his old home he seems to have taught there until Galba brought him back to Rome in 68 A.D. Under Domitian, who made him consul, he taught the Emperor's two grand-nephews. He had had much actual experience in the law courts and had occupied for years a chair established by Vespasian. Himself the father of promising children who died in childhood, he begins his system almost with infancy, laying great stress upon home influences and sound training in character. The orator is to be a good man, as required by Cato (p. 213), and not to use his gifts for unworthy ends. A thorough, liberal education is insisted upon, though the lines are less broad than those of Cicero. The student's reading in poetry and general literature must be carefully directed; hence a famous muster of the best Greek and Roman writers in the tenth book, with brief but sound criticisms. In rhetoric he reduces the technicalities and simplifies the rules, preferring rather to show what successful orators have done. Those who made light of careful study and preparation, or exalted form above content, or made display an end in itself, found no support in Quintilian. Sound counsel, sane judgment, a deep sense of the dignity of human speech at its best, a contempt for mere artifice, a conviction that speaking and writing should never be divorced, such are the leading characteristics of this master of them that teach. An ardent admirer of Cicero, he has little patience with the tendencies represented by Seneca in his "sand without lime," as Caligula had put it. He even wrote on reasons for the decline in oratory, a work which has not been preserved, but was no doubt known to lawyers and others who came from the Basilica Ulpia into the adjoining library.

A very different prose writer, read for information or consulted by specialists, was Frontinus, a contemporary of Quintilian, distinguished in the public service, governor of Britain, and three times consul. Nerva put him in charge of the aqueducts of Rome, and his principal surviving work is on that subject—a straightforward, matter-of-fact account of all the aqueducts of the city, with much engineering detail. He wrote on military science also, a work lost to us, supplemented by a book, entitled *Stratagems,* which is extant. Fragments remain of another treatise for land surveyors.

One of the best-known orators of Trajan's time was Pliny the Younger, nephew of the author of the *Natural History,* and adopted by him in his will. Born and brought up by the Lake of Como, Pliny had for his guardian a distinguished man of affairs, Verginius Rufus, eminent also as a general, for his master in rhetoric Quintilian, and he early

won distinction at the bar. His speeches were carefully revised for publication, but only one has survived—the
Panegyric, enlarged and overelaborated from a speech in
honor of Trajan delivered by Pliny as consul. He wrote
trifles in verse and published one book of them—probably
no loss to us. His enduring reputation rests upon his *Letters.*
Nine books of these are addressed to friends and relatives.
Here, as in his orations, he is a conscious imitator of Cicero,
without shaking off Silver Latin habits entirely. Point and
epigram are conspicuous aims, and the offhand, conversa-
tional manner of Cicero in intimate letters is rarely caught
by Pliny. In two well-known letters to Tacitus he describes
as an eyewitness the eruption of Vesuvius and tells of the
death of his uncle in that catastrophe. Other letters deal
with notable cases in the courts, public readings by authors,
ghost stories, anecdotes, his seaside villa and his country-
seat in the upper valley of the Tiber (p. 174), visits to the
country, a few days as a guest at the Emperor's villa on the
coast, the founding of a school, the deaths of notable persons, literary questions, kindness to slaves, and many other
subjects. Though written with an eye to publication, and
hence more artificial than those of Cicero, they hold the
reader's interest and give a very entertaining picture of the
cultivated society in which this kindliest of men moved. A
tenth book of letters contains official correspondence with
Trajan while Pliny was governor of Bithynia and Pontus,
and is a prime source for the history of provincial administration, since the questions raised by Pliny involve petty
details of routine as well as large issues, such as the treatment of the Christians. Trajan's replies (*rescripta*) reveal
the enlightened and conscientious head of a great government. As the series of official letters comes to a sudden end
it is to be inferred that the governor died at his post (probably 113 A.D.) and never saw this library of his friend the

he did not rest content with his history of his own times. Turning back to the death of Augustus he recounted in the so-called *Annals* the reigns of Tiberius and his successors to the fall of Nero in 68 A.D. For us, who cannot visit a Roman library or the bookstalls near the Forum of Nerva, the text of this great work, which no less narrowly escaped total loss, is made up of two large but defective sections separated by a gap of ten years. Our books 1-6 and 11-16 cover little more than half of the original, ending abruptly a year and a half before the death of Nero.

These two historical works followed the general method of the annalists, but with much freedom. In style they show marked differences. Even from the beginning of the *Histories* he has an incisive manner all his own, out of which the still more concentrated style of the *Annals* was developed. The power of a few words aptly chosen and reset with inimitable skill was never more brilliantly demonstrated than by this dramatic poet in prose. The vivid scenes, the caustic epigrams, the searchings of the human heart, no reader can forget, nor easily return to sunlight from those somber colors and heavy shadows. A work on the happier times of Nerva and Trajan was projected long before, but if ever undertaken was cut short by death early in the reign of Hadrian.

For one reader of the austere Tacitus in our public library,[7] it is safe perhaps to reckon ten readers of the journalistic Suetonius. This author of the *Lives of the Caesars* (Julius to Domitian) was a younger friend with whom Pliny corresponded, and later secretary to Hadrian, having access presumably to archives of state. On a lower plane than Tacitus he caters to popular tastes, lavishing petty details such as the people craved, and that in a matter-of-

[7] Every such library was required by the Emperor Tacitus (third century), who claimed kinship, to possess the works of the historian.

fact language regardless of polish. He was a painstaking
biographer, writing lives in considerable numbers. Those
of the *grammatici* and the *rhetores* we have, as well as those
of a few famous authors, such as Terence and Horace, mere
relics of entire series of biographies of poets, historians, and
others. Commentators and editors ran to the libraries to get
information from Suetonius or merely to abridge one of his
lives, as that of Vergil (lost to us). Other works of his, not
preserved, were on manners and customs, dress, and the like.
Some of these books were in Greek, and accordingly to be
found in the Greek section of the library, on the other side
of the court. Two generations later one would have asked
there for the *Thoughts* of Marcus Aurelius (pp. 265 ff.).

Inquirers for a handbook of Roman history may have
been referred to the outline covering 700 years written by
Florus early in the reign of Hadrian. The facts are drawn
mainly from Livy, but the book is in reality a eulogy of
the Roman people. Speeches of Hadrian himself were published and accessible to readers, later perhaps some of his
verses also, not omitting the last of them, his famous lines
to his departing soul, *Animula, vagula, blandula.*

Professional poets' works were there in numbers, including long-drawn tales in verse by men who read them to a
circle of admiring or much-enduring friends. Among these
epic poets was Valerius Flaccus, who under the Flavian
emperors produced an unfinished tale of the *Argo* and her
crew in eight books, based on the work of Apollonius of
Rhodes and under great obligations to Vergil.

Another epic poet whose books seldom perhaps strayed
from orderly piles on their shelves was Silius Italicus, who
after an official career (consul in 68 A.D.) settled down in
his comfortable villas, well stocked with books and statues,
to write the story of the Hannibalic War, with help or
hindrance from the gods and goddesses sidetracked by

Lucan. Owning one of Cicero's villas and Vergil's tomb, he is the type of the rich dilettante, whose uninspired *Punica* in seventeen books has accidentally been preserved.

A far more gifted poet of the same period was Statius, who was born at Naples and wrote under Domitian. He is at his best in occasional poems, due to some occurrence or under some particular impression—a wedding, a visit to a friend at his villa, the sailing of another friend, the death of a relative or a parrot, a tame lion, the birthday of Lucan (to his widow), a tribute to his own father, insomnia. Most of these are in hexameters and not without their attraction for modern readers, in spite of straining after effect and the fear of being direct and natural. In contrast with these *Silvae* in five books are the two epics. The *Thebais* in twelve books, reviving the tale of the Seven against Thebes, is his chief work and, especially in the Middle Ages, found many admirers, including Dante. Equally artificial and lacking in sustained inspiration is his second epic, the *Achilleis*. This was begun on an ambitious scale, but remained at his death a fragment broken off in its second book. Homer's tale was to be supplemented by recounting all the deeds of his chief hero before and after the Trojan expedition.

A poet whose works were best-sellers was Martial, the last of the brilliant series of writers from Spain. Coming from the same region as Quintilian, Martial at about twenty-five reached Rome while Seneca and Lucan were still alive, and then waited fifteen years and more before publishing anything. Many gifted Romans had written epigrams on occasion; Martial was the first to win a name by working this vein to the exclusion of all others. It was for greater poets to sing of lofty themes, for him to ensure for his mere trifles incessant reading. So he tells us in an inscription for a bust of himself in the library of a friend.

Many of the epigrams are exceedingly brief and the prevailing form is the couplet of elegy, while hendecasyllables and other meters also are used. Two books (13 and 14) are made up of appropriate couplets to be sent with gifts at the Saturnalia (p. 188). The preceding books are a mirror of the social life of the capital. You are not reading about Rome, you are *in* Rome, among his friends of every class, from Quintilian and Pliny down to the very lowest levels. What he does not see and describe in daily life at Rome was not there. Always impecunious, he is unabashed in his dependence upon gifts from rich patrons. Ridicule, caricature, and satire abound in these pointed verses, stooping often to please depraved tastes. Yet real poetry now and again comes to the surface, and more rarely deep feeling. To appreciate their popularity at the time we should think of them as circulating singly and repeated from memory among the loungers, fashionable or shabby, in the porticos and the baths, after the manner of limericks today. In 98 A.D. the poet returned to his native Bilbilis, in Spain, and wrote one more book of epigrams. And there after five or six years the master of epigram died, unrivaled in his own day or since.

The last and most powerful poet of the Silver Age was Juvenal, a friend of Martial, but at that time known only as a rhetorician. It was as a middle-aged man, in the time of Trajan, that Juvenal became a satirist. Little is known of his life; but he was born, it seems, at Aquinum in Latium in the time of Nero; and reaching an age of some eighty years he lived on probably into the reign of Antoninus Pius (138-161 A.D.). In subject matter he ranges over all the ways of men and women, with a strong tendency to use a merciless lash. He is not the kindly spectator, including himself in the mass of frail humanity, as did Horace. In the heat of righteous indignation he forged verses of which many became almost household words. All the gross vices, excoriated in direct proportion to their unspeakableness, the miseries of life in a degenerate Rome, the dangers of the streets, fires, the humiliation of the poor retainer, the folly of pedigrees, and the vanity of all human ambitions, the neglect of children's training, the sham and the boredom of literary readings—such are the themes of his sixteen satires. The language, strained and often obscure, is again and again unforgettable. His shadows are blacker than those of Tacitus, his colors very different from those in which social life is pictured in Pliny; and he left no successor in satire, the one original contribution to literary forms made by the Romans.

PROVINCIAL AND LATER LIBRARIES

If it were possible to continue our visits to Roman libraries, widening our range both in space and time, we should first of all seek out those of provincial cities. For municipal libraries founded by private donors were numerous in Italy and the provinces. The best preserved is that of Ephesus, capital of the province of Asia. This also dates from Trajan's time and resembles that in which we have lingered so long at Rome. Its stately rectangular hall facing east had a podium from which rose columns to support a gallery, and behind the colonnade niches containing the bookcases, while others were reached from a gallery (possibly two galleries). Opposite the door was a semicircular niche for a statue of Athena. There were adjoining small rooms for the storage of books. Remains of the façade show that it was adorned with lower and upper columns after the manner of a scene wall in a theater. At Pergamum has been excavated one of the most celebrated libraries of antiquity, in a more ruined state. At Athens Hadrian's library was architecturally imposing, but nothing is known of its internal arrangements. Not far from it the recent excavations in the agora have revealed another library of private foundation in the time of Trajan. At Timgad in Numidia (Thamugadi) we visit a library of the third century (illus., p. 415). This hall was semicircular, with its columns and niches disposed as in the library at Ephesus, except that the gallery was lacking. A forecourt with columns led up to the doorway. Stateliness was thus a feature demanded for a library even in a small city.

At Rome the Thermae of the emperors, as those of Caracalla and Diocletian, added libraries to their varied facilities for recreation. Two halls for this purpose in Caracalla's Baths are in part preserved, a Greek and a Latin library, illustrating the arrangements described above. From the fourth century on, libraries came to be connected with churches, as previously with temples. The roll form by that time had been displaced by the *codex,* the book form familiar to us; and parchment was now the material instead of papyrus (illus., p. 416). A Christian library was built by Pope Damasus (died 384 A.D.) in the Campus Martius. Constantinople had its important collections and Ravenna, even under the Ostrogothic kings and later exarchs, had its libraries. And now, with the sixth century begins the rise of the monastic library, so important in preserving the ancient writings from complete extinction. Influential was the library established in the extreme south of Italy by Cassiodorus, who had held high offices under Theodoric and his successors, but retired to his estates and founded there the monastery of Vivarium, near Scylaceum. There he spent the latter years of a very long life, writing and providing for the enlargement and maintenance of a library in connection with which copying and binding were carried on by the monks. It was the beginning of that enlightened activity for which the order then recently founded by St. Benedict (in 529 A.D.) at Casinum (Monte Cassino) in southern Latium became justly famous.

Christian literature in Latin had had its beginning in the time of Antoninus Pius and Marcus Aurelius, when a defense of the new religion in the form of a charming Ciceronian dialogue, the *Octavius,* was written for the intellectuals by Minucius Felix. He was answering an attack by the noted African orator Fronto, the tutor of Marcus Aurelius, whose bookish correspondence with his teacher has been in part preserved. Fronto and his admirers affected a new and singular style, sprinkled with obsolete words and other vanities. But the prince abandoned rhetoric and all these its frivolous works for Stoic philosophy, and as Emperor wrote his *Meditations* in Greek (p. 303).

The fashionable new style, however, was followed by another African, Apuleius, in the *Metamorphoses,* his long romance, with inserted tales such as the famous story of Cupid and Psyche, and in his other works. Meanwhile Gaius was writing on the Roman law in his direct and lucid style (pp. 312, 314). And in that same Antonine period Gellius in his *Attic Nights* was studying curiosities in language, literature, and customs, discussing them in his own pedantic manner, and preserving many valuable quotations and choice morsels of every kind for the learned.

With the age of Septimius Severus (died 211 A.D.), Caracalla, and Alexander Severus, jurisprudence reached its peak in the able and ample works of Papinian, Ulpian (both of these from Syria), and Paulus. Their terse and simple language contrasted strongly with the artificial perversities of prose writers on other subjects. Another lawyer, but a convert to Christianity and later to a heretical sect, is the fiery Tertullian, an African and author of many theological works in an original style, often strained and obscure. This earliest of the Latin Fathers was followed by

Cyprian, Bishop of Carthage until his death as a martyr in 255 A.D. His writings show a clearer style and are far more readable.

In the middle of this third century fall the crude beginnings of Christian poetry in a careless popular Latin and uncouth verse. Commodian of Gaza employed a new kind of hexameter for uncultivated ears, substituting word accent in large part for the traditional ictus based on quantity, and making use of acrostic in many of his poems.

The age of Diocletian brought Gaul and its rhetorical schools, particularly those of Bordeaux, Autun, and Trier, to the fore. Elaborate orations in praise of emperors were produced, a literature of panegyrics, such as those of Eumenius. These fulsome speeches were matched by a series of biographies of the emperors, known to us in their few survivals as the *Historia Augusta,* written by Spartianus, Capitolinus, and others.

At the end of the third century come two more of the African Fathers. Arnobius was a rhetorician from Numidia who as a recent convert to the new religion made haste to attack the old. His far more influential pupil Lactantius was summoned by Diocletian to teach Latin rhetoric in the eastern capital, Nicomedia, where he was probably converted to Christianity. Lactantius was a fertile writer in a lucid, almost Ciceronian style, so that Jerome calls him "a river of Tullian eloquence." He wrote verse as well as prose, and often quotes the classic writers, especially in his best-known work, the *Divine Institutes* in seven books. As an old man he was tutor to Constantine's son Crispus in Gaul, probably at Trier.

Christian poetry in the age of Constantine was cultivated by a Spaniard, Juvencus, who made a metrical version of the four Gospels in creditable hexameters in imitation of Vergil. The same century promoted a whole literature of grammatical learning and commentary on the classics, so that its libraries must have been well stocked with facilities for literary study. Servius's large commentary on Vergil still remains; that of Donatus is reduced to a fragment, while we have his notes on Terence, also his grammatical works, together with those of Nonius Marcellus, Charisius, and Diomedes.

In poetry there were translations from Greek poets, represented for us by those of Avienus, who made one more version of the astronomical poem of Aratus (p. 281) and translated, also in verse and with the same freedom, two geographical poems: a *Descriptio Orbis* and an *Ora Maritima,* the latter still an important source for the geography of the fourth and third centuries B.C. But the chief poet of the fourth Christian century is Ausonius of Burdigala (Bordeaux), a teacher of oratory, tutor to Gratian and, after his pupil became emperor, a high official. From his numerous poems of many different types we have a complete picture of life and learning in Gaul in that period of transition, when a Christian poet owed all his inspiration to pagan sources. Most appealing to modern readers is his *Mosella,* describing a journey up that river. The official Christian poet of the time was Pope Damasus, who wrote metrical inscriptions for churches, still identified by the calligraphy of the papal stonecutter, not to mention equally uninspired poems on saints and martyrs—all no doubt to be had from his new library near a church of St. Lawrence (p. 264).

Defenders of the old faith were not lacking, such as the orator Symmachus (consul in 391 A.D.), a leading aristocrat whose speeches survive only in a fragmentary state, while his *Letters* imitating the Younger Pliny are extant, as also his official reports as prefect of the city. But his few ideas are shrouded in a mist of empty words. To such a pass had style been reduced by the stylists.

History languished between uncritical biographies of the emperors, of the type written by Lampridius and Vopiscus, and mere outlines compiled from older works, as those by Aurelius Victor and Eutropius. The only real historian we possess from this late period is Ammianus Marcellinus, a Greek soldier from Antioch who wrote in a highly artificial style, not without a singular admixture of popular Latin. Beginning as a continuator of Tacitus, that is, with Nerva, he covered nearly three centuries in thirty-one books, of which the first thirteen, spanning two centuries and a half, have been lost.

An ardent champion of the new religion was Ambrosius (St. Ambrose, died 397 A.D.), the eminent Bishop of Milan, who had previously held high government offices. He was the author of many theological works and of letters, some of these of the length of a pamphlet; also of discourses, including funeral orations for Valentinian II and Theodosius, and hymns. The last are iambic stanzas based upon quantity and rhyming frequently but not with regularity. A more accomplished writer, Hieronymus (St. Jerome, died 420 A.D.), is best known for his famous translations of the Old and New Testaments, undertaken at the suggestion of Pope Damasus and forming the basis of the Vulgate. Born on the borders of Dalmatia and Pannonia, he traveled far and wide, finally settling himself in a cloister at Bethlehem. He published many treatises, sometimes in the form of letters, and wrote numerous real letters, picturing for us cultivated society and elect ladies in Rome under Christian auspices. The chronological tables of Eusebius he translated from the Greek and continued them to his own time— a work of great value for the history of Roman literature, but by no means free from errors.

The greatest of Christian Latin poets belongs to this same period, Prudentius, who was born in eastern Spain and served as judge, governor, and at the court of Theodosius. He wrote lyrics and hexameters for the cultivated and rarely descends to the simple and natural. There are long hymns, very different from those of Ambrose, and tales of the martyrs, theological tractates in verse, attacks upon pagans such as Symmachus. Nevertheless he is a real poet, to be rated among the classics of Christian literature. Another able contemporary poet, himself a convert, was Paulinus, a Gaul from Burdigala, but Bishop of Nola near Naples.

Against these we may balance a master of classic verse in the pagan mode, Claudian, a Greek from Alexandria. Events of the day furnished many of his subjects: the praises of the Emperor Honorius and his general, Stilicho; a victory of the latter over Alaric the Goth; attacks upon personal enemies of Stilicho. Best known now is an incomplete epic *De Raptu Proserpinae,* containing beautiful descriptions and revealing Claudian as a latter-day Vergil. There are also many clever briefer poems. Their gifted author was probably a nominal Christian, though reckoned a pagan by St. Augustine. His statue stood in the Forum of Trajan and we have its inscription.

In the fifth century the great figure in Latin literature, pagan or Christian, is St. Augustine, who was born at an inland town in Numidia, Thagaste, and educated chiefly at Carthage. He was a teacher of rhetoric at both places and later at Rome and Milan. Converted at thirty-three under the influence of St. Ambrose, after a wild youth, he returned to Africa. For thirty-five years he was Bishop of Hippo (Bône), an old Punic seaport in his native Numidia. And there he died in 430 A.D., not long before the besieging Vandals destroyed the city. Of his many works, some of them epoch-making in the history of Christian thought, we may mention only two. In his *Confessions* we have the one great autobiography which has come down to us from antiquity, the self-portrait of a rare soul who had known all the spiritual heights and many of the human depths. More studied in style is his *City of God* in twenty-two books, a monumental work (some 1,200 pages) replying to pagan charges that desertion of the old gods and their temples had laid Rome low, and to many other arguments in favor of the ancient religion; and then building up in the last twelve books an elaborate structure of Christian teaching. Drawing upon rich stores of learning derived from Cicero, Varro, Plato, and many others, and quoting frequently from the classic poets, the greatest in the long line of African champions of the new faith produced this real masterpiece in an imposing Latin, destined to dominate centuries of Christian writers.

At Augustine's suggestion Orosius, a Spanish priest, wrote an ambitious general history from the creation down, with every vain and foolish rhetorical artifice and none of the mastery shown in the *City of God*. In the classical literature there was still an enlightened interest, as is proved by the learned conversations imagined by Macrobius in his *Saturnalia,* a large work of varied content, keeping Vergil in the foreground; also by his very detailed commentary on Cicero's *Dream of Scipio.*

Poetry had its surprising afterglow not only in Claudian, but also in Rutilius Namatianus, whose charming description in elegiac verse of a journey from Rome back to his native Gaul is still pagan, but confident of the high destiny of the *urbs aeterna,* in spite of its sack by Alaric six years before.

Letter writing with the intention to publish survived in distant imitation of Pliny the Younger, but marred by a style even more unnatural than that of Symmachus. Nine books of such letters we have, many of them of uncommon interest, likewise versified eulogies and other poems by the same hand, that of a cultivated Bishop of Arverni (Clermont-Ferrand), Apollinaris Sidonius, who survived by a few years the last of the western emperors (p. 75). Grammarians too had not disappeared, witness the much-used work of Priscian, from Mauretania, writing at Constantinople early in the sixth century.

We have reached the age of Theodoric, the Ostrogothic king of Italy, whose ministers Boethius and Cassiodorus exercised a great influence in letters, the former a philosopher and scientist and author of the celebrated *Consolation of Philosophy,* partly prose, partly verse, written in prison. Cassiodorus's writings and his labors for the preservation of the classical heritage have been already mentioned (p. 264).

Not exactly literature, but of immense importance and bulking large in all the libraries were the legal works compiled and published at Constantinople by authority of Justinian and in modern times collectively known as the *Corpus Iuris Civilis.* Out of the great mass of works of the jurists, such as Gaius, Ulpian, Paulus, and the rest, belonging to the best period of the Roman law, from Marcus Aurelius to Alexander Severus, and from earlier writers were culled thousands of extracts to be edited and systematically arranged in the *Digest* in fifty books (p. 314). What we should call statute law was assembled in the *Codex,* a collection of all the laws still in force, including many that were due to Justinian himself. There is also a manual for students, the *Institutes,* based upon a work of Gaius. After the completion of the *Corpus* in 534 A.D. a collection of later laws by the same emperor was made and published after his death in 565 as the *Novellae.* In this new legislation Latin has been almost entirely displaced by Greek.

Returning from Constantinople to the West, it remains for us to recall the services to learning of Isidore, Bishop of Hispalis (Seville) in the seventh century. His chief work, his *Origines* (also called *Etymologiae*) in twenty books, is a veritable storehouse, stocked from older sources such as Varro, Suetonius, and the Elder Pliny. The name itself compels us to look backward to those very different *Origines* of Cato the Censor, thus retracing nearly eight centuries in the history of Latin prose. Spain alone could have produced such an encyclopedic work in the days of St. Isidore, the very last writer who could still claim to be a belated Roman.

X

KNOWLEDGE AND THOUGHT

SCILICET ARMA MAGIS QVAM SIDERA, ROMVLE, NORAS,
CVRAQVE FINITIMOS VINCERE MAIOR ERAT.

OVID, FASTI, 1, 29

NOSTRI OMNIVM VTILITATIVM ET VIRTVTVM RAPACISSIMI.

PLINY, NATURAL HISTORY, 25, 4

VENIET TEMPVS QVO POSTERI NOSTRI TAM APERTA NOS NESCISSE MIRENTVR.
. . . RERVM NATVRA SACRA SVA NON SEMEL TRADIT. INITIATOS NOS CREDI-
MVS; IN VESTIBVLO EIVS HAEREMVS. . . . ALIVD HAEC AETAS, ALIVD QVAE
POST NOS SVBIBIT DISPICIET.

SENECA, NATURAL QUESTIONS, 7, 25, 5; 30, 6

QVANTVM ENIM GRAECI PRAECEPTIS VALENT, TANTVM ROMANI, QVOD EST
MAIVS, EXEMPLIS.

QUINTILIAN, 12, 2, 30

IN OMNIBVS QVIDEM, MAXIME TAMEN IN IVRE AEQVITAS SPECTANDA EST.

PAULUS, DIGEST, 50, 17, 90

SCIENCE to the Roman mind was a field in which the whole duty of discovery had fallen to the Greeks, whose results needed only to be mastered and turned to account by their successors. *Illis haec invenienda fuerunt, nobis cognoscenda sunt,* as Quintilian phrases it. If such was the attitude of the Spanish master of oratory as he penned his last pages, nearly a hundred years after Christ, Romans of the third and second centuries B.C., in the early period of Hellenization and long after, must have been overpowered by the intellectual superiority of the Greeks in all that concerned mathematics and the other sciences. The cultivated Roman could only wonder at the universal respect and admiration bestowed in Greek cities upon those who had carried geometry to its heights. He could but admit with Cicero that his countrymen had merely the applications, mensuration and surveying. In every department of science we are struck with the amateur spirit in which men approached these subjects at Rome. The few Greek intellectuals who were really admitted to the inner circles of Roman society, as Panaetius to the coterie of the Younger Scipio, created no such enthusiasm for pure science or the higher levels of philosophy as to lead young men over the bounds of a merely dilettante interest.

An excellent example from that period is Sulpicius Gallus, who showed extraordinary knowledge of astronomy by calculating eclipses, to the amazement of his friends. Not that he claimed original discovery, or as a Roman gentleman could conceivably have devoted himself singly to astronomical research. He was only applying intelligently what had been learned from Greeks of the century of Hipparchus.

For pure mathematics the gift was lacking to the limited Roman imagination. Nor could these studies appeal to those who supposed that the ultimate limits would soon be reached, and felt no real call to join in the quest of truth. Even the example of Archimedes of Syracuse, who was equally great in theory and in its practical application to ingenious inventions, failed to inspire any contemporary Roman, so far as we know, to imitate him.

To be sure the application of physical principles to catapults and other engines of war, to pulley, crane, lever, pump, water clock, sundial, etc., had been so completely anticipated in the Hellenistic age that there probably seemed little left to be done by Roman inventors. There were of course gradual improvements in the military and engineering field, as in building construction, but few of these were distinctively Roman inventions. And under the Empire there was a decline in invention, so that even the stimulus of the barbarian invasions failed to bring marked advances in means of attack or defense. No Italian or Gallic Archimedes arose to make the frontiers secure, or at least delay the irruption.

Nevertheless some Romans had made themselves at home in mechanics, as in optics, and we may see from Vitruvius that their range of knowledge in these branches was not inconsiderable. But deeper research in physics did not exist. Chemistry was limited to practical uses connected with metals, distillation, dyeing, and medicines.

Botany and zoölogy had been extensively cultivated by Greek specialists, but here again we find the Roman an amateur and a country gentleman. The habits of plants and animals were observed and recorded mainly with reference to agriculture and breeding. Minute observations over considerable periods in a scientific spirit must have been of rare occurrence. Hunting was indeed a national sport, and yet it yielded small results for natural history. A keen observer was Lucretius, but rather as poet and teacher of men, seeking everywhere for the most convincing illustrations, than as an original investigator. Yet in scientific imagination he has no Roman rival.

Unquestionably the scientific type of mind was very rare among the Romans. And the question, "Who was their leading scientist?" is a veritable poser. If an academy of sciences wishes to adorn its new building with the names of the greatest in that domain Greek names at once suggest themselves in numbers. But how is the one blank space for a Roman to be filled? Who could bear comparison with Aristotle, Eratosthenes, Euclid, Hipparchus, or Ptolemy? Certainly not Pliny, unless the influence of his vast compilation through darkened centuries is to weigh far more heavily than personal achievement. Nor shall it be Varro, who better deserves to be classed among the scientific spirits, yet as an encyclopedist rather than a discoverer of truth. Nor is it to be Seneca, in spite of his forward look into ever-expanding knowledge, or the great influence of his *Natural Questions* with their superficial studies of physical nature turned to ethical account. No other candidate appearing eligible, the stone is sure to be assigned to another Greek. So completely is Roman science eclipsed by that of Athens and Alexandria.

Yet no picture of Roman life is complete without some account of its amateur attitude toward these studies, its readiness to avail itself of talented Greek specialists, rather than to develop its own professions, its willingness to consult the foreign astrologer, imperfectly differentiated from the astronomer. And to such a picture must be added more cheering sketches of philosophy and of the one Roman science, jurisprudence. Not that the new contribution was of the highest order in the field of pure thought. Though long a stranger within the gates, philosophy became in time a mentor and for the best of men the only guide through the maze of life, while logic and equity applied to law brought to Latin civilization its most enduring distinction.

ASTRONOMY AND MATHEMATICS

In astronomy the thoughtful must have been dazed by the facility with which the Greeks could offer no less than four or five different solutions—all purely geometrical—of the problem presented by the movements of the heavenly bodies. There was the theory of concentric spheres revolving about the earth as a center. Eudoxus of Cnidus, who died about 355 B.C., assumed no less than twenty-seven such spheres, of which three accounted geometrically for the movements of the sun, three for those of the moon, four each for the five planets, and one for the fixed stars. This theory was accepted with modifications by Aristotle and his school, and it still lives a ghostly existence in the phrase "the music of the spheres."

Another system, that of Heraclides Ponticus, a pupil of Plato, made Venus and Mercury revolve about the sun, while the sun and the rest of the planets revolve, he maintained, about the earth, rotating on its axis. Others assumed that each of the five planets had the type of motion accepted by Heraclides for the nearest only, moving, that is, along the circumference of its own circle, whose center was in motion along the circumference of a larger circle, the center of which in the case of Mercury and Venus was at the center of the earth. This complete system of epicycles (circles upon circles) was developed by Apollonius of Perge in Pamphylia, the famous mathematician and father of conic sections, and was adopted by Pliny and Ptolemy.

For the superior planets, Mars, Jupiter, and Saturn, there was also a theory of eccentric circles, each revolving about a point other than its center and carrying with it one of these planets, the point of revolution in each case being on a line between the earth and the sun. This also was proposed by Apollonius.

Finally there was the theory which placed the sun in the center and made all the planets and the earth revolve about it, the earth turning on its axis as well. This heliocentric system was announced by Aristarchus of Samos (ca. 310-230 B.C.), but, strange to say, was adopted by only one other ancient astronomer, Seleucus, about 150 B.C., and for its revival had to wait for Copernicus in 1543.

Each of these was an ingenious, purely geometrical solution, unsupported by evidence from physics. In fact physics in the ancient world always remained in so backward a state compared with mathematics that no conclusion could be reached as to which of these theoretical systems corresponded most closely with physical facts. Meantime the Greek astronomers and the few Romans who tried to follow them into the rare atmosphere of astronomical speculation had to rest content with their individual choice among the rival theories which ingeniously illustrated what was in each case geometrically conceivable but which offered no suggestion of a physical cause. The least probable explanation, as it was thought, that of Aristarchus, in which no Roman seems to have taken the least interest, was proved after eighteen centuries to be correct.

It is in an extant book of Archimedes that we first hear of the sun-centered theory of Aristarchus, and as Archimedes invented the first known machine to show the motions of the heavenly bodies we might be tempted to conjecture that his remarkable mechanism, of which we have no detailed account, may have been so constructed as to illustrate the hypothesis of Aristarchus, the earth also revolving about the sun, as in a modern orrery. For confirmation or refutation of such a conjecture we look to Cicero, since he had a personal interest in the Sicilian scientist, whose forgotten tomb he had himself rediscovered and whose celestial globe and the mechanism just mentioned he describes. This *sphaera* was preserved in a temple just outside the Porta Capena, and could have been visited at any time. He speaks of its operation—how it reproduced the various motions and even simulated eclipses. Yet he omits to state whether earth or sun occupied the central position. However, if all the planets and the earth revolved about the sun it is not easily conceivable that Cicero should fail to mention the fact that the machine illustrated a theory which no one at that time accepted.[1]

If the Romans had little interest in astronomical theory they at least gave the science a place among the liberal arts. Thus Varro in his lost encyclopedic treatise on nine such *artes liberales* [2] assigned one book (*liber*) to *astrologia, i.e.,* astronomy. And in the same spirit Pliny in the second book of his much more extensive *Natural History* described the structure of the universe. But it is a mere outline of a nonprofessional character. Seneca too remained an amateur, employing others to gather material for him and interpreting the heavens from the standpoint of the preacher. A smattering of astronomy was required for the construction of sundials, as set forth in Vitruvius, or for the study of

[1] We know that Archimedes wrote a book on the construction of such *sphaerae,* and there is no reason to think that he mentioned any other possibility than that the earth should be in the center. Posidonius (p. 284) also devised a machine for the same purpose, but how it differed from that of Archimedes is not known. Later on we hear of others, of which some, if not all, were driven by water power. Claudian, the fifth-century poet, describes a *sphaera* which had one globe of glass. It is supposed by modern authorities that the system selected was the first of those mentioned, that of the Eudoxian concentric spheres, and the mechanism must have been highly complicated (p. 278).

[2] The traditional list of seven was made by dropping the last two, medicine and architecture, from Varro's list.

chronology and the calendar, as in Censorinus (third century). The confusion into which the calendar had fallen under the Republic is one more evidence of the Roman lack of interest in astronomy. For Julius Caesar's much-needed reform a Greek astronomer, Sosigenes, was summoned from Alexandria.

A certain knowledge of the constellations was fairly general—far more so than at present. The farmer, so long as the disordered calendar gave no reliable clue to the seasons, had to depend upon the risings and settings of certain constellations as his guide for planting and other duties. And the mariner, who lacked a compass as well as a nautical almanac, was even more dependent upon his acquaintance with the stars. In literature the lore of the constellations was much in evidence. A Greek poem on this subject was translated first by Cicero, then by Germanicus Caesar, and again in the fourth century by Avienus. The original by Aratus (ca. 270 B.C.) was based on the books and the celestial globe of Eudoxus.

Astronomy was very generally confused with astrology, all the more that the term *astrologia* was applied to both. The latter was an eastern "science" practised by *Chaldaei,* also called *mathematici,* which in Cicero's day had meant mathematicians. They pretended to know the "influence" each planet exerted upon the lives and fortunes of men, as determined by the precise hour of birth. Each of the twenty-four hours was assigned by them to one of the seven planets, sun and moon being reckoned as planets. Their list in the inverse order of distance was: Saturn, Jupiter, Mars, sun, Venus, Mercury, moon. If the first hour of a given day fell to Saturn that planet would again exert its "influence" over the eighth, fifteenth, and twenty-second hours, while Jupiter in his turn would claim the twenty-third hour and Mars the twenty-fourth. The first hour of the next day would be under the "influence" of the sun, its last hour under that of Mercury. The next day, beginning with the moon, would end with Jupiter. Thus when the seven days acquired names, each from the heavenly body supposed to preside over its first hour, the familiar list of the days of the week came into existence: the day of Saturn, of the sun, of the moon, of Mars, of Mercury, of Jupiter, of Venus.[3] This purely astrological week was known at Rome by the time of Augustus, but for centuries it showed no signs of displacing the Roman week of eight days, the *nundinum,* in which each day was given merely a letter, A, B, C, etc., in a calendar (p. 114).

But astrologers ranged beyond their seven planets, and professed to detect "influences" of stars at the moment of their rising or in some other position; also of constellations, especially those of the zodiac. That our personal destinies are to be read in the heavens was so commonly believed that it occasioned no surprise if a poet, such as Manilius in the time of Tiberius, wrote a versified treatise on astrology. Though repeatedly forbidden both under the Republic and during the Empire the art was practised in the face of exile and executions. Elaborate works on the subject kept appearing, as that of Firmicus Maternus in the fourth century. For some emperors privately consulted the masters of what posed surreptitiously as a science; and Severus Alexander even established a professorship of astrology.

Pure mathematics was so far from being a favorite study with the Romans that we hear with surprise of an uncle of Pompey, a Sextus Pompeius, who devoted himself to geometry, but evidently as an amateur, like Gallus in astronomy (p. 275), and with an eye to practical applications.

[3] It did not mean that *solis dies* was sacred to the sun, *lunae dies* to the moon, and so on, for there was no religious significance in the names.

As for arithmetic, we hear of no real advances. Everyday experience naturally developed the skill required for operations recurring in trade and affairs generally, in reckoning interest, in determining shares, as when the settlement of an estate involved complicated fractions, or in computing the profits or losses of partners. The inconvenience caused by the Roman numerals (cumbrous except in addition and subtraction), and the consequent all but universal use of the abacus, have been already mentioned (p. 210). Specimens of calculations remain for us in Vitruvius and in Frontinus's work on the aqueducts, as also in books of the surveyors (*agrimensores*). On the educational side were such books as that of Varro, who treated both of arithmetic and geometry in his work on the nine liberal arts (p. 280) ; and Quintilian's educational plan for the future orator stressed the need of timely schooling in mathematics, to avert humiliating errors arithmetical and geometrical when he came to argue cases before a court. He is confident too that these studies train the reasoning powers. On the other hand Varro's interest was not limited to the pedagogical side, for he wrote some other mathematical books of which we know little.

It was for the Greeks to carry on more serious mathematical studies. Such Romans as really pursued the subject did so with the help of Greek teachers and Greek books. This in fact was the general situation for all branches of advanced study except the law. Even Euclid's *Elements,* a much-used book, appears never to have been translated into Latin until the sixth century (by Boethius).

GEOGRAPHY

Geography, at first purely descriptive even for the Greeks, had become largely mathematical at Alexandria in the effort to make latitude and longitude prime requisites. In general the Hellenistic geographers aimed to treat scientifically a subject which had suffered much from travelers' tales, such as those of Pytheas of Massilia, an adventurous contemporary of Alexander. It was the aim of Eratosthenes, the first great geographer (ca. 276-194 B.C. at Alexandria), to raise his subject to the rank of a science. Yet the historians could not willingly relinquish what had long been a part of their province. Alexander's eastern expedition had enormously enlarged the horizon of geographical knowledge. And other wars often brought new peoples and strange lands to the fore, so that without a suitable digression on such land and people the reader of a history would lose much of his interest in the narrative. Polybius in his Roman history had continued the tradition which linked descriptive geography with the historian's art. He had traveled widely and did some actual exploration of the north and northwest coast of Africa with a fleet furnished by his friend Scipio the Younger for the purpose (146 B.C.). He gave up one whole book (the lost thirty-fourth) to the geography of the Roman world. A generation later Posidonius, philosopher and traveler, combined the mathematical with the descriptive element, the physical with the ethnological in a work much read at Rome.

Geography appealed to the Romans more than almost any other science, but on the practical side exclusively. Cicero planned to write a work on the subject, but was discouraged by the formidable mathematics in a Greek work in which he was reading up. The absence of any thoroughgoing Roman geographer is a notable fact. And hardly known among them until the third century was the great work of Strabo, a Greek from Pontus, who is our chief source for ancient geography. A historian as well, he had traveled extensively except in the West, and wrote for the general reader, avoiding the mathematical and the scien-

tific, but including an immense store of information as vari-
egated as the map itself. This voluminous work in seventeen
books appeared in his old age under Tiberius. By comparison the small Latin manual of Pomponius Mela (p. 248)
in the time of Claudius is meager indeed, yet the best that
has come down to us in Latin. From Vespasian's time we
have the four geographical books (3-6), a dry abstract
crowded with names, in Pliny's *Natural History*.

Julius Caesar planned to find the sources of the Nile, and
Nero revived the project, but serious exploration hardly
existed in Roman times except in connection with military
operations, in spite of the improved facilities for travel and
the increasing need of information in regard to lands beyond the frontiers. Pompey reached the Caucasus, and
Caesar opened the way into regions beyond the Rhine and
across the Channel. Drusus pushed on to the Cimbric Peninsula (Denmark). Suetonius Paulinus first led an army
over the Atlas Mountains. Corbulo penetrated the wilds of
Armenia. The memoirs of such generals became an important source for historian and geographer, exploration being
a by-product of distant campaigning. Provincial governors
by their expeditions into little known regions added to the
general stock of information. Balbus, governor of Africa,
reached the Sahara; Petronius, prefect of Egypt, about the
same time (under Augustus) advanced up the Nile far beyond the limits of his province. Merchants wandered into
many a *terra incognita,* but their information, even where
they were not deliberately misled by the natives, was of
limited value. Caesar could trust few of the statements made
by such traders when he was about to invade Britain. The
report that it was an island was not confirmed by circumnavigation until Domitian's reign and the governorship of
Agricola. The tale of a midnight sun in the north of Cale-
donia could be credibly retold by his sober biographer

Tacitus. Had not Caesar repeated without protest the fiction of earlier writers that islands north of Britain had in winter a night lasting thirty days?

Books of travel were written, yet hardly in the modern sense. A monograph on Egypt by the Younger Seneca, who spent some time in that country, might suggest to us a traveler's impressions. But he wrote also a similar work on India with which he had no personal acquaintance. And if Tacitus ever visited German territory no positive evidence of such contacts remains in his famous pamphlet. Intimate and detailed accounts of travel were probably confined to letters. There was no Marco Polo to inspire adventurous spirits, nor were there mariners bold to do what Hanno had done for Carthage as early as 500 B.C. as a pathfinder for Phoenician colonies toward the West, or to rival the Greek Eudoxus (not the astronomer), who in the second century B.C. made voyages to India and attempted to circumnavigate Africa.

The spherical form of the earth was fully accepted by the science of the first century B.C., and it was understood that the inhabited part of the world, the *orbis terrarum,* occupied something like half of the temperate zone in the northern hemisphere. From the farthest shores of India to Gibraltar the distance was estimated at from 8,500 to 10,000 Roman miles. Posidonius thought that if one sailed westward from Spain one would reach India in a direct voyage of about the same distance. And the same idea of reaching India by sailing west meets us again in Seneca, with the distance reduced to a short voyage—a text not overlooked in the great age of discovery. Another theory posited four *orbes terrarum,* of which three were unknown and judged to be inaccessible, the antipodes being placed in the southern half of a western hemisphere. Some who held to the spherical form argued that there were no habitable lands beyond the ocean, or that, if such existed, they could never be reached.

Artists represented the earth in the form of a globe, as, for example, on a coin of Pompey. But to the popular mind it was neither spherical nor flat, but like a round shield, convex but flattened out near the edges. It was possibly a reaction against what they could not quite accept as fully demonstrated which led even cultivated men such as Plutarch and Tacitus to adopt the popular view, the former ridiculing sphericity and antipodes, while the latter gravely accounts for a midnight sun as appearing along the rim of the world.

A map of the known world, it was admitted by the geographers, should not be flat, but laid out on a part of the surface of a large sphere. Such a globe (the only one of which we seem to have positive mention) had been made, probably at Pergamum, by the Stoic Crates of Mallos in the second century B.C. Strabo recommends that the globe have a diameter of ten feet. But an ordinary map of the world was drawn on a plane surface, and probably showed the known orbis terrarum as roughly elliptical and about twice as long from east to west as its breadth from north to south.

The best known map of the world as the Romans knew it was that of Agrippa on a wall of his Porticus Vipsania in the Campus Martius (p. 382). Its shape, however, is uncertain, as no description has survived. Based in part on official information gathered by Agrippa, it was not limited to the Roman Empire. There, in a place much frequented, it remained one of the sights for visitors from every quarter. In a temple of Tellus, Mother Earth, a proper patroness for geography, there was a painted map of Italy, and perhaps others of provinces. From the time of Septimius Severus one could study a large map of the city engraved on a marble wall in the Forum of Vespasian (p. 385), and many of its fragments still remain.

In Propertius a wife, desolate while her husband serves in the East, pores over a map and reads about the customs of the Parthians. For schools we must assume the use of maps in various forms, though our positive information is late and carries us away to Gaul and Augustodunum (Autun), where the school map mentioned was in a portico (end of the third century; p. 217). In private possession a common form must have been that painted on parchment, such as the map of the *orbis terrae* of which we read in Suetonius's life of Domitian.

For the convenience of travelers the map-makers devised what must be called a diagram rather than a map, showing the *orbis terrarum* flattened out into a narrow belt many times longer from east to west than its breadth. Rolled up on a short rod it required little space, though it might attempt to cover the known world, with all the most important roads marked. One such colored map is known to us in a medieval copy (twelfth to thirteenth century), the celebrated Tabula Peutingeriana in Vienna.[4] In this the Mediterranean, Adriatic, Black Sea, and Red Sea appear as very long and narrow lakes, Italy as a horizontal strip much elongated. The aim was to indicate not the relative position of cities but the roads and distances, even in India and China. It was in effect a graphic itinerary, and we must imagine similar guides for travelers' use restricted to single provinces or groups of provinces, with a larger scale and less violent distortion. Such were probably some of the maps carried, together with simple itineraries, by generals on campaign.[5]

[4] At the left or west end of this parchment roll (over 22 feet long and 13.4 inches wide) one sheet is missing, so that most of Britain and all of Spain are lacking.

[5] For the extant itineraries cp. pp. 101 f.

A condensed guide to be read of all passers-by was some-times set up in a public place in the form of an inscribed itinerary with distances. Such in effect was the Golden Milestone of Augustus in the Roman Forum. One inscrip-tion of this class, on the road from Capua to the Straits of Sicily, goes back to 132 B.C. At distant Gades (Cadiz) there was probably a monument bearing the complete list of sta-tions and distances to Rome, over 1,800 miles away. This seems to have been imitated in the silver cups already de-scribed (p. 101). Similar pillars are perhaps to be assumed for other remote termini.

In the second century A.D. we hear of maps of the world made by Marinus of Tyre, whose work was revised by a younger contemporary, Claudius Ptolemaeus, a Greek of Alexandria. Ptolemy's *Geography* aimed at rigorous scien-tific method founded on longitudes and latitudes, but seri-ous distortions appear in maps based on his figures. A large part of the text consists of little more than names, some 8,000 in all. Yet since it was accepted as a definitive work it has exercised an immense influence, especially in the Latin and Arabic translations, even down to the fifteenth century, and is still of great historical value.

No Roman was inspired to carry on the work, and in geography, as in astronomy and medicine, the culmination of ancient knowledge came in the age of Antoninus and Marcus Aurelius. A Pausanias in the same period could describe Greece, its sacred places, temples, and works of art for intelligent tourists. But no Baedeker in Latin is known. It was for the historians to keep up the tradition of geographical excursuses, for the poets to describe scenes of their travels or to translate from the Greek. Thus for a his-torian we may cite Ammianus in the fourth century, and his mention of the Wall of China; and among the late poets Avienus, or Ausonius in his *Mosella,* or Rutilius Namatianus, narrating his homeward journey into Gaul in the fifth century (pp. 267, 270).

MEDICINE

Medicine at Rome down to the Second Punic War meant household remedies, often combined with charms and other superstitious practices in the entire absence of physicians. The way for the coming of the Greek physician was indeed paved by the introduction in 291 B.C. of the cult of Aesculapius, the god of healing, on the island in the Tiber. The first doctor, however, reached Rome from the Peloponnesus in the year 219 B.C. This Archagathus was made a citizen and an office for his use was provided at the public expense. Much appreciated at first for his treatment of wounds, he soon acquired a bad name by unsparing use of the knife and cautery. Prejudice against foreigners who came to Rome in that period to practise medicine still speaks for us in an amusingly violent fragment from the writings of the Elder Cato, who scented a clever conspiracy of the Greeks to destroy all barbarians by their medicine. Rome had survived, as Pliny remarks with some exaggeration, more than six centuries without doctors, but not without medicines.

For the kind of remedies employed we have only to turn to Cato's book *On Agriculture* (pp. 66, 230). There are assorted prescriptions, cabbage being a favorite ingredient; also such abracadabra as *huat hauat huat ista pista sista dannabo dannaustra,* repetition of which was commended as helpful in reducing a dislocation. Much of this no doubt represents old tradition, to be esteemed above the imported wisdom of those despised Greeks. Lost to us is a whole book of remedies with the help of which Cato ventured to practise upon his own household—a book of which Pliny made some use when writing on medicine.

Greek physicians had come to stay. Prominent among

them was Asclepiades, who came from Bithynia early in the first century B.C. as a teacher of rhetoric. But, though a friend of Crassus the orator, he turned to medicine as more profitable. His eminence is shown by an invitation, which he declined, to become court physician to Mithridates. In spite of some charlatanism he wrote important medical works, being apparently the first to distinguish acute from chronic diseases.

Physicians at Rome were generally Greek freedmen, especially from Asia Minor. Slaves who had had the necessary Greek training were often maintained as physicians in large households. Cicero was much attached to such a slave, Alexio. From these associations with foreigners, freedmen, and slaves medicine was considered no profession for a Roman of social standing, and in this respect the *medicus* was commonly rated no higher than the architect or the teacher. Nor did the scientific and humanitarian aspects of the profession prove attractive to Romans of ability. Not one holds a real place in the history of medicine.

Julius Caesar encouraged the practice of medicine by giving Roman citizenship to Greek doctors at Rome. Augustus treated them with similar favor. His own physician, Antonius Musa, a freedman, was richly rewarded for success in treating a critical illness. He was made a knight and his statue was placed on the island in the Tiber, the nearest approach that Rome had to a medical center. Of the physicians with Roman names the majority were doubtless of Greek origin, having taken the name of a patron, or having assumed a Roman name on becoming citizens. Their social position improved under the Empire. Women were permitted to practise, but are rarely mentioned. There were specialists, in particular surgeons (*chirurgi*) and oculists (*ocularii medici*).

The physician usually compounded his own prescriptions, purchasing the needed ingredients from a dealer, the *pharmacopola,* who was not a pharmacist. In this as in other matters the physician had the assistance of pupils and apprentices, for medical education was thus received rather than in schools. Often he had what might be termed a nursing home or small hospital (*valetudinarium*) under his own roof. On large estates there was such an establishment for the slaves. Most of our knowledge of Roman hospitals comes from legionary stations in the provinces under the Empire. The development of hospitals for the public did not come until Christian times, near the end of the fourth century.

With the army were surgeons, adequate instruments, and a well-regulated medical service (p. 464). Municipalities also had in the time of the Empire their appointed physicians, exempted from taxation up to the number of ten for the largest cities, five for a small city—an exemption parallel to that allowed to a smaller number of teachers. There were public physicians for the gladiators. Rome itself had from the year 370 A.D. one head physician for each of the fourteen regions.

Medical books were written almost exclusively in Greek, the professional language. The limited demand for works on medicine in Latin was satisfied by books which could not be called technical. They were designed for the general reader, and proved useful for students in a different field requiring only a résumé of the subject, for example, the prospective architect, who is advised by Vitruvius to include medicine among his preparatory studies. In this spirit Varro, who was no more a physician than he was architect or astronomer or rhetorician, shaped his liberal arts so as to embrace a cursory treatment of medicine (p. 280). Augustus's physician, Antonius Musa, wrote in Greek on medicine, a work lost to us, but frequently mentioned by Galen.

From the time of Tiberius we have in Latin the important work of Celsus. Without claiming an expert's knowledge he employed much sound sense and no small talent as a writer of excellent Augustan Latin in producing a medical work based on the best Greek authorities. He too, like Varro and Pliny, is to be rated with the encyclopedists, rather than with the professionals, since he wrote similar works (not extant) on agriculture, rhetoric, and the military art. In his very readable treatment of medicine in eight books it is significant that he mentions only one physician who even bore a Roman name, Cassius. A little later Scribonius Largus, a physician probably from Sicily, who went to Britain with the Emperor Claudius in 43 A.D., compiled an extant book of prescriptions, 271 in number. Incidentally he finds that the famous Hippocratic oath, to which all doctors subscribed, forbids the giving of an injurious drug even to national enemies.

Fashionable physicians earned large incomes, especially those who advertised themselves by some novelty. In Nero's time we hear of Crinas from Massilia, who combined astrology with medicine, leading his patients to understand that the "influence" of the stars at favorable moments would second the beneficial effect of the prescribed diet and medicines. Greek Massilia produced many doctors, among them another fashionable practitioner of Nero's day, Charmis, noted for his cold-water cures and the high fees his renown enabled him to charge.

Pliny the Elder in his *Natural History* approached medicine from the standpoint of *materia medica*.[6] He did not limit himself to plants which yielded drugs, but included also animals and other creatures that contributed in any

[6] A recent predecessor in this field, Dioscorides, a Greek from near Tarsus in Cilicia, had produced in Greek an authoritative work still extant on medical botany, one of our earliest examples of an illustrated book.

way to the resources of the physician. In this way no less than thirteen books are largely devoted to what nature has provided for the fight against disease and pain or for the maintenance of health.

With Galen of Pergamum (129-199 A.D.) ancient medicine reached its culmination. The study of anatomy was still hampered by the infrequency of dissection and the rare use of skeletons. Vivisection was practised on monkeys, no longer on criminals, as had been permitted long before by the Hellenistic kings. Galen was an eclectic, intolerant of those who were the slaves of a particular school. More than half of his life was spent in Rome. His very voluminous writings became standard works and were gradually translated into Latin. They exercised a dominant influence down to very modern times, as did those of his contemporary, Ptolemy, in astronomy and geography. Later medical works in Latin were translations or abridgments—nothing of original value. The end of progress had been reached.

The diseases of animals were not neglected, especially in the army, where veterinary medicine was fostered, and on the large estates. The writers on agriculture of course touched upon the subject. A few special works have survived, among them a single book of Pelagonius, of the fourth century, in which recipes are seasoned with incantations, such as "Once born, once cured," to be said into the right ear of a horse, after which one spits into the ear! Later in the same century came Vegetius Renatus, who wrote on military science also. A man of rank with stables of his own, he finds the horse "an animal born for pleasure." His authorities were only those accessible in Latin, such as Columella (p. 250), Pelagonius, and Chiron, the last evidently the pseudonym of some Greek veterinary who took the name of the centaur who taught Achilles—quite appropriate for one whose works were translated into the Latin of the stables. Vegetius eliminates the vulgar Latin and writes interesting introductions, the only original parts of his four books.

PHILOSOPHY

Philosophy at Rome, like the sciences, produced no commanding figure, to win a place among the original thinkers, to found a new school or remake an old one, to exercise a dominant influence because of substantial contributions. It was not until after the conquest of Macedonia (168 B.C.) that Greek philosophers began to make an impression in Latium. We first hear of them, without mention of particular names, in 161 B.C., when the senate expelled philosophers and teachers of rhetoric. That their teachings were thought to be sophistical and their influence bad, is clear from the experience of the well-known embassy of the three philosophers from Athens in 155 B.C. Officially they were to defend Athens for an act of palpable injustice, but a more unfavorable impression was created by the fact that the three, Carneades, Critolaus, and Diogenes (the Stoic), exhibited a dangerous fluency in debate. Conservatives noted with uneasiness that the younger generation was charmed by their facile eloquence, regardless of the thesis they were defending, and blunt Cato urged that they be sent away at once.

A few years later, however, we find a Greek philosopher domiciled in the house of one of those young men, Scipio Africanus the Younger, and attending him on his travels. This was the Rhodian Panaetius, who both in the intimate circle of Scipio and his friends and beyond it exerted a strong influence toward a less rigid type of Stoicism. With some accommodation to Roman needs this school of thought made its way. Panaetius returned to Athens as head of the Stoic school and trained a Syrian, Posidonius, his most eminent pupil. And Posidonius in turn was eagerly heard by Cicero, Pompey, and many other Romans in lectures at Rhodes and again at Rome.

The rival school of the Epicureans reached Rome with much less éclat, but spread more widely, as its doctrine of pleasure had a popular appeal and could easily be brought down from the high plane on which the founder, Epicurus, had placed it. Among the prominent adherents of this school in Cicero's time were his friend Atticus, Cassius the Caesaricide, a late convert, and Pansa. In general it may be said that from the first century B.C. on most Romans of the upper classes inclined either to the Stoic school or to the Epicurean, neither of which produced a Roman Zeno or an Epicurus. Of the other two leading schools, the New Academy and the Peripatetic, only the former can be said to have been really represented at Rome. It was not until a much later age that Aristotle was destined to have his day in Italy. The Academic doctrines based upon the teachings of Socrates and Plato, but much modified by later heads of the school, such as Arcesilas and Carneades, were preferred by Cicero, who with his fondness for debating both sides of any question was captivated by their method of approaching the truth through the probable, it being conceded that the truth itself is beyond our reach. There could thus be no occasion for dogmatic positiveness nor any narrow-minded claim that one school was self-sufficient. He felt free to adopt important teachings from other schools, notably the Stoic, and is therefore classed as an eclectic; but he found nothing to commend either in the materialistic physics or in the self-centered ethics of the Epicureans. Academic in their philosophical writings were also his friends Varro and Brutus.

With the Epicureans had begun the production of works on philosophy in Latin. In the first century B.C. we hear of three such prose writers, Amafinius, Rabirius, and Catius, the last an Insubrian Gaul from Ticinum (Pavia). These endeavored in simple language to popularize the doctrines of Epicurus, who had himself written much with little attention to style. And the Latin treatises, though unattractive in form, were widely read. Critics, such as Cicero, carped at their lack of finish. It was perhaps in part to rescue the school from reproach as incompetent to express itself that a new defender of that faith arose in Lucretius. Far more important for him, however, was an intense conviction that his school alone could rid men of their superstitious fear of gods and their dread of death. Thus he was led to compose his powerful didactic poem (p. 234). Yet in spite of the poet's apostolic fervor in winning new converts and his canonization of the founder, no one would have accounted him a professional philosopher.

No more is Cicero to be raised from the rank of a highly cultivated and widely read amateur in philosophy to that of a master. A great work he did in bringing the messages of the leading philosophers of Greece to many readers in Italy and the provinces whose command of Greek was too limited to permit independent study of the texts or real profit from half-understood lectures. Commanding a very wide knowledge of Greek thought and able to apply it for the most part from memory without verification, he rapidly produced in temporary retirement from public life a series of works destined to exert an immense influence on later ages (p. 233). This was due to sustained enthusiasm, charms of style, lucid exposition, a general avoidance of the profound, the glamour of a great name, and, for the medieval period, the all but universal ignorance in the West of his Greek sources. A lifelong student with unabated ardor, he has preserved for us much that would otherwise have perished. Hence he holds his own place in the history of philosophy, though neither his age nor ours would dream of numbering him in any strict sense among the philosophers.

The professional remained as before a Greek, often the intimate friend and adviser of a prominent Roman. Thus a Stoic, Diodotus, lived for some years in Cicero's house, and such a practice was not uncommon. Philosophy had become the preferred avocation of intellectuals, not merely as a stimulating study and topic of conversation, but as a guide much needed in trying times. The house-philosopher was in effect a spiritual adviser and a consoler in times of sorrow, to be compared with a domestic chaplain or father confessor in more recent times; with the important difference that he represented no superhuman authority. If a Stoic he was not bound to agree at all points with the founder, Zeno, or any more recent head of that school, but could adopt at discretion views and maxims of any other thinker. Such was the academic freedom of the Greek philosopher in the house, as also of those who established no such personal relation. Augustus had his own philosopher, Areus, highly appreciated by the Empress Livia for his consolation upon the death of her son Drusus by an accident in Germany.

Since a religion of externals had no comfort for the sorrowing and could not furnish even to the most stalwart defenders of old customs the kind of inward strength needed in an age of strain and stress, it was philosophy that nerved men to meet their fate with fortitude. The canonical example for later generations was the Younger Cato, whose Stoicism supported him to the bitter end at Utica (46 B.C.), and whose memory was revered almost as that of a saint by the Stoics. In the very next year there died in political exile an aristocrat of the most varied learning who had endeavored to revive the teachings of Pythagoras, with a strange admixture of mysticism and magic. But at least this Nigi-

(Orvieto) in Etruria. Cornutus was the teacher of the poets Lucan and Persius, and a writer on philosophy in Greek, on grammar and rhetoric in Latin, a commentator on Vergil as well, but was banished by Nero. Musonius, evidently a strong personality, attracted even Greek disciples who attained celebrity, such as Dion of Prusa and Epictetus. It was he who converted Dion from rhetoric to philosophy. For the content of his teachings we are dependent upon his pupils and admirers, for he seems to have written nothing. He too was banished—this in 65 A.D.—to one of the Cyclades. In the lives of these philosophers there was much austerity. Plain fare, self-denial, high ideals marked them out as preachers of a sober way of life. They did not tend toward the mystic, and would not have felt at home in a dimly lighted conventicle like that by the Via Praenestina.

Seneca the Younger, though not their pupil, was strongly influenced at first by the ascetic tendency, until persuaded by his father to spare his health. He too was not destined to become a professional, and yet the range of his works and their lasting influence give him a significant place in any outline of philosophy at Rome. A Stoic, trained by pupils of the independent Sextius, Seneca followed them in their willingness to borrow from other systems, but retained little or nothing of the Pythagorean. His nearest approach to the professional attitude is in the *Consolationes,* where in the rôle almost of a spiritual director he chooses those consoling arguments best suited to the temper and state of mind of the bereaved person; and again in the so-called *Letters* (p. 251). He is untroubled by lack of consistency with standard Stoic teaching, if one can speak of such a standard at Rome. His interest is in human lives and human hearts, and he draws his sage counsels from various sources, often quoting maxims of Epicurus. By that time the reader of books on philosophy had ceased to care for well-ordered logical arguments as compared with terse words of wisdom, sage counsel reduced to the form of an epigram or a maxim that could not be forgotten. Seneca meets this demand of the times, if he did not do more than anyone else to create it. He is sententious and many of his pointed utterances became familiar quotations: "God is near you, is with you, is within"; "A sacred spirit abides within us"; "God comes to men, or rather . . . comes into men; no mind without God is good"; "All this that you see . . . is one: we are the members of a great body." Had he chosen to imitate Sextius he might have won a much higher place as a real philosopher. But prominence at the court, as tutor and then minister of Nero, kept him a man of the world. Single-minded quest of truth was not for him amid such surroundings and hampered by the fatal gift of an excessively pointed style. And yet those very utterances, with all their artifice, have brought help and comfort to many of his readers.

The Stoics of Seneca's generation and for some time after were strongly opposed to tyranny and by their outspokenness often gave offense to the authorities as forming a nucleus of opposition. This attitude was hereditary in some families, as that of Thrasea Paetus, a prominent victim of Nero. To be addicted to philosophy, especially of that school, was in itself suspect.

The next important product of philosophy at Rome was another Stoic, Epictetus, a disciple of Musonius. Coming from Phrygia as a slave he was emancipated by his master Epaphroditus, himself a freedman and minister of Nero. He taught in Greek a tempered Stoicism until philosophers were banished by Domitian (93 A.D.). Retiring to Epirus he continued his teaching, cheerful in poverty, writing nothing, leaving it to his disciples, Arrian and others, to take down and publish what he had said. Once more it is a rule of life, not a logical system. Practical ethics is everywhere in the foreground, and the Stoic law of life is still to act in conformity with Nature. Not to be deceived by appearances is an important stage in learning the art of living, that essence of philosophy, so much more vital than the hearing of many lectures of the philosophers or the devouring of whole volumes before you can swallow a morsel. The wise man examines and tests the rules of conduct, and then does not fail to apply them. He knows, with Cleanthes, that we are all sprung from God, the father both of men and of gods. He realizes that there is a great community composed of God and men, so that he is at once a citizen of the world and a son of God, afraid of nothing that can happen to men.

Thus Stoicism at Rome continued to produce noble counsels for the guidance of the high-minded. The studied, epigrammatic words penned by Seneca, always aiming to achieve sharpest point and utmost brevity, are followed by simple, direct utterances from the lips of Epictetus, indifferent to form so long as he reached the heart; and finally in the highest place of all we have the musings of Marcus Aurelius in his closet and in his tent. In these three very different collections are preserved to us the life-philosophies of one brilliant mind, the gift of Spain to Rome, and of two of the rarest characters, one an unmatched product of Greek slavery, the other an equally unrivaled product of princely education at Rome, uncontaminated by a court, unspoiled by the possession of a power at first shared with Verus, and then all but unlimited, had it ever occurred to him to use it as such.

At twelve Marcus Aurelius was studying philosophy and imitating his teachers of the ascetic type who slept on the bare floor, until he was dissuaded by his mother. At twenty-five he did not reckon himself an adept in these studies, but had turned his back upon rhetoric, in spite of affection for his teacher Fronto, perhaps because of Fronto (p. 265). Adopted at seventeen by Antoninus Pius he saw his adoptive father succeed Hadrian in the same year (138 A.D.). Marcus himself became emperor in 161, ruling for eight years with his brother by adoption, Lucius Verus, and then alone, except that for the last three years his son Commodus was his colleague. A great war with Parthia, a pestilence of unheard-of violence, and endless campaigns on the Danube and beyond marked that reign, in which it was a double irony of fate that the philosopher on the throne should be obliged to spend years in fighting off German and Sarmatian tribes, and that the kindest of men should find it his duty to repress the Christians with stern measures, as representing to his mind a rising tide of organized opposition to his government.

Out of such an overburdened life, largely spent on the frontier in the face of dangerous foes, come to us the famous *Meditations* in twelve books, of which the first was written north of Budapest and the second below Vienna, at Carnuntum. That he wrote in Greek, the language of learning, rather than in his mother tongue, should occasion no surprise, though there are good reasons for our vain regret. Yet with all the defects in the text the book remains one of the treasures in the world's literature of the spirit. But better than pages of comment on his quest of moral perfection, his deep devotion to his duty as man and ruler, his submission in all things to a higher will, are a few examples:

According to your usual thoughts will be the character of your mind. For the soul is dyed by the thoughts. Therefore dye it with a series of such thoughts as, "Where it is possible to live, there a good life is possible. But it is possible to live in a palace; therefore a good life is possible in a palace."

. . .

Do not hope for Plato's ideal state; but be content if the smallest thing moves forward, and consider even that result no slight matter.

. . .

What is not good for the hive is not good for the bee.

. . .

To those who ask, "Where have you seen the gods, whence apprehended their existence, that you so worship them?" In the first place they are visible even to the eye; [7] in the second place I have not seen my soul either, and still I reverence it. So then with the gods also, from repeated experience of their power I apprehend their existence and venerate them.

. . .

Simple and modest is the task of philosophy.

. . .

The Pythagoreans bid us look up at the sky at daybreak, that we may be reminded of those who always perform their own task according to the same laws and in the same way, and also of their order and purity and nakedness. For a star has no veil.

. . .

The one fruit of the earthly life is a religious spirit and social acts. In everything be a disciple of Antoninus.

. . .

Short is this time that remains. Live as on a mountain.

. . .

Therefore pass this brief time according to Nature and die contented, as an olive ripens and falls, blessing her who produced it and thanking the tree its parent.

For Marcus the end came at the post of duty, still commanding his armies on the Danube. And as he approached so closely the Christian ethics we may close our brief sketch of philosophy at Rome with Marcus Aurelius. Not that there were no more thinkers of the traditional type. But much of Greek and Roman thought entered into the minds

[7] Since the stars are divine according to the Stoics.

and teachings of the Church Fathers, with whom begins another age. Looking backward one is once more impressed by the fact that if Rome added little or nothing to the content of philosophy, there were Romans who made a memorable contribution by living it and pointing others to a way of life. "Ours are not high-sounding words, but noble lives," [8] said one of the earliest of Christian apologists, Minucius Felix (p. 265). And we may well adapt the words to his contemporary, the philosopher emperor, of whom in every sense of the words we may say *magna vixit*.

THE LAW

The one field of intellectual activity in which the Romans attained a manifest superiority to all other ancient peoples was the study of the law. Many other states had their laws and their codes. None developed so masterly a system of jurisprudence, in which logical reasoning, precise definition, and lucid exposition in the simplest terms were dominant notes. Typical of the direct and unpretending language of this whole branch of learning is its definition by Celsus, a jurist of the time of Trajan and Hadrian, repeated at the very beginning of the *Digest* of Justinian: "Jurisprudence is the study of the good and the just," *Ius est ars boni et aequi*. Another definition, that of Ulpian a century later, makes jurisprudence "the knowledge of things divine and human, the science of the just and the unjust." Such discrimination of the lawful from the unlawful, the equitable from the unjust, was the prime task of the jurist, who was figuratively described as a "priest of justice."

In the early Republic jurists were literally priests, sole guardians of the old customary law, both sacred and secular. Even after the Laws of the Twelve Tables (p. 14) were drawn up and posted, the monopoly of the pontiffs,

[8] *Non eloquimur magna, sed vivimus.*

their esoteric treatment of legal knowledge, remained unchanged except that the text of the laws could be read by
anyone who came to the Rostra. Disputes as to the actual
wording were now at an end. But the exact meaning? The
application to a particular case? The steps to be taken in
bringing a suit? An aggrieved citizen seeking to protect his
rights and recover his loss was in no position to bring or
conduct a lawsuit, or in any way to safeguard his interests
without aid and advice from the pontiffs.

These leaders of the patricians found it becoming to furnish such assistance without tangible compensation. Of such
legal wisdom they retained an almost complete monopoly
for a century and a half longer, keeping control of the
calendar also (p. 114). It was theirs to interpret the laws
and gradually to develop forms of procedure to supplement the meager outlines furnished by the Twelve Tables.
Thus without changes in the letter of the code other forms
of procedure were added from time to time, and the fact
that the pontiffs formed a "college" gave these innovations
a certain sanction almost legal. And precisely as in the Roman religion the exact wording of the ritual was of vital
import, so in these forms, the *legis actiones,* the slightest
variation from the prescribed wording vitiated the entire
action. The law too had its ritual and its superhuman associations. Hence it was natural that priests charged with maintaining sacred usages should at first be the only authorized
interpreters of the secular law as well. In the process of interpreting they virtually expanded the clauses of the old
code by applying given forms to purposes not originally
intended, or by removing some restriction. As a result there
came with changing times to be a body of such interpretations, more or less stereotyped and known collectively as the
Civil Law. In practice this was another source of law, of no
less consequence than the Twelve Tables, which remained

unamended. Necessary adaptations to changed conditions
had been by degrees effected by the labors of the pontiffs
without resort to a vote of approval.

With the time of Appius Claudius, who as censor in 312
B.C. had built the Via Appia and the first of the aqueducts,
we reach a new period in legal progress. A clerk of Claudius, Gnaeus Flavius, no doubt with the approval, if not at
the instigation of the ex-censor, published the series of *legis
actiones,* hitherto closely guarded by the pontiffs. With the
help of this work, the *Ius Civile Flavianum,* a litigant had
no need to consult a pontiff, all the more that the same
Flavius as aedile in 304 B.C. published the calendar also,
setting it up in the Forum, so that all could now know on
what days cases might be heard.

The first plebeian Pontifex maximus, Tiberius Corun-
canius, who had been consul many years before in 280 B.C.,
introduced a new practice, that of admitting auditors when
he was asked to give a legal opinion (*responsum*). The veil
of secrecy being thus removed young men had an opportunity to study the law at the feet of their elders, especially
when discussion or explanation followed the interpretation.
It was the beginning of a legal education no longer esoteric.
A small class of experts was being recruited in this way,
mainly from the old families.

These jurists were not advocates, but specialists consulted
by the practical lawyers, clients, and magistrates. It was the
business of the *iuris peritus* to give an opinion on points of
law when consulted; to furnish the precise wording for
valid legal documents; also less commonly to give desired
advice as to the conduct of a case.[9] He did not give lectures
nor as yet write books in that age of undeveloped prose.

[9] His duties were accordingly summed up in the three words, *respondere,
cavere, agere.* Those who wished to consult him found him at his own house
or in the Forum.

In the second century B.C. began the literature of jurisprudence with Sextus Aelius Paetus Catus, censor in 194, and Cato, censor in 184. The *Tripertita* of the former was accounted the "cradle of the law," containing the Twelve Tables with brief commentary, further developments of the law in the interpretations of the jurists, and the forms of procedure. More extensive and more important than the legal writings of Cato were those of his son Marcus. Other eminent jurists took up the pen, among them Manius Manilius, Publius Mucius Scaevola, who wrote a treatise in ten books, and a Brutus, who used the dialogue form for a work in three books on the Civil Law, an experiment which no one seems ever to have repeated.

Meanwhile the specialists were exerting their influence in another characteristically Roman fashion, that is, in contributing to that original method by which the old laws in many respects no longer applicable without injustice were in effect modified in the direction of equity by the praetor. As we have seen (p. 18) it was the custom of the *praetor urbanus* upon entering office to set up an edict stating his understanding as to what the laws would mean during his administration, offering relief from undue severities, legalizing evasions of the strict letter in some cases, and in general allowing for the changes which three centuries had brought. If the praetor was not a jurist himself he usually consulted those who had the special knowledge required in drafting proposed new clauses of the edict, a large part of which was merely repeated according to custom from that of the previous year.

Among the lumber which the praetors replaced with better things was the whole series of *legis actiones,* the ritualistic forms of procedure which were now considered obsolete, and which with certain exceptions were abolished by a law of uncertain date in the second century B.C., the *lex*

Aebutia. In place of the old method the praetor introduced
a simpler procedure. In a preliminary hearing at which
he was to appoint a judge or judges to try the case he formu-
lated the complaint in a document called a *formula*—an instruction for the guidance of the judge. Such *formulae* for
cases of different kinds were included in the edict, along
with the other innovations or promises of relief, if any,
which the praetor for a particular year announced upon his
inauguration. It was by this means that the inflexibility of
statutory law—the Twelve Tables and subsequent legislation—was made to yield to the demands of equity. Legislation to modernize obsolete provisions became unnecessary
when the same object could be accomplished by a few words
added to the praetor's white-board (*album*) set up near his
tribunal in the Forum. With expert opinion behind him the
praetor was in small danger of going too far, while if he did
do so the mischief could readily be corrected by his successor in the next edict.

In the first century B.C. the activity of the jurists took another direction—that of systematic, methodical treatises on
the law. Another Scaevola, Quintus, the more famous son
of the Publius mentioned above, and a teacher of Cicero,
produced the first orderly treatment of the *ius civile* in
eighteen books. Still more eminent was Servius Sulpicius
in the next generation, a friend and correspondent of
Cicero. The loss of his legal works in some 180 books is the
more to be regretted as we know from his letters with what
a master's hand he wrote. We may well believe Cicero that,
thanks to his logical gift and command of expression, his
legal works, of which only fragments remain, were unmatched. Among these was the first of many commentaries
on the edict of the praetor; for this had already become one
of the most important sources of the law. Servius, who was
well read and an orator, evidently possessed rare talent as

a teacher. His pupils were well known in the Augustan Age and continued the tradition of productivity. Unfortunately of all this literature of jurisprudence during two entire centuries nothing remains to us except fragments, detached citations mainly preserved in the works of later jurists who are quoted in the *Digest* of Justinian.

The prestige of the jurisconsults was increased by Augustus, who gave to the most eminent specialists the privilege of delivering opinions (*responsa*)[10] which the judge was required to accept as binding, if not in conflict with the *responsum* of another jurist. This right, the *ius respondendi,* was conferred by Tiberius also and his successors, without depriving other specialists, not formally privileged, of their right to give *responsa* to those who consulted them.

Under Augustus the leading jurist and most prolific writer on the law was Antistius Labeo, who gave six months every year to his pupils and for the remaining months retired from the city to write his books. Independent in his attitude toward the *princeps* and recent changes in the state, he was himself an innovator in the private law. A single one of his works, which reached a total of 400 books, now known from fragments only, would be of great value to us. Ateius Capito, consul in 5 A.D., was hardly less distinguished in a lifetime which lasted well into the reign of Tiberius (to 22 A.D.). He was a supporter of the new régime, but in law a conservative, less influential in later times than Labeo, in part because the range of his works was much more limited. These eminent jurists were described as the "two ornaments of peace," and from their teachings came the two schools of opinion which flourished for a century and a half —the Sabinians and the Proculians, taking their names from successors of Capito and Labeo respectively. That the rival schools inclined to perpetuate their tendencies is prob-

---

[10] These concerned the law only, not the facts of the particular case.

able, but their differences cannot be shown to rest on basic principles.

In the absence of law schools in our academic sense the rival groups furnished a large part of the legal education of the day, with a strong emphasis upon close reasoning and clear-cut statement. Even the most tyrannical emperors seldom interfered with the development or the practice of private law, in spite of the fact that the leaders in jurisprudence were almost exclusively senators and in their philosophy Stoics, hence inclined to side with the opposition. Through the teachings of this school of philosophers Greek thought continued to exercise a certain influence upon Roman law under the Empire, but chiefly upon other branches than the private law, with which the jurists were chiefly concerned.

The praetor continued to issue his annual edict, and commentaries upon that part of it which remained almost unchanged continued to appear. Yet as the Emperor was himself the highest court of appeal the praetor could no longer exercise independence in proposing changes from year to year. His customary powers to modify and adapt the old, to introduce new interpretations and other innovations, naturally became anomalous. It was inevitable that such power be taken over by the Emperor, the edict sooner or later reduced to a permanent text subject to no further revision. This was done under Hadrian by Salvius Julianus, who was later honored by a consulship, the friendship of Marcus Aurelius, and the government of important provinces, including his native Africa. Whatever changes proved desirable thereafter were made by special order of the Emperor. The praetorian edict, after filling a large place in the historical progress of the Roman law, had now ceased to be a *viva vox*.

Nevertheless the active labors of the jurists were undiminished. The "living voice" was now that of the Civil Law, that is, a body of accumulated interpretations continually renewed and revised by the living members of a very small profession, headed by those licensed by the Emperor to give *responsa* with the virtual effect of law. When the audible voice of the law was that of the Emperor it was seldom without the approval of the same experts. From their pens still came voluminous legal works, such as a commentary in upwards of eighty books on the now codified edict, among the other treatises of Sextus Pomponius, a writer and teacher but not in public life.

With his contemporary Gaius, under Hadrian, Antoninus, and Marcus Aurelius, we reach in the long succession of jurists the first whose works are not reduced to fragments. By a happy discovery made by Niebuhr at Verona in 1816 we have Gaius's handbook for beginners in the law, his *Institutiones* in four books, though the old manuscript of the fifth or sixth century is not without gaps. Here we have law Latin at its best, direct and simple, avoiding all display. Other jurists wrote similar manuals, but that of Gaius was chosen by Justinian's editors as a basis for the *Institutes* prepared for a like purpose by order of that Emperor. Who Gaius himself was, why he has only a *praenomen,* whence he came, where he lived, are much debated questions still very far from solution. He was clearly a teacher, like Pomponius, and wrote many other works during the reigns mentioned above. Among these was one more commentary on the Twelve Tables, one on the praetorian edict, another on the provincial edict, which was a similar declaration issued for a particular province by its governor.

Under Septimius Severus and his immediate successors jurisprudence flourished with a brilliance all the more striking in comparison with every other form of literature or intellectual occupation in the whole period, or with every art except portrait sculpture. The leading masters were Papinian, Ulpian, and Paulus, of whom the first came probably from Syria, the second certainly from Tyre. All three produced important works, all three reached the rank of *praefectus praetorio,* Ulpian and Paulus as colleagues in that office under Alexander Severus.

Papinian's works survive for us only in the many concise and logical citations in the *Digest* of Justinian, and in meager fragments from Egypt. Ulpian and Paulus produced almost a law library of their own, with the apparent aim of rendering the writings of earlier jurisconsults superfluous.[11] From these treatises there are a very large number of quotations in the *Digest,* including passages from their very ample commentaries on the praetorian edict, each in about eighty books. One brief work of Ulpian is extant in an abridged form—his *Rules,* designed for beginners. From Paulus also we have an abridgment of his *Sententiae* in five books, but far the larger part of the work has been lost.

The first third of the third century is called the classic period of Roman jurisprudence, and the last important jurist of that age was Ulpian's pupil Modestinus, whose works were in large part manuals for students and practising lawyers. So high was the respect paid to the legal ability of the jurisconsults of the Severan age, so much more accessible were their writings than the vast mass of the productions of their predecessors, that their opinions dominated the profession ever after. Several of the emperors relieved the embarrassment of judges and magistrates by narrowing the range of their quest for authoritative guidance, a quest made all the more difficult by the perishable nature of papyrus rolls and their inconvenience at best. In the fifth century Theodosius II and Valentinian III issued the Law

[11] Ulpian's works filled about 287 books, those of Paulus about 305.

of Citations, giving the fullest authority to all the writings of Papinian, Paulus, Gaius, Ulpian, and Modestinus, together with such opinions of earlier jurists as any one of these five had quoted.[12]

The editors of the *Digest* of Justinian in fifty books, published in November, 533 A.D., were more considerate of the older jurists (cp. pp. 309 f.). They consulted and abstracted over 1,600 books (*libri*), reaching back as far as Quintus Mucius Scaevola in the beginning of the first century B.C., but rarely quoted works of the Republic or even of the Augustan Age. An outline of the succession of the jurists, extracted from a manual by Pomponius, was inserted near the beginning. Most of the opinions quoted are from the five named above, while fully a third of the entire space is given to quotations from Ulpian. Such freedom, however, was taken by the editors in making verbal alterations that the accuracy of the citations has to be discounted.

In fact, the *Institutiones* of Gaius is the only classic of Roman jurisprudence which has reached us in anything like its original condition, to represent for us many generations of devoted interpreters of the Roman law, most of whom combined with logical powers of a high order the gift of expression in the plainest terms—a trait all the more remarkable since the law had had its beginnings in an atmosphere of mystery. While oratory was submerged in the flood of its own rhetoric, while prose in general was losing contact with the natural, while "constitutions" of the emperors grew more and more stilted, the language of the Civil Law remained terse, clear, and unaffected. From that limpid source no one could dream of tracing the descent of modern legal verbiage.

[12] Thus only Gaius was placed on a par with the Severan masters. All the previous writers on the law were relegated to obscurity except in so far as they were frequently cited by Papinian and the rest.

XI

FINE ARTS

EXCVDENT ALII SPIRANTIA MOLLIVS AERA,
CREDO EQVIDEM, VIVOS DVCENT DE MARMORE VOLTVS.
VERGIL, AENEID, 6, 847

FICTILIBVS CREVERE DEIS HAEC AVREA TEMPLA.
PROPERTIUS, 4, 1, 5

VT PICTVRA POESIS: ERIT QVAE, SI PROPIVS STES,
TE CAPIAT MAGIS, ET QVAEDAM, SI LONGIVS ABSTES;
HAEC AMAT OBSCVRVM, VOLET HAEC SVB LVCE VIDERI,
IVDICIS ARGVTVM QVAE NON FORMIDAT ACVMEN;
HAEC PLACVIT SEMEL, HAEC DECIENS REPETITA PLACEBIT.
HORACE, ARS POETICA, 361

FOR Roman studies all the arts are upon a single plane, and if space permitted we should treat them all as of equal importance to the Roman mind. There was no gulf between the fine arts and handicraft, and if in that leveling process "major" arts suffered in social prestige, at least there were no "minor" skills. Painter, sculptor, architect, chaser of gold and silver or bronze, engraver of gems, worker in mosaic or terra cotta or glass, maker of fine furniture, were all on a par—a low level in popular esteem, in spite of the high respect in which the Greek old masters were held by the more cultivated. If cameo cutting was a trade, so was mural painting. There were to be sure a few Romans of standing who indulged such a plebeian taste, a *sordidum studium,* as a writer of the Empire calls it. But the prejudice against artificers and those who seemed to be no better, the artists, was hard to overcome, since they represented a foreign element; and patriotic pride appeared to demand a measure of contempt for almost everything which came from without, in particular from the Greeks. Art as a profession may be said to have lived in a Subura or a Ghetto, emerging from its un-Latin quarter from time to time, but never quite admitted to respectable citizenship.

Literary men, even of humble origin, were accepted socially, but in that company of patrons of letters, poets and other writers, we look in vain for the artist. With few exceptions he was a person to be employed when his services were required. We cannot discover that he counted with the critics or was thought worthy of the distinction so freely bestowed upon his kind in Greece; nor can we find many personal touches. No extant work of a master writing about his craft remains except that of the architect Vitruvius, nor do we read of painters or sculptors who wrote on sculpture or painting. Education prepared for oratory or philosophy, but gave no training in artistic taste. One could take lessons in painting in one's youth, as did Nero, without entering the ranks of the painters, which would have been a shock to family and friends, almost as if one should appear on the stage as concert performer or as charioteer in the circus— again as Nero did. And the same prejudice helps to explain why the professional musician also was without the social gates and his art never fully domesticated.

Appreciation of art in any form was in large part a luxury of the critical upper class, able to follow its years of schooling at home with further study at Athens or Rhodes and travel in Greece and Asia Minor. But once he had entered public life in the days of the Republic a prudent man kept his interest in art and artists very much to himself, as a Greek taste, not yet seemly for a full-blooded Roman.

The demand for artistic surroundings, however, kept on increasing, and how far that demand had been met by the year 79 A.D. is clearly shown by the treasured wall decorations, sculptures, and other works of art furnished us by a single town, Pompeii, especially if we ask ourselves what would be the artistic yield of one of our towns of 25,000 inhabitants if similarly overwhelmed and preserved for the eyes of remote descendants.

With the Empire and under official patronage the general level of taste had been notably raised. One clear evidence of this change is seen in the lettering of inscriptions. No longer could a triumphing general dedicate artistic spoils with a crudely lettered slab, as did Mummius after deleting Corinth. Inscriptions were now in faultlessly studied capitals, with careful adjustment to fill the given space. Lettering thus ennobled was a peculiarly Roman contribution, exerting a marked influence ever since. Trajan's inscription on the pedestal of his Column continues to this day an undisputed canon for draftsmen (illus., p. 427). A large inscription of Hadrian recently discovered in Britain shows the same mastery of letter forms. One has only to compare modern examples such as that which bears Poliziano's epitaph of Giotto, in the cathedral of Florence, that of Raphael in the Pantheon, or of Erasmus in Bâle, or instances of more recent date, in order to see how general has been the imitation of Roman practice. Not less striking is the obligation of printers' fonts in every country using a Latin alphabet to Roman letters.in their best forms, as still found in inscriptions surviving in every land that once was Roman.

The taste which demanded that inscribed letters should bear the closest criticism in form and finish was not satisfied with carelessly copied books. Many were the handsomely written texts in stately square capitals, such as are shown by some of our oldest parchment manuscripts of the fourth century (illus., p. 416), and a little later in the more flowing rustic capitals, better suited to the reed pen or the brush. Even a more rapidly written papyrus fragment from Herculaneum, containing a few verses from a poem on the Battle of Actium and fairly assumed to represent the average book of the first century of the Empire, shows the hand of a calligrapher. One needs only to *know* one's alphabet in order to refute the familiar charge that the Roman had no taste.

PAINTING

In the last period of the monarchy and during the early years of the Republic paintings at Rome must have differed little from the mural paintings then to be found in the temples and palaces of Etruria, where methods and motives imported from Ionia still prevailed. The character of

the Etruscan painter's art at that time is known to us only
from the frescoed tombs hollowed out of the rock near such
cities as Veii, Caere, Tarquinii, and Clusium. He painted
chiefly animals, real or imaginary; but scenes from Greek
mythology had begun to appear.

Within a generation after the founding of the Republic
Etruscan art entered upon a period of temporary decline
which lasted to about 400 B.C. The favorite themes on the
walls of the tombs were now banquet scenes, dances, spec-
tacles, and sports, such as hunting and fishing. Natural
backgrounds appear—rocks and trees, flowers, the sea; and
the Greek influence grows stronger. From such wall decorations painted in the darkness of tombs we try to reconstruct
in imagination the more finished murals which adorned
temples and palaces in the cities of Etruria, and then we
have to think of that style transferred to Roman shrines and
a few of the statelier houses—not to the tombs, for that was
no Roman custom. At such towns as Ardea and Lanuvium
there were very old paintings, presumably Etruscan, mentioned by Pliny.

As early as 493 B.C. we hear of Greek artists, Gorgasus
and Damophilus, painting the cella walls of the Temple of
Ceres (p. 127) and adorning it with reliefs. Greek artists
continued to arrive, and Etruscan painting, revived and renewed in the fourth century B.C., was itself strongly influenced by the Hellenistic through the third century. By the
end of the fourth century B.C. we hear for the first time of
a native Roman painter, the patrician Fabius, who is said
to have painted the Temple of Salus on the Quirinal. From
about the same date we have part of a fresco from a tomb
on the Esquiline—a rare exception to the general rule—
representing another Fabius in scenes from a war with the
Samnites. But there is no reason to think they were the work
of Fabius Pictor. In the second century B.C. we know that

the tragic poet Pacuvius painted the walls of a temple of Hercules.

By that time panel pictures (*tabulae*) painted on wood in melted wax[1] were being brought in from the Greek cities, or even produced in Rome by imported artists. With the wars in Macedonia and Greece came an influx of valuable paintings of this class, many of them first seen in the triumphal procession of such generals as Aemilius Paulus, to be hung in some temple or handed down in the family of the victor. The sack of Corinth in 146 B.C. added immensely to the treasures of art in Roman hands. If Greek painters at Rome were saddened by such plundering of the home land they at least found work in plenty when a triumph brought a sudden demand for hastily painted pictures of battles and sieges to be borne in the procession. And the votive temple presently to be erected would require frescos depicting similar scenes and often a portrait of the founder. Thus in Livy's youth one could study many famous events portrayed on temple walls or in porticos by artists of the two preceding centuries, with the names of the leading persons inscribed. The panel pictures which also adorned such a temple might be old masters, but they do not seem to have inspired many artists at Rome to imitate them.

The easel picture, as we might call it, to be hung or let into the wall, often with doors hinged to its frame like those of a triptych, was to be found in great houses, but we have no evidence that many who were not portrait painters confined themselves to these wooden panels. None of the *tabulae,* whether portraits or others, have survived, and we may hardly hope that Herculaneum, which is yielding many objects in wood, is yet to give us a panel picture in fair preservation. Encaustic portraits (that is, painted in

---

[1] Never in oil. Even ships were painted with melted wax, as there were no lead paints.

melted wax) and others of later date in tempera have been preserved in considerable numbers with mummies in Roman Egypt. Interesting as these are, they do not enable us to judge whether the Roman sculptor's unquestioned talent in portraiture was fully equaled by that of the painter, plausible though such an inference would seem to be. It is safe to say that a historian of art, writing, let us say, in the age of Marcus Aurelius, when examples of every kind were abundant, would have given much space to the portrait, rating this as one of the three fields in which the painter's art accomplished most at Rome, the others being landscape and decorative painting.

Painted wall decoration moved on two very different levels—a higher plane on which the pictured wall or room tells its story in a series of scenes carefully planned before the first stroke of the brush, as in the adornment of a temple or other stately interior, and a lower plane of mere decoration. On this latter and more popular level material for our study outruns all limits down to a certain date, that of the first known eruption of Vesuvius, and then becomes scanty and scattered until the age of the catacombs. Pompeii and Herculaneum with their suburban villas have furnished innumerable specimens of the decorator's art, and excavation is continually adding to their number.

The celebrity of the buried cities has led to the impression that this method of decoration, these designs and colors, belonged somehow to that Campanian region, instead of being in more general use. It was not that Herculaneum and Pompeii could claim originality, but only that Hellenistic novelties in this field rapidly reached a region of Italy open to Greek influence through the commerce of Puteoli, and in close touch with the fashionable world of Rome as it flocked to its villas around the Bay of Naples for the season. Could we recover entire frescoed rooms from some of the more celebrated villas at Baiae or Misenum we should have more brilliant examples both of the decorator's skill and taste and of the higher art which produced whole scenes, admirably disposed, with life-sized figures. As it is we must base our study upon what may be seen in and about Pompeii and Herculaneum, in the Museum of Naples and other great collections; also upon the more limited material in and around Rome, showing, as if in compensation, a higher average of excellence than the Campanian.

At first, in the second century B.C., the costly veneering or revetment of walls with slabs of colored marble was imitated at slight expense by the decorators, who marked off blocks in relief in the wet plaster and at once colored them to correspond with the tints or even the grain of favorite marbles. The older and statelier houses of Pompeii have atria and rooms decorated in this manner from floor to ceiling, the wall spaces divided vertically by painted columns or pilasters. Even after this Incrustation Style ceased to be applied to the whole wall, "marbles" continued to find their place in a dado, a frieze, or other details. With such imitations of marble slabs in various colors the interiors of the better houses in Rome were decorated, we must assume, in the second century B.C. and the first decades of the first, in other words, even in the youth of Cicero and Caesar. A few rooms, in particular the tablinum (p. 162), might be enriched by a mosaic floor of elaborate design, even reproducing some well-known painting.

About the year 80 B.C., or a little later, a new style was introduced from Asia Minor. In this the decorator escaped the rigid formalism of the older manner and was free to imitate architectural features, shaded to give the impression of reality. The dado, often painted to simulate marbles, becomes a podium on which columns or pilasters appear to rest, usually dividing the main wall space into three panels and supporting an entablature, above which is a frieze, perhaps suggesting glimpses of sky, thus seeming to enlarge the room. In the central space, where a panel picture would have been hung, such a painting was often imitated in a frescoed picture, the subjects being drawn from Greek mythology. Smaller scenes such as had been painted on wood were reproduced in fresco to adorn less conspicuous parts of the wall. Frequently the wall is treated as a needless obstruction of the view, something which can even be reduced to a few columns or pilasters between which we seem to look out. The vista plays an important rôle.

This Second, or Architectural, Style is distinguished by a semblance of structural forms, tending to grow lighter and more graceful, but usually compatible with actual construction at least in wood. This was the classical Roman style of interior decoration, and must be borne in mind whenever we picture to our imagination a well-appointed house in the last half century of the Republic and during the reign of Augustus. In fact in the house on the Palatine in which it is now thought that he lived, the so-called House of Livia (p. 381), are found some of the best examples of this type of decoration. From the Augustan Age are also the frescoed walls, now in the Museo delle Terme at Rome, from a house on the left bank of the Tiber near the Villa Farnesina—these too in the architectural manner and signed by a Greek artist, Seleucus.

An entire room thus decorated may be seen in the Metropolitan Museum of Art in New York (illus., p. 417). This comes from a villa at Boscoreale, on the lower slopes of Vesuvius above Pompeii. It is an oblong vaulted chamber, each of its long walls divided into four large panels by red columns (painted) with yellow capitals. Each panel is com-

pletely filled with an architectural perspective—houses
with stately doorways, balconies, terraces; villas and their
colonnades; shrines in a garden or a stately peristyle, not
without repetition both in alternate panels and in those of
the opposite wall. A garden scene with pergolas, terraces,
a fountain, rocks, and ivy fills the alcove end of the room,
which still keeps its grilled window. The window, however,
was a later insertion, with serious injury to the painter's
symmetrical scheme. The whole room with its rich coloring
is a notable example of the scenic method, with its vistas
and an approach to perspective, creating an impression of
ample space in a small room.

This Second Style, which must originally have been designed for large and stately interiors rather than for private
houses, went through some three different phases. Even in
the first half of Augustus's principate it was becoming
more imaginative, with the help of innovations probably
brought in from Asia, to the disgust of the academic
Vitruvius, who rails at painters who let mere reeds or the
slenderest of candelabra pretend to be columns, who devised other fanciful impossibilities, and who are addicted
to striking colors.

The trend toward fantastic architectural forms conjured
out of a blank wall by a painter's brush was not to be re-
tarded by conservative opposition. Such intricate elaboration was not the only development, however, when the Second, or Architectural, Style yielded to newer methods in
design. It was followed in fact by two radically different
styles about the beginning of Tiberius's reign. These Third
and Fourth Styles have regularly been treated, in deference
to the well-deserved reputation of August Mau, as successive chapters in the history of Roman decorative painting,
with the beginning of Nero's reign as approximately the
dividing line between them. But the lack of material out-

side of Campania makes it difficult to accept such rapid succession. More plausible is the theory that these two styles represented rival schools of painters and were practised side by side until the more showy manner prevailed.

The issue was between the recognition on the one hand of the wall as something substantial, to be adorned, not to be charmed away by the witchery of an artist, and on the other hand the willingness to go any length in simulating fantastic architecture unrestrained by mere practical considerations. Masters of the former school and their pupils developed, probably at Rome, what we call the Third Style, in which the architectural framework of the Second Style is replaced by more delicate ornament from which the element of illusion is almost completely banished. An extremely attenuated column or a very slender candelabrum fancifully treated serves to divide wall spaces, or bands of pure ornament perform the same function. The wall is not something to be painted away. Emphatically it is there, often in solid color, even black, to be decorated, not to be ignored. Rooms painted in this style have many charming details, as we see them in the Metropolitan Museum's frescos from Boscotrecase, also near Pompeii (illus., p. 418). Some details suggest Egypt, but this type of decoration is known only in Italy—a further reason for not assigning it a whole period of its own. Pure forms and delicate coloring characterize this Third Style, which seems to have competed with the Fourth, not without mutual influence; but it never gained the upper hand.

The Fourth, or Intricate, Style carried on the architectural basis of the Second, but developed highly imaginative forms producing a complex far removed from realities, increasingly elaborate in its forms and intense in coloring. When Pompeian decoration is mentioned it is this style that is generally meant, as being much more abundantly represented than the others, since the earthquake of 63 A.D. caused so much rebuilding and redecorating. It has often been compared with the rococo or the baroque of modern times, and is now described as a degenerate stage, now as the culmination of the decorator's art in Roman times. Fanciful architecture serves to frame and subdivide wall spaces. Landscapes fill narrow bands, never the whole wall, seldom one of the main divisions. The painter of landscapes, usually on a small scale, delighted in views of colonnaded villas along the coast or rising one above another against a background of mountain. Seldom does he give us purely natural scenery, always inserting at least a shrine or sacred tree. Vesuvius, Capri and Ischia were not in his repertory. Garden scenery was appropriated especially to the open-air triclinium or the walls of a garden, that this might seem more spacious. Grapevine arabesques sometimes encircle the bright red columns of a peristyle, as in recently excavated houses at Herculaneum.

Through the fanciful architecture of an elaborate frieze human figures often seem to be looking down as from an upper story. Central mythological paintings are still in vogue, as also the floating figures in other panels. Vistas and street scenes continue to retain their popularity, as do the narrow bands on which are pictured the trades, occupations, and sports of men, often in a playful version in which Cupids play the masculine rôles, while the female parts are taken by Psyches with butterfly wings. Or if a chariot race is pictured the horses in this fairyland are stags. In the well-known House of the Vettii such scenes show the hand of a very able miniature painter.

Naturally this, the last style that is known to us from the cities of Campania, did not end abruptly among their more fortunate neighbors. In Rome, from which it came, there are still numerous remains of contemporary decorations, in the Golden House of Nero or on the Palatine, but mostly ruined or else as yet inaccessible and unpublished. No style so exuberant could fail to produce a reaction in the direction of sobriety, probably not later than the reign of Trajan. A sober, classic manner may be assumed for Hadrian's time, to match the taste of that day in sculpture. We may be sure that his villa at Tibur (p. 172) had painted rooms more stately than any that have been preserved, in harmony with the rich mosaic floors and the wealth of statues and other works of art. And it is reasonable to suppose that several different styles were represented, even local types to recall his extensive travels. The imperial palaces at almost any period must have had not a few masterpieces of mural decoration, to say nothing of the houses and villas of the aristocracy down to the fourth century.

By the second century A.D. painted tombs were more common, though the decoration of such chambers was frequently in stucco relief with some use of color, as in the well-known tombs of the Via Latina. One vaulted ceiling, probably later, has a graceful vine arabesque—this in a tomb chamber later incorporated in the Catacombs of St. Domitilla. The white background had become common. In general decorative painting of a humbler sort may be studied\ in the corridors and occasional chambers of the catacombs. The decoration of churches fortunately availed itself of mosaic so that many remarkable examples remain from the fourth and fifth centuries, continuing the mural art in another medium, but with many of its methods unchanged.

Turning from the purely decorative painting to murals of the higher order, covering walls with large scenes and life-sized figures or with ample landscapes, we have to deplore the almost total loss of such works. Many of them,

depicting scenes from the national history or from mythology, must have been comparable to the best of the reliefs,
and certainly represented the acme of the painter's art in
ancient Italy.

We have indeed but one complete series of mural paintings of the highest class, with almost life-sized figures, and
these were not discovered until 1909, at the Villa dei Misteri, outside the walls of Pompeii (illus., pp. 420, 421).
The mysteries of Dionysus furnished the theme of these
extraordinary scenes from the worship of the god, who is
represented seated with Ariadne. Beginning at a narrow
door in a corner a series of Bacchic scenes is carried along
two unbroken walls and part of a third. The decorative
features [2] are of the Second, or Architectural, Style. The
date is thus approximately determined to about 50 B.C.,
though the walls are perhaps two hundred years older.

Against the red background and often directly in front of
a pilaster are painted groups of figures, some of them preparing for the ceremonies, some taking part in the ritual
of Dionysus, while others suggest the romance of his mystic
cult. A wreathed Silenus of portly figure has been singing
and accompanying himself on the lyre, and is resting for
a moment in ecstasy, having just struck his last note. There
is the noble form of a frightened, fleeing woman; also a
formidable female figure, winged and raising her whip—
the lash that purifies—as if to strike the young woman who
has sought refuge on the knees of a seated matron, her com-
forter. Evidently initiation had its terrors, superbly depicted in these scenes. The series culminates in one nude
Bacchante whirling in excited dance, her rapid motion

[2] That is, a dado simulating colored marbles in horizontal bands, surmounted by a green podium cornice; dark violet pilasters, dividing the
main wall spaces in brilliant red, not broken by any pilasters in the angles
of the wall; finally a rather intricate frieze, including a maeander and
a broad central band imitating alabaster.

vividly indicated by a perfect arc of filmy scarf. The four
figures on this wall are a very remarkable example of subtly
organized geometrical composition, in which a circle plays
a leading part.

From the rapt expression of votaries, devout, inspired, or
terror-stricken, relief is given by peaceful scenes from the
haunts of the god—young satyrs and goats forming a pastoral interlude, while a Silenus and satyrs, one of whom is
drinking, serve to relieve the tension. There is one quiet
ceremonial scene—a priestess with her back to the spectator,
assisted by two female attendants; another of a little boy
at his mother's knee, reading a hymn from a scroll.

To the mystic rites of Dionysus only women were admitted, and it is probable that the painter aimed to give
scenes from the initiation through which brides must pass
if they wished to be enrolled among the votaries.[3] Detached
paintings in other corners picture a bride being decked for
her wedding, the real or the mystic, and a matron seated
alone. The painter probably aimed to recall, rather than
to reproduce, with adaptation to limited space, some great
series which adorned the walls of a temple or portico, perhaps in Asia Minor.

No other ancient paintings yet discovered bring us so
near to an understanding of what the work of the old Greek
masters must have been in the fifth and fourth centuries B.C.
When provincial Pompeii could possess frescos inspired by
masterpieces and on so high a level of artistic attainment
no one can believe that the capital in the first century B.C.
lacked splendid examples of interiors of the kind which
we habitually associate with the learned art of the Renais-

[3] Much still remains to be explained as to the meaning of these paintings.
There seems to be no valid reason for supposing that here a group of
enthusiasts met for secret orgies such as had greatly alarmed the Roman
government in 186 B.C., four generations earlier (p. 128).

sance, combining apt choice of theme and studied arrangement with mastery in every detail of execution, precisely
the type which we have now before us in that one room of
the Villa of the Mysteries.

To the same period belong the decorations from the large
triclinium of the villa at Boscoreale already mentioned (p.
324), now in the Metropolitan Museum of Art in New
York. Here again are life-sized figures against a vivid red
background: a man and a woman seated, suggesting portraits, possibly of some Hellenistic royalties; another group
of a seated woman playing the cithara, while a little maid
stands behind her chair. There is also a single female figure
holding a shield. Such works are presumably typical of
much that could be seen in that region of the Bay of Naples,
and leave no possible doubt as to the competence of the
painter.

Somewhat later in date, but Augustan and much more
widely known, since it was discovered more than three
hundred years ago, is the Aldobrandini Marriage, from a
house on the Esquiline and now in the Vatican. In this
there is nothing to compare with the art of the Bacchic
scenes at Pompeii; but the colors are pleasing and the total
effect suggests an excellent Greek tradition followed by a
painter who was no great master.

Landscape painting at Rome is best represented for us
by a series of scenes from Homer's *Odyssey* painted on the
walls of another house on the Esquiline but now in the
Vatican. Scenes from Homer were popular, as we know
from Vitruvius, and in these the landscape element pre-
dominates, the figures being small with their names added
in Greek letters. Red paneled pilasters (painted only),
bearing yellow Corinthian capitals, divide the wall spaces,
and as from a portico we seem to look out upon the perils

of Odysseus among the wild Laestrygonians, who stone and wreck all but one of his ships. A central scene shows the palace of Circe, resembling a seaside villa, to which the hero is admitted by the goddess, who a little farther on kneels before him. More striking are the scenes in the lower world, dimly lighted through its rocky entrance.

Landscapes also, but of a different type, are the decorations of a vaulted room in the Villa of Livia at Prima Porta (p. 169; illus., p. 419). Here no attempt is made to provide a distant background or long vistas through the garden which is pictured. The foreground is made by a fine latticework fence separated by a narrow strip of green lawn from another fence enclosing a thicket of shrubs and trees, some bearing brightly colored fruits. Flowers abound and birds of varied colors. The whole effect is very charming, the coloring still fresh, the drawing that of a master— possibly the Ludius [4] mentioned by Pliny as noted for works of a somewhat different character.

In the western provinces we have only very fragmentary specimens of fresco or other painting, though it is safe to assume that southern Gaul, with an artistic stimulus from Massilia, was in this respect, as in others, a second Italy. In the East we are more fortunate, but anything like a Roman influence on the local painters can seldom be claimed, except in some trite theme, as in figures of gladiators in the theater of Corinth. For temples religious subjects are to be assumed wherever their walls were frescoed. And the same art on a humbler plane is represented by scenes from Scripture occasionally found in the remains of early churches and in a single synagogue, as far away as the banks of the Euphrates. [5]

[4] Or Studius, for the reading is uncertain. Similar scenes are found in gardens recently excavated at Pompeii.

[5] Frescos of the third century from a church and a synagogue at Dura on the Euphrates are now in the museum of Yale University.

At Rome the transition to Christian decorative art may be studied in the mosaics of Santa Costanza. The vaulting of this circular mausoleum of Constantine's daughter has mosaics on a white ground representing vintage scenes in the classic manner, showing marked decline in the artist's skill, but charming and naïve in their symbolism so lightly worn. Other mosaics (in glass) of the fourth century may be seen in the church of Santa Pudenziana, continuing the tradition of the fresco painters. From the fifth and sixth centuries there are many notable examples at Rome and Ravenna, not to mention those produced in the new capital, Constantinople. And it must be admitted that few interior decorations anywhere in the Roman world charm the visitor more than the blue-ground mosaics in the very small Mausoleum of Galla Placidia at Ravenna. For the seventh and eighth centuries the frescos of Santa Maria Antiqua in Rome [6] furnish valuable material for the further history of wall decoration, now far removed from the antique.

SCULPTURE

In sculpture also the Etruscan influence dominated the whole early period of the art as practised at Rome. Etruscan sculptors followed Greek models, but with great independence, developing in their own individual manner a native power to reproduce with lifelikeness and vigor, even to the point of brutal realism. To what extent the temple statues in terra cotta and other works in bronze were brought in from Etruria or produced in Rome by Etruscan artists, we have no means of deciding.

The general character of early images of the gods in the temples can best be appreciated from a study of the Apollo found at Veii in 1916, and probably the work of the master

[6] These were discovered in 1902 just outside the Forum Romanum, near the Temple of Castor.

Vulca (illus., p. 406). This is not a cult statue, however, but part of a terra-cotta group representing a contest between Apollo and Heracles for the possession of a deer in the presence of Hermes and Artemis. The date is about 500 B.C. and the style Ionic archaic, vigorous and masterly. For early temples we are to imagine whole pediment groups in the same material, produced by Etruscans at Rome or under their influence.

Sculpture at Rome was like painting in being primarily decorative, and many pages in the early history of the art are written, as it were, on clay—the terra-cotta plaques, friezes, and other forms of revetment borrowed from the Etruscans (p. 366). This method of adorning buildings had reached a high level of artistic achievement in the time of the Tarquins. Scenes from Greek mythology are often represented, while many show conventional designs. For several centuries these colored reliefs must have played an important part in cultivating taste for graceful decoration in low relief.

More ambitious sculpture had been produced at Rome as early as the sixth century B.C. as the work of Etruscan masters. From such a hand and at that time probably came the best-known of the oldest sculptures, the bronze Wolf of the Capitol, rediscovered in the early Middle Ages. Lean and fierce, she stands defiant and menacing—not nursing the twins, as was supposed when Romulus and Remus were added, probably in the fifteenth century.

Terra-cotta statues in the Etruscan manner must have been common in early Republican times, not merely in the temples. Striking examples of such Tuscan sculpture may be seen in the Metropolitan Museum of Art in New York, especially the two heroic figures of warrior-gods or warriors ready for the fray, in all their national ferocity; also the helmeted head of a colossus.

Much influence on Roman sculpture was exerted by Etruscan portraits on sarcophagi and cinerary urns. Such likenesses in terra cotta seem never to have been flattering. The artist concentrated on the head and expression of the face, while the reclining body was summarily treated and even shortened. Homeliness and ugliness were reproduced with unsparing sincerity, leaving no doubt in our minds that the aim was to portray an individual and his usual expression, not merely a certain type of humanity. More ambitious are the Etruscan bronze portrait statues, of which few remain, notably that of an orator, the so-called Arringatore, now at Florence, representing late Etruscan art of the third or possibly of the second century B.C. With the help of this statue we are able to restore in imagination the general type of bronze likenesses of prominent Romans in and about the Forum in the last two centuries of the Republic.

Meanwhile Greek sculptors from the South and from Sicily were increasingly in demand, and while temples still wore an Etruscan look their statues were more and more thoroughly Greek in spirit. Quaint examples of early date were the equestrian statues of Castor and Pollux, now reduced to fragments, at the Fountain of Juturna (p. 372). In the third century B.C. Etruscan art, reviving after a period of decline, itself became almost Hellenistic and merged with the Hellenized Roman.

For the greater part of the Republican period we have few memorable examples of really Roman sculpture. The ancestral religion furnished no picturesque myths of the gods, no elements out of which imagination could create such legendary groups and scenes as were sculptured and painted in every Greek city. That world of imagination had no appeal for the practical Roman. Sculpture to please him inevitably kept in close touch with the visible and tangible, both in the direction of realistic portraiture and in that of historical reliefs, taking their themes from the immediate past, with rare recourse to legendary history in tales of Aeneas or Romulus and the rest.

The realistic portraits of the Republican age are in large part prosaic reliefs in somber peperino, once no doubt stuccoed and colored, representing husband and wife or several members of a family—homely faces looking out from a roadside tomb as from a window, to meet the eye of the passer-by. Statues of the same period have seldom survived, though once so numerous that Rostra and Forum had to be cleared at times to make room for new celebrities.

Busts resembling in features the wax masks of the ancestors (p. 162) were probably common in great houses. A laureled head in peperino found in the tomb of the Scipios, and too hastily labeled Ennius, may represent for us the portrait sculpture of the second century B.C. In that period there must have been many such busts carved from blocks of common volcanic stone, but coated with white stucco, a procedure which made it easy for the sculptor to effect slight changes before laying on his colors. Marble busts of a later date are illustrated on p. 424.

For extant historical reliefs of note the long series begins in the very end of the Republic with those of an altar [7] to Neptune set up near the Flaminian Circus about 31 B.C. as the gift of Domitius Ahenobarbus, who stands by an altar in the center ready to offer a sacrifice of thanksgiving for a naval victory, while soldiers with oval shields and waving plumes fill the spaces to right and left.

The Augustan Age saw an immense increase in the number of marble reliefs. Many of these, particularly on altars and tombs in the new altar form, have figures in high relief,

[7] Now in the Louvre; a part in Munich.

approaching the round. Much taste and skill were expended upon the decorative features. Ornament was highly developed, studied and yet natural, with no subjection to the Greek rule that nature must be conventionalized when used as ornament. Details of plant forms, wreaths, festoons, and other favored motives were usually treated with care to preserve the natural form, while convention governed the decorative scheme as a whole. Leaves of olive, laurel, oak, vine, or plane were studied from nature, flowers less minutely; and not a little is merely sketched or suggested. The purely geometrical and strictly conventional, the painfully accurate, are all avoided. Even the acanthus, so long traditionally stereotyped, recovers the movement of a living plant. It was a marked change, and the new freedom was used with a fineness of touch which gives an unmistakable stamp to Augustan relief.

Much of this delicate designing was applied to pilasters and other architectural members in that age of building and rebuilding. The Basilica Aemilia (p. 358) had clerestory windows too far above the ground for any close inspection of the carving; yet the mullions of those upper windows are perfect specimens of the new spirit in their slender plant and flower forms climbing gracefully out of a cluster of acanthus leaves (illus., p. 422).

Naturalistic ornament rapidly reached its culmination in the Altar of Peace, on the Via Lata in the Campus Martius, dedicated in 9 B.C. (illus., p. 422). The actual altar has not been recovered, but of the small, nearly square marble enclosure in which it stood a considerable part is preserved, unfortunately scattered in several different museums. The exterior wall spaces, framed in ornate pilasters, were divided between a purely decorative dado and a sculptured frieze. In the former a delicate framework of graceful spirals springs out of acanthus leaves or from other spirals, often interlaced by tendrils, until the whole space is covered. But however artificially combined, the plant forms (acanthus, palmetto, rose, and others) retain much of the natural, so that swans with outspread wings do not seem out of place. In contrast the interior wall spaces have the solemn air of a temple in their frieze of ample festoons suspended between ox skulls with pendent and floating fillets. The relief decoration of these walls reaches the highest known level in Roman art. That they were not unique is to be inferred from the absence of any mention of them in literature.

Historical reliefs filled the upper part of the enclosing wall on its exterior face. These at least were colored. The long panels on the north and south sides represent a religious procession—lictors, flamens, pontiffs with attendants, the Emperor with his whole family, including several small children, senators also and magistrates, all moving solemnly to the west. It is a gallery of contemporary portraits, few of which can be identified. For the shorter walls flanking the two entrances allegorical and mythological subjects were chosen.

Portraits and busts of the same period are numerous, especially those of Augustus himself, including two celebrated marble statues at different ages and one bust of him in his youth. In the Prima Porta statue (illus., p. 423), now in the Vatican, but found in the villa of his widow Livia, he is the *imperator,* in military garb, addressing his troops, the right arm extended, the left holding a staff. The beautifully carved cuirass reproduces an original in silver repoussé. Yet no skillfully wrought detail distracts attention from the whole. For the original impression of this, the best of all Roman portrait statues, we must restore the purple of his cloak, the silvering of the cuirass, and the other colors.

A statue of more recent discovery (1910) the Augustus
of the Via Labicana (frontispiece), now in the Museo delle
Terme, represents him as Pontifex maximus, with a fold
of the toga drawn over the top of his head. A weary expression of the face, emaciated but majestic and of the finest
mould, beneath tumbled locks, reveals the great ruler overburdened. Here the toga was doubtless left white except for
its purple border, while flesh and hair were colored; and
the solemnity of the white figure must have been increased
by the rarity of statues having so little color.

Another branch of the sculptor's art—now applied to
pure decoration—was that of the worker in stucco relief.
The older tradition of low relief in terra cotta, inherited
from the Etruscans, was carried on in this new application
to large surfaces for the adornment of entire walls and
vaults. The artist worked not in clay as before, but in fine
stucco made of marble dust. His designs drew upon the
architect's resources in their general framework, as in their
use of mouldings, rosettes, and other motives, but borrowed
more from the painter-decorator in the choice of idyllic
scenes or floating figures for the center of panels. A painter
simulated mouldings and other projecting members by the
use of light and shade. The worker in stucco achieved actual
relief in quite literal mouldings, colored as a rule while the
plaster was still wet. From the time of Augustus we have
excellent examples of this decorative work in stucco, usually
for interiors and commonly colored. Special mention should
be made of those from a house by the Tiber, noted for its
frescos as well (p. 324; illus., p. 425).

In a subterranean hall of the time of Claudius, known as
the Basilica of Porta Maggiore (p. 299), we see graceful
winged figures floating in air and many other designs disposed with great taste. Contrary to the rule, these seem

never to have been colored. Vaulted corridors in particular, as the cryptoporticus of the Palatine, received this type of decoration. At Pompeii, in the Stabian Baths and elsewhere, are elaborate designs in stucco relief. The panels often picture idyllic scenes, a wayside shrine, a sacred tree, cattle at a spring, shepherds and flocks—the type made familiar to us by old wall paper.

With the reign of Vespasian begins another period in Roman sculpture, in portraits as well as in reliefs. Busts and statues now show greater skill in grasping personality and rendering character. The Flavian emperors, as we see them sculptured, are men of common mould faithfully reproduced, with no toning down of plebeian or repellent features. And there is no misguided effort to reproduce literally the texture of skin or garment.

In historical reliefs, such as those under the Arch of Titus (p. 384), there was a marked advance in technique. One of these shows Titus standing in the triumphal chariot, while a winged Victory is placing a laurel wreath on his head and the goddess Roma leads his horses. Near her and behind are the lictors with their tall fasces. The other relief represents that part of the procession in which the golden and silver spoils of the Temple in Jerusalem are borne aloft —the seven-branched candlestick, the table of the shewbread, the silver trumpets. In both of these reliefs we find a very important innovation, marking a complete break with the traditions of Greek relief. Even without their original coloring and gilding these figures, some in very high relief, seem to have air behind them and between. This new technique in the art of relief gives the illusion of distance and perspective.

Widely known and often imitated is Trajan's eagle of the SS. Apostoli, superbly poised with outspread wings in a wreath of oak. Particularly rich in reliefs was his Forum with its adjacent buildings. Some of these, among them those which enrich the Arch of Constantine (p. 345), were used again elsewhere. Two large reliefs still stand in the Forum Romanum, but not on the original site. These have the added interest of an architectural background showing the basilicas and other structures in the Forum as they were at that time. The scenes depicted have to do with Trajan's charitable measures and the remission of taxes. His arch at Beneventum (p. 35) preserves almost intact an entire series of reliefs, here also picturing not battles but the triumphs of peace, the beneficent rule of a kindly father of his people.

The monumental column standing by his ruined Basilica Ulpia (p. 355) is the most striking single work of Roman sculpture. A spiral band of continuous relief turns twenty-three times around the shaft and contains no less than 2,500 figures in a total length of 660 feet (illus., pp. 426 f.). His two wars against the Dacians were literally pictured in painted reliefs. Many scenes from these campaigns succeed one another with no marks of division, except that a Victory stands amid trophies at the end of the first war. This is the so-called continuous method, appropriate to a band winding spirally about a column. In all this diversity a sense of unity is conveyed by the reappearance of the figure of the Emperor, in fact about once in every seven feet. The background offers every variety—towns and camps, forest or buildings, or a narrow strip of sky. Roman realism dominates everywhere, delighting in the exact reproduction of every detail of military equipment, every feature of the soldier's life and service, which are at the same time ennobled and, as it were, commended to rising generations. The sculptor has turned historian and practises a new narrative art destined to have a long history of its own. For us the highest part of the spiral with the story of the second

Better known is his column in the Campus Martius, imitating that of Trajan in its spiral band of reliefs. Here too we have the continuous style, the art of plastic chronicle in scenes which melt into one another. Again two wars are narrated, that with the Germans on the upper Danube and beyond, and that with the Sarmatians (p. 303). Many of the scenes invite comparison with like situations in Trajan's Dacian campaigns, but the imitations reveal a declining power, figures more crowded, shadows handled with less skill. For the beholder, unable to achieve a spiral ascent, there is the same difficulty, increased by a lofty pedestal and street traffic in a busy square.

In compensation for the lost statue of the philosopher emperor which once stood on the top of the column we have many of his busts, realistic and as unsparing as he was to himself. And there is the famous gilt-bronze equestrian statue on the Capitol, with right arm stretched out to give an order or summon the enemy to submit. Nothing in feature or pose suggests the careworn prince or the thinker, nothing prompts comparison with the statues of the first *princeps*. Yet the sculptor's skill is not to be denied, and if it were this statue would claim attention as the only extant equestrian portrait of an emperor, and as having always remained above ground.

Decorative sculpture had flourished under Trajan and Hadrian, and although the carvers of ornate detail seldom reached the Augustan standard, they were still capable of excellent work in the time of Marcus Aurelius. Stucco relief also held its own through the second century and beyond, as is shown by the vaulted ceilings of some well-known tombs on the Via Latina and the Appia.

Already in the time of Hadrian sarcophagus reliefs had begun to be more frequent, and in all the later history of decorative sculpture in Roman lands they claim an important place. Some continue an older tradition with a division into panels by small columns or pilasters. More usually scenes from mythology or other purely sculptural designs fill the entire surface. Rarely was a scene taken from the career of the deceased. The myth selected might suggest a premature or sudden parting. Favorite themes of this type were Hippolytus and Phaedra, Adonis, the Niobids, Diana and Endymion, or Persephone. But there are happy scenes as well, especially those drawn from the legends of Dionysus. The labors of Hercules also had their vogue, intimating rewards won by a strenuous life, trials and sufferings that deserved immortality. Battle scenes were frequent, as also the dangers of the chase.

The old classicism combined with a new romantic symbolism, scarcely comprehensible at an earlier period. The background disappears in the effort to cover the whole surface uniformly. The relief is high, the shadows deep, the style continuous—a narrative in scenes undivided. Even the coming of a new religion affected the sculptors little, beyond the substitution of themes from the Scriptures for the traditional myths.[8] Ravenna and Arles, as well as Rome, have many specimens of the Christianized sarcophagus.

While commercially produced sarcophagi grew more crude, realistic busts were often admirable down to the fourth century. Those of Caracalla show great skill in grasping and expressing an odious personality at a time when the decline in all the other branches of sculpture was painfully evident. Admirable is the portrait of an unknown Roman, dating from the middle of the third century—a very recent discovery (illus., p. 424). But even in portraiture a corrupted taste showed itself in the common use of colored marbles, alabaster, or porphyry for the drapery of

[8] It was to the Etruscans rather than to the Greeks that the Romans were indebted for the mythological trend in sarcophagus designs.

busts, while head and neck were of white marble, probably still colored.

Historical reliefs of the third century may be studied on the Arch of Septimius Severus. In the confused battle scenes in bird's-eye view, as in other reliefs, figures are massed upon figures. Credit may perhaps be given for experiments in perspective, but few of the figures have escaped serious damage.

A century later we find sculptured reliefs hastily executed for the Arch of Constantine (p. 394), to fill spaces for which older and better reliefs were not available. Among these is the battle of the Mulvian Bridge, and Constantine on the Rostra haranguing the crowd. These and others give plain proof of the condition to which the art was reduced after a century which had produced no creditable sculpture of its own except in portraits. Yet one must admit that it was better to begin again and work a new vein than slavishly to copy, and that there is after all in these untutored reliefs some promise for the future.

From the age of Constantine we have also the red porphyry sarcophagi, now in the Vatican, of Helena his wife and Constantia his daughter. With a prodigal expenditure of labor very high reliefs were wrung from one of the hardest of stones, probably in Egypt, certainly in a style almost oriental and not far from barbaric. The continuous historical reliefs of Roman tradition were carried over to Constantinople, particularly in the spirally banded Column of Theodosius, still standing in the sixteenth century, and that of his son Arcadius, which survived into the eighteenth.

On the whole sculpture at Rome, always lacking the pure genius of the Greeks and hence incapable of the greatest achievement, had distinguished itself most in portraiture, meeting the Roman's demand for uncompromising realism, with a closeness of observation and directness of rendering which increased almost steadily during several centuries. The second rank would no doubt have been assigned by any Roman critic to historical reliefs—imposing lessons for the masses, more impressive in the subjects chosen and the technical resources employed than in the evidence of very marked talent. In this field sculpture, making use of rich coloring, came into closest contact with historical painting. From a modern standpoint the decorative relief in marble or stucco, in clay or silver, would claim the second place, as more original, more universal, more inspiring to designers and artists of later ages. Relief ornament was as indispensable to the Roman architect as his borrowed egg and dart, so that here again two arts were merged.

Medieval sculpture as a matter of course borrowed much from the Roman, and in the Renaissance obligations to the antique become even more obvious. Busts and statues revived the ancient realism and decorative reliefs were everywhere inspired by Roman examples, especially those of the period from Augustus to Hadrian, which were often rivaled in graceful forms by the sculptors of Florence, Rome, and other cities in the Italy of the fifteenth and sixteenth centuries.

ARCHITECTURE

The materials of which early Rome was built were of the simplest kind. A soft stone formed of volcanic ashes was quarried from the hills in and about the city. This tufa, especially the grayish variety now known as cappellaccio, was in common use, usually laid in oblong blocks forming courses made up of "headers" [9] and "stretchers" without mortar. Many houses were of sun-dried bricks (*lateres*), often with timber framing. Walls of these perishable materials were coated with plaster, and wooden parts came to

[9] *I.e.,* blocks set at right angles to the plane of the wall.

be protected by thin plaques of terra cotta ornamented in low relief (p. 334). Shingle roofs gradually gave way to tiles. (For materials and construction see illus., p. 428.)

Soft varieties of tufa were in general replaced by the harder yellow and brown kinds in the second century B.C. and by better volcanic stones from the Alban Hills or Gabii. *Lapis Albanus* (peperino) and *lapis Gabinus* (sperone) were hardly affected by fire. Travertine (*lapis Tiburtinus*),[10] a hard, cream-colored limestone quarried near Tibur (Tivoli), came into use in the last century of the Republic. At first sparingly employed for arches or architraves and at other points of special strain, it found unlimited use under the Empire.

In general solid masonry in squared stone blocks (*opus quadratum*) without mortar [11] was almost entirely displaced by a less costly and more durable method of construction in concrete, since excellent volcanic materials were available, such as the chocolate-colored earth of Puteoli (pozzolana), found also near Rome. This was much used with lime to form a cement which hardened even under water. By the addition of small pieces of stone or broken brick to these ingredients was produced the well-known concrete (*caementum*) which revolutionized Roman construction, making wide vaults and great domes possible.

From the first century B.C. the typical Roman building had walls of this concrete faced with small stones or with brick or both combined. It was at first used for foundations, either concealed by a casing of stone, or simply poured, or rather pressed, into a mould of timber, the marks of which often remain visible. Above ground the facing of a wall in the second century and early in the first century

---

[10] Much used now in this country for floors and stair-treads.

[11] The use of lime at Rome seems not to be proved before the third century B.C.

B.C. was of small irregular pieces of tufa but showing a smooth face. This *opus incertum* was succeeded in the time of Sulla by a very regular system suggestive in its appearance of network and hence called *opus reticulatum*. The lines of mortar always ran diagonally and the small blunt pyramids of tufa reaching back into the solid concrete turned neatly squared bases outward. This reticulated facing prevailed for two centuries, through the reign of Hadrian. Many such walls had occasional bonding courses of thin triangular bricks. Angles of the wall also were faced with brick.

Even in the first century A.D. a concrete wall frequently had a complete facing of brickwork (*opus testaceum* or *latericium*), in which the triangular form was used, except for occasional courses of large square bricks to bind the wall together. After Hadrian this was the almost invariable type of facing. Seldom were entire brick buildings to be found without concrete, but arches were regularly of large square bricks, often thinner at the lower edge. Where the bricks are thin and the joints very close we know that the building is of the early Empire; for both tended to grow thicker from century to century.

The introduction of marble about 150 B.C., whether for actual construction or for purposes of adornment, was an imitation of Hellenistic splendor. Hence the importation of many different marbles, chiefly from Asia Minor, the Greek islands, and Greece, in endless variety of grain and coloring. To mention only a few favorite kinds, there was the Numidian (giallo antico), deep yellow varied with pink; Phrygian (pavonazetto), white with purple veining; Carystian (cipollino) from Euboea, white and green with showy markings; white marble of Pentelicus in Attica, or of Paros in the Aegean, or of Luna (Carrara near Pisa), the only Italian marble extensively used, and that not in quantity until the time of Augustus. Other costly building stones were highly prized, as the red and the green porphyry from Egypt, which also sent its gray and its red granite (syenite) from the upper Nile (p. 92).

Mechanical contrivances were not lacking and slave labor was always available. Columns and other massive blocks were raised by means of a crane with its system of pulleys. Motive power was supplied by men in a treadmill —a huge wooden wheel, represented in operation on a well-known tomb-relief at the Lateran.[12]

Passing on from the resources at the disposal of the architect to his art, we may conveniently divide Roman architecture into three distinct phases, in the first of which column and lintel dominate, in the second, pier and arch, in the third, vault and dome. Needless to say, the architecture of the lintel, that is, of the horizontal entablature, did not in practice forbid combination with that of the pier and the arch; and both of these systems entered into the design of every vaulted or domed structure of consequence.

As in the other arts, there was much imitation, and models were readily to be found among Etruscan neighbors to the north and Greek cities to the south, finally in Hellenistic centers after the Second Punic War. It was imitation, however, not slavish reproduction of a given design. No architect at Rome would have thought of taking the design of a Greek temple complete and then fitting into it a house or other incongruous structure—the error so frequently committed in the days of our Greek Revival.

For the architecture of the column and lintel the so-called orders were fundamental. To each of these belonged a tra-

---

[12] An old drawing shows a similar machine in use in the building of St. Peter's in the sixteenth century.

ditional type of column and capital, base (where this is not lacking) and entablature, with more or less rigidly fixed proportions. Each order was in itself a definite system, permitting variation only within rather clearly marked limits. There were but four such orders: Tuscan, Doric, Ionic, and Corinthian.

The Tuscan order, the first to be used at Rome, was until recently treated as an Etruscan modification of the Doric, which was known from many examples in Greek cities of southern Italy and Sicily. But now, in the light of Cretan monuments, it must be granted that the Tuscan is more ancient and may fairly be described as Pre-Doric, imported into Latium by the Etruscans with little change, and not a perversion, as was formerly thought, of the Greek Doric.

This Tuscan order has an unfluted shaft resting upon a simple base above a square or round plinth (illus., pp. 429, 430). Its capital is merely a rudimentary echinus (a swelling cushion member) supporting a square slab, and with no carving or other enrichment than simple mouldings. The frieze commonly has triglyphs, suggesting beam ends conventionally grooved and alternating with metopes, i.e., plain slabs or carved. A rosette often adorned the metopes. In the earliest temples, as that of Jupiter on the Capitol, the columns were wooden posts, supporting great beams as architraves, the latter protected from the weather by terra cotta. Temples of this order, owing to the distance between the columns, often retained their wooden architraves even after the shafts were of stone or marble. In general the Tuscan order had given way to the more decorative Ionic and Corinthian before the end of the second century B.C. It continued to be used chiefly for half-columns and pilasters, especially in combination with the other orders on the façades of secular buildings of various kinds (p. 357).

The Doric order was seldom used by Roman architects,

although the Greek cities of the South were full of Doric temples of massive construction, some of which are still imposing in their ruin. How these ponderous proportions were modified in the direction of lightness by an architect of the time of Sulla, following in this his Hellenistic predecessors, we may see in a temple at Cori (Cora) in Latium (illus., p. 429). Slender columns were placed much farther apart, the size of capital and weight of cornice reduced, simple bases added, and the shafts fluted, while the frieze was given more than the normal number of triglyphs in proportion to that of the columns. No example of this modernized Doric remains at Rome, though in the church of San Pietro in Vincoli on the Esquiline we may see rows of Doric columns of the time of the Empire.

The Ionic order has a taller column, fluted except when a very hard stone or a rich marble was to be used (illus., p. 431). The capital retains the bolsterlike member of the Greek Ionic, with spirals on two opposite faces (adjacent faces in the case of a corner column). Another type of Ionic capital was square with four identical faces and no cushions. The base was that commonly known as Attic-Ionic, having two *tori* (cushions) separated by a concave member and resting on a thin square plinth. The architrave usually had three plane surfaces (*fasciae*), the upper projecting beyond the lower (a system familiar to us in the flat surfaces of doorframes), and each wider than that below in the proportion of 5, 4, 3. The frieze, plain or sculptured, was enriched by dentils and mouldings beneath the cornice. This order, never very widely used in Italy as compared with the others, played its part also in the applied ornament of façades.

The Corinthian order, less delicate in its proportions, less refined in its ornament, was everywhere the general favorite under the Empire (illus., pp. 430, 431). Here too

a tall shaft was often unfluted, that polished marble, granite, or porphyry might be more effective. The capital suggests in its form a bell-shaped basket about which have
grown up two rows of alternating acanthus leaves, while
higher up emerge volutes curving out to meet the angles
of a narrow abacus concave on all four sides. The utmost elaboration was expended upon the cornice—dentils,
mouldings, brackets, alternating with rosettes. There was
often a richly sculptured frieze, separated from the architrave and its three *fasciae* by delicate mouldings. An innovation due to the taste for ornate detail was the Composite
capital, distinguished by an unhappy substitution of an
Ionic capital of the four-faced type for the normal volutes
of Corinthian—a hybrid form seen on the Arch of Titus.
Variant forms of Corinthian or Composite capitals show
forms of animals or even cornucopias in place of volutes,
or human figures rising out of the acanthus leaves. Like the
Tuscan and the Ionic was the Corinthian in its frequent
employment in lofty and elaborate façades, as that of a theater, or on its scene wall. Superposition of the orders was to
be found also in porticos, where a lower tier of columns
(usually Tuscan) supported an upper tier (usually Ionic
or Corinthian) on a smaller scale, as in the Forum of
Pompeii.

Temple architecture was almost restricted to that of the
column and lintel. In plan the normal temple was at first,
and so long as the Etruscan influence was strong, nearly a
square, later a rectangle, about twice as long as it was broad,
following Greek proportions, since most of the architects
were Greeks. The simplest type had columns only in front,
forming a deep porch. Such a prostyle temple most frequently had four or six columns across the front and one or
two more on each side, the line of columns being continued
in the form of half-columns along the side walls of the cella,

the rear of which was often a blank wall. Half-columns across the rear were common, whole columns rare. A good example of a Republican temple with four Ionic columns across the front (prostyle tetrastyle) and its cella encased in half-columns is the so-called Temple of Fortuna Virilis (perhaps of Mater Matuta) by the Tiber (p. 373; illus., p. 431). A similar Corinthian temple without the half-columns is that of Augustus at Pola in Istria. Of the prostyle hexastyle temple (six columns in front) the best preserved example is the Maison Carrée, the gift of Agrippa to the city of Nemausus (Nîmes) (illus., p. 431). Another is the Temple of Augustus and Livia at Vienna (Vienne).

Peripteral temples, *i.e.,* with columns all around, were less commonly built by the Romans than those which had columns on three sides but none at the rear. A magnificent instance of the latter type is Augustus's Temple of Mars Ultor in his Forum, an octastyle backing up against a lofty fire-wall enclosing the Forum (p. 381). Entirely encircled by columns (peripteral) were the Temple of Castor and Hadrian's double Temple of Venus and Rome, the latter having ten columns beneath each pediment (decastyle; illus., p. 438). Few of the old square temples on an Etruscan plan survived into the Empire, though the great Capitoline temple retained its original ground plan to the end (p. 386).

In contrast with the much more numerous rectangular temples was the circular plan, suggestive of the old Italic straw hut, but found in Greek lands also. Such was the Temple of Vesta in the Forum, where a reërected section may now be studied (illus., p. 435). Larger and higher is the unidentified temple by the river, perhaps that of Portunus, which has lost one of its twenty columns and the whole entablature. At Tivoli (Tibur) is another round temple of great interest, dating from about 80 B.C.

Characteristic of Roman temples in general, though Hel-

lenistic in origin, is the lofty podium, or platform. One entered after mounting a flight of steps only at the front and
between two short walls—a contrast to the accessibility of
classic Greek temples, surrounded by a few steps on all
sides.

In the interior of large temples much use was made of
columns, either placed on a high podium and close to the
walls for mere decoration, or in rows on the floor level to
divide into nave and aisles. The Temple of Concord may
illustrate the former method, the Temple of Mars Ultor
the latter.

To provide a sacred enclosure about a temple a colonnaded *porticus* was often erected. In its usual form this
court with columns carried around all four sides differed
little, if at all, from the Hellenistic peristyle of a house or
villa (p. 165). One or more temples stood within such a
porticus, being located centrally or near one end. A single
temple sometimes closed the farther end of the court, as did
Caesar's recently excavated Temple of Venus Genetrix (p.
380). In the Campus Martius we may still see the remains
of four temples in a single enclosure (p. 377). Other porticos were public lounging places, not connected with a
sacred building. The Porticus Liviae on the Esquiline was
a quadrangle enclosed by a double row of columns and similar to the Porticus Octaviae, which sheltered two temples
near the Theater of Marcellus. Pompey's Theater and
others had porticos of their own, a refuge for spectators in
case of rain. In the imperial fora we find other courts of
this kind, as in palaces and in the Thermae.

Another use of the colonnade was to border important
streets, after the manner of the arcades in many medieval
and modern cities. This custom reached Rome as early as
193 B.C., when two roads outside the city gates received such
shelter. After the great fire of 64 A.D. Nero, besides broad-

ening his new streets, ordered the erection of porticos of
this kind along the fronts of the houses. Many towns had
similar colonnades, especially around the market places,
and often in two stories. But colonnaded streets were more
usually met with in the East, for example at Palmyra, and
in Africa (illus., p. 430).

Libraries often had a peristyle for an entrance court and
columns purely ornamental, or to support a gallery, along
the walls of the interior (pp. 246, 263). In basilicas also the
column and architrave style of architecture was the rule.
This form may best be studied in the basilica of Pompeii,
where tall columns divide a broad nave from the side aisles.
At Rome the Aemilia and Ulpia followed the same scheme,
the latter having a nave and four aisles (pp. 387 f.). Numerous examples might be cited from the provinces, even
Britain, where Calleva (Silchester) had an aisled basilica.
By exception that at Timgad (Thamugadi) in Numidia
has no columns.

To this division of our subject belong also the monumental columns, small and large, with base, shaft, and
capital. Republican examples, not the very earliest and no
longer extant, were the column of Maenius, near the Carcer, for his naval victory over Antium (338 B.C.), and the
two columns of Duilius (one of them by the Rostra) for a
naval victory over Carthage (260 B.C.), the latter columns
adorned with beaks of ships. The shaft of columns of this
class was commonly plain, of polished marble or granite,
or later of red porphyry, and the monument was often surmounted by a winged Victory. Such columns abounded in
public places, frequently in pairs. More impressive were
the huge sculptured shafts, such as the Column of Trajan
or that of Marcus Aurelius (pp. 341 ff.), or that of Jupiter
at Mainz (Moguntiacum) from the time of Nero.

Here too may be placed the tombs which made use of

the order, if only for details. And any of the roads leading out of Rome would have shown an astonishing variety of architecture to the passing crowds, from the simple altar form with cushion members borrowed from an Ionic capital to an Egyptian pyramid. The Etruscan tumulus type had a drum of masonry, faced with travertine or marble and adorned with a cornice if not also with pilasters, the whole supporting a conical mound of earth, often planted with trees. Not materially different from this form of mausoleum were trophy monuments, except that they were entirely of masonry. Best-known, and very recently restored in part, is that at La Turbie above Monaco—the Trophies of Augustus, with tall columns around a circular upper story (p. 47; illus., p. 429). Trajan's trophy at Adamklissi in Roumania was raised high above a great monument of the same general type but lacking columns.

The architecture of the pier and arch was developed from purely utilitarian structures, such as aqueducts and bridges, in which art might be revealed merely in studied proportions, with no attempt at ornament. Reducing to a single unit (or bay), we find the essential elements in the arch, much used by the Etruscans, and in two supports of substantial masonry, that is, rectangular piers. An entire building constructed by mere repetition of this simple unit would be massive and durable but so ponderous as to be out of keeping with everything in its neighborhood, particularly with any example of the architecture of column and lintel. Sculpture might have relieved the bareness and heaviness of such an arcade; but instead of casting about for a method of adornment strictly consistent with the construction, architects fell back upon the orders as surface ornament. A half-column or pilaster applied to the front of each pier gave the appearance of supporting a complete entablature (architrave, frieze, and cornice) above the crown of the arch. This was to rob the order of all constructive function and reduce it to a decorative frame enclosing the arch and partly masking the pier. But the repetition of this illogical scheme across a whole front or around an entire building, and then again in a second or even a third story, produced a remarkable effect of unity in multiplicity, and in addition marked contrasts of light and shade in the several stories, set off by their cornices and varied by the conventional use of the Tuscan order for the first story and of the Ionic and Corinthian for the second and third respectively.[18]

This was the famous Roman arcade system, constructively only alternating piers and arches camouflaged by the orders illogically applied. Found in Hellenistic countries also, it cannot be considered a purely Roman invention. Familiar examples are the Theater of Marcellus and the Colosseum (pp. 382, 384), but this was the accepted style for the exterior of any theater, amphitheater, or circus, and much used for basilicas, as it was sometimes for porticos (illus., pp. 408, 433). The earliest extant example is the Tabularium (p. 374). Reduced to a single unit, this system yields the simplest form of the triumphal arch. In three such units combined we have the essential scheme of the more ornate triumphal arches or other gateways.[14]

The employment of this massive architecture of the pier and arch for some of the porticos in the Forum and the Campus Martius suggests an instructive comparison with the colonnaded street fronts. That is, we are dealing in

[18] Other means of securing variety are sometimes found, as the use of entire columns or three-quarter columns, or the employment of a different stone for the shafts.

[14] There were many other uses of this motive, as for blind arcades, for mausolea and smaller monuments, and on a diminutive scale it served as pure decoration in place of a frieze.

these cases with a corridor, similar in its use to the shady colonnade. Even in that first example, the Tabularium, the main feature of its front was two open galleries or loggias, one above the other, the lower actually used as a thorough-fare in passing from the Capitolium to the Arx. As the Forum Romanum lacked the porticos which surrounded fora of smaller cities, Augustus in rebuilding the basilicas provided such shelter by his arcades parallel to the two streets. Through that on the north side one passed into a row of shops and on beyond them into the Basilica Aemilia —the hall itself, in a different style of architecture. The main hall had in fact its three rows of columns, and no arches. On the south side of the Forum one entered a sim-ilar portico with its arches also framed in the Tuscan order; and then passing up two steps and under a second row of arches one found oneself in the side aisle of the Basilica Iulia, separated from the nave by another row of arches. But here the entire structure, *porticus* included, was in the architecture of the pier and arch. Standing at one end of the broad nave one looked down its length between two arcades in two stories, and upward to a flat, wooden, paneled ceiling above the clerestory windows. Side aisles and por-tico were vaulted, as was the rule with corridors in this style.

In the Campus Martius, along the Via Lata, was the most remarkable *porticus* of the arcaded and vaulted type. The Saepta Iulia had seven aisles side by side (p. 382). That nearest the street, the modern Corso Umberto, served as an arcaded thoroughfare for foot passengers—virtually a covered sidewalk. Considerably more than twice the length of the Colosseum, this was the longest building in the city except the Circus Maximus (p. 388). Agrippa's Porticus Vipsania was probably on a similar plan, an unusual one for a *porticus*.

A theater, an amphitheater, a circus or a stadium all demanded ample corridors and many entrances. The pier-and-arch type of construction was all but inevitable, especially as no other combined such solidity with the needed openness. The elliptical corridors around the entire circuit of an amphitheater, the semicircular corridors of a theater, and those of a circus and a stadium (straight and curved) furnish numerous examples, while the façades of all of these almost invariably have applied orders.

For gateways and monumental arches of every kind the same system was employed—the arches set in a purely ornamental frame consisting of columns, half-columns, or pilasters, commonly on high bases and supporting a complete entablature. City gates were sometimes imposing, as we see at Turin (Augusta Taurinorum) and Trier (Augusta Treverorum), both of these gates still retaining their flanking towers, as is not the case with those of Nîmes (Nemausus) and Autun (Augustodunum). At Rome the one really monumental city gate extant became such by accident, having been built by Claudius to carry his two aqueducts across two roads meeting at a sharp angle. This Porta Praenestina (Maggiore) has rusticated masonry, with the order subordinated and unimportant—a framing for niches against the piers.

Triumphal arches furnish particularly ornate examples of the same architectural type, and these are widely dispersed in the western provinces and North Africa, which alone has more than fifty (illus., p. 402). Besides those at Rome, touched upon in another chapter (pp. 384, 391, 394), we may name only a few. The earliest still extant, and of Republican date, is the arch at Saint-Remy, near Arles, in honor of Caesar's victories in Gaul. The much larger triple arch of Orange (Arausio), with elaborate reliefs, was probably begun under Julius Caesar and completed by Augustus and Tiberius. Some of the monumental arches erected by Augustus had to do with important roads, as that which marked the end of the Flaminian Way at Ariminum (Rimini). Another at Augusta Praetoria (Aosta) spanned a road leading up to an Alpine pass, as did that at Susa in the Cottian Alps, pleasing in architecture but crude in its sculpture. More ornate, with engaged columns in pairs, is the Arch of the Sergii at Pola, slightly later in date. Trajan's arches are well known, especially the richly sculptured arch at Beneventum on the Appian Way (p. 341). A simpler arch of his stands by the harbor of Ancona on the Adriatic, another at Timgad (Thamugadi) in Numidia. Other African arches are those of Marcus Aurelius at Oea (Tripoli) and that of Caracalla at Tebessa, each of these with four faces, being placed over the crossing of streets. A simpler arch of Caracalla is at Djemila (Cuicul) in Numidia. Tasteful and original is Hadrian's arch at Athens.

Commemorative arches on a bridge or at one end of it were not infrequent, as at Saintes in France (Tiberius, a double arch) and Alcántara and Martorell in Spain. At Saint-Chamas near Marseilles is a bridge of Augustan date with an arch of attractive form at each end.

Bridges and aqueducts must be passed over with the briefest mention. Every province has remains of this kind, and Roman bridges still in use are encountered by the traveler in the most unexpected places. Mérida and Alcántara have the best-known Roman bridges in Spain. At Rome are the Republican Pons Mulvius, Pons Fabricius (62 B.C.), and Hadrian's Pons Aelius. Others still in use may be seen at Rimini and Verona (two arches are ancient), not to mention the many picturesque ruined bridges such as that at Narni or the Ponte Rotto (Aemilius) at Rome. Wooden arches on stone piers were sometimes employed, as for Trajan's great bridge over the Danube.

Aqueducts also are widely scattered in their ruin from one end of the empire to the other. Familiarly known are those of the Roman Campagna, especially the Marcia, Claudia, and Anio Novus, with their miles of arches on lofty piers. Another celebrated ruin of the kind is the Pont du Gard, a triple arcade 160 feet high, which supplied the city of Nîmes with water flowing most of the way underground, as was the usual Roman practice (illus., p. 432). Tarragona in Spain has another with arches upon arches. Segovia also and Mérida have notable aqueducts, as have Carthage and Cherchel (Caesarea in Mauretania).

City walls would seem at first sight to require no use of the arch except at gates. The third-century Wall of Aurelian, however, as seen from within, shows a series of tall arches behind the curtain wall from one tower to the next, rising not from the ground but from a gallery from which arrows could be shot through loopholes. An upper gallery at the top of the wall is supported by these arches.

Finally the arcade motive was applied to many a mausoleum or lesser tomb, especially for its more massive first story.

A totally different arcade system was that in which the weight of the arches was actually borne by the columns (illus., p. 433). In this the order recovered its logical constructive function and the element of camouflage disappeared. Greater lightness was secured, especially if the arches were wide in proportion to the height of the columns. Conservative Roman builders no doubt viewed the innovation with disapproval as lacking stability owing to the slenderness of a column as compared with a sturdy pier. The arch might be quite plain, as in the earliest known examples in two peristyles at Pompeii, or moulded in the manner traditional for an architrave. Sometimes the arches rested

directly upon the capitals, in other cases upon an entablature borne by the capitals, as we see them pictured in fresco
in the Villa dei Misteri at Pompeii. The best-known arcade
of this type resting upon columns instead of on stout piers is
that in the principal court of the Palace of Diocletian at
Spalato on the Dalmatian coast (p. 168). This system was
used in Syria and Asia Minor, and if in Italy it was dis-
trusted as unsubstantial, there must surely have been such
arcades which have not survived earthquakes.[15] They were
imitated in Christian churches and descended through Byzantine and Romanesque into Gothic architecture, to be
revived and widely used in the Renaissance.

Another employment of an arch supported by columns
appears especially in Syria, but also in the palace at Spalato.
Here the familiar triangle of a pediment was radically
altered by springing an arch over the two central columns.
In fact the frieze and cornice on nearing the center deserted
their horizontal lines for a curve up and over the arch. No
pediment of this baroque type is known at Rome.

The architecture of the vault and dome belongs to the
Empire and was still flourishing when Rome ceased to be
the capital. The materials were, as we have seen, largely
volcanic and lighter than cut stone. It was concrete construction which led up to vaulting and made possible domes
of great size (illus., pp. 410, 434). Vaults were most frequently of the type known as barrel vaults, that is, with a
semicircle or lesser arc for a cross section. The under surface was often relieved by panels, rectangular or polygonal,
with stuccoed details painted or gilded. Groined vaults
(cross vaults) consist of one barrel vault pierced, so to
speak, crosswise by another, so that the weight is concen-

[15] The light arcade motive appears also on a small scale in decorative
design, as on sarcophagi and in late Roman architecture.

trated at four points. The lines of intersection in different lights become conspicuous features. This was the method of vaulting applied to the great halls such as those of the Thermae, having three bays, the thrust of the vaulting being concentrated at eight points, beneath which huge columns were placed, though quite unnecessary, since the vault is supported by the massive walls and buttressed by those of the adjoining halls.[16] A third type of vaulting is that known as the cloister vault, in which the weight is not concentrated at the angles but rests upon the four walls, the inconspicuous intersections being like the wall-angles and simply meeting at the top. If placed over an octagonal room such a vault makes an octagonal dome. Multiply the sides to infinity, and we have the typical dome, which among the Romans was as a rule nearly or quite hemispherical.

Domes rested either upon circular walls, such as the great drum of Hadrian's Pantheon, or upon a structure of polygonal plan, pierced by lofty arches, such as the calidarium of the Baths of Caracalla (an octagon). Concrete was the usual material of domes, but some had ribs of brick like so many meridians, others, relieving arches of brick. Besides using pumice stone as an ingredient in the concrete to lighten the weight of a broad vault or of a dome, Roman architects placed courses of empty earthen jars (*amphorae*) in the mass of concrete, especially near the top.

In this architecture of vault and dome all emphasis was placed upon the interior, adorned with columns or arches or both. The exterior of the great vaulted halls and domes was usually very plain, the total effect largely due to masses, as in recent buildings of the skyscraper class, in which the scale of the whole would completely dwarf conventional types of ornament. Thus the exterior of such a rotunda as

[16] Flying buttresses were sometimes added, as in the Baths of Diocletian and the Basilica of Constantine.

the Pantheon was not relieved by arcades, whether blind or open, similar to those of the Colosseum, nor by columns except at the entrance, while the elaborate decoration of the interior included arches resting on entablatures supported by colored marble columns and pilasters. In fact we know of no Roman dome whose exterior made an impression of studied architectural form, like that of St. Peter's or that of St. Paul's in London, with their display of orders encircling the drum, of moulded ribs, and a lantern to crown the whole.

The vaulted halls of the Thermae were equally plain as seen from without, though so surrounded by other buildings that there was no need of a façade. Constantine's basilica (p. 393) fronted directly on the Sacred Way and was plainly seen from the Forum and Palatine, but there is no reason to think that its front was imposing otherwise than in its great mass.

On the Palatine the Domus Flavia of Domitian (p. 383) had some notable vaulted halls, one of nearly a hundred feet span, but even in this case the exteriors were probably simple except for a colonnade.

Under the Empire vaulting sometimes replaced the wooden ceiling of a temple cella, as in the double temple which Hadrian dedicated to Venus and Rome, at least as this was restored by Maxentius; or in a great temple at Baalbek in Syria. In such cases there was of course no neglect of the exterior. Small round temples and halls were often domed. Barrel vaulting was much used for tombs large and small, the surface being adorned with relief designs in stucco, as in well-known tombs on the Via Latina and the Appia.

In general the public places and streets of Italian cities showed two radically different types of façade, that with colonnades in a single story, almost limited to temples, and that with arcades masked by use of the orders in two or three stories. The contrast of the two types, the lintel versus the arch, must have been especially striking in the Forum Romanum. Some buildings constructed on the pier-and-arch system had windows and wall spaces in place of the open arches. Of this our best illustration is the Porta Nigra, an ornate gate of Trier (Augusta Treverorum). In other less pretentious buildings arches and blank wall spaces dominated and the order was reduced to narrow pilasters and mere stringcourses.

Elaborate façades without the use either of the colonnade or arcade were adorned with pairs of small columns sustaining a pediment, triangular or curved, framing niches for statues—a theatrical style in two or three stories, best represented by the scene walls of such theaters as those of Aspendus in Asia Minor or Orange (Arausio, near the Rhone). A baroque front of this type is that of a library of Trajan's time at Ephesus (p. 263); another was Severus's Septizonium in Rome (p. 391). In the later period a façade was sometimes adorned by a series of niches framed by small columns resting on brackets and supporting small arches in place of pediments—a method illustrated by the Porta Aurea of Diocletian's seaside palace at Spalato (p. 362).

Naturally one asks if there were no buildings worth mentioning in which the arch was effectively used without help from the stereotyped orders. Such architecture was presumably thought suited only to a work of utility and excessively sober. A monumental city gate at Fano (Fanum on the Adriatic), where Vitruvius built a basilica, has indeed the complete entablature, but no columns nor pilasters, except for an upper gallery on a smaller scale, and similar are the two city gates at Autun (p. 359).

In all the three phases of Roman architecture an important place was taken by revetment, the use of facings of several different kinds. The wooden lintel or architrave of the early period was encased in terra cotta. These thin plaques had relief designs and were highly colored. This method had been employed by the Greeks, especially in Sicily, but came to Rome from the Etruscans (p. 334). Many admirable specimens have been preserved. In the first century B.C. and the first A.D. walls of houses and temples were often decorated by attached plaques of terra cotta representing mythological or historical scenes, or purely ornamental. Placed side by side they formed a continuous frieze. Ornament was also produced by patterns in stone or by using brick of different colors.

For the closing age of the Republic and under the Empire the common form of revetment was in marble after the fashion of the Hellenistic cities. These slabs (*crustae*) of polished marble from three-quarters of an inch to an inch in thickness were attached by iron clamps to the stone or brick facing of the concrete wall (p. 348). Such a revetment might be merely a dado; more rarely it covered the whole wall. In temples or other public buildings, in the fora of the emperors, in palaces, the marble revetment took on an architectural character, with much use of the orders, especially of fluted Corinthian pilasters and their entablatures, the whole made more striking by the different colors of polished marbles. Beautiful examples have been found in recent years in the Fora of Augustus and Trajan. As for the exteriors of "marble" buildings, these too were almost invariably facings only, after concrete had all but banished squared masonry (*opus quadratum*). White marble slabs of greater thickness were carved in relief, and a good part of the effect of many celebrated buildings was due to revetment in this its most artistic form.

Reflections upon this method, which separated construction from adornment, have often led to unfavorable comparisons with the best Attic construction in solid marble, a material ready to hand in Greece, and to the statement that such facings were expressive of a veneered civilization. Much can be said, however, for the Roman method on the score of durability and of adaptation as well to the materials locally available. The skillful development of these resources alone made wide vaults and great domes possible —an immense achievement, and not merely from the standpoint of engineering. For with these marvels of construction came the hardly less admirable elaboration of vast plans symmetrically disposed and notable triumphs in the treatment of interiors. The Roman architect became indeed an engineer and his gifts were eminently practical, in designing public works, utilities of every kind, apartment houses and shops, warehouses, city walls and gates. Nevertheless and in spite of all his obligations to Hellenistic predecessors and colleagues his artistic accomplishment deserves full recognition.

Temple architecture remained academic and Roman in little more than the name, producing nothing new of importance until vaulting afforded the means of achieving impressive interiors, and even then the Pantheon was unique. It was in secular architecture that the greatest results were attained by developing two distinct styles, the one (pier-and-arch) capable of application to buildings as essentially different as a theater and a basilica, the other (vault-and-dome) flexible enough to serve for palaces as well as for baths. Above all it was an imperial art, almost to the exclusion of local styles in the provinces, and stamped as plainly as was the coinage with an unmistakable image and a superscription which might have read *urbi et orbi*.

XII

THE CITY OF ROME

"HAEC SVNT FORA CAESARIS," INQVIT,
"HAEC EST A SACRIS QVAE VIA NOMEN HABET,
HIC LOCVS EST VESTAE, QVA PALLADA SERVAT ET IGNEM,
HAEC FVIT ANTIQVI REGIA PARVA NVMAE."
INDE PETENS DEXTRAM "PORTA EST" AIT "ISTA PALATI,
HIC STATOR, HOC PRIMVM CONDITA ROMA LOCO EST."

OVID, TRISTIA, 3, 1, 27

REGINA ET DOMINA ORBIS

FRONTINUS, DE AQUIS, 88

IN QVA VNICA TOTIVS ORBIS CIVITATE SOLI BARBARI ET SERVI PEREGRINANTVR.

APOLLINARIS SIDONIUS, EPISTOLAE, 1, 6, 2

THE outward aspect of a city with a long history can best be realized in its successive phases by selecting certain moments and imagining ourselves as visiting the city at each of the selected dates, to make at least a partial round of its chief centers, principal streets, and most conspicuous buildings as they then were; or else by reconstructing in imagination a bird's-eye view of the city at each particular time.

For early Rome we lack the material necessary either for a sight-seeing tour or for a panorama, and must be content with a few generalizations. From the very beginning of the Republic we should have found the most conspicuous hill, the Capitoline, crowned by the one temple of notable size— the Temple of Jupiter, high above the Forum. Like all Roman temples of the fifth century B.C. it would be so completely Tuscan in its architecture that the visitor from any of the cities of Etruria must have felt much at home, though doubtless impressed by its imposing scale. Naturally Etruscan kings in developing a capital had given to buildings their national stamp, some traces of which remained long after the Greek influences from the South and East had brought momentous changes in the growing city. Passing over the prosperous period under the Etruscan kings, a subsequent century of material decline, and then gradual recovery, and further growth through the fourth and third centuries B.C., we come to the age of the Elder Scipio and that of Cato the Censor.

ROME IN HER SIXTH CENTURY

If we could have walked about the city of Rome with Cato as our guide, let us say in the year 170 B.C., he would no doubt have pointed with pride to the historic monuments, such as the Curia Hostilia, or Senate House, older, it was imagined, than the Etruscan Tarquins. He would perhaps have shown us the only prison, the Carcer, facing on the same small square, the Comitium. Adjoining the prison stood his own Basilica Porcia, the first of its kind at Rome, and no doubt exhibited by him with unconcealed satisfaction as the work of his censorship, to serve as an exchange and a courthouse. Passing the Rostra, or speakers' platform, and the so-called Tomb of Romulus on our way out of the Comitium into the more open Forum, he would have pointed out the primitive altar of Vulcan on a higher level toward the Capitoline. Behind the Vulcanal and against the hill was the Temple of Concord, built to commemorate the passage of the Licinian laws of 367 B.C., after the long struggle between the classes. This no doubt was in the Tuscan style, as was the Temple of Saturn, farther to the south, facing toward the Curia and dating from the first decades of the Republic. Thence he would have led us past the shops on the south side of the Forum and past Scipio's house, to be removed the next year for the erection of Sempronius's basilica. Then to the Temple of Castor, dedicated in 484 B.C., this also Tuscan. Thence farther east to the Lacus Iuturnae, a sacred spring with its basin and quaint old equestrian statues of Castor and Pollux. For here the twins were said to have watered their horses after reporting the victory of Lake Regillus. Then to the Temple of Vesta, rebuilt after a fire in 241 B.C., but still recalling in its circular plan the primitive Italic hut, though probably Greek in its architectural forms. Behind a row of shops, Tabernae Novae, on the north side of the Forum he would have shown us how his example had been imitated by the next censors in building another basilica, the Aemilia.

Italian Air Service

AERIAL VIEW, PIAZZA VEN

1

—

2

—

3

—

4

—

5

—

6

HE COLOSSEUM

On the Palatine we should have been escorted to the
thatched Casa Romuli and other antiquities; then to their
new neighbor, the Temple of the Great Mother, Cybele,
with its fluted and stuccoed columns, dedicated twenty
years before. From the ramparts of the Palatine we should
have looked down upon the Circus Maximus, in the valley
between Palatine and Aventine, while our guide preached
his oft-repeated sermon on the habits of the populace and
the degeneracy of the times. At the farther end of the Circus
could be seen a section of the Servian Wall (fourth century) and the Porta Capena, spanning the Appian Way.
Our guide would have pointed to the temples on the opposite hill, the Aventine: that of Diana, of the sixth century
B.C., and that of Juno Regina, a century and a half younger;
also in the low quarter to the right, near the Tiber, another
temple, possibly that of Mater Matuta, rebuilt during the
Second Punic War.[1] Near it was the old wooden bridge,
Pons Sublicius, and two shorter wooden bridges connecting
the island with both banks, replacing those swept away by
a flood in 192 B.C. Just below the island we should have observed a new bridge built by the censors of 179 B.C., the
Pons Aemilius, with stone piers and wooden arches.

Then up to the Capitol to visit the chief of Roman temples, that of Jupiter Optimus Maximus, nearly square and
completely Tuscan, as built by the last of the kings, but
dedicated in the first year of the Republic. With its long
timber architraves resting upon wide-spaced columns, with
its terra-cotta ornamentation, this great temple must have
appeared to Cato the historian the focus of national history.
And there on the Capitol he might have left us to look
down upon the broad meadow of the Campus Martius and
the public buildings which had already encroached upon

---

[1] It was rebuilt again a century after Cato and is still well preserved, the
so-called Temple of Fortuna Virilis (p. 353).

its nearer portion—a second circus, that of Flaminius, and the temples in that vicinity, including Apollo's of the fifth century B.C.

THE ROME OF SULLA

In the year of Sulla's death, 78 B.C., we may imagine ourselves standing upon the roof of a great new building across the western end of the Forum and against the slope of the Capitoline. This Tabularium, or Record Office, dedicated in that very year by Lutatius Catulus, still stands in large part, with added stories and tower. From its roof we should then have looked down upon a small irregular place, formerly a market. Out of this always busy center opened toward our left a much smaller square, the Comitium, no longer used for popular assemblies. It was separated from the Forum in part by a platform, the convex front of which was adorned by the beaks of ships, and hence known as the Rostra. On this platform, then recently rebuilt, we might have chanced to see a speaker addressing a crowd. Behind him and farther to our left, on the north side of that smaller place, stood the old Senate House, facing south and dating, it was said, from the seventh century B.C., but largely rebuilt by Sulla in 80 B.C. Our view would be obstructed in part by the Temple of Concord and two basilicas designed for law courts and as business exchanges. The rear wall of this temple, built about 360 B.C. and restored in 121, actually touched the front wall of our Tabularium. Of the two halls, the Basilica Opimia (121 B.C.) lay close to the temple on its northern side, while the Porcia faced the side wall of the Curia (p. 372). Between the basilicas lay the small, low Carcer, also facing east. Not far beyond the Rostra we should have observed the bronze shrine of Janus, its doors always open except at those rare moments when peace prevailed. Once only in some 600 years previous to Sulla's

time was it said to have been closed, and that after the First
Punic War. Beyond the diminutive temple lay a row of
shops occupied by bankers and money changers—the Tabernae Novae, with open galleries above them; and directly
behind these the Basilica Aemilia, a century old (p. 372),
but just restored by Aemilius Lepidus.

At its farther end, in the distance, the Forum grew somewhat narrower, and was not as yet closed by any conspicuous building. Beyond its limits, as marked by the triumphal
arch of Fabius (121 B.C.), we should have seen the Regia,
where the Pontifex maximus had his office, and a little
nearer and more to the right the round Temple of Vesta,
encircled by its Tuscan columns. Behind it lay the Atrium
Vestae, the ample dwelling of the six priestesses charged
with the duty of maintaining the sacred fire in the temple.
More conspicuous and nearer would appear the Temple of
Castor on its lofty foundation, with a speaker's platform on
the stairs leading up to its stuccoed columns (p. 372). It
had been rebuilt forty years before. Nearer still we should
look down on the roof of the Basilica Sempronia (*ibid.*),
behind another row of shops along the right (southwest)
side of the Forum. Nearest of all, and almost directly beneath us, would be the Temple of Saturn, just where the
street leading up to the Capitol made a sharp turn. This
temple was then over four hundred years old, with Tuscan
columns of soft tufa or harder peperino coated with white
stucco. It contained the public treasury, while the offices
were near by.

What would have impressed us most in this view of the
Forum of the Republic from the roof of its newest and larg-
est building, is its absence of plan and consistent purpose.
In spite of Sulla's many improvements a visitor from the
smallest Greek city must have thought the civic center of
Rome barren of interest, its old temples, with a single

exception, that on the Capitol, no more imposing than those to be found in towns of small importance. Low rows of very small shops seemed to jostle the basilicas half-hidden by them, while the halls themselves lacked real stateliness. The one imposing building in the Forum was this Tabularium, on whose roof we have perched in imagination. Above the massive substruction rose a story having an open gallery whose arches rested on heavy piers adorned with half-columns of the Tuscan order (p. 350). Over this was a second open gallery of similar construction, but with half-columns of the Ionic or Corinthian order.[2]

Toward the southwest we look off from our point of vantage on the same roof to the Capitolium, formerly crowned by the ancient Jupiter temple, at this time (78 B.C.) slowly rebuilding after its destruction by fire five years before. Its restoration in the same Tuscan architecture, retaining its wide intercolumniations and wooden architraves faced with terra cotta, was begun by Sulla, to be finished by the same Catulus who completed the Tabularium and, nine years after the dictator's death, dedicated the temple.

Turning northward we should have before us the Arx, a citadel with walls and towers, and rising above them at the highest point the Temple of Juno Moneta, of the fourth century B.C., and probably still Tuscan with stuccoed columns. In a building connected with the temple the mint was established, and there were coined the silver and other coins of the Republic.

Between that crest of the Capitoline and the western height, on which we have watched the rebuilding of Jupiter's temple, we look down upon the connecting ridge or saddle toward which the Tabularium has another façade on an open place high above the Forum level, but considerably lower than the two crests. In spite of the temples

---

[2] Probably replaced later by a Corinthian colonnade.

large and small and the citadel we note that there are still many dwellings on these heights.

Farther away we look off westward and northwestward into the Campus Martius, in the distance a place of exercise and military training, but in the foreground largely covered with public buildings. Most conspicuous is the Circus Flaminius, where popular assemblies also are held. As yet there are no theaters and few porticos, such as that of Metellus, a colonnaded court surrounding two Greek temples of Jupiter Stator and Juno. Below us are the roofs of a number of other temples, including four which stand within the same enclosure,[3] and stretching away to the north is the long ribbon of the Via Flaminia, leading to the Mulvian Bridge over the Tiber (p. 98).

Turning more to the right the eye follows the line of the so-called Servian Wall from the Capitoline around the northwest side of the Quirinal. Thence from a point near the distant Porta Collina the wall turns to the southeast, being strengthened by a great earthwork, the Agger, and a wide trench where it crosses the level ground to the Porta Esquilina. From that gate on the Esquiline the wall turns in the general direction of the river until it has enclosed the Caelian and Aventine, ending at the Porta Trigemina, close to the Tiber. In the quarters included in this sweep of the eye there are at this date of 78 B.C. no very conspicuous monuments. The Quirinal to be sure has its old Temple of Quirinus (sixth century). On the Esquiline are some large residences, especially on the Carinae. But the day of veritable palaces has hardly arrived.

It is on the Palatine to the southeast, particularly on that side which looks down on the Forum, that stately houses are beginning to rise. On the western angle which looks toward the Tiber we see the Temple of Cybele, begun in 204 B.C. to

[3] The recently excavated Foro Argentina.

receive the Phrygian goddess, and near it the straw Hut of Romulus showing just above old walls (p. 373). On the lower level is the northwest end of the Circus Maximus. As for the Tiber itself, we have glimpses of the river and a view of the island and its Temple of Aesculapius, reached by a wooden bridge from either bank. Of the two bridges across the full width of the river the old wooden Pons Sublicius remains as before, but the Aemilian has stone arches which replaced wood in 142 B.C. Beyond the bridges we see a poor quarter, and high above it a fort on the top of the Janiculum.

The view of Rome from any of its heights in the age of Sulla must have been very disappointing to a traveler from Greek lands. Largely built of sun-dried brick, so far as dwellings and shops were concerned, and relieved by few imposing structures effectively placed, straggling beyond its walls, and only just beginning to think of the art of city planning, it had much to learn from every Hellenistic city.

ROME OF THE FIRST CAESARS

The period immediately preceding the feverish building activity of Julius Caesar produced one conspicuous group which was the work of Pompey. His theater in the Campus Martius was the first permanent stone theater in Rome, seating at least 10,000 persons and containing at the center of the highest row of seats a temple of Venus Victrix, so that the whole building was dedicated in 55 B.C. as a temple. Pompey provided a large *porticus* also with a central garden, and a hall, the Curia Pompeii, in which Caesar was assassinated at a meeting of the senate. The hall was walled up as an accursed spot by Augustus, who restored the theater, as did Tiberius also after a fire.

Caesar had vast projects for the remaking of Rome. His unfinished buildings were completed or reconstructed by

Augustus, and the combined efforts of these founders of the Empire and of their friends produced at last a worthy capital. Among these countless improvements only a few of special significance may be mentioned here.

To begin with the Forum, its appearance was completely changed by new buildings and the renewal of nearly all its existing structures. Most conspicuous, and almost opposite each other, were the two great basilicas, the new Aemilia on the northeast side, with shops behind the arches of its long portico, while back of these lay the broad nave and aisles of the basilica itself; and on the southwest side the larger Basilica Iulia, entered through an arcaded portico (without shops) directly adjoining a side aisle, beyond which lay a nave and two more side aisles (p. 358). These spacious buildings of white marble in the arcaded style contrasted strongly with the purely Greek architecture of the reconstructed temples. The long façades of the basilicas consisted of open arcades similar to those of the Tabularium, borne by square piers to which the Greek orders were applied as ornament. For the first story it was the Tuscan order, for the second Ionic (a "setback" in the case of the Aemilia). Higher still, but hardly seen at short range, rose a clerestory to light the interior. Caesar was unable to finish his Basilica Iulia and on its completion by his successor fire destroyed the building. It was then rebuilt on a larger scale by Augustus, who was obliged to renew the Aemilia also after a fire.

In spite of the great floor space—sumptuously paved with colored marbles—provided by these basilicas, with a virtual enlargement of the Forum, further extensions were projected. Julius Caesar, having decided to add a new Forum of his own to the north, removed the Curia, which had been rebuilt after its destruction by fire in 52 B.C., when the Basilica Porcia also was burned. A new Senate House

was erected on a site nearer the old Forum and facing southwest, and behind this new Curia lay the eastern end of the
new Forum Iulium, in part surrounded by shops that were
entered from a colonnaded court (illus., p. 436). At the farther end of this court he built a splendid Temple of Venus
the Mother.⁴ These new works involved encroachment upon
the old Comitium, which now became merely a corner of
the Forum Romanum, with the removal of the Rostra to a
new position near the northwest end, looking down the
length of the Forum.

Caesar's example was followed by other leading men,
such as Munatius Plancus, who in 42 B.C. rebuilt the Temple of Saturn on its lofty podium with a façade of Ionic
columns. Under Augustus the other temples of the Forum
were rebuilt. The Temple of Concord at its northwest end
was completely renewed, though retaining its unusual
ground plan. The wide and shallow cella of this, one of the
most beautiful temples in Rome, was placed against the
Tabularium and entered from the center of a long side.
From its lofty Corinthian porch one looked down upon the
new Rostra and to the farther end of the Forum—a vista
closed (since 29 B.C.) by the Temple of the Deified Julius,
erected by Augustus on the spot where Caesar's body had
been burned. This temple stood on an elevated platform the
front of which, adorned with ships' beaks from the battle
of Actium, provided another platform for speakers.

Close to the south side of this temple stood the triple
Arch of Augustus, commemorating a diplomatic victory—
the return of the standards captured from Crassus by the
Parthians in 53 B.C. The adjoining Temple of Castor was
rebuilt by Tiberius under Augustus in 6 A.D. in the Corinthian style, on a lofty podium. No more beautiful examples
of Hellenistic architecture in Rome remain than the three

⁴ A large part of this forum and its temple has been recently excavated.

columns of white marble supporting a part of the entablature (illus., p. 435). An unusual feature due to lack of space
was that the steps at the front were broken by a landing
from the ends of which narrow staircases led down to the
level of the Forum.

Thus before the end of Augustus's reign all the buildings
around the Forum Romanum, except the Tabularium and
the Carcer, had been rebuilt with a splendor unknown to
the previous period. The demand for ampler spaces and the
example of Julius led Augustus to add another forum of
his own beyond that of Caesar and on a more magnificent
scale (illus., p. 436). Its axis was at right angles to that of
the Forum Iulium and at the farther end, toward the Quirinal, he built a great Temple of Mars the Avenger, vowed
by him at the battle of Philippi (42 B.C.). Caesar's Venus
Genetrix, ancestress of the Julian family, was to be matched
by Mars Ultor, commemorating the vengeance upon Brutus
and Cassius. Protected by a lofty fire wall over a hundred
feet in height, of which a large part still remains, this
Forum Augustum and its temple, even now very imposing
in their ruins, were lavishly adorned with rich marbles. To
gain room for statues of all the generals who had triumphed
the rectangular space was enlarged by two immense, almost
semicircular apses (*exedrae*) to right and left of the temple.

More famous and certainly no less splendid was Augustus's new temple of Apollo on the Palatine, commemorating
the victory at Actium. It stood in its own *porticus* adorned
with works of art and giving access to a Greek and a Latin
library. The site is still debated, but it was close to the house
in which Augustus lived, a modest dwelling, once the residence of Hortensius the orator. The house is probably that
known as the House of Livia and still in part preserved
(p. 324).

In the same reign the Circus Maximus assumed a more

permanent form, and two stone theaters were erected in the Campus Martius, that of Marcellus, of which a large part remains and has recently been excavated and freed from some of its encumbrances (illus., p. 408), and the Theater of Balbus. Agrippa, the Emperor's son-in-law and minister, built the first of the great Thermae, or public baths (p. 156), also in the Campus, and in connection with them a temple, known as the Pantheon, destroyed by fire with the Baths in 80 A.D. Agrippa also completed the so-called Saepta Iulia, extending along the west side of the Via Lata (Flaminia) for a distance of some 1,400 feet (p. 358). Replacing an earlier structure designed for the conduct of elections, it was soon devoted to other purposes, since popular elections ceased with the accession of Tiberius. Its seven aisles, separated by rows of piers, came to be a favorite lounging place parallel to that busy street, the modern Corso Umberto. On the east side of the same Via Lata Agrippa finished the Porticus Vipsania, which opened upon a park and contained his famous map of the world (p. 287). And near the Theater of Marcellus another *porticus* was built by Augustus, to bear the name of his sister Octavia. Surrounding two reconstructed temples it contained a library and many works of art. Another similar *porticus* he laid out on the Esquiline in honor of his wife Livia. Between the Tiber and the Via Lata, in a public park, he erected more than forty years before his death a circular mausoleum for the imperial family and his successors. Crowned by a mound of earth planted with trees, or by concentric terraces, and at the very top by his statue in bronze, it was a glorified version of an old Etruscan tumulus. At the entrance one could read on bronze tablets the history of his reign from his own pen—the famous inscription known as the Monumentum Ancyranum, since the best copy is at Angora (Ancyra) in Turkey.

In artistic merit probably no single monument of the Augustan Age surpassed the Altar of Peace, on the Via Lata, small in size, but a notable achievment (p. 337). An impressive result of the peace Augustus had brought to the world was the virtual rebuilding of the city which he had found of brick (sun-dried brick at that) and had left, as he ventured to claim, of marble.

To complete our mental picture of Rome at the beginning of the Christian era we should recall one fact of a different kind, that the old walls, the so-called Wall of Servius Tullius, had been completely outgrown. Whole stretches of the old defenses had been removed or utterly neglected, and there was no thought of a new line of fortification.

ROME OF THE FLAVIAN EMPERORS

If we now pass over more than two generations to the mild rule of Nerva we may imagine ourselves making another tour of the city of Rome in the year 96 A.D. Most of the changes we note will be due to the three Flavian emperors, Vespasian and his two sons, since the great fire in Nero's time and the impossible character of some of his rebuilding gave great opportunities to his successors. The passion of the Flavians for building was given further scope by a disastrous fire in the short reign of Titus, which ravaged the Palatine, the Capitol, and part of the Campus Martius.

We may begin our circuit on that hill of the palaces, and first wander through the Domus Flavia, the work of Domitian. It is a group of state apartments, lavish in their marbles and other adornments, and all on a grand scale, surrounding a huge peristyle. There are halls for every occasion of state, including a sumptuous triclinium. Much of this group was built directly over a palace of Nero, his Domus Transitoria (burned in the fire of 64 A.D.) and older houses in the low central portion of the hill. For purposes of residence Domitian rebuilt the Domus Tiberiana, or Palace of Tiberius, to which Caligula had made additions, so that this palace with its large courts extended to the angle of the hill looking down upon the Forum. We may wander through the long vaulted corridor (*cryptoporticus*) which with several arms linked the different parts of the group together. Or, walking southward, we reach the Domus Augustana, another residential palace, also rebuilt by Domitian, looking down upon the Circus Maximus. Continuing our ramble toward the southern angle of the hill we come to the gardens of the same emperor, laid out in the form of a stadium (p. 174).

Returning to the front of the Domus Flavia we descend the Clivus Palatinus to the Arch of Titus, at the highest point of the Sacra Via. A single arch of the simplest type, it is framed by engaged columns with capitals of the Composite form and adorned with celebrated reliefs recalling the triumph of Titus over the Jews and his capture of Jerusalem (p. 340). It was completed by Domitian after the death of his brother.

From the arch we go down the slope of the Velia to the Flavian Amphitheater,[5] the largest of its kind. This immense ellipse, 617 by 512 feet and 159 feet high, has 80 arches at the ground level serving as entrances.[6] The arches rest upon massive piers of travertine adorned with half-columns of the Tuscan order. The second and third stories have the same number of open arches, but the half-columns against the piers are Ionic and Corinthian respectively (p. 357). Above the arcades is a loftier story, its solid wall relieved by Corinthian pilasters and broken at regular inter-

[5] Usually called by its medieval name the Colosseum, from the neighboring Colossus.

[6] Thirty-four such arches of the exterior arcade are still standing.

vals by windows, also by corbels for the awning masts. Passing through a vaulted corridor we find ourselves in the arena, completely surrounded by ascending rows of seats [7] with a probable capacity of 45,000. At the top is a colonnade [8] affording shelter to the highest seats; but over a part of the vast space awnings can be spread, supported by masts at the top of the outer wall. Opened by Vespasian in 79 A.D., it was formally dedicated the next year by Titus, but actually completed by Domitian.

This low and formerly swampy site had been converted by Nero into a lake, the Stagnum Neronis, in the extensive park of his Golden House, which with its gardens covered an immense area mostly on the Palatine and Esquiline, with an entrance court between the lake and the Velia, toward the site of the Arch of Titus. In the court was placed yonder colossal statue—his own likeness until Vespasian changed the head and converted it into an image of the sun god. [9]

On this southern slope of the Esquiline are the Baths of Titus, opened by him at the time of the dedication of the amphitheater. These too lie within the former area of the Domus Aurea of Nero (p. 157).

Proceeding now in the direction of the old Forum we come to the newer Forum of Vespasian, in the center of which stands the Temple of Peace [10] erected by him to commemorate the reëstablishment of order after civil wars, and containing the spoils of the Temple in Jerusalem. On beyond, toward the Capitol, we enter the newest addition to the Imperial Fora, the narrow Forum of Nerva, and confront the Temple of Minerva. Both were the work of Domi-

[7] All of these have disappeared.
[8] No longer to be seen.
[9] Nothing now remains of the Colossus Neronis except a part of the foundation.
[10] Nothing is now visible, although a new street has been carried across the site.

tian, but completed by his successor. Passing between the lofty columns [11] on this side and that we enter the Forum Romanum between the Curia and the Basilica Aemilia. Crossing in front of the Temple of Concord we come at once to the Corinthian Temple of Vespasian and Titus,[12] with its face turned toward the distant amphitheater.

While ascending the winding street which leads to the Capitol we look back upon the whole of the Roman Forum, almost unchanged, and across to the Palatine, completely altered in appearance since the time of Augustus. Beneath its western corner we see the temple of the first of the emperors.

On the Capitol we have before us the magnificent new Temple of Jupiter, with its glistening roof of gilt bronze tiles and its three gilded doors. Domitian rebuilt the temple once more after the fire of the year 80 A.D. His father also had found it in ruins on reaching Rome from the East; for it had been burned in the fierce struggles between the partisans of Vitellius and those of Vespasian at the end of the revolution year, 69 A.D. Thus the temple has been twice rebuilt by the Flavians, with increasing splendor and in the Corinthian order (p. 376).

In the Campus Martius we visit the Stadium of Domitian, erected by him for the contests of athletes,[13] and near by the Thermae of Nero, the second establishment of the kind in Rome. Moving southward we come to the new Pantheon, Agrippa's temple, rebuilt by Domitian after the fire of Titus.[14]

At this point our guide would probably give us our choice between several longer walks to more distant sights. We

[11] Two of these are still standing.
[12] Three columns remain.
[13] Cp. p. 154. The lines of the arena are still plainly marked by the long, narrow Piazza Agonale (Navona).
[14] Not to be confused with Hadrian's rotunda, p. 389.

might cross the Tiber by Agrippa's bridge or that of Nero
to the Circus of Caligula and Nero, in gardens once the
property of Agrippina.[15] We may prefer a turn in quite the
opposite direction to the Camp of the Praetorians, the fortified post of the praetorian cohorts, first concentrated at
Rome under Tiberius and established a short distance beyond the Porta Collina. In returning we might follow at
first the line of Claudius's two aqueducts, Claudia and Anio
Novus, pausing at the double arch [16] which spans the meeting of two roads, Via Praenestina and the Labicana. Thence
we may return across the Caelian along the line of lofty
arches by which Nero carried water of the Aqua Claudia
to the Palatine.

ROME OF THE ANTONINES

The chief public work of Trajan at the capital was his
new Forum with its adjacent buildings.[17] Its central feature
was a great rectangular *porticus* with semicircular extensions toward the Quirinal on one side, toward the Capitoline
on the other, the whole space being paved with choice
marbles. A triumphal gateway toward the Forum of Augustus (p. 381) was the principal entrance, directly opposite one side of the Basilica Ulpia with its three entrances.
In the center of the open space stood an equestrian statue
of the Emperor. The apse toward the Quirinal adjoined a
concentric street with a hemicycle of shops whose upper
stories rose in terraces,[18] while on a higher level to the
north stood a vaulted hall (an "arcade" we should now call

[15] Over one side of this circus, the scene of Nero's cruel treatment of
the Christians, was built the old basilica of St. Peter.

[16] Later a gate (Praenestina) in Aurelian's Wall, and now Porta Maggiore (p. 359).

[17] Recent excavations have brought to light much that was hitherto unknown.

[18] There was no corresponding hemicycle of shops toward the Capitoline.

it) with several stories of shops (illus., pp. 434, 437). The basilica itself, larger and more stately than any of its predecessors, had a nave and four aisles, and at each end of this forest of columns was a large apse for law courts.

Just beyond the basilica stood a Greek and a Latin library (p. 245), and in a very small court between them rose the famous Column of Trajan,[19] sculptured for the whole height of its shaft (p. 341) and supporting his statue. In a chamber in the pedestal his ashes were laid away. And to complete the imposing group—the most impressive thing in ancient Rome—Hadrian added a temple to the deified Trajan in a colonnaded court beyond the libraries.

Trajan provided the capital with another bathing establishment, on the Esquiline, near the Baths of Titus (p. 385), but on a much larger scale, certain parts being erected directly over halls and rooms of the Golden House of Nero. The central structure, with its caldarium projecting to the southwest, to be warmed as far as possible by the sun, with its great hall, tepidarium, and frigidarium, was surrounded on three sides by open spaces bordered by rooms for various forms of exercise or recreation. Four of these were semicircular projections (exedrae), and a fifth, much larger and facing the caldarium, was used as a theater. These Thermae, like the Forum of Trajan, were designed by Apollodorus, a celebrated Greek architect from Damascus.

In this same period the Circus Maximus was much enlarged by carrying the upper tiers of seats above the street and up the slope of the Palatine. With a length of nearly 2,000 feet there were now probably seats for 150,000 people. The exterior was much like that of the Colosseum, but of marble.

Hadrian gave Rome the greatest of her temples, that of Venus and Rome, and the most enduring, the present Pan-

[19] Not including the pedestal, it is 100 feet high.

theon. The double temple was surrounded by a large
porticus, extending from the Arch of Titus almost to the
Flavian Amphitheater, occupying an elevated platform on
the Velia. Designed by the Emperor himself, it contained
two cellae having their apses back to back, one for Venus
and the other for the Goddess Roma. Ten Corinthian columns distinguished each of the façades, and of the brick-
faced concrete great masses, including the apses, still remain. The court surrounding the temple had many columns
of gray granite, some of which have now been reërected.
Much of what we still see is probably due to Maxentius
after a fire early in the fourth century (illus., p. 438).

In a totally different style, except for its façade, is the
Pantheon (illus., p. 434), reared by Hadrian in place of
Domitian's temple, which was burned in the time of Trajan
(p. 386). A rotunda open to the sky and entered through a
deep Corinthian porch, it remains unrivaled among Roman
structures. The hemispherical dome, 142 feet in internal
diameter and the same in height, massively constructed of
concrete and brick, lavishly adorned with marbles within,
is lighted only from an "eye" overhead—an unroofed opening 30 feet in diameter—and from the lofty doorway when
its bronze doors (still in place) are open. The exterior of
the huge drum was as plain as possible, except for simple
stringcourses. As previous Pantheons had been members of
a larger group, the Baths of Agrippa, the new temple was
a part of the same Thermae, as enlarged and restored by
Hadrian.

One other conspicuous monument of the city today was
the work of the same emperor—the Castle of St. Angelo,
the mausoleum of the emperors to the time of Caracalla,
and later the principal fortress of Rome for some fourteen
centuries, down to 1870. Upon a massive base 275 feet
square and 33 feet high, faced with Parian marble, rose a

drum also marble-faced, 210 feet in diameter and 69 feet high. Above the cylinder was a cone of earth planted with cypresses, or a garden, above which rose a small circular structure, probably supporting a colossal statue of Hadrian driving a quadriga. As an approach to his tomb the same emperor built a stone bridge still in use, the Pons Aelius.

On the Palatine, aside from some rebuilding of the Palace of Tiberius, Hadrian appears to have added little more to the complex of palaces than the huge exedra, or semi-circular projection, looking down upon the stadium-shaped garden (p. 384). After his years of extensive travel it is probable that he lived mainly at the immense villa he had built near Tibur (p. 328).

To mark the reigns of Antoninus Pius and Marcus Aurelius there were fewer monuments of note. In the Campus Martius stood a red granite column nearly fifty feet high in memory of Antoninus and surmounted by his statue. The elaborately sculptured white marble pedestal, depicting on its principal face the deification of this emperor, is now in the Vatican.

More imposing was the Column of Marcus Aurelius, nearer to the Via Lata and opposite the Porticus Vipsania. It still stands in one of the busiest squares of modern Rome, the Piazza Colonna. Like the Column of Trajan and of the same height, it pictures continuous scenes from campaigns against barbarian invaders (p. 343).

Antoninus built a temple on the Sacred Way, just before that street enters the Forum Romanum, in memory of his wife Faustina, who had been deified. Upon his death in 161 A.D. the temple was dedicated to the deified emperor as well. Preserved in large part by use as a church it still retains its Greek marble columns on a very lofty podium and a large part of its entablature with the two inscriptions.

ROME IN THE AGE OF CONSTANTINE

To realize the appearance of the city in the time of the first Christian emperor, and just before the removal of the capital to the Bosporus, we must bear in mind the principal changes due to Septimius Severus, his son Caracalla, Aurelian, and Diocletian.

A serious fire in 191 A.D. encouraged the building propensities of the first emperor from Africa, Severus, whose most notable building was done on the Palatine. There he made conspicuous enlargements of the palaces, especially to the south, where the slope toward the Circus rendered very high arched and vaulted substructions necessary. At the extreme southern angle of the hill he erected a sham façade closing the vista for one approaching by the Appian Way. It was similar in its excessive elaboration to the scene walls of many theaters, but even more lavish, with niches, fountains and sculpture. This Septizonium was only an apparent front, and not an entrance to his new palace (p. 365).

With equal disregard for taste Severus spoiled the upper end of the Forum Romanum by his triple triumphal arch, 75 feet high, almost directly in front of the Temple of Concord and alongside of the Rostra. His victories in the East are represented in reliefs, now damaged (p. 345), on this otherwise well-preserved monument. The inscription fills the entire attica, and one can see that the name and titles of Geta were erased after his murder by his brother Caracalla.

Imitating the essential features of Trajan's Baths Caracalla built his much larger Thermae in the southern part of the city, on a new street parallel to the Via Appia (p. 97). The central block alone is no less than 708 feet long and 367 feet broad. The hot bath (caldarium) projected to the southwest in the form of a lofty dome, 115 feet in diameter and raised on towering piers. In the center of the whole was the great vaulted hall without heating arrangements, while the cold bath, a swimming pool, was placed against the northeast wall and probably open to the sky. From each end of the main hall one reached a palaestra with columns on three sides. This entire block of buildings, with many smaller rooms in addition to the halls, stood in a vast garden nearly square and surrounded by a *peribolus,* or outer range of buildings, designed for different kinds of recreation and exercise, including libraries and the half of a stadium, behind which were reservoirs. The main structures were dedicated in 216 A.D., the outer range added later and probably finished by Alexander Severus. The materials used, in almost incredible quantities, were concrete, brick facing, columns of marble and granite, marble slabs, mosaic floors and ceilings, stucco.

With Aurelian (270-275 A.D.) Rome once more became a walled city. His walls and gates of brick-faced concrete included a much larger area than the old walls of the fourth century B.C. (the Wall of Servius Tullius). Constructed in haste they were so located that much material was spared by the use of existing structures of every kind—aqueduct arches, retaining walls, the fortifications of the Castra Praetoria, a small amphitheater on the east side of the city, and a tomb on the road to Ostia, the marble-faced Pyramid of Cestius. In the Campus of Agrippa, near the Via Lata, Aurelian erected a magnificent Temple of the Sun, whose cult he had introduced from the East.

Diocletian cleared away whole streets with their houses in what had been the northern angle of the old Servian city to make room for his Baths, of which the central building alone was to be 919 feet long by 525 broad. These Thermae closely resembled those of Caracalla in plan, as in materials and methods of construction, but the capacity was doubled. The caldarium was a rectangular hall, as in the Baths of

Titus and those of Trajan, having a southwest exposure. The great vaulted central hall (incorrectly called the tepidarium), with its colossal columns, is still in use as a church. Another hall now serves as a Planetarium. Without lay a large garden surrounded by an outer range of buildings containing many rooms for different purposes, exedras and a much larger semicircle serving as a theater, also two rotundas, one of which is now a church.

In the Forum the old Senate House, which had been restored by Domitian, was burned shortly before Diocletian's accession. He now rebuilt the Curia in simpler style without a portico, its walls of brick and concrete coated with white stucco and faced with marble slabs near the ground (illus., p. 435). Since the seventh century it has been a church, Sant' Adriano. The Basilica Iulia had suffered in the same fire and was restored by Diocletian.

A striking change in that quarter of the city was made by the erection of a new basilica totally different in plan and construction from its predecessors. This was in large part the work of Maxentius, usurping emperor in 306-312 A.D., and after his defeat and death at the Mulvian Bridge was completed by Constantine, from whom it takes its name. Instead of rows of piers or columns dividing nave and aisles —the system of the earlier basilicas—Maxentius followed a plan suggested by that of the main halls of the baths. A nave 82 feet in breadth had groined vaulting (about 115 feet high) which appeared to rest upon eight huge columns, but in reality upon concrete masses just behind them. There were three transepts, and broad doorways between them gave the effect of side aisles. An east porch faced the neighboring Temple of Venus and Rome, restored by Maxentius. At the opposite end is an apse in which stood a statue of Constantine, who added another entrance from the Sacra Via and a second apse in the farther end of the central transept.[20] The whole building was lavishly decorated with showy marbles, but was much more remarkable as a triumph of bold concrete construction on a great scale. These three ruined vaults, casting their somber shadows, are now all the more impressive in contrast with the slender Lombard campanile of Santa Francesca Romana.

Besides completing this colossal hall Constantine early in his reign added the last of the great Thermae on the Quirinal, to the southward of the present Royal Palace. These differed from the others in ground plan, owing to an irregular site, but retained the familiar features of the other Baths. Space being unavailable for an enclosing garden and peribolus, some open ground was reserved before the entrance on the north side. A west entrance was at the top of a long flight of steps leading down into the Campus Martius. Both caldarium, to the south, and tepidarium had domes and even these latest of the Baths were enriched by many works of art.

Constantine's famous triumphal arch near the Colosseum belongs also to the beginning of his reign. To commemorate his victory over Maxentius in 312 A.D. this arch was hastily erected, or as we might say, assembled. In elevation it has nearly the same dimensions as that of Septimius Severus, and the same grouping of a smaller archway on each side of a much larger central arch. The total effect is far more successful, since the purely ornamental yellow marble columns at least serve to support statues sculptured for Trajan of Dacian captives, and the inscription, less portentous in length, is confined to the central portion of the attica, the remainder being occupied by reliefs. Comparatively little of the sculpture belongs to the time of Constantine; for older buildings, including the Forum of Trajan and an arch of the philosopher emperor, were plundered to adorn this

[20] Behind this an entire street has recently been excavated.

latest of the commemorative arches (p. 359). It is a composite masterpiece, designed to glorify a single victor, but on close inspection inviting us to reflect upon a synthetic civilization which borrowed many elements and combined them in a solid structure of which so much still endures.

The removal of the capital to Constantinople a few years afterward could not rob the elder Rome of her place in the mind of succeeding ages. If her primacy was henceforth largely ideal it was in its own way still dominant. Not for nothing had the western world so long trained its eyes upon a single focus.

Spiritually speaking there could be but one *urbs aeterna,* her unique and undisputed title gradually taking on new meanings while enshrined in the memory and imagination of the Middle Ages. Later centuries, less fervent in their *Salve per saecula!* are united in critical appreciation of her part in the making of modern nations. To the historian's eye, no less than to that of the Renaissance poet,

le plan de Rome est la carte du monde.

ILLUSTRATIONS AND MAPS

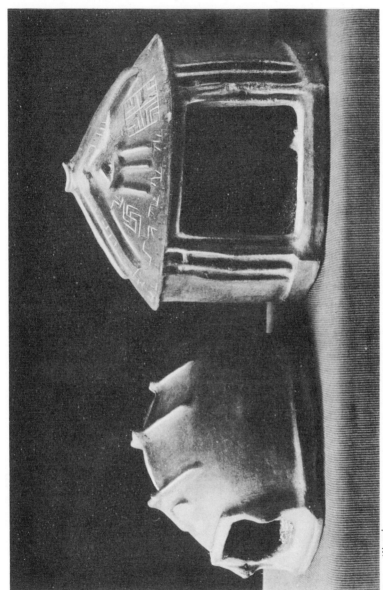

Photo. Alinari   PREHISTORIC HUT-URNS FROM CASTEL GANDOLFO, VATICAN

Photo. D. Anderson, Rome

FORUM ROMANUM, LOOKING TOWARD THE CAPITOLINE

WALL OF HADRIAN IN BRITAIN, AT HAYDON BRIDGE

PRAETORIUM AT LAMBÈSE, NUMIDIA

Lévy et Neuardein

ORANGE, GALLIA NARBONENSIS
TIBERIUS

SUSA, COTTIAN ALPS
AUGUSTUS

DJEMILA (CUICUL), NUMIDIA
CARACALLA

Lévy et Neuardein
TIMGAD, NUMIDIA
TRAJAN

TRIUMPHAL ARCHES

Photo. Luce

SHOP FRONTS, VIA DELL' ABBONDANZA, POMPEII

Photo. D. Anderson, Rome

COURT OF WAREHOUSE, OSTIA

SHOP FRONTS WITH APARTMENTS AND BALCONIES ABOVE, OSTIA

CASA DI DIANA

Photo. Alinari

VIA APPIA, NEAR ROME, WITH A VILLA OF THE QUINTILII

APOLLO OF VEII, VILLA PAPA GIULIO

ETRUSCAN, 500 B.C.

Photo. D. Anderson, Rome

THE FOUR FACTIONS OF THE CIRCUS

MOSAICS, MUSEO DELLE TERME

THEATER OF MARCELLUS: AUGUSTUS

Photo. Alinari

THERMAE OF TRAJAN

THERMAE OF CARACALLA, AERIAL VIEW

Photo. Alinari

Photo. Luce   ATRIUM, HOUSE OF THE MENANDER, POMPEII
ROOF RESTORED

TABLINUM WITH ORIGINAL FOLDING DOORS, HERCULANEUM

HOUSE OF CORNELIUS RUFUS, POMPEII

VIEW THROUGH TABLINUM TO GARDENED PERISTYLE

Photo. T. D. Price

SABINE VILLA, PROBABLY THAT OF HORACE

Photo. Luce

SILVERWARE FROM THE HOUSE OF THE MENANDER, POMPEII

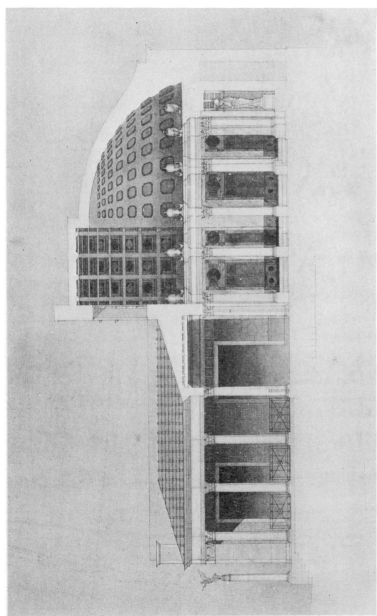

SECTION OF THE LIBRARY AT TIMGAD, PFEIFFER'S RESTORATION

SHOWING BOOKCASES AND THE FORECOURT

VERGIL MANUSCRIPT AT ST. GALL

AENEID I, 685-702; FOURTH OR FIFTH CENTURY

DETAIL OF FRESCO FROM BOSCOREALE, SECOND STYLE

AN ENTIRE ROOM IN THE METROPOLITAN MUSEUM OF ART, NEW YORK CITY

418

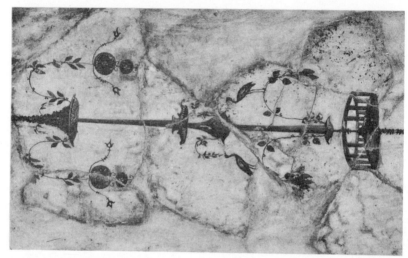

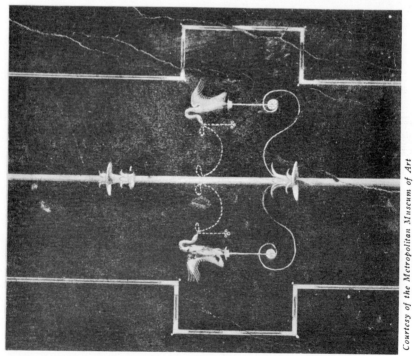

DETAILS OF FRESCO FROM BOSCOTRECASE, THIRD STYLE

LANDSCAPE FRESCO, VILLA OF LIVIA AT PRIMA PORTA

420

DETAIL OF FRESCO, VILLA OF THE MYSTERIES, POMPEII

Photo. D. Anderson, Rome

DETAIL OF FRESCO, VILLA OF THE MYSTERIES, POMPEII

PILASTER, ALTAR OF
PEACE

MUSEO DELLE TERME

INTERIOR FRIEZE, ALTAR OF PEACE

MUSEO DELLE TERME

DECORATIVE RELIEFS

Photo. Alinari

BASILICA AEMILIA

FORUM ROMANUM

AUGUSTUS AS IMPERATOR
FROM VILLA OF LIVIA AT PRIMA PORTA, VATICAN

Photo. D. Anderson, Rome
UNKNOWN BUSTS, FIRST CENTURY B.C.

UNKNOWN BUST, MIDDLE OF
THIRD CENTURY A.D.
FOUND IN EXCAVATIONS FOR THE NEW
VIA DEL IMPERO

Photo. D. Anderson, Rome

STUCCO DECORATION OF CEILING FROM A HOUSE BY THE TIBER

MUSEO DELLE TERME

COLUMN OF TRAJAN, LOWER PART OF THE SHAFT

Photo. D. Anderson, Rome

COLUMN OF TRAJAN, PEDESTAL WITH INSCRIPTION

OPUS INCERTUM
POMPEII

OPUS MIXTUM
NEAR VIA APPIA

OPUS RETICULATUM
VILLA OF HADRIAN

TUFA
SERVIAN WALL

OPUS LATERICIUM
OSTIA

PEPERINO
FORUM OF TRAJAN

CONCRETE POURED INTO MOULD
PALATINE

TRAVERTINE
PONS FABRICIUS

MATERIALS AND METHODS OF CONSTRUCTION

Foto. D. Anderson, Rome

DORIC: TEMPLE AT CORI

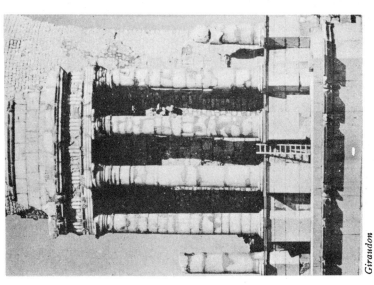

Giraudon

TUSCAN: AUGUSTUS'S MONUMENT AT
LA TURBIE, UPPER STORY

THE ORDERS

Lévy et Neuardein

Lévy et Neuardein

CORINTHIAN AND TUSCAN COLONNADES AT TIMGAD, NUMIDIA

THE ORDERS

Photo. D. Anderson, Rome
IONIC: "TEMPLE OF FORTUNA VIRILIS"

CORINTHIAN: TEMPLE AT NÎMES (MAISON CARRÉE)

THE ORDERS

PONT DU GARD, AQUEDUCT OF NÎMES

Lévy et Neurdein

PIER AND ARCH: AMPHITHEATER OF NÎMES

COLUMNS
BEARING
ARCHES:

DIOCLETIAN'S
PALACE,
SPALATO

Photo. Anton Schroll

Photo. T. Warscher
COLUMNS BEARING ARCHES: PERISTYLE OF THE
CASA DELLA FORTUNA, POMPEII

THE TWO ARCADE SYSTEMS

Photo. Alinari

MERCATO OF TRAJAN, INTERIOR OF AULA

Photo. D. Anderson, Rome

PANTHEON OF HADRIAN, INTERIOR

VAULT AND DOME

Photo. D. Anderson, Rome
SENATE HOUSE, DIOCLETIAN'S FAÇADE

Photo. D. Anderson, Rome
TEMPLE OF CASTOR AND POLLUX, AND TEMPLE OF VESTA

FORUM ROMANUM

Photo. D. Anderson, Rome
FORUM OF JULIUS CAESAR, WITH TEMPLE OF VENUS GENETRIX

Photo. D. Anderson, Rome
FORUM OF AUGUSTUS, WITH TEMPLE OF MARS ULTOR

HEMICYCLE OF TRAJAN'S FORUM AND SHOPS AGAINST THE QUIRINAL

HADRIAN'S TEMPLE OF VENUS AND ROME, FROM THE COLOSSEUM

ARA PACIS

TEMPLE OF JUPITER

COLOSSEUM

HADRIAN'S TEMPLE
OF VENUS AND ROME

CIRCUS MAXIMUS

HADRIAN  ROMA AETERNA

COINS OF THE EMPERORS

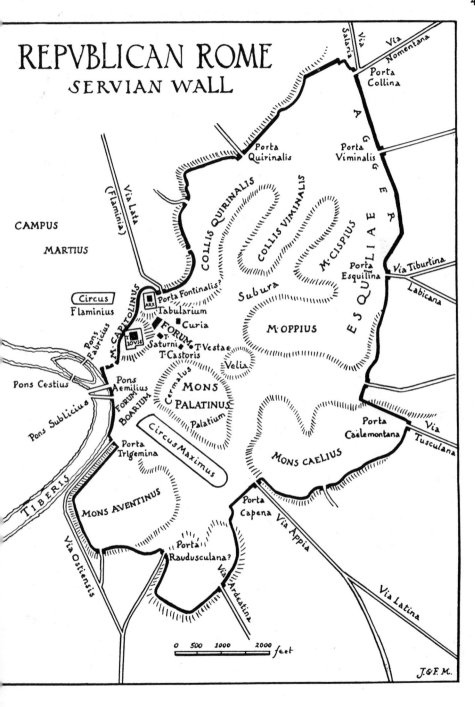

REPVBLICAN ROME
SERVIAN WALL

CAMPUS
MARTIUS

COLLIS QUIRINALIS

COLLIS VIMINALIS

M. CISPIUS

ESQVILIAE

AGGER

Via Salaria

Via Nomentana

Porta Collina

Porta Quirinalis

Porta Viminalis

Porta Esquilina

Via Tiburtina

Labicana

Via Lata (Flaminia)

Circus Flaminius

ARX

Porta Fontinalis?

Tabularium

Curia

FORVM

T. Jovis

T. Saturni

T. Castoris

T. Vestae

Subura

M. OPPIUS

Velia

M. CAPITOLINUS

Pons Fabricius

Pons Cestius

Pons Sublicius

Pons Aemilius

FORVM BOARIVM

Cermalus

MONS PALATINVS

Palatium

Porta Trigemina

Circus Maximus

Porta Caelemontana

Via Tusculana

MONS CAELIVS

TIBERIS

Via Ostiensis

MONS AVENTINVS

Porta Raudusculana?

Via Ardeatina

Porta Capena

Via Appia

Via Latina

0   500   1000   2000 feet

J.&F.M.

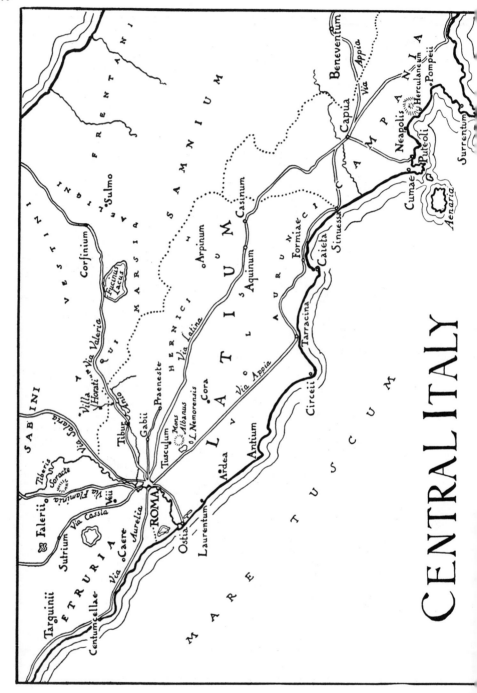

CENTRAL ITALY

ITALIA

GALLIA CISALPINA

Comum
Mediolanum
Segusio
Augusta Taurinorum
Cremona
Mantua
Placentia
Verona
VENETIA
Patavium
Aquileia
HISTRIA
Pola
LIBURNIA
DALMATIA

LIGURIA
Genua
Bononia
Ravenna
Ariminum
Fanum Fortunae
Ancona
Salonae
Narona

Nicaea
Luna
Pisae
Arnus
Faesulae
Florentia
Arretium
UMBRIA
PICENUM
MARE HADRIATICUM

Populonia
Clusium
Perusia
Volsinii
Tiberis
SABINI
Hadria

Ilva
ETRURIA
Corfinium

Aleria
CORSICA
ROMA
LATIUM
SAMNIUM
APULIA
Arpi

Capua
CAMPANIA
Venusia
Brundisium

Puteoli
Tarentum
CALABRIA

Paestum
LUCANIA

MARE TUSCUM

SARDINIA

Thurii

Carales
Croton

BRUTTII
Scylaceum

Messana
Rhegium

Aegates Iae.
Panormus

MARE
AFRICUM

Lilybaeum
SICILIA

Agrigentum
Syracusae

Hippo Regius
Utica
Carthago

NUMIDIA
AFRICA
Zama
Melita

J.&F.M.

SPAIN
1 Gades
2 Corduba
3 Emerita
   Augusta
4 Tarraco

GAUL
1 Tolosa
2 Nemausus
3 Arelate
4 Massilia
5 Lugdunum
6 Burdigala
7 Augustodunum
8 Augusta
   Treverorum

ITALY & SICILY
1 Mediolanum
2 Aquileia
3 Pisae
4 Perusia
5 Puteoli
6 Tarentum
7 Brundisium
8 Panormus
9 Syracusae

NORTH AFRICA
1 Tingis
2 Cirta
3 Lambaesis
4 Thamugadi
5 Carthago
6 Leptis Magna

BRITAIN
1 Londinium
2 Camulodunum
3 Eburacum
4 Vallum Hadriani
5 Vallum Antonini

GERMANY
1 Colonia Agrippinensis
2 Moguntiacum

PANNONIA
1 Carnuntum

a ALPES MARITIMAE
b ALPES COTTIAE
c ALPES GRAIAE & POENINAE

ROMAN
A·D

EUROPE
1 Athenae
2 Sparta
3 Thessalonica
4 Byzantium

ASIA MINOR
1 Nicomedia
2 Pergamum
3 Sardis
4 Ephesus
5 Trapezus
6 Ancyra
7 Tarsus

SYRIA, JUDAEA ARABIA
1 Antiochia
2 Zeugma
3 Berytus
4 Tyrus
5 Palmyra
6 Hierosolyma
7 Petra

EGYPT & CYRENAICA
1 Alexandria
2 Koptos
3 Myos Hormos
4 Berenice
5 Cyrene

a LYCIA
b PAMPHYLIA

SARMATAE

MARE CASPIUM

DACIA

MOESIA

THRACE

MACEDONIA

PONTUS EUXINUS

BITHYNIA PONTUS

GALATIA

CAPPADOCIA

ARMENIA

ASSYRIA

MESOPOTAMIA

EPIRUS

ACHAIA

ASIA

CILICIA

SYRIA

CRETA

CYPRUS

MARE INTERNUM

ARABIA DESERTA

JUDAEA

ARABIA

ARABIA FELIX

CYRENAICA

AEGYPTUS

SINUS ARABICUS

EMPIRE
117

J. & F.M.

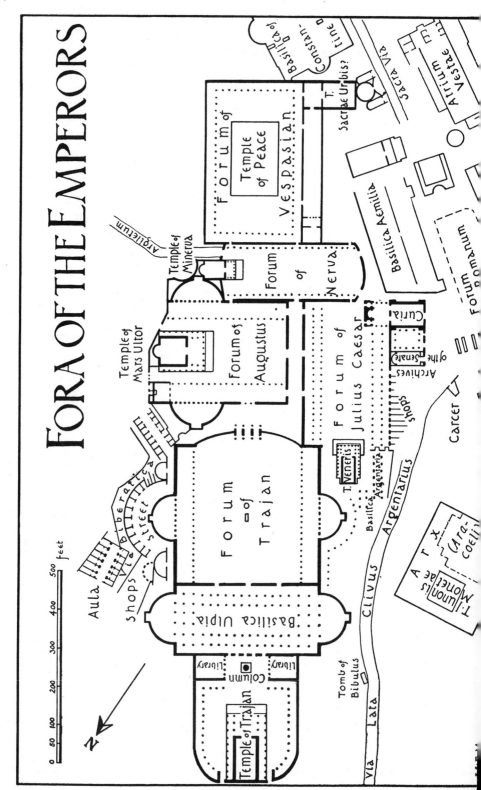

FORA OF THE EMPERORS

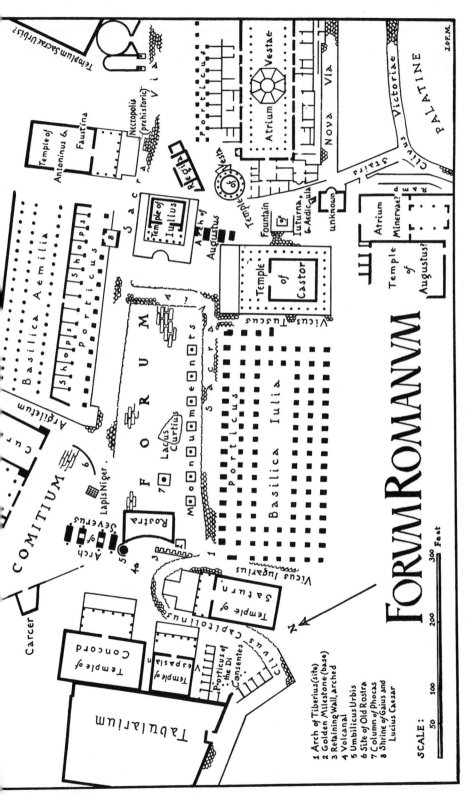

FORVM ROMANVM

SCALE:

50   100   200   300   Feet

1 Arch of Tiberius (site)
2 Golden Milestone (base)
3 Retaining Wall, arched
4 Volcanal
5 Umbilicus Urbis
6 Site of Old Rostra
7 Column of Phocas
8 Shrine of Gaius and
    Lucius Caesar

J.E.M.

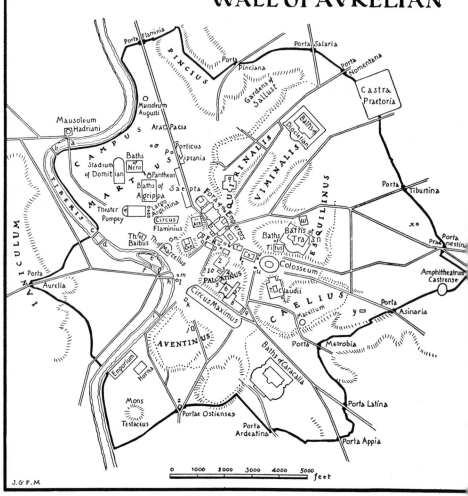

ROME IN THE FOVRTH CENTVRY
WALL OF AVRELIAN

J.&F.M

Cap   Capitolium, with Temple of Jupiter   F·R   Forum Romanum

1	Temple of Ceres	d	Pons Aurelius	p	Column of M. Aurelius
2	Domus Tiberiana	e	Pons Fabricius	q	Baths of Constantine
3	Domus Liviae (Augusti)	f	Pons Cestius	r	Basilica of Constantine
4	Domus Flavia	g	Pons Aemilius	s	Temple of Venus and Rom
5	Palatine Temple of	h	Pons Sublicius	t	Arch of Titus
	Apollo (?)	i	Pons Probi	u	Arch of Constantine
6	Domus Augustana	j	Temple of Diana	v	Colossus Neronis
7	Hippodromus (Garden)	k	Temple of Ceres	w	Porticus Liviae
8	Domus Severi	l	Temple of Portunus (?)	x	Nymphaeum ("Minerva
9	Septizonium	m	Temple of "Fortuna		Medica")
a	Pons Aelius		Virilis"	y	Domus Lateranorum
b	Pons Neronianus	n	Temple of Apollo	z	Pyramid of Cestius
c	Pons Agrippae	o	Column of Antoninus Pius		

A dotted line marks the Servian Wall, a large part of which had already disappeared.

APPENDIX
ARMY AND NAVY

SERVICE in the army was in the earliest period a matter of course. Only the aged and disabled were exempt. Raids of active neighbors, especially after harvest time, had to be resisted or punished by shepherds and farmers turned soldiers. Nor was aggression absent. With the end of summer hostilities as a rule were over, and no further service required until the following season. More serious wars grew frequent, but were followed by the usual return to the plow before winter came. With the growth of the city under the kings a more serviceable army organization had been developed, not without much borrowing from the Etruscans, a race of warriors.

In the nine centuries to be covered in following the history of the Roman army five periods are to be distinguished: (1) an early period down to the war with Pyrrhus (280 B.C.); (2) from Pyrrhus to Marius (100 B.C.); (3) from Marius to Augustus, or rather to the battle of Actium (31 B.C.); (4) from Augustus to Severus (200 A.D.); (5) from Severus to Constantine (337 A.D.).

THE ARMY: FIRST PERIOD

By the beginning of the Republic, or perhaps somewhat later, the body of male citizens was organized as an army on the basis of a property qualification. Tradition ascribed to Servius Tullius this system under which the whole body of freemen was divided according to their property in land into five classes, graded from 20 *iugera* (13 acres) down to two.[1] In each class the younger men were separated from the older in an equal number of subdivisions called centuries (*centuriae*). Each century had to furnish 100 men if needed from its number. The older men, *seniores,* from 45 to 60, were liable for garrison duty and as reserves, the *iuniores* for active service in the infantry. There were 40 centuries of each in the first class, while the four remaining classes included no more than 90 centuries. The most prosperous, without regard to age, formed a separate

[1] Later, reckoned on a money basis, the census of the highest class was 10,000 denarii, or 100,000 asses.

group, the *equites,* and furnished the cavalry, largely but not entirely patrician. Thus including the cavalry more than one-half of the army was drawn from the ranks of the comparatively well-to-do, the rest from those who had some property at stake. In addition to the centuries of the five classes were three more centuries of engineers, artisans, and trumpeters, one of supernumeraries, and finally one century—a very large one, no doubt —of the *proletarii,* having little or no property and unable to serve except when the state furnished them arms.

On the basis of such a property classification an army was raised each year—commonly two legions for active service during the early Republic, that each consul (at first called *praetor*) might command one legion in the field. A legion was made up of ten cohorts, each of them divided into three maniples, the smallest unit of importance in battle. A maniple, however, had two centurions, each in charge of a century, the senior centurion being at the same time commander of the maniple.[2] The legion at that time was commanded by a consul, having as his staff six military tribunes. Later, when there were two legions or more with auxiliaries for each consul, command of the legion devolved upon its tribunes.

The line of battle closely resembled the Greek phalanx, presenting to an enemy masses of men rank behind rank. For each of these the state required specific arms and equipment to be furnished by the soldier.[3] In order that the tactical units might keep together and execute orders promptly each maniple had a *signum,* a standard borne by a *signifer,* who kept near the centurion in command. The shaft was surmounted by an uplifted hand or the head of a lance. Below this was a crossbar with short ribbons. Shod with iron, the standard could be set up in the ground, to remain until the *signifer* was ordered to advance,

[2] The century was composed normally of 60 men, except that in the third line in battle 30 of the older men made a century. Thus a legion had for its regular complement 3,000 heavy infantry (20 maniples at 120 men and 10 at 60) besides 1,200 light armed (p. 452).

[3] Details are given by Livy: for the first class helmet, cuirass, greaves, round shield, spear, and sword; for the second class the same, except that the shield was rectangular (*scutum*) and that they had no cuirass; and so on down to the fifth, which had only slings and stones and served as skirmishers.

the whole maniple moving with him. The cavalry units, *alae* and *turmae* (the latter 30 men) had a different type of standard— a small square banner (*vexillum*) on a pole. The legion had as yet no single standard,[4] but cherished certain symbolic figures also called *signa*—eagle, wolf, minotaur, horse, and boar, each mounted on a pole and carried into battle.

In this early period much use was made of the lance (*hasta*), as in the Greek phalanx, while the sword was of secondary importance. But with the slow evolution of a more open order of battle the *hasta* was gradually replaced by the *pilum*, a short javelin. This and a short sword became the characteristic weapons of the Roman heavy infantry. And as the state in time furnished the necessary accouterment a certain amount of uniformity was attained. From 406 B.C. both cavalry and infantry began to receive pay out of the state treasury.

THE ARMY: SECOND PERIOD

With such armies Rome survived many conflicts with warlike neighbors, Latin, Etruscan, Samnite, and the rest. In the war with Pyrrhus—and here begins our second period—came the first clash with highly trained soldiers armed and led according to the most approved Hellenistic tactics, as developed and brilliantly employed by Alexander the Great. The Greek phalanx led by a master and supplemented by a terrifying novelty, trained elephants, had to be met by Roman armies in three important battles. But the gradual introduction by the Romans of a more open method of fighting in the years preceding the war and the further improvements to which the two serious defeats inflicted by Pyrrhus at Heraclea and Ausculum had forced them, gave Rome her ultimate victory at Beneventum (275 B.C.). From the close order there had been a gradual change to open ranks, in which the individual soldier had an opportunity to display his skill with the sword. This was the famous maniple formation in three ranks. In front stood 1,200 *hastati*, now armed with the *pilum* in place of the *hasta*, but retaining the name. A second line was formed by the *principes* (1,200), no longer in the front rank, a third by the *triarii*, the oldest men (600). In each of these three ranks were 10 maniples. And in addition to the heavy

---

[4] For the legionary eagle of later times cp. p. 458.

troops each legion had light-armed (*velites*), about 1,200 in number, but not forming maniples. In an emergency the complement of a legion might be raised to 5,000 infantry. Between the maniples of the front rank an open space was left through which the enemy could see a maniple of the second rank ready to close that interval. Behind the similar intervals of that second rank stood the maniples of the third, the *triarii*. Within the maniples the formation was probably six men deep, so that something of the solidity of the phalanx remained, but the long bristling spears had disappeared. Each legion was regularly supported by an equal number of allied infantry in cohorts, not maniples, and forming wings (*alae*). Cavalry also was furnished by the allies.

Such was the Roman army and its battle formation in the wars with Carthage, until in the Second Punic War the genius of Hannibal by three terrible defeats, culminating at Cannae (216 B.C.), revealed the fact that Roman troops thus organized were incapable of adjusting themselves promptly to unexpected maneuvers. There were years of careful preparation in Spain under a general of great ability, the Elder Scipio Africanus, who armed his troops with a new weapon, the Spanish sword (*gladius*), 24 to 27 inches long and sharp on both edges and at the point, serving equally well for a blow or a thrust. This became the standard sword for the legionary, and with an army so equipped, officered by men of mature experience, the defeat of Hannibal at Zama in Africa was made possible (202 B.C.).

From that time on the army contained an increasing non-Italian element among the auxiliary troops—slingers from the Balearic Islands, archers from Crete, Numidian cavalry, and even mercenaries. The cavalry became less Roman or even Italian, while the heavy infantry of the legions remained national and homogeneous. The maniple formation was unchanged, but all three ranks were now armed alike. The larger unit, the cohort, containing three maniples, one in each of the three ranks, was of increasing importance, both as a possible detachment and for particular movements in battle. By 182 B.C. the legion, which at times had reached the number of 6,200 men, was virtually fixed at 5,200 men; but 6,000 was not an unknown figure.[5]

[5] For the Empire cp. p. 463.

There was as yet no military profession. In practice, however, wars long continued or frequent provided highly competent officers. The commanders, in theory magistrates elected for a year, or given a second year of authority outside of the city, to carry on a campaign or govern a province, were at critical times and by special extension retained for the duration of the war. Under the commander stood a quaestor, who was a magistrate elected by the people and responsible for stores, equipment, pay, etc., but who could be entrusted with a command. There were *legati* also, to whom a special duty was often assigned, though they did not normally command a legion or other unit of the forces. Each legion still had its six military tribunes, two of whom commanded it for a month, each apparently having sole authority on alternate days. The other tribunes performed staff duties. It often happened that a former commanding officer took service again as *legatus* or tribune for another campaign. Each legion had its 60 centurions, but in battle the significant unit was still the maniple made up of two centuries, and it was commanded as before (p. 450).

The standards remained as in the previous period, the term *signa* regularly meaning the standards of the maniples. They were further differentiated by metal discs (*phalerae*), metal wreaths, and other ornaments extending down the shaft. By the end of this second period, about 100 B.C., the figures of wolf, minotaur, horse, and boar were left behind in the camp, while the eagle was carried into battle, thus becoming the familiar standard of the legion. There was no military music in the modern sense—only trumpets and horns to give and repeat signals, i.e., the *tuba*, a long straight trumpet, the *cornu*, a curved horn. Every maniple had at least one of each. Another horn, the *bucina*, was used in camp.

For the organization and equipment in the second century B.C. we have much detailed information in the pages of the Greek historian Polybius, himself on intimate terms with the Younger Scipio and other commanders. The legionary soldier of his time had a bronze helmet (*cassis*) with a crest of red or black feathers, a long rectangular shield of wood covered with canvas and curved cylindrically (protected by a leather cover on the march), a *lorica,* or cuirass of sole leather, the short sword of Spanish origin worn at the right side,[6] and a javelin (*pilum*)[7] to be thrown before the sword was drawn. The *pilum* was about six feet long, a barbed iron rod inserted in a wooden shaft.

The cavalry had the *cassis* and *lorica,* also a light round shield (*clipeus*), a *hasta*, apparently no sword. Light-armed *velites* had only a leather helmet (*galea*), a small round shield (*parma*), a sword, and a short dart (*iaculum*).

The pay of the legionary was only 120 *denarii* a year, that of a centurion 240, and from this pay deductions were made for rations and equipment. As for the food supply, the simple fare of the Italian farmer still prevailed in the army, the chief article being wheat gruel (*puls*). And with small pay and simplest food went severe discipline. The centurion's rod, cut from a grape-vine, saw frequent use, and from a general's sentence there was no appeal. Punishments were severe, the mildest being the loss of pay. Capital punishment took the form of scourging to death, the ax of the lictor being reserved for the beheading of officers. Where an entire unit was to be punished rations of barley might be ordered instead of wheat; or the unit might be compelled to bivouac outside of the camp; or for the most serious offenses decimation was the penalty. This meant that every tenth man was put to death by scourging, while the rest suffered lesser indignities. On the other hand there were rewards for special bravery (p. 460). The general himself could be acclaimed by his own troops as *imperator*, a coveted distinction. It was his ambition to earn a triumph, an honor in which his army would have a conspicuous share.

Subject to fixed conditions [8] a successful general was permitted by the senate to enter the city at the head of his army or of representative units. Formed in the Campus Martius and fol-lowing a fixed itinerary the triumphal procession made its way through shouting crowds to the Circus Maximus, passed the whole length of the arena and thence to the Sacra Via, through the Forum and up the Clivus Capitolinus: magistrates and sena-tors; trumpeters; spoils taken from the enemy; gold and silver;

---

[6] The *balteus,* a sword-sling, passed over the left shoulder.

[7] Actual specimens found at Numantia show great variety of form.

[8] Failing these an ovation was granted in place of a triumph. In this the general was on foot or mounted, but the pomp and ceremony, the display of spoils might be no less impressive.

works of art; models of captured cities; pictures of battles; images of river gods and countries; numerous victims for the sacrifice, usually white cattle with gilded horns; priests and attendants; singers and musicians; captives in chains; the king or general of the enemy; hostages and prisoners; the Roman general standing in his chariot and clad in a historic purple and gold-embroidered tunic and toga from the treasury of Jupiter, wearing a laurel wreath and holding a scepter and a laurel branch, while a slave standing behind him held a heavy golden wreath (also Jupiter's) above his head, and lictors in red escorted the chariot.[9] Mounted officers followed, and finally the soldiers shouting *Io triumphe* and singing rude songs in their commander's honor, but mixed with coarse abuse. Mounting the Capitol, while the chief captive was led away to execution or to prison and others to be sold into slavery, the general entered the Temple of Jupiter, presented his laurels and crown to the god and offered sacrifice. Feasting and entertainments of every sort brought the great pageant, the crowning ambition of every Roman, to a close.

Most important for the success of the Roman arms was the morale of the soldiers, the product of a hereditary sense of discipline from a time when every citizen-soldier knew that he was defending hearth and home from immediate attack. Service at a distance, especially in over-seas provinces, weakened that old-time sense of direct responsibility, but the tradition of a national discipline remained one of the greatest of Roman assets until the age of Marius, when armies became more permanent, devoted to a leader rather than to the *patria*.

Particularly characteristic of the Roman army was the care bestowed upon the fortification of camps, even when the march was to be resumed at daybreak. No other armies were so secure against night attacks. Polybius in his famous excursus on the Roman army has fully described the normal plan of a camp. Of course in many situations no such square form and mathematical regularity was possible. Excavations around Numantia in Spain have yielded remains of seven Roman camps of Scipio the Younger, showing how flexible was the camp plan when the

[9] His young children might be with him in the chariot or astride its white horses, while older children rode behind.

nature of the ground required variations from the norm.[10] Most essential for the temporary camp were the ditch (*fossa*) and earthwork (*agger*) crowned with a palisade (*vallum,* but this term was applied to the *agger* also). In exceptional cases the soldier carried three or more stakes (*valli*) to form a palisade. There were usually four gates at least fifteen feet wide, broad enough to admit a column of sixes. That toward the enemy was the *porta praetoria,* from which the *via praetoria* led to the quarters of the general, the *praetorium,* which faced upon the broad *via principalis* leading to a gate at either end, the *porta principalis dextra,* and *sinistra* respectively—these twice the width of the others. In front of the headquarters was an altar and a platform from which the commanding officer could address his men. Behind the *praetorium* (often placed on the highest ground in the camp), was an open space, the *forum,* leading to the *quaestorium,* or tent of the quaestor, near the remaining gate, *porta decumana,* opposite the *porta praetoria.* Where possible a wide space, *intervallum,* was left between the fortifications and the tents of the troops. Guard duty was strictly maintained day and night, the night watches, *vigiliae,* being of three hours each, from sunset, when the trumpet (*classicum*) sounded in front of headquarters, to sunrise, while a *bucina* from the tent of the first centurion announced the beginning of the other watches. There were ten light-armed sentries at each gate and a guard line on the wall.

On the march the column (*agmen*) made up of legions and *alae* (of the allies), each with its own cavalry and baggage train, was normally preceded by an advance guard only a short distance ahead of the column. If in the immediate neighborhood of the enemy a special form, called *agmen quadratum,* was used, with *hastati, principes,* and *triarii* (p. 451) marching in parallel columns some distance apart, leaving space for baggage between the advancing maniples. Thus the familiar battle line could be quickly formed in case of an attack by the enemy.

The tactics in the second century B.C. were still based upon the open formation by maniples, with wide spaces between them

[10] These camps encircle the site of Numantia at nearly uniform distances from one another, and since the siege began with the winter and lasted many months much stone was used in their construction.

and an appreciable interval between the front ranks (*hastati*) and the second (*principes*), and then a still wider interval between the latter and the third rank (*triarii*). A battle was begun by a skirmish of the light-armed troops, slingers, archers, etc., who then retired through the openings in the lines of the heavy infantry. The legions stood in the center, flanked by the infantry of the allies on the right and left. On the wings were the Roman horsemen, usually on the right, and those of the allies, commonly on the left. The legionary soldiers first threw the *pilum* into the ranks of the enemy, and then advanced to the attack. This charge (*concursus*) was immediately followed by the *impetus*, an attack with the sword, and upon the skillful swordsmanship of the soldier, fighting behind his tall shield, depended the fortune of the battle. Long training was required both in throwing the *pilum* with force and accurate aim and in handling the short sword. The frontal attack was not, however, invariable. The general might order either cavalry or a part of his infantry to turn the flanks of the enemy and attack them in the rear.

If a war involved the siege of a walled city the usual method was still to enclose the place with a number of fortified camps connected so far as possible by earthworks and trenches. Thus the inhabitants could be starved into submission. When opportunity offered attacks would be made, but the main dependence was upon the severing of all communications. Such an investment sometimes lasted many months. Famous examples are the siege of Syracuse by Marcellus (214-212 B.C.), of Carthage and Numantia (146 and 133 B.C. respectively) by the Younger Scipio. At times, however, a well-organized attack with catapults and other machines and with all the resources of Greek strategy forced the city or stronghold to a prompt surrender. It was thus that the Elder Scipio possessed himself of New Carthage in Spain (209 B.C.).

THE ARMY: THIRD PERIOD

With the end of the second century B.C. begins a third, and a highly important, period in the history of the Roman army. The names of Marius and Sulla, of Pompey and Julius Caesar, are associated with this age. Beginning in a very thorough reorganization, chiefly the work of Marius, this period reached its culmination in the brilliant strategy of Caesar, but it includes also the time of the second triumvirate, when even larger forces were massed for such momentous battles as Philippi (42 B.C.). The army was in theory still a militia, based upon the census and made up of men paid by the state, but destined to return to civil occupations after service. In actual practice it was virtually a professional army from the days of Marius, who for his campaign against Jugurtha accepted many volunteers from the proletariat, the mass of whom had no occupation. The army which defended Italy from the first great invasion of the Germans had no thought of a return to the plow or the shop. It remained dangerously devoted to a popular leader and inclined to ignore the claims of the state where these conflicted with the ambitions of their general. Such services with promised rewards at the end of the term of enlistment attracted masses of men from the city population. The civil war between Marius and Sulla, together with long service outside of Italy, completed the breach between the militia of former times and the reorganized army. Not yet was it to be called a standing army, though with a term of sixteen years (later twenty) it was rapidly moving in that direction.

To Marius is probably due the important change by which the maniple ceased to be the tactical unit. In its place the cohort, nominally 600 men and still composed of three maniples, became the unit of chief importance in the formation of the line of battle and in all military maneuvers. The senior centurion of the cohort was its commander and was called *primus pilus*. And henceforward the *signum* of the *triarii* seems to have served as a standard for the cohort.[11] It was Marius who reorganized the baggage train,[12] relieving its burden by requiring the soldier to carry more. A regulation load, including probably an emergency ration for three days, and neatly packed, was carried by each soldier on a pole. Due to Marius was also the adoption of the silver or plated eagle with uplifted wings as the standard of the legion (p. 453). It was sacred and not regularly used to indicate movements or orders to be executed. The staff was like that of the *signa* of the maniples, but without ornaments or distinctions.

[11] This was a larger standard than those of the *hastati* and *principes,* which bore the letters H and P respectively.

[12] Pack animals with some wagons. In Caesar's train there seem to have been no wagons.

This standard was borne by an *aquilifer,* who was under the special charge of the first centurion of the legion. In camp the eagle was kept in a shrine at the *praetorium.*

Now that the army had reached a more permanent basis the legions had fixed numbers and often names as well, for example, Caesar's *Alaudae* (The Larks). Each legion had some of the lighter *tormenta* (artillery) manned by men from the cohorts. There was no artillery arm of the service. The command of the legion remained in the hands of the six tribunes (p. 453) until Caesar made a *legatus* the legionary commander. It was not yet a permanent system, however, as a *legatus* might be given the command of a unit as small as a cohort, or on the other hand of a whole army. Important officers were *praefecti,* including those of the cavalry and the *praefectus fabrum,* an officer of engineers or even an adjutant general. The tribunes were knights as a rule and were gradually losing their importance, being more and more assigned to mere staff duties. The higher officers wore a red tunic under a cuirass, while the general was distinguished in battle by his purple cloak (*paludamentum*).

As for the weapons of the legionary soldier, his *pilum* was now lighter and shorter than in the previous period (p. 454). That it might all the more embarrass an enemy whose shield it had struck, Marius devised a method of attaching the iron to the wooden shaft by an iron nail and a wooden peg. The breaking of the latter left the shaft hanging down. Caesar improved upon this by making the iron shank of soft iron, only the barbed head being hardened.[13] The range of the *pilum* was perhaps 100 feet. Sword and shield[14] and helmet remained almost unchanged. The heavy cavalry, regularly Spanish or Gallic, probably had long swords as well as lances. The light-armed infantry still carried bow and arrows and slings, the latter hurling lead *glandes,* often bearing an inscription, as many specimens show.

Pay of the soldier continued as before (p. 454), until Caesar raised it to 225 denarii, and 450 for a centurion. Their savings were in the care of the standard-bearers. A share in the booty (increased as a reward for conspicuous courage) and, from the time of the civil wars, a special gift or donative of the general added to their resources. Officers above the grade of centurion

---

[13] Many of the iron parts have been unearthed around the site of Alesia.
[14] In the civil wars shields were inscribed with the name of the general.

received substantial benefits in food allowances and in rewards at the end of the campaign, but they had no pay.

The traditional military decorations may be mentioned here, though most of them came down from at least the age of the Punic Wars. Some were reserved for the general, as the laurel wreath worn at his triumph (a myrtle garland if he received the lesser honor of an ovation); a *corona obsidionalis* or *graminea,* a wreath of grass, if he had rescued a beleaguered fort or camp. Others were for an officer or soldier in recognition of some conspicuously brave act: a *hasta pura,* simply a lance without a head; *phalerae,* medallions, worn on the breast like modern *croix de guerre;* collars (*torques*); arm bands (*armillae*); various *coronae,* such as the *civica,* of oak, for saving the life of a fellow citizen; the *corona muralis* or *castrensis,* for the first man to scale the walls of a town or a camp respectively; also the *corona aurea* for bravery in general.

In Caesar's time we find great variety in battle formations. The triple line was still more usual than any other disposition, but the third might be held in reserve, as at Pharsalus. Trenches had been used by Sulla to protect his flanks in a battle with Mithridates. Caesar carried their use in battle much further, notably on the Aisne, the scene of much trench warfare in the Great War, and at Dyrrhachium on a vast scale.

There were great sieges in this period: three memorable examples in the Gallic War, culminating in that of Alesia, where the elaborate works required in investing a high-perched stronghold were complicated by the rare feature of a formidable contravallation, to defend the besiegers of the town against the hordes of Gauls coming to the relief of its starving inhabitants. And later, in the civil wars, the sieges of Massilia, Mutina, and Perusia were notable.

In besieging a city it was usual to prepare the way by constructing an *agger,* in this case not an embankment, but an elevated causeway of logs, leveled up and broad enough to carry a wooden tower. The latter was built at a distance, beyond the range of catapults on the walls, and was advanced on wheels or rollers along the *agger* up to the wall, from which the defenders had by this time been driven by artillery, including that mounted on the upper stories of the moving tower (*turris ambulatoria*), 50 to 60 feet high. Great use was made of the battering-ram

(*aries*) also in making a breach in the wall, the soldiers oper-
ating it being protected by a heavy wooden shed (*musculus*)
covered with hides and connected with the rear by lighter sheds
(*vineae*). Mines, or tunnels to undermine the wall, or to cut the
water supply, were dug in places.

Military camps were as before, but guarded with greater vig-
ilance by a cohort stationed at each gate, with others in readiness, and by cavalry patrols outside. Marches were sometimes
forced, Julius Caesar being especially noted for his rapidity of
movement. Yet the ordinary march was, as before, not above
12 miles a day, as the soldier carried a total burden of about
60 pounds. What technical resources were available for armies
obliged to cross a wide river, is clear from Caesar's two bridges
across the Rhine (54 and 52 B.C.), with a probable length of
1,300 feet, completed in 10 days, or less in the case of the
second bridge. Pontoon bridges were little used in this period.

THE ARMY: FOURTH PERIOD

With Augustus begins a new age in military matters. The
impossibly large armies of the civil wars had to be brought down
to reasonable limits. On such a reduced scale—surprisingly small
when we consider the vast territory to be defended—he organized a standing army. As commander in chief he placed the legions in the provinces that fell to him in the partition by which
the senate was allowed to keep only the peaceful provinces. The
one exception was Africa, which though senatorial retained one
legion (p. 54).

An entirely new feature was the organized frontier policy,
under which the larger part of the army was stationed with direct reference to an exposed frontier. The legions posted at a
distance from any front were holding regions recently or imperfectly subdued, or from which they could readily be transferred to the zone threatened by an invader. Such regions were
Spain (especially in the northwest), Dalmatia, and Egypt. Thus
the legions in Spain could support the Rhine legions in case Gaul
should revolt or be invaded either from Britain or from Germany; those in Dalmatia were a reserve for Pannonia or Moesia
in case of trouble on the Danube; the two in Egypt could be
shifted to Syria to meet Parthian aggression or could be employed against Arabia.

In the last years of Augustus we find 25 legions with their normal contingents of auxiliaries stationed as follows:[15]

The Far West	Spain	3	IV Macedonica
			VI Victrix
			X Gemina
Rhine Front	Gallia Belgica [16]		
	Lower Rhine	4	I (Germanica)[17]
			V Alaudae
			XX Valeria
			XXI Rapax
	Gallia Belgica		
	Upper Rhine	4	II Augusta
			XIII Gemina
			XIV Gemina
			XVI (Gallica)
Danube Front	Pannonia	3	VIII Augusta
			IX Hispana
			XV Apollinaris
	Moesia	2	IV Scythica
			V Macedonica
	Dalmatia	2	VII (Claudia)
			XI (Claudia)
Parthian Front	Syria	4	III Gallica
			VI Ferrata
			X Fretensis
			XII Fulminata
	Egypt	2	III Cyrenaica
			XXII Deiotariana
Southern Front	Africa	1	III Augusta

The legions of the Rhine formed the *exercitus Germanicus*, and distance gave them a dangerous sense of solidarity as a powerful unit, capable of defying the central authority. So it was in the revolution year, 69 A.D., when rival emperors were set up by different provincial armies. For there was also an

[15] The missing numbers, XVII, XVIII, XIX, were those of Varus's legions lost in the Teutoburg forest, and hence were never used again.

[16] See p. 47.

[17] Later names are in parentheses.

exercitus Syriacus and an *exercitus Pannonicus*. And while a legion was liable to be shifted from one front to another for a war, some of them remained, except for brief intervals, in the same province for many years, even centuries. Their permanent winter camps (*hiberna*) with the adjoining settlements of sutlers and traders and their extensive granaries often grew into towns of importance. This was the history of Cologne (Colonia Agrippinensis), Bonn (Bonna), Mainz (Moguntiacum), and later of Chester (Deva), York (Eburacum), Vienna (Vindobona).

A legion (10 cohorts of infantry, each having 480 men) had its own cavalry, 120 in number, its own artillery (*tormenta*) drawn by mules. Attached to the legion were non-Italian auxiliary troops, raising the total to about 10,000 men. Later under Vespasian the auxiliaries were detached from the legion and stationed in different camps. The legionaries, if not already citizens, became such on entering the service. In Italy there were no regularly stationed legions, at Rome only the guards and the forces of law and order.

The praetorian guards (*cohortes praetoriae*) were concentrated just outside the city by Sejanus in the time of Tiberius. Nine such cohorts of 1,000 men each (with some cavalry included) were commanded by two prefects (*praefecti praetorio*) who were knights, while each cohort had its tribune as commander. To the guard was added a mounted *garde du corps*, part of which consisted of German (Batavian) horse. Three *cohortes urbanae* (later four) shared the quarters of the praetorians, but were normally under the orders of the prefect of the city (*praefectus urbi*). Fire protection and ordinary police duty were entrusted to the *vigiles*, the watch—7 cohorts of 1,000 each, with their barracks dispersed among the 14 wards. Except for their officers they were not rated as soldiers.

In the disposition of the legions an unusual number of changes were made between the time of Tiberius and the year 69 A.D., largely owing to the ambitious designs of Caligula and Nero, also to the conquest of Britain and the Jewish War. For his German expedition Caligula formed two new legions, XV Primigenia and XXII Primigenia; and Nero for his proposed campaign against Parthia two more, I Italica and I Adiutrix, the latter being drawn from the marines. One more legion, VII Galbiana, was raised by Galba in Spain to aid him in dethroning Nero. For Claudius's expedition against Britain and the occupation of that new province three legions were required, two being transferred from the Rhine and one from Pannonia. For the war which ended in the capture of Jerusalem by Titus (70 A.D.) three legions from Pannonia, Moesia, and Syria had been assigned to Vespasian as general. Other changes were entailed by these larger movements, and in all 14 of the legions listed in the table on page 463 had been removed to a different province by or in 69 A.D., and the total had risen from 25 to 30. Two of the new legions were temporarily stationed, one in Rome and one at Lugdunum (Lyons)—extraordinary measures due to the confusion of the times.

In the Rhine legions further changes were made by Vespasian after the rebellion of 70 A.D. He also formed the new II Adiutrix, composed of former marines. New legions were added by Trajan, Marcus Aurelius, Septimius Severus, and Alexander Severus, while others meeting with disaster had disappeared from the list. But it remains a marvel that the widely dispersed forces, numbering in all no more than 300,000, which alone held off the swarming invaders, were always so small compared with modern armies, defending incomparably shorter frontiers.

The second century A.D., particularly the reign of Marcus Aurelius, faced greatly increased danger on the Danube front and in the East. Consequently by the time of Septimius Severus we find 12 legions in the Danube provinces, compared with only 4 defending the Rhine in Upper and Lower Germany. At the same period the eastern frontier had 11 legions, including one in reserve in Egypt. The total was 33, only 8 more than in the time of Augustus.

The pay of the legionary, still 225 denarii a year under Augustus, but raised to 300 by Domitian, had reached 450 under Severus—a nominal advance, since the currency had been more than once depreciated. In peace as in war the commissariat was of course maintained and care taken of the soldiers' health. At a permanent station there was a military hospital (*valetudinarium*), larger and better than that at a summer camp. Surgeons (*medici*), however, had only a low rank in the service. Discipline and a high standard of excellence were steadily maintained in this period, especially under such emperors as Trajan, Hadrian, and Marcus Aurelius.[18] The centurion with his grape vine cudgel was a terror to idlers and cowards. As rewards of merit the *dona militaria* (p. 460) continued to be awarded, until abolished early in the next period by Caracalla. The highest distinction, that of a triumph, was reserved from the time of Augustus for the Emperor,[19] or in a few cases for a prince of his family; and even the ovation (p. 454, n. 8) came to be similarly restricted, the last private citizen to receive the latter honor being the conqueror of Britain, Aulus Plautius (47 A.D.).

As regards the camp of an army in the field during this period, we have for comparison with the plan derived from Polybius (p. 455) that of Hyginus in the third century (probably), with strikingly similar internal arrangements, but much reduced in space per man. It is a rectangle with rounded corners—a standard plan, to be freely adapted in actual practice as might be dictated by the nature of the site. The permanent stations were planned on similar lines, but with more attention to comfort. Most of these were placed near the frontiers, the defense of which by lines of forts, earthworks and walls is an interesting chapter in Roman military history, their imposing remains speaking for themselves.

The most impressive of these is the Wall of Hadrian in northern Britain (p. 33). At first a series of forts with a connecting road was carried across from the Tyne to the Solway. Then two lines of earthworks with a trench between them for the whole distance served rather to mark the *limes* as the farthest limit of the civil administration than to establish a real line of defense. Conversion into a strictly military work followed only a few years later when the same Emperor, Hadrian, in 122 A.D. carried a massive stone wall and its trench across from Wallsend below Newcastle (Pons Aelii) to Bowness below Carlisle (Luguvallium), a distance of over 73 English miles. The wall was placed a short distance north of the now needless earthworks, and in addition to the camps it had "mile-castles" with intervening watchtowers. The defense of the entire line required a garrison of about 10,000 auxiliaries. Twenty years

[18] Slaves were allowed to serve by Marcus Aurelius, not by Trajan or Hadrian.

[19] Agrippa might have been the sole exception, but he more than once declined the honor.

later Antoninus Pius advanced this northern front some 80 miles by carrying a wall of turf across the much shorter line (35 miles) from the Firth of Forth below Edinburgh to the Clyde below Glasgow, along the line of former forts established by Agricola in 81 A.D. (p. 49). But this more northerly frontier was abandoned by Commodus.

Other fortified lines connected the Rhine with the Danube and were completed under Antoninus and Marcus Aurelius. These ran from the Rhine below Andernach to the Danube above Regensburg, a distance of 370 Roman miles, and protected Upper Germany and Raetia, which had expanded in the first century beyond the old line of the rivers. Many remains of these works are still to be seen and a large part of the line has been determined by excavations in recent years. Both the Upper German and the Raetian *limes* were lost by 260 A.D., that is, within a century after the accession of Marcus Aurelius. Similar military works, but less extensive, ranging in date from Domitian to Constantine or even later, are found in the lower Danube country, especially in Roumania, some of them near the mouths of the river.

Of memorable sieges in this long period from Augustus to Severus we may mention only two, that of Jerusalem by Titus and that of Sarmizegetusa, chief town of the Dacians, by Trajan. The former is narrated in detail by Josephus, the latter pictured on the famous column. Notable military bridges with pontoons were Corbulo's over the Euphrates in Nero's time, probably at Zeugma (p. 34) and provided with towers for catapults; and Trajan's over the Danube, represented on the column. Shown elsewhere in the same reliefs is also the more substantial bridge of Trajan on lofty stone piers, from which, however, Hadrian removed the wooden arches or stone arches which had soon replaced them. Less imposing but more lasting were the fortified bridges across the Rhine at Mainz and Cologne (Moguntiacum and Colonia Agrippinensis).

Foreigners were admitted to the legions from the time of Antoninus Pius, receiving citizenship upon enlistment, while auxiliaries became citizens only at the end of their service. The latter in their variety of half-barbaric races were less unlike the legionaries, now that these were ceasing to be Italians.

THE ARMY: FIFTH PERIOD

With Septimius Severus we may mark the beginning of a final period. It was his aim to eliminate Italians entirely from the army, even centurions; and the praetorians were dismissed. More significant were the altered conditions on the frontiers. He permitted soldiers at the permanent stations to marry, to live with wife and children on farms granted them in lieu of adequate pay, reporting at certain times for military duty. In time, if not at first, land grants carried with them the hereditary obligation to serve in the army. We have reached an age in which the contrast with the Roman army of early days is startling. Identity of *populus* and *exercitus* had been a corner stone of the old Roman state. And now the overgrown, polyglot empire was creating an army as far removed from the people as possible, and that by two methods: the selection of conscripts from races known for their warlike spirit, and an inbreeding process under the land-grant system at the permanent military stations. The hereditary soldier was thus the counterpart of the hereditary *colonus* and the hereditary artisan (pp. 74, 96). Each of these great groups formed a caste.

Under Diocletian the number of the legions was doubled and the auxiliaries somewhat increased. He appears to have placed 46 legions in the frontier provinces, 16 more as reserves, so disposed that they could be moved up to a particular front, and as a general reserve for duty anywhere, 3 legions for the West and 3 for the East—a total of 68 legions.

With Constantine came even more sweeping changes—complete separation of garrison troops from field armies. The former kept their old names and formations, but were of inferior material and assigned to fixed stations. The field armies, one for the East and one for the West, comprised guards, called *Palatini,* in place of the old praetorians, and *Comitatenses,* troops of the line. Both were largely composed of men of German or Sarmatian or other warlike races, such as Illyrians, Thracians, Britons.

Cavalry now ranked above infantry and the legion was reduced to 1,000 men. It still bore its eagle, but the cohort had a dragon (*draco*), a new standard borrowed from Dacians or Parthians. The Christian *labarum,* with its monogram of Christ, was not accounted one of the regular military *signa*. The familiar weapons of the legionary had changed, a longer sword (*spatha*) having displaced the *gladius,* and a different form of javelin with a triangular point having taken the place of the *pilum.*

In the fortification of camps and permanent stations there was a marked decline, while sieges were conducted as heretofore. New titles were given to the higher officers, field armies being commanded by *comites,* frontier armies usually by *duces;* and now that the *praefecti praetorio* (p. 463) were civil magistrates, not generals, the high command was divided between a *magister peditum* and a *magister equitum.*

THE NAVY

As the Romans did not take naturally to the sea they looked upon naval warfare as entirely secondary. Through the whole period of the Republic they regarded a navy as potentially a necessity, in case an emergency required it, not as one of the obvious means of defense to be continuously provided for in time of peace. The earliest trustworthy mention of a warship is in 394 B.C., presumably furnished by the allies, as were no doubt those with which the first Roman naval victory was won, that over the fleet of Antium in 338 B.C. (p. 29).

At the outbreak of the First Punic War the almost complete lack of naval resources is seen in the fact that the Romans had suddenly to create a fleet, though they had no experienced ship-builders. Taking as their model a Carthaginian five-banker, they hastily constructed of green timber 100 such warships and 20 three-bankers (triremes). For crews they had in part sailors from the allies, but for fighting men had to depend upon legionary soldiers taught in all haste to board an enemy's ship and fight hand to hand on its deck. To make boarding easier a species of weighted bridge, the *corvus* (raven), was invented, to be slung over the bow to starboard or to port and dropped on the enemy's deck. Thus in 260 B.C. under Duilius the Romans won their first naval victory over Carthage off Mylae in Sicily. By the same methods they gained other victories, but suffered disasters where seamanship was needed, as when a whole fleet was lost off Drepana (Trapani) in 249 B.C. Yet in 241 B.C. a new fleet of 200 warships was built by private contributions, and the long war was brought to an end by the brilliant success of

Catulus off the Aegates Islands. As always, even under the Empire, they depended far more upon the fighting powers of the individual soldier serving on board than upon skillful seamanship and adroit maneuvering.

In the Second Punic War the fleet, which had been much neglected in the interval, was useful chiefly in connection with the transporting of troops to Spain, Sicily, and Africa. Similar service was rendered in the wars with Syria and Macedonia. The few naval victories of that time were not sufficient to establish a continuous seapower for the Republic of the West. As soon as peace was made the navy was again neglected. So it was once more after the destruction of Carthage. While Mithridates had 400 warships, Lucullus found the greatest difficulty in gathering a force able to defeat the king's fleet twice in 85 B.C. And in the next war, in 73 B.C., he lost 70 of his ships in one battle, and owed his ultimate success largely to a storm which wrecked many of Mithridates' vessels.

The lack of an efficient navy held in readiness allowed piracy to increase to an alarming extent, until Pompey was given such unheard-of powers in 67 B.C. that he was able to clear the Mediterranean of pirates in a single season. Julius Caesar built a fleet on the west coast of Gaul to operate against the Veneti in Brittany—the first Roman fleet to encounter the strange tides of that coast. For the siege of Massilia he built 12 warships at Arelate (Arles). For convoying and active service as well in various other phases of the civil war he required many more, while Pompey depended largely upon ships furnished by his eastern allies.

Naval warfare on a large scale was carried on by the son, Sextus Pompey, in his struggle against the triumvirs, and the issue between Octavian and Antony was decided by the greatest naval battle of ancient times, that at Actium, 31 B.C. Agrippa, the real victor, then reorganized the navy, consisting of some 800 ships. He established a naval station on the Bay of Naples, at Misenum, another on the Adriatic, near Ravenna, a third at Forum Iulii (Fréjus) in Gallia Narbonensis. There were small fleets or flotillas also in provincial waters, in the Black Sea, on the Rhine and Danube, and elsewhere. Much use was made of light craft, somewhat like the Liburnian galleys of the upper Adriatic, which had done such good service at Actium. These had one to three banks of oars. Real ships of the line, so to speak, the large vessels with many banks of oars and towers for artillery, remained theoretically the standard for important conflicts. They ceased, however, to be built in Augustus's time, since there was now no rival naval power. In a war naval vessels might transport or convoy troops or be used against an enemy. In the civil war of 69 A.D. they were employed by Otho against Vitellius, that is, by one usurper against another. No foreign foe could be reached by sea, except at a great distance, as when Drusus and later Germanicus in their campaigns against the Germans were supported by warships in the North Sea and on the lower Rhine.

Acts of conspicuous bravery, especially in boarding, were duly rewarded by the *corona navalis* or *rostrata* (cp. p. 460). Yet the navy was always an inferior service compared with the army, and included freedmen and even slaves among the sailors and oarsmen. Marines who were transferred to a legion congratulated themselves on their promotion. The commanding officers were *praefecti,* of the rank of knights, the admiral of one of the major fleets (*praefectus classis praetoriae*) ranking with the *legatus* commanding a legion. Pliny the Elder was admiral of the fleet at Misenum at the time of the eruption of Vesuvius. An important naval harbor had been constructed there by Agrippa, after a previous attempt a few years before to make a harbor (Portus Iulius) by connecting the Lake of Avernus with the Lucrine Lake. The sailing of a fleet from the port of Ancona is represented on the Column of Trajan.

The navy had seldom aroused enthusiasm among the Romans. With the establishment of peace under the Empire its duties came to be those of a coast guard, serving police purposes and of potential utility to the army. Piracy was allowed to exist in such distant waters as the eastern end of the Black Sea and on the Indian Ocean. In the third century it became once more a terror to Mediterranean commerce.

SELECT BIBLIOGRAPHY

In addition to the more general works named below, a brief bibliography is provided for each chapter and for the Appendix. Books on the same special subject, or closely related in range or mode of treatment or in the scale of importance, are grouped together. This arrangement, largely topical, will prove more serviceable, it is believed, than an alphabetical order. Roman numerals are used only for volumes (except periodicals), or for chapters of the present work.

To the few works of a general character which are named first a short list of references is given for each chapter, to suggest collateral reading and in the case of larger works to furnish a clue to the ancient sources.

GENERAL

Blümner — H. Blümner, Die römischen Privataltertümer, 3d ed., Munich, 1911.

Cambridge — The Cambridge Ancient History, VII-X, Cambridge, 1928-34.[1]

Cagnat — R. Cagnat et V. Chapot, Manuel d'archéologie romaine, 2 vols., Paris, 1917-20.

Daremberg — Daremberg-Saglio-Pottier, Dictionnaire des antiquités grecques et romaines, 10 vols., Paris, 1877-1919. (In the last volume is a conspectus of particular articles grouped under general heads.)

Frank — T. Frank, An Economic Survey of Ancient Rome, I, Baltimore, 1933.

Friedländer — L. Friedländer, Darstellungen aus der Sittengeschichte Roms, 10th ed., 4 vols., Leipzig, 1920-22; in English from the 7th ed., Life and Manners under the Early Empire, 4 vols., London, n.d.

Johnston — H. W. Johnston, The Private Life of the Romans, 2d ed., Chicago, 1932.

Jones — Sir H. S. Jones, Companion to Roman History, Oxford, 1912.

[1] With very ample bibliographies.

Legacy C. Bailey and others, The Legacy of Rome, Oxford, 1923.

Marquardt J. Marquardt and T. Mommsen, Handbuch der römischen Altertümer, 7 vols., Leipzig, 1881-88; in French, Manuel des antiquités romaines, 15 vols., Paris, 1887-93.

Pauly Pauly-Wissowa-Kroll, Realencyclopädie der classischen Altertumswissenschaft, Stuttgart, 1894- (still in progress).

Rostovtzeff M. I. Rostovtzeff, Social and Economic History of the Roman Empire, 2 vols., Oxford, 1926; 2d ed. in German, Leipzig, 1931; 3d ed. in Italian, 1 vol., Florence, 1932.

Sandys Sir J. E. Sandys and others, A Companion to Latin Studies, 2d ed., Cambridge, 1913.

Rostovtzeff, M. I., A History of the Ancient World, II, Oxford, 1928.

Zielinski, T., Histoire de la civilisation antique, Paris, 1931.

Gercke, A., und E. Norden, Einleitung in die Altertumswissenschaft, II, 4th ed., Leipzig, 1932-33; III, 2d ed., 1914.

Baumgarten, F., F. Poland, and R. Wagner, Die hellenistisch-römische Kultur, Leipzig, 1913.

Goetz, W., K. J. Beloch, and others, Hellas und Rom, 1931.

Birt, T., Das Kulturleben der Griechen und Römer, part 4, Leipzig, 1928.

Glover, T. R., The Ancient World, London, 1935.

Chapot, V., The Roman World, New York, 1928.

Frank, T., A History of Rome, New York, 1923.

Homo, L., La Civilisation romaine, Paris, 1930.

Giles, A. F., The Roman Civilization, London, 1926.

Rogers, H. L., and T. R. Harley, The Life of Rome; Illustrative Passages from Latin Literature Selected and Translated, Oxford, 1927.

Abbott, F. F., Roman Politics, Boston, 1923.

Showerman, G., Rome and the Romans, New York, 1931.

———— Monuments and Men of Ancient Rome, New York, 1935.

———— Eternal Rome, New Haven, 1924.

Greene, W. C., The Achievement of Rome, Cambridge, Mass., 1933.

Fowler, W. W., Social Life at Rome in the Age of Cicero, New York, 1909.

Kroll, W., Die Kultur der ciceronischen Zeit, Leipzig, 1933.

Dill, Sir S., Roman Society from Nero to Marcus Aurelius, 2d ed., London, 1905.

———— Roman Society in the Last Century of the Western Empire, 2d ed., London, 1898.

McDaniel, W. B., Guide for the Study of English Books on Roman Private Life, New York, 1926.

I. FROM VILLAGE TO CITY-STATE

Cambridge, VII, chs. 10 ff.; VIII, chs. 2-12; 15; IX, chs. 1-8; 11-17.

Daremberg, *aedilis, comitia, consul,* etc.

Jones, ch. 1.

Marquardt, I-III; in French, I-VII.

Pauly, *aedilis, comitia, consul,* etc.

Rostovtzeff, ch. 1.

Sandys, ch. 1 §2; ch. 3; ch. 6 §§1, 5, 7-9.

Randall-MacIver, D., Villanovans and Early Etruscans, Oxford, 1924.

———— Italy before the Romans, Oxford, 1928.

———— The Etruscans, Oxford, 1927.

Rose, H. J., Primitive Culture in Italy, London, 1926.

Fell, R. A. L., Etruria and Rome, Cambridge, 1924.

Ducati, P., Etruria antica, Turin, 1925.

Nogara, B., Gli Etruschi e la loro civiltà, Milan, 1933.

Johnstone, M. A., Etruria Past and Present, London, 1930.

Seta, A. della, Italia antica, 2d ed., Bergamo, 1928.

Bryan, W. R., "Italic Hut Urns and Hut Cemeteries," *Papers and Monographs of the American Academy in Rome,* IV, 1925.

Duhn, F. von, Italische Gräberkunde, I, Heidelberg, 1924.

Homo, L., Primitive Italy and the Beginnings of Roman Imperialism, New York, 1926.

———— Roman Political Institutions from City to State, London, 1929.

Piganiol, A., Essai sur les origines de Rome, Paris, 1917.

Pais, E., Storia dell' Italia antica, 2 vols., Rome, 1925.

Heitland, W. E., The Roman Republic, 3 vols., Cambridge, 1909.
See also the next section.

II. MAKING AN EMPIRE

Cambridge, VII, ch. 14 §10; ch. 25 §8; VIII, ch. 11 §3; IX; X.
Daremberg, *colonia, municipium, provinciae.*
Jones, ch. 1.

Legacy, ch. on "Administration."
Marquardt, I-IV; in French, I-IX.
Pauly, *coloniae, municipium.*
Sandys, ch. 3; ch. 6 §1.

Piganiol, A., La Conquête romaine, 2d ed., Paris, 1930.
Pais, E., Storia di Roma durante le grandi conquiste mediterranee, Turin, 1931.
Homo, L., L'Empire romain, Paris, 1925.
Frank, T., Roman Imperialism, New York, 1914.
Holmes, T. R., The Roman Republic and the Founder of the Empire, Oxford, 1923.
———— The Architect of the Roman Empire, 2 vols., Oxford, 1931.
Marsh, F. B., History of the Roman World, 146-30 B.C., London, 1935.
———— The Founding of the Roman Empire, 2d ed., Oxford, 1927.
Hammond, M., The Augustan Principate, Cambridge, Mass., 1933.
Jones, Sir H. S., The Roman Empire, New York, 1908.
Nilsson, M. P., Imperial Rome, New York, 1926.
Albertini, E., L'Empire romain, Paris, 1929.
Cavaignac, E., La Paix romaine, Paris, 1928.
Dessau, H., Geschichte der römischen Kaiserzeit, 2 vols., Berlin, 1924-30.
Domaszewski, A. von, Geschichte der römischen Kaiser, 2 vols., Leipzig, 1909.
Paribeni, R., Optimus Princeps (Trajan), 2 vols., Messina, 1926-27.
Pelham, H. F., Essays, Oxford, 1911.
Mommsen, T., The Provinces of the Roman Empire, 2d ed., 2 vols., London, 1909.

Arnold, W. T., The Roman System of Provincial Administration, 3d ed., Oxford, 1914.

Jullian, C., Histoire de la Gaule, III, 2d ed., and IV, Paris, 1920, 1913.

Brogan, O., "An Introduction to the Roman Land Frontier in Germany," in *Greece and Rome,* 3, 1933, 23 ff.

Haverfield, F., The Romanization of Roman Britain, 4th ed., Oxford, 1923.

―――― and Sir G. Macdonald, The Roman Occupation of Britain, Oxford, 1924.

Macdonald, Sir G., Roman Britain, London, 1931.

Collingwood, R. G., Roman Britain, London, 1923.

Windle, B. C. A., see under VII.

Other books on Britain under Appendix.

III. TILLING THE SOIL

Blümner, pt. 3, ch. 2.
Cagnat, II, bk. 3, ch. 3.
Cambridge, VIII, chs. 5-6.
Daremberg, *rustica res.*
Frank, ch. 3 §6; ch. 5 §7.
Johnston, ch. 12.

Jones, ch. 5.
Legacy, ch. on "Agriculture."
Pauly, *Ackerbau.*
Rostovtzeff, esp. chs. 1, 6, 7.
Sandys, ch. 5 §7.

Heitland, W. E., Agricola, Cambridge, 1921.

Frank, T., An Economic History of Rome, 2d ed., Baltimore, 1927.

Billiard, R., L'Agriculture dans l'antiquité, Paris, 1928.

―――― La Vigne dans l'antiquité, Lyons, 1913.

Day, J., "Agriculture in the Life of Pompeii," in *Yale Classical Studies,* III, New Haven, 1932.

Brehaut, E., Cato the Censor on Farming (translation with notes), New York, 1933.

Hooper, W. D., and H. B. Ash, M. Porcius Cato on Agriculture; M. Terentius Varro on Agriculture, in Loeb Classical Library, Cambridge, Mass., 1934.

IV. CRAFTS, TRADE, TRANSPORTATION

Blümner, pt. 2, ch. 7; pt. 3, chs. 3-4.

Cagnat, II, bk. 3, chs. 3-7.

Cambridge, VIII, ch. 11; X, ch. 13.

Daremberg, *fabri, mercator, mercatura, via.*

Frank, ch. 3 §7; ch. 4 §§7-8; ch. 5 §§6, 8.

Friedländer, I, ch. 6; in English, ch. 7.

Johnston, chs. 10-11.

Jones, chs. 1 and 5.

Legacy, ch. on "Communications and Commerce."

Marquardt, VII, pt. 2; in French, XV.

Pauly, *collegium, fabri, Seewesen* (in Suppbd. V).

Rostovtzeff, esp. ch. 5.

Sandys, ch. 6 §10.

Frank, T., see under III.

Louis, P., Ancient Rome at Work, New York, 1927.

Toutain, J., The Economic Life of the Ancient World, New York, 1930.

Waltzing, J. P., Étude historique sur les corporations professionelles chez les Romains, 4 vols., Louvain, 1895-1900.

Liebenam, W., Zur Geschichte und Organisation des römischen Vereinswesens, Leipzig, 1890.

Déchelette, J., Les Vases céramiques ornés de la Gaule romaine, 2 vols., Paris, 1904.

Rostovtzeff, M. I., Caravan Cities, Oxford, 1932.

Torr, C., Ancient Ships, Cambridge, 1895.

Köster, A., Das antike Seewesen, Berlin, 1923.

Westermann, W. L., *Sklaverei,* in Pauly, Suppbd. VI, 944 ff.

———— "On Inland Transportation and Communication in Antiquity," in *Political Science Quarterly,* 43, 1928, 364 ff.

Charlesworth, M. P., Trade-Routes and Commerce of the Roman Empire, 2d ed., Cambridge, 1926.

Warmington, E. H., The Commerce between the Roman Empire and India, Cambridge, 1928.

Rawlinson, H. G., Intercourse between India and the Western World, Cambridge, 1926.

Hirth, F., China and the Roman Orient, Shanghai, 1885.

Schoff, W. H., Arrianus, Flavius, The Periplus of the Erythraean Sea, New York, 1912.

V. GODS AND MEN

Cagnat, II, bk. 3, ch. 1.

Cambridge, VIII, ch. 14; X, ch. 15.

Friedländer, III, ch. 13; in English, ch. 2.

Johnston, ch. 15.

Jones, ch. 4.

Legacy, ch. on "Religion and Philosophy."

Marquardt, VI; in French, XII-XIII.

Sandys, ch. 4.

Moore, G. F., History of Religions, I, chs. 21-22, New York, 1913.

Wissowa, G., Religion und Kultus der Römer, 2d ed., Munich, 1912.

Bailey, C., The Religion of Ancient Rome, Chicago, 1907.

———— Phases in the Religion of Ancient Rome, Berkeley, 1932.

———— Religion in Virgil, Oxford, 1935.

Fowler, W. W., The Religious Experience of the Roman People, London, 1911.

Carter, J. B., The Religion of Numa, London, 1906.

Rostovtzeff, M. I., Mystic Italy, New York, 1927.

Macchioro, A., Roma capta, Messina, 1928.

Pais, E., Storia interna di Roma, bk. 5, ch. 1, Turin, 1931.

Grenier, A., The Roman Spirit in Religion, Thought and Art, New York, 1926.

Toutain, J., Les Cultes païens dans l'Empire romain, 3 vols., Paris, 1907-20.

Cumont, F., Les Religions orientales dans le paganisme romain, 4th ed., Paris, 1929.

———— The Oriental Religions in Roman Paganism, Chicago, 1911.

———— The Mysteries of Mithra, 2d ed., Chicago, 1910.

La Piana, G., Foreign Groups in Rome during the First Centuries of the Empire, chs. 4-5, Cambridge, Mass., 1927.

Taylor, L. R., The Divinity of the Roman Emperor, American Philological Association Monograph, 1931.

Nock, A. D., Conversion: the Old and the New in Religion from Alexander the Great to Augustine of Hippo, London, 1933.

Glover, T. R., The Conflict of Religions in the Early Roman Empire, 11th ed., London, 1927.

Boissier, G., La Fin du paganisme, 6th ed., 2 vols., Paris, 1909.
Laing, G. J., Survivals of Roman Religion, New York, 1931.
Conway, R. S., Ancient Italy and Modern Religion, Cambridge, 1933.

VI. FESTIVALS AND DIVERSIONS

Blümner, pt. 2, ch. 6.

Cagnat, II, bk. 3, ch. 2.

Daremberg, *feriae, ludi publici, gladiator, circus, amphitheatrum, balneum, thermae,* etc.

Friedländer, II, chs. 8-9; in English, chs. 1-3.

Johnston, ch. 9.

Jones, ch. 4 §3; ch. 7.

Marquardt, VI, 462 ff.; in French, XIII, 247 ff.

Pauly, *ludi publici* (in Suppbd. V), *gladiator* (in Suppbd. III), *circus, theatron, Bäder,* etc.

Sandys, ch. 6 §§15-16.

Fowler, W. W., The Roman Festivals of the Period of the Republic, London, 1908.
Wissowa, G., §§63-64; see under V.
Frazer, Sir J. G., Publii Ovidii Nasonis Fastorum libri sex (translation and commentary), 5 vols., London, 1929.
Gardiner, E. N., Athletics in the Ancient World, Oxford, 1930.
Schröder, B., Der Sport im Altertum, Berlin, 1927.

VII. THE PATERNAL ROOF

Blümner, pts. 1-2.

Cagnat, II, bk. 3, chs. 9-12.

Cambridge, IX, ch. 19.

Daremberg, *domus, villa, funus, sepulcrum,* etc.

Friedländer, II, ch. 11; in English, ch. 2.

Johnston, chs. 1-8 and 14.

Jones, ch. 2 §§11-13.

Legacy, ch. on "Family and Social Life."

Marquardt, VII, pts. 1-2; in French, XIV-XV.

Pauly, *Römisches Haus, Gartenbau, Bestattung, columbarium,* etc.

Rostovtzeff, chs. 2 and 5-7.

Sandys, ch. 5 §§3-6, 8; ch. 6 §6.

Boethius, A., "Domestic Architecture in Rome," in *American Journal of Archaeology,* 38, 1934, 158 ff.
Mau-Kelsey, Pompeii, Its Life and Art, New York, 1899.
Maiuri, A., La casa del Menandro e il suo tesoro di argenteria, 2 vols., Rome, 1933.

Maiuri, A., La villa dei misteri, see under XI, where titles of other books on Pompeii and on Herculaneum will be found.

Tanzer, H. H., The Villas of Pliny the Younger, New York, 1924.

Paribeni, R., The Villa of the Emperor Hadrian at Tivoli, Milan, 1932.

Gusman, P., La Villa impériale de Tibur, Paris, 1904.

Lugli, G., Horace's Sabine Farm, Rome, 1930.

Gauckler, P., in *Monuments Piot,* III, 1896, 177 ff. (for villa at Uthina, Africa).

Gnirs, A., in *Jahreshefte des österreichischen archäologischen Institutes;* XVIII, 1915, Beiblatt, 101 ff. (for villas at Brioni Grande, Istria).

Joulin, L., in *Mémoires de l'Académie des Inscriptions,* XI, 1901, 219 ff. (for villa near Martres-Tolosanes).

Grenier, A., in *Bibliothèque de l'École des Hautes Études,* fasc. 157, Paris, 1906 (for villas near Metz).

Windle, B. C. A., The Romans in Britain, ch. 11, London, 1923 (for houses in Britain).

Richter, G. M. A., Ancient Furniture, Oxford, 1926.

Heuzey, L., Histoire du costume antique, Paris, 1922.

Houston, M. G., Ancient Greek, Roman, and Byzantine Costume and Decoration, London, 1931.

Bieber, M., Entwicklungsgeschichte der griechischen Tracht (Roman included), Berlin, 1934.

Wilson, L. M., The Roman Toga, Baltimore, 1924.

McClees H., The Daily Life of the Greeks and Romans as Illustrated in the Classical Collections, Metropolitan Museum, New York, 1925.

Quennell, M., and C. H. B. Quennell, Everyday Life in Roman Britain, London, 1924.

VIII. SCHOOLS AND MASTERS

Blümner, pt. 2, chs. 1-2.

Daremberg, *ludus, educatio.*

Friedländer, III, ch. 14; in English, ch. 3.

Johnston, ch. 4.

Marquardt, VII, pt. 1, ch. 3; in French, XIV, pt. 1, ch. 3.

Pauly, *Schulen.*

Sandys, ch. 5 §9.

Duff, J. W., "Education" (Roman), in Hastings, Encyclopaedia of Religion and Ethics, New York, 1912.

Gwynn, A., Roman Education from Cicero to Quintilian, Oxford, 1926.

Dobson, J. F., Ancient Education and Its Meaning to Us, New York, 1932.

Monroe, P., Source Book of the History of Education for the Greek and Roman Period, New York, 1902.

Wilkins, A. S., Roman Education, Cambridge, 1905.

Boissier, G., La Fin du paganisme, I, bk. 2, ch. 1; see also under V.

———— Tacitus, New York, 1906 (a chapter on the schools of declamation).

Winter J. G., Life and Letters in the Papyri, pp. 64 ff., Ann Arbor, 1933.

Schubart, W., Einführung in die Papyruskunde, pp. 380 ff., Berlin, 1918.

Haarhoff, T., Schools of Gaul, Oxford, 1920.

Sandys, Sir J. E., A History of Classical Scholarship, 3d ed., I, chs. 10-12, Cambridge, 1921.

IX. IN A ROMAN LIBRARY

Cagnat, I, bk. 1, ch. 11; II, bk. 3, ch. 15.

Cambridge, VIII, ch. 13; IX, ch. 18; X, ch. 16.

Daremberg, *liber, bibliotheca.*

Friedländer, II, ch. 10; in English, III, ch. 1.

Johnston, ch. 10.

Jones, ch. 2 §8.

Legacy, ch. on "Literature."

Marquardt, VII, pt. 2, ch. 4; in French, XV, pt. 2, ch. 4.

Pauly, *Bibliotheken, Buch, Buchhandel.*

Sandys, ch. 5 §10; ch. 8 §1.

Kenyon, Sir F. G., Books and Readers in Ancient Greece and Rome, Oxford, 1932.

Schubart, W., Das Buch bei den Griechen und Römern, Berlin, 1921.

Cagnat, R., Les Bibliothèques municipales dans l'Empire romain, Paris, 1906.

———— Carthage, Timgad, Tébessa, ch. 5, Paris, 1909.

Pfeiffer, H. F., "The Roman Library in Timgad," in *Memoirs of the American Academy in Rome,* IX, 1931, 157 ff.

Sisson, M. A., in *Papers of the British School at Rome*, XI, 1929, 58 ff. (Hadrian's library at Athens).

Wilberg, W., in *Jahreshefte des österreichischen archäologischen Institutes*, XI, 1908, 118 ff. (library at Ephesus); cp. *ibid.* VIII, 1905, Beiblatt, 61 ff.

Boyd, C. E., Public Libraries and Literary Culture in Ancient Rome, Chicago, 1916.

Duff, J. W., A Literary History of Rome from the Origins to the Close of the Golden Age, 2d ed., London, 1920.

———— A Literary History of Rome in the Silver Age, New York, 1931.

———— The Writers of Rome, Oxford, 1923.

Sandys, Sir J. E., chs. 10-14; see under VIII.

Mackail, J. W., Latin Literature, New York, 1895.

Humbert, J., Histoire illustrée de la littérature latine, Paris, 1932.

Schanz, M., and C. Hosius, Geschichte der römischen Literatur, 4th ed., 3 vols., Munich, 1927.

Teuffel, W. S., and others, Geschichte der römischen Literatur, 6th ed., 3 vols., Leipzig, 1910-16; in Eng. from the 5th edition, London, 1891-92.

Bailey, C., and others, The Mind of Rome, Oxford, 1926.

Grenier, A., see under V.

Summers, W. C., The Silver Age of Latin Literature, New York, 1920.

Glover, T. R., Life and Letters in the Fourth Century, Cambridge, 1901.

Wright, F. A., and T. A. Sinclair, A History of Later Latin Literature, New York, 1931.

Many of the authors are accessible in the Loeb Classical Library (text and translation), and in the similar French series of the Association Guillaume Budé.

X. KNOWLEDGE AND THOUGHT

Cambridge, IX, ch. 21 (law).

Daremberg, *astronomie, géographie, medicus, juris consulti.*

Friedländer, I, ch. 3 §4, c; III, chs. 14-15; in English, I, ch. 3 §4, 3-5; III, chs. 3-4.

Legacy, chs. on "Science"; "Religion and Philosophy"; "The Science of Law."

Pauly, *Arithmetik, Geometrie, Astronomie, Astrologie, iu-* *risprudentia, Geographie* (in Suppbd. IV).
Sandys, ch. 8 §§2-4; ch. 6 §2.

Heiberg, J. L., Mathematics and Physical Science in Classical Antiquity, Oxford, 1922.
Grenier, A., ch. 6; see under V.
Dreyer, J. L. E., History of the Planetary Systems from Thales to Kepler, Cambridge, 1906.
Smith, D. E., History of Mathematics, 2 vols., Boston, 1923-25.
———— Mathematics, Boston, 1923.
Tozer, H. F., A History of Ancient Geography, 2d ed., (M. Cary), Cambridge, 1935.
Warmington, E. H., Greek Geography, London, 1934.
Cary, M., and E. H. Warmington, The Ancient Explorers, London, 1929.
Burton, H. E., The Discovery of the Ancient World, Cambridge, Mass., 1932.
Miller, K., Die peutingersche Tafel, 2d ed., Stuttgart, 1929.
Taylor, H. O., Greek Biology and Medicine, Boston, 1922.
Elliott, J. S., Outlines of Greek and Roman Medicine, London, 1914.
Allbutt, Sir T. C., Greek Medicine in Rome, London, 1921.
Hicks, R. D., Stoic and Epicurean, New York, 1910.
Arnold, E. V., Roman Stoicism, Cambridge, 1911.
Martha, C., Les Moralistes sous l'Empire romain, 7th ed., Paris, 1900.
Sedgwick, H. D., Marcus Aurelius, New Haven, 1921.
Girard, P. F., A Short History of Roman Law, Toronto, 1906.
———— Manuel élémentaire de droit romain, 8th ed., Paris, 1929.
Declareuil, J., Rome the Lawgiver, New York, 1926.
Buckland, W. W., The Main Institutions of Roman Private Law, chs. 1-2, Cambridge, 1931.
———— A Text-book of Roman Law from Augustus tó Justinian, 2d ed., ch. 1, Cambridge, 1932.
Kübler, B., Geschichte des römischen Rechts, Leipzig, 1925.
Krüger, P., Geschichte der Quellen und Litteratur des römischen Rechts, 2d ed., Munich, 1912.
Costa, E., Storia delle fonti del diritto romano, Turin, 1909.

XI. FINE ARTS

Cagnat, I; II, bk. 2.

Cambridge, IX, ch. 20; X, ch. 17; Plates, Vol. IV.

Friedländer, III, ch. 12; in English, ch. 3.

Jones, chs. 2 and 8.

Legacy, chs. on "Architecture and Art"; "Building and Engineering."

Sandys, ch. 7.

Strong, E., Art in Ancient Rome, 2 vols., New York, 1928.

Pijoán, J., History of Art, I, New York, 1927.

——— Summa artis, historia general del arte, V, Madrid, 1934.

Seta, A. della, see under I.

Contenau, G., and V. Chapot, L'Art antique, Orient-Grèce-Rome, Paris, 1930.

Rodenwaldt, G., Die Kunst der Antike (Hellas und Rom), 2d ed., Berlin, 1927.

Walters, H. B., The Art of the Romans, 2d ed., London, 1928.

Ducati, P., Storia dell' arte etrusca, Florence, 1927.

Martha, J., L'Art étrusque, Paris, 1889.

Grenier, A., The Roman Spirit; see under V.

Swindler, M. H., Ancient Painting, New Haven, 1929.

Curtius, L., Die Wandmalerei Pompejis, Leipzig, 1929.

Pfuhl, E., Masterpieces of Greek Drawing and Painting, New York, 1926.

——— Malerei und Zeichnung der Griechen, 3 vols., Munich, 1923.

Rizzo, G. E., La pittura ellenistico-romana, Milan, 1929.

Spinazzola, V., Le arti decorative in Pompei e nel Museo Nazionale di Napoli, Milan, 1928.

Maiuri, A., La villa dei misteri (with atlas of colored plates), Rome, 1931.

Wirth, F., Römische Wandmalerei (79-300 A.D.), Berlin, 1934.

Anthony, E. W., A History of Mosaics, Boston, 1935.

Strong, E., Roman Sculpture from Augustus to Constantine, London, 1907.

——— La scultura romana, etc., 2 vols., Florence, 1923-26.

Wickhoff, F., Roman Art, London, 1900.

Paribeni, R., Ara pacis Augustae, Rome, 1932.

Chase, G. H., and C. R. Post, A History of Sculpture, New York, 1924.

Hekler, A., Greek and Roman Portraits, London, 1912.

Paribeni, R., Il ritratto nell' arte antica, Milan, 1934.

Toynbee, J. M. C., The Hadrianic School; a Chapter in the History of Greek Art, Cambridge, 1934.

Delbrück, R., Antike Porphyrwerke, Berlin, 1932.

Robertson, D. S., A Handbook of Greek and Roman Architecture, Cambridge, 1929.

Anderson, W. J., R. P. Spiers, and T. Ashby, The Architecture of Ancient Rome, London, 1927.

Rivoira, G. T., Roman Architecture and Its Principles of Construction under the Empire, Oxford, 1925.

Brooks, A. M., Architecture, Boston, 1924.

Morgan, M. H., and H. L. Warren, Vitruvius, the Ten Books on Architecture, Cambridge, Mass., 1914.

Granger, F., Vitruvius on Architecture, 2 vols., London, 1931, 1934.

Delbrück, R., Hellenistische Bauten in Latium, 2 vols., Strassburg, 1907-12.

Frank, T., Roman Buildings of the Republic; an Attempt to Date Them from Their Materials, Rome, 1924.

Gest, A. P., Engineering, New York, 1930.

Mau-Kelsey, see under VII.

Maiuri, A., Pompeii (in English), Rome, 1929; Pompei (in Italian), Novara, 1929.

——— Herculanum (in French), Paris, 1932; Ercolano, Novara, 1932.

Rusconi, A. J., Pompei, Bergamo, 1929.

Mau-Ippel, Führer durch Pompeji, 6th ed., Leipzig, 1928.

Warscher, T., Pompeji; Ein Führer durch die Ruinen, Berlin, 1925.

XII. THE CITY OF ROME

Cambridge, VIII, ch. 12 §7;   Pauly, *Rom; Forum Romanum*
IX, ch. 20 §7; X, ch. 17 §6.   (in Suppbd. IV).

Jones, ch. 1 §3.   Sandys, ch. 1 §3.

Platner, S. B., and T. Ashby, A Topographical Dictionary of Ancient Rome, Oxford, 1929.

Platner, S. B., The Topography and Monuments of Ancient Rome, 2d ed., Boston, 1911.

Lugli, G., The Classical Monuments of Rome and Its Vicinity,

I, Rome, 1929. (A second volume has appeared in Italian, 1934.)

Bartoli, A., The Roman Forum, the Palatine, Milan, 1922.

Hülsen, C., Forum und Palatin, Munich, 1926.

―――― The Forum and the Palatine, New York, 1928.

Paribeni, R., I fori imperiali, Rome, 1930.

Ricci, C., La via del impero, Rome, 1932.

Säflund, G., Le mura di Roma repubblicana, Uppsala, 1932.

Richmond, I. A., The City Wall of Imperial Rome, Oxford, 1930.

Ashby, T., The Aqueducts of Ancient Rome, Oxford, 1935.

Van Deman, E. B., The Building of the Roman Aqueducts, Washington, 1934.

Gusman, P., La Rome antique, Grenoble, 1934.

Lanciani, R., Ancient and Modern Rome, New York, 1925.

Discoveries both in Rome and in the provinces are reported in the *American Journal of Archaeology,* the *Journal of Roman Studies, The Year's Work in Classical Studies* (Bristol, England), the *Bullettino Comunale di Roma (Notiziario),* the *Jahrbuch des archäologischen Instituts,* the *Jahreshefte* of the Austrian Archaeological Institute in Vienna, and frequently in the *Illustrated London News.*

APPENDIX: ARMY AND NAVY

Cagnat, II, bk. 3, chs. 7-8.

Cambridge, IX, ch. 10 §2; X, ch. 8.

Daremberg, *exercitus, classis.*

Jones, ch. 3.

Marquardt, V, pt. 3; in French, XI.

Pauly, *legio, exercitus, limes, Geschütze, Kriegskunst* (in Suppbd. V), *Seekrieg* (Suppbd. IV).

Rostovtzeff, chs. 3-4, 9-10.

Sandys, ch. 6 §§13-14.

Kromayer, J., and G. Veith, Heerwesen und Kriegführung der Griechen und Römer, Munich, 1928.

Couissin, P., Les Armes romaines, Paris, 1926.

McCartney, E. S., Warfare by Land and Sea, Boston, 1923.

Parker, H. M. D., The Roman Legions, Oxford, 1928.

Cheesman, G. L., The Auxiliaries of the Roman Imperial Army, Oxford, 1914.

Bruce, J. C., The Handbook of the Roman Wall, 9th ed., Newcastle-upon-Tyne, 1933.

Collingwood, R. C., A Guide to the Roman Wall, Newcastle-upon-Tyne, 1933.

Brown, P., The Great Wall of Hadrian in Roman Times, London, 1932.

Macdonald, Sir G., The Roman Wall in Scotland, 2d ed., Oxford, 1935.

Pelham, H. F., "The Roman Frontier in Southern Germany," in Essays, ch. 9; see under II.

INDEX